BRITAIN
AND
AMERICA

TRADITION
AND
CHANGE

LEHRERBUCH

Cornelsen

Britain and America · Tradition and Change
Lehrerbuch

Im Auftrag des Verlags herausgegeben von
OStR Georg Engel, Garmisch-Partenkirchen · OSchRn Dr. Rosemarie Franke, Berlin ·
StD Armin Steinbrecher, Kaiserslautern · Professor Dieter Vater, Weinheim ·
StD Dr. Gerhard Weiß, Kaiserslautern · StD Dr. Egon Werlich, Dortmund

Verlagsredaktion
Dr. Annelore Naumann-Schütze, Neil C.F. Porter, Dr. Christian v. Raumer,
Allen J. Woppert (Projektleitung)

1. Auflage 1989

© 1989 Cornelsen Verlag, Berlin

Druck: Adolph Fürst & Sohn, Berlin

ISBN 3–464–05488–8
Vertrieb: Cornelsen Verlagsgesellschaft, Bielefeld
Bestellnummer: 54888

Inhaltsverzeichnis

Kommentar

The United Kingdom

The United States

Universal Topics

Vorwort

I. Allgemeine didaktische Konzeption und Zielsetzung

1. Adressatenkreis

Britain and America · Tradition and Change wurde für die gymnasiale Oberstufe konzipiert. Bei der Auswahl der Stoffe ebenso wie bei ihrer didaktischen Bearbeitung wurden sowohl die in den Lehrplänen der Bundesländer beschriebenen Anforderungen als auch der gegenwärtige Stand der Fachdidaktik berücksichtigt. In seiner Strukturierung nach inhaltlich ausgerichteten Großkapiteln folgt das Werk dem allseits anerkannten Prinzip der themenorientierten Textsequenzen. Das vielseitige Angebot an Themen und Textformen, die Palette sprachlich und gedanklich unterschiedlich schwerer Texte und die im Anspruchsniveau differenzierten Aufgabenstellungen entsprechen den Bedürfnissen der Kursphase, *Britain and America* bietet sich also vor allem für Grund- und Leistungskurse an.

2. *Britain and America* – ein landeskundliches Lesebuch

Es ist das Hauptanliegen dieses Buches, das durch die Lehrwerke der Sekundarstufe I vermittelte Bild Großbritanniens und der USA oberstufengemäß zu erweitern und zu vertiefen. Die Herausgeber legten ganz bewußt das Schwergewicht auf diese beiden Zielsprachenländer, über deren Gesellschaft und Kultur alle Lehrpläne umfassende Kenntnisse vorschreiben. Eine solche Konzentrierung ermöglicht eine repräsentative und ausgewogene Darstellung der Inhalte sowie deren intensive, niveaugerechte Erörterung. Dies schließt jedoch nicht aus, daß in *Britain and America* neben landesspezifischen Sachverhalten auch allgemeine, länder- und kulturübergreifende Themen und Probleme vorgestellt werden, sinnvollerweise dann aber in ihrer britischen oder amerikanischen Ausprägung.

Durch die sorgfältige Auswahl verschiedenartiger Originaltexte sowie deren Kombination mit visuellen Materialien und "Info-Boxes" (vgl. S. vi) sichert *Britain and America* sowohl den Erwerb eines von den Lehrplänen erwarteten überblickartigen Grundwissens als auch einen auf tieferes Verständnis zielenden Einblick in Sach- und Problemzusammenhänge. Darüber hinaus ermöglicht das Werk exemplarisch die für Jugendliche unerläßliche emotional nachvollziehbare Begegnung mit Aussagen, Verhaltensweisen und existentiellen Erfahrungen wirklicher oder fiktional gestalteter Repräsentanten der Zielsprachenkulturen. Da die Gegenwart nur vor dem Hintergrund vergangener Ereignisse und Entwicklungen zu verstehen ist, werden – wo immer es sich anbot – auch historische Perspektiven eröffnet. Durch diesen didaktischen Ansatz verhindert *Britain and America*, daß landeskundliches Lernen sich in einer bloßen Institutionenkunde erschöpft oder Problemstellungen ohne die entsprechenden Vorkenntnisse unsachgemäß und unsachlich diskutiert werden.

3. *Britain and America* und politische Bildung

Indem die Schüler/innen die von Vertretern der beiden Zielsprachenländer verfaßten Texte in *Britain and America* erschließen und sich mit den darin dargestellten Sachverhalten, Problemen und Meinungen auseinandersetzen, lernen sie nicht nur andere Denkweisen und Normen kennen, sondern vergleichen diese auch mit den Gegebenheiten und Wertvorstellungen ihrer eigenen Kultur sowie mit ihren persönlichen (Vor-)Urteilen, Ansichten und Erfahrungen. Ausgehend von der Vermittlung landeskundlicher Kenntnisse und Einsichten trägt *Britain and America* damit zur sachlichen Auseinandersetzung mit anderen Nationen und zum Verständnis für eine fremde, teilweise andersartige Gesellschaft bei. Es führt zur Überwindung von Klischees und ethnozentrischen Sehweisen und beugt unkritischer Identifikation oder auch Ablehnung vor. Es erzieht zu Toleranz und Verständigung und fördert somit die Persönlichkeitsentwicklung und Identitätsfindung der jungen Menschen. Auf diese Weise leistet dieses Buch auch einen Beitrag zur Verwirklichung wichtiger fächerübergreifender Erziehungsziele der Schule.

4. *Britain and America* und Textunterricht

Bei der Arbeit mit *Britain and America* werden die Zielsprachenkulturen über die verschiedensten Arten schriftlich fixierter und auditiv dargebotener Texte (vgl. S. viii) sowie über visuelle Darstellungen erfahrbar und verstehbar. Um die beabsichtigten fachspezifischen und allgemeinen Zielsetzungen zu erreichen und um die Lernenden anzusprechen und zu motivieren, wurde bei der Auswahl auf eine große Vielfalt von Texttypen und Textformen – mit unterschiedlichem Abstraktionsniveau – geachtet, die sowohl in fiktionaler als auch nicht-fiktionaler Gestaltung ein breites Spektrum von Sachverhalten, Meinungen, Absichten und Verhaltensweisen repräsentieren. Bei der Erschließung dieser Materialien begegnen die Schüler/innen unterschiedlichen Formen der Textbildung, lernen Strukturen, Argumentationsstrategien, Wirkungsweisen, Sprachebenen und -varianten, stilistische wie auch sprachliche Besonderheiten kennen. Sie erweitern und vertiefen somit ihre Kenntnisse von Texten und üben sich in Analyse und Interpretation. Indem sie darüber hinaus ihr Textverständnis, ihre persönliche Meinung zu einem Sachverhalt, ihre Reaktionen auf die Aussage eines Autors und die Stellungnahmen ihrer Mitschüler/innen in spezifischer Form mündlich oder schriftlich artikulieren oder Informationen, etwa im Rahmen von Kurzreferaten, an die Lerngruppe weitergeben, fördern sie gleichzeitig ihre Fähigkeit, eigene Äußerungen in der fremden Sprache adressatenbezogen und intentionsgerecht zu entwickeln und zu formulieren. Ein landeskundliches Lesebuch wie *Britain and America* dient so auch der Erweiterung und Festigung methodischer und arbeitstechnischer Kenntnisse und Fertigkeiten.

5. *Britain and America* und Sprachunterricht

Auch auf der gymnasialen Oberstufe bleiben der Aufbau und die Erweiterung einer differenzierten Kommunikationsfähigkeit in der englischen Sprache ein vorrangiges Ziel des Englischunterrichts. Die Schüler/innen sollen sich über Themen aus wichtigen Sachbereichen, insbesondere der Zielsprachenländer, auf sprachlich und gedanklich angemessenem Niveau mitteilen und verständigen können. Da Sprache nicht nur Teil der Kultur einer Nation ist, sondern auch deren Ausdruck und Spiegel, besteht ein unmittelbarer Zusammenhang zwischen sprachlichem und landeskundlichem Lernen. Bei der Erschließung der verschiedenartigen, unter thematischen Gesichtspunkten verknüpften Texte begegnen die Lernenden nicht nur wichtigem allgemeinsprachlichem Vokabular mit seinen kulturspezifischen Inhalten, sondern vor allem auch themenbezogener Lexik sowie sach- und texttypischen Registern, die wiederum im Unterrichtsgespräch sowie in der mündlichen und schriftlichen Auseinandersetzung mit den jeweiligen Themen und Problemen verwendet werden sollen[1]. Die anwendungsbezogene Zusammenstellung semantischer Felder und themenspezifischer Kollokationen, wie sie im Lehrerbuch angeboten wird (vgl. S. viii) und in den Unterricht integriert werden kann, ist ein Beispiel, wie sich durch die Arbeit mit *Britain and America* unmittelbar auch die Sprachkompetenz der Schüler/innen fördern läßt.

II. Das Schülerbuch (SB)

1. Auswahl und Abfolge der Themen und Texte

Ausschlaggebend für die Auswahl der in *Britain and America* angebotenen Themen waren der Anspruch der Sache, die Erfordernisse der Lehrpläne sowie der Kenntnisstand und die Interessenlage der Schüler/innen. Die Herausgeber berücksichtigten in erster Linie solche Aspekte, die für das jeweilige Zielsprachenland wichtig und charakteristisch sind. Daneben wurden aus überwiegend bildungstheoretischen Gründen Themen angesprochen, die auch für andere Industrienationen der heutigen Welt allgemein von Bedeutung sind. Für die Gliederung des Buches ergab sich hieraus eine Dreiteilung: Jeweils vier der insgesamt zwölf Kapitel repräsentieren Großbritannien und die USA, das letzte Drittel weist eine für beide Länder relevante allgemeinere Thematik auf.

Der erste Textblock befaßt sich mit Großbritannien. Kapitel I gibt zunächst einen Überblick über die Entwicklung des Landes vom Weltreich zum Mitglied der Europäischen Gemeinschaft. Kapitel II, III und IV gehen genauer auf verschiedene Teilaspekte des öffentlichen Lebens in Großbritannien ein. Sie behandeln z.B. das englische Schulwesen, gesellschaftliche Strukturen, Probleme der heutigen Arbeitswelt und der wirtschaftlichen Entwicklung von der Industriellen Revolution bis zur Gegenwart, den Wohlfahrtsstaat, die Entstehung sowie einige Besonderheiten des modernen britischen Staatswesens und enden mit einem Blick auf die spezifischen Verhältnisse in Nordirland.

Der USA-Teil beginnt mit einem Kapitel über die Besiedlung des Landes, verschiedene Einwanderergruppen und Minoritäten sowie ausgewählte Regionen. Dabei werden einige für Amerika bedeutsame Konzepte, etwa "Frontier", "American Dream", "Melting Pot vs. Ethnic Diversity", vorgestellt. Kapitel VI und VII des Buches bieten Texte zur Bedeutung religiöser Gruppierungen in den USA, zu Fragen der Erziehung, des Sports, der Arbeitswelt, zu sozialen und wirtschaftlichen Problemen sowie zur Stellung der amerikanischen Frau und zur Bürgerrechtsbewegung. Kapitel VIII widmet sich politischen Themen, auch unter historischem Aspekt, etwa der amerikanischen Unabhängigkeitserklärung und Verfassung, dem amerikanischen Bürgerkrieg, der Rolle wichtiger politischer Institutionen (Präsidentenamt, "Supreme Court", Parteien), der Entwicklung der Menschenrechte sowie der heutigen Stellung Amerikas als Weltmacht.

Der letzte, beide Zielsprachenländer betreffende Textblock behandelt Probleme der Stadtsanierung sowie der verantwortungsbewußten Gestaltung und Veränderung der Umwelt, Funktionen von Sprache allgemein und Aspekte der englischen Sprache im besonderen, die modernen Massenmedien, Fragen der Rezeption von Literatur – u.a. Shakespeares –, Musik und Kunst. Er befaßt sich mit möglichen Konsequenzen naturwissenschaftlicher Entdeckungen und technologischer Erfindungen für die gesamte Welt und betont schließlich die Notwendigkeit der Völkerverständigung, damit ein friedliches Zusammenleben der Nationen gesichert wird und Katastrophen verhindert werden.

Die maßgebenden Kriterien für die Auswahl der authentischen Einzeltexte[2] waren ihre exemplarische Aktualität, ihre thematische Eignung, der Grad, in dem sie zur inhaltlichen Ausgewogenheit eines jeden Kapitels beitragen, die Vielfalt der Texttypen und -formen, der Wechsel zwischen Personalisierung und Abstrahierung, der Motivationsgehalt und die Angemessenheit des sprachlichen und gedanklichen Schwierigkeitsgrads.

Neben Illustrationen, Schaubildern und Tabellen, die der Veranschaulichung sowie Motivierung dienen und vielfältige Sprechanlässe bieten, enthält jedes Kapitel von *Britain and America* ein bis drei von den Herausgebern erstellte "Info-Boxes". Da hier die wichtigsten Sachinformationen zu den jeweiligen thematischen Schwerpunkten knapp, sprachlich ausformuliert und gut verständlich zusammengefaßt und verknüpft werden, erfüllen die "Info-Boxes" im Rahmen des Gesamtwerks eine bedeutsame didaktische Funktion. Sie erlauben es, bei der Textauswahl auf rein informative Sachtexte zu verzichten, da sie die für das Verständnis der Texte nötigen Basisinformationen anbieten. Mit ihrer Hilfe lassen sich die aus den vorwiegend problematisierenden Einzeldarstellungen gewonnenen Kenntnisse und Einsichten verbinden und systematisieren. Darüber hinaus stellen sie ein kleines Nachschlagewerk für die Schüler/innen dar. Die konsequente Einbettung der "Info-Boxes" in die einzelnen Kapitel bedeutet einen neuen didaktischen Weg in der Erstellung eines landeskundlichen Lesebuchs.

2. Didaktische Bearbeitung der Einzeltexte

Jedem Text wurde eine kurze Einführung ("Note") vorangestellt. Sie umreißt den Kontext, ordnet ihn in das jeweilige Kapitel ein, verknüpft ihn gegebenenfalls mit anderen Texten und regt die Schüler/innen zum Lesen an. Um eine zügige Erschließung vorzubereiten, wurden alle Texte mit Annotationen versehen, die lexikalische Hilfen und Sachinformationen bereithalten. In den Fällen, in denen sich erfahrungsgemäß Aussprachefehler einstellen, wurde die phonetische Umschrift oder das *stress pattern* hinzugefügt. Erstmals in einem Oberstufenlesebuch wurde, wo erforderlich, neben der Aussprache im *Standard British English* auch die des *Standard American English* angegeben, beide wurden durch das Symbol ☆ getrennt[3].

Die Textrezeption selbst kann in **Britain and America** auf unterschiedliche Weise erfolgen. Bei etwa einem Viertel aller Texte, insbesondere den sprachlich leichteren, fiktionalen oder solchen mit starkem Appellcharakter, wurde auf einen Aufgabenapparat im Schülerbuch verzichtet, um den Jugendlichen einen möglichst unmittelbaren, unverstellten, individuellen Zugang zu erlauben. In diesen Fällen finden sich etwa fünf bis zehn Arbeitsaufträge (mit den zugehörigen Lösungsvorschlägen) im Lehrerbuch. Bei den übrigen Texten entschieden sich die Herausgeber für die Aufnahme von vier bis sechs Aufgaben in das Schülerbuch, die durch weitere Fragen im Lehrerbuch ergänzt werden. Diese sehr variabel einsetzbaren Erschließungshilfen sind als Leitlinien gedacht für die erste Textbegegnung der Schüler/innen zu Hause oder in der Schule; sie können aber auch das nachfolgende Unterrichtsgespräch steuern und mündlich oder schriftlich, vollständig oder in Auswahl behandelt werden. Ein schematisches Vorgehen sollte jedoch vermieden werden.

Die einzelnen Arbeitsaufträge zielen auf die zentralen thematischen Aspekte eines Textes, heben insbesondere landeskundlich relevante Erscheinungsformen hervor und leiten zum Erkennen bedeutsamer Merkmale und Entwicklungen der Zielsprachenkulturen an. Darüber hinaus führen sie zur Untersuchung von Zusammenhängen zwischen Textform, struktureller Gestaltung, sprachlich-stilistischer Realisation und Wirkungsabsicht, setzen die Auseinandersetzung mit der Autorenintention in Gang, fordern zu eigenen Reaktionen und zu Vergleichen mit bereits behandelten Texten und persönlichen Lebenserfahrungen auf und regen zu Projekten und Kurzreferaten (durch ● gekennzeichnet) an, die bestimmte Teilthemen ergänzen und weiterführen können.

3. Variable Verwendungsmöglichkeiten im Unterricht

Jeder der in **Britain and America** angebotenen Texte wurde, was Annotierung und Aufbereitung anlangt, als in sich geschlossene Einheit betrachtet. Auch die einzelnen Kapitel setzen sich nicht gegenseitig etwa im Sinne einer Sequenz voraus. So ist größtmögliche Freiheit in der Themen- und Textwahl gewährleistet. Je nach den Unterrichtszielen, den Erfordernissen der Lehrpläne und den Interessen der Schüler/innen lassen sich speziell auf eine Lerngruppe zugeschnittene Textfolgen wählen oder anders zusammenstellen. So ist es z.B. möglich, von der Trennung in britische und amerikanische Themenbereiche abzugehen und unter länderübergreifenden thematischen Schwerpunkten wie "Education", "Work", "Religion" oder "Politics" Texte aus den Kapiteln II und VI, III und VII, IV und VI oder IV und VIII zu verknüpfen. Hierdurch erhöht sich die Zahl der Texte zu einem bestimmten Thema, eine willkommene Gelegenheit, längere Unterrichtssequenzen zusammenzustellen.

Man kann auch andere thematische Schwerpunkte setzen, die sich mit Texten aus ganz verschiedenen Kapiteln bearbeiten lassen. Themenbereiche, die sich hier anbieten, sind etwa "Science and Technology", "Aggression and Violence", "Human Rights". Das in das

Lehrerbuch aufgenommene „Didaktische Inhaltsverzeichnis" (vgl. unten und S. x ff.) enthält die erforderlichen Kurzinformationen zu den Texten und Vorschläge für geeignete Themenkombinationen, in den „Didaktischen Hinweisen" (vgl. unten) finden sich weitere Anregungen.

III. Die Cassetten

Das Textangebot von **Britain and America** wird durch zwei Toncassetten von je ca. 90 Minuten Spieldauer vervollständigt. Die Cassette "Selected Texts on Cassette" bietet 18 ausgewählte Texte aus dem Schülerbuch. Die drei Gedichte werden jeweils in einer vom Autor gesprochenen Version präsentiert, alle anderen Texte wurden von professionellen Sprechern/Sprecherinnen gesprochen, und zwar je nach Textquelle im Britischen oder Amerikanischen Englisch. Damit ist die Cassette multifunktional einsetzbar: zur Einführung in den Text, zur Nachbereitung, zur akustischen Präsentation der Ausspracheunterschiede zwischen Britischem und Amerikanischem Englisch sowie unterschiedlicher Sprachebenen und Register – und nicht zuletzt zur Motivation.

Die "Listening Comprehension Cassette" bietet zu jedem der 12 Kapitel des Schülerbuchs mindestens einen zusätzlichen, die angesprochene Thematik weiter auffächernden Text, darunter Interviews, Lieder und Reportagen. Transkriptionen dieser Texte liegen der Cassette als Script bei. Die Arbeit mit dieser Cassette wird zwar in erster Linie der Schulung des Hörverständnisses dienen, doch läßt sie sich auch heranziehen, wenn es um die Vertiefung eines im Schülerbuch angesprochenen Themas geht. Die konsequente Nutzung der beiden Cassetten wird langfristig auch die Aussprache der Schüler/innen verbessern.

IV. Das Lehrerbuch (LB)

Das „Didaktische Inhaltsverzeichnis" (S. x ff.) gibt zu jedem der Texte tabellarisch knappe Hinweise zur Wortzahl, zur Sprachvariante, zur Textform, zum Inhalt und zu den semantischen Feldern und nennt Themen für weitere Textsequenzen. Hierauf folgt der detaillierte Kommentarteil, der für jeden Text eine Reihe verschiedenartiger Informationen anbietet mit dem Ziel, die Unterrichtsvorbereitung und -durchführung zu entlasten.

Die „Didaktischen Hinweise" ordnen den Text in den thematischen Gesamtzusammenhang ein, machen auf seine Besonderheiten und auf mögliche Querverbindungen zu anderen Texten aufmerksam und geben Anregungen (und bibliographische Hinweise) zur thematischen Erweiterung mit Hilfe von Zusatzstoffen.

Unter "Background information" – einer logisch konsequenten Fortführung der im Schülerbuch enthaltenen "Info-Boxes" – findet man wichtige weiterführende Sachinformationen in englischer Sprache zum Autor/zur Autorin, zum Thema, zum Text und seinem Hintergrund, die je nach Bedarf an die Schüler/innen weitergegeben werden können.

Die "Semantic and collocational fields" bieten zu jedem Text den auf den jeweiligen thematischen Schwerpunkt bezogenen Themenwortschatz und seine Kollokationen. Diese Felder bilden ein wichtiges Instrument bei der Entwicklung und Festigung einer differenzierten Sprachkompetenz, da sie als assoziationsstützende Netze fungieren. Sie können die Erschließung eines Textes sprachlich entlasten, Wörter und Kollokationen können schriftlich festgehalten, durch bereits verfügbaren Wortschatz ergänzt, im weiteren Verlauf der Textbehandlung wieder aufgegriffen und zu größeren Feldern zusammengeschlossen werden[4]. Eine intensive Beschäftigung mit ihnen trägt zur Sicherheit in der Anwendung eines themenspezifischen Wortschatzes bei und fördert damit langfristig auch die selbständige Textproduktion[5].

Die "Suggested answers" schließlich bieten zu allen Aufgaben ausformulierte Lösungsvorschläge – mit Ausnahme der Anregungen zu Diskussionen, Kurzreferaten und Projektarbeit. Die in eckigen Klammern stehenden Hinweise sind als Hilfen für die Gesprächsführung, Leitlinien für die Diskussion und Denkanstöße für eine vertiefte Auseinandersetzung mit dem Text zu verstehen. Die Lösungsvorschläge wurden bewußt auf dem Sprachniveau des *educated native speaker* angesiedelt, sollen also nicht als Norm für erwartete Schülerantworten verstanden werden.

Die Herausgeber von **Britain and America** hoffen, mit dem Schülerbuch, den beiden Toncassetten und dem Lehrerbuch ein Oberstufenlehrwerk vorgelegt zu haben, das zu einem zeitgemäßen, interessanten und ertragreichen Englischunterricht beiträgt.

––––––––

1 Die Entscheidung darüber, welcher Wortschatz als produktiv anzusehen ist, sollte der Unterrichtssituation angepaßt werden.

2 Bereits in der Textvorlage vorhandene Auslassungen wurden durch ..., von den Herausgebern vorgenommene Kürzungen durch [...] gekennzeichnet. – Das Prinzip der Authentizität führt im übrigen zu scheinbaren orthographischen Inkonsequenzen. So steht etwa *organise* neben *organize, per cent* neben *percent*. Diese Unterschiede in der Schreibung spiegeln die Realität.

3 Die phonetische Transkription basiert auf den Lautschriftzeichen von Daniel Jones, A.C. Gimson: *Everyman's English Pronouncing Dictionary.* London, Dent [14] 1988

4 Eine ausgezeichnete Hilfe bei der Arbeit mit Kollokationsfeldern ist M. Benson, E. Benson, R. Ilson: *Student's Dictionary of Collocations. Mit einem Vorwort von F.J. Hausmann.* Berlin, Cornelsen Verlag 1989 (Best.-Nr. 23249).

5 Eine systematische Einführung und einen praktischen Wegweiser zur Textproduktion bietet E. Werlich: *Student's Guide to Text Production.* Berlin, Cornelsen Verlag 1988 (Best.-Nr. 20290).

Didaktisches Inhaltsverzeichnis

Chapter I: Commonwealth and Common Market

Chapter II: Education and Class

Text	Titel	SB, S.	LB, S.	Wortzahl	Sprach-variante	Textform/-variante	Inhalt/landeskundliche Thematik	Semantic and collocational field	Weitere thematische Verknüpfungen
1	Arnold Wesker: Education – It's Asking Questions All the Time	37	24	1199	BE	drama (excerpt)	the importance of education for the development of greater awareness and personal freedom	Approaches to life	growing up; family; individual in society; class; culture; mass media; men and women; language
2	Jilly Cooper: Everyone Has an Accent	40	27	723	BE	comment (excerpt)	language and class	Language and class	stereotypes; mass media; individual in society
3	John Wain: Silly Notions of an Upper-Class Herrenvolk	42	29	1252	BE	novel (excerpt)	class distinctions and class-determined values	Arguing	individual in society; stereotypes; work; social mobility
4	School Fees Made Possible	44	32	–	BE	advertisement	financing private education for one's children	Specialist help	family; individual in society; class
5	William Trevor: The World in Miniature	46	34	1306	BE	novel (excerpt)	the aims of public school education	Secondary education (public school)	growing up; sport and class
6	Robert Holman: Cricket Snobbery Must End	50	37	236	BE	letter to the editor	class and sport	Cricket	sport and recreation; individual in society; education; class
7	Peter Shaffer: How Are You Settling Down at Cambridge?	51	39	712	BE	drama (excerpt)	the purpose of a university education	University education	growing up; family; individual in society; class

Chapter III: Work and Welfare

Text	Titel	SB, S.	LB, S.	Wortzahl	Sprach-variante	Textform/-variante	Inhalt/landeskundliche Thematik	Semantic and collocational field	Weitere thematische Verknüpfungen
1	Barry Hines: At the Careers Office	61	52	845	BE	novel (excerpt)	the difficulty of finding a job for a young person	Looking for work	growing up; economics
2	Bill Hewitt et al.: The Haves and the Have-Nots	63	55	897	AE	interpretive news story (excerpt)	the economic and social situation of present-day Britain	Britain's economic situation	life in the cities; class system; work; welfare state; industrialization
3	Family Income Supplement	66	57	–	BE	leaflet	information on welfare benefits for families	Income Supplement	individual in society; welfare state
4	Paul Harrison: Adding Insult to Injury	69	58	733	BE	feature story (excerpt)	a woman's experiences of the welfare system	Social Security support	poverty; life in the cities
5	Katharine Whitehorn: The Paula Principle	71	59	481	BE	essay (excerpt)	women's self-image and work	Career	men and women; social mobility
6	John Wyndham: No Ordinary Robot	72	62	748	BE	short story (excerpt)	a humanoid robot as a household servant	An electric mechanism	science and technology
7	Benjamin Disraeli: Children's Work	74	64	468	BE	novel (excerpt)	children's work in 19th century coal mines	Work in a mine	industrialization; Victorian England; trade unions; industrial relations
8	Henry Brougham: Address to Labourers on Destroying Machinery (1830)	76	66	529	BE	speech (excerpt)	the effects of labour-saving machines on the lives of workers in the 19th century	Introduction of new machinery	industrialization; Victorian England; economics; crime and violence; science and technology; industrial relations; trade unions

Chapter IV: Constitutional History and Present Politics

Text	Titel	SB, S.	LB, S.	Wortzahl	Sprach-variante	Textform/-variante	Inhalt/landeskundliche Thematik	Semantic and collocational field	Weitere thematische Verknüpfungen
1a	Excerpts from the Magna Carta (1215)	85	74	374	BE	legal document (excerpt)	eight of the 63 articles of the Magna Carta: essential liberties	–	Crown vs. Parliament, 1215–1688; system of government
1b	Excerpts from the Bill of Rights	87	76	220	BE	legal document (excerpt)	the rights of parliament over the Crown	Law	Crown vs. Parliament, 1215–1688; system of government
2	James Callaghan: The Fixed Centre	90	78	608	BE	feature story	the role of the Queen in society as seen by an ex-prime minister	The Monarchy	system of government; political parties
3	Spencer Reiss, Donna Foote: New Life in the House of Lords	92	80	501	AE	interpretive news story	the role of the House of Lords in the British system of government	Parliament	system of government; political parties
4	Anthony Sampson: A Disaster for the Middle	96	83	1042	AE	comment	the British party system and the position of the SDP	Party system	system of government; political parties; political changes
5	Jasper Ridley: The Birth of the Established Church	99	89	471	BE	historical study (excerpt)	Henry VIII's split with the Catholic Church	The Church	Anglicanism; system of government; religion, religious groupings
6	Colin Hughes: The Bishop and and the Lord	101	90	531	BE	report (excerpt)	religion and politics	Religion and politics	Anglicanism; political parties; elections
7	Peter Carter: Things Weren't as Nice as They Had Been	103	93	1459	BE	novel (excerpt)	the differences between Catholics and Protestants in Northern Ireland as seen by two boys	–	(Northern) Ireland; war and peace; growing up

Chapter V: The Frontier and the American Dream

Text	Titel	SB, S.	LB, S.	Wortzahl	Sprach-variante	Textform/-variante	Inhalt/landeskundliche Thematik	Semantic and collocational field	Weitere thematische Verknüpfungen
1	Archibald MacLeish: A Country of Extremes	113	101	305	AE	impressionistic description	the vastness and variety of the USA	–	mobility; national identity; regions/regionalism
2	Michel-Guillaume Jean de Crèvecœur: The American – A New Man	115	102	452	AE	essay (excerpt)	an 18th century settler's view of the American national identity	–	auto-stereotypes; national identity; American Dream; melting pot; immigration
3	E.L. Doctorow: A Crazy Quilt of Humanity	116	104	979	AE	novel (excerpt)	immigrants' life in New York City in the early 20th century	Immigration	melting pot; national identity; immigration; ethnic minorities; poverty; life in the cities
4	Frederick Jackson Turner: The Frontiersman's Prophetic Dream	119	106	501	AE	essay (excerpt)	Western settlement and the myth of the frontier	The opportunity of the West	manifest destiny; American Dream; national identity; auto-stereotypes; regions
5	David Galloway: The American Frontier – The Line of Potential	122	108	321	AE	lecture (excerpt)	the continuance of the frontier myth in the age of space technology	The new frontier	American Dream; manifest destiny
6	Dave Martin Nez: New Way, Old Way	124	110	288	AE	poem	the clash between the Native American tradition and the white American way of life	Blending two American cultures	national identity; culture; ethnic minorities
7	Vern E. Smith: A Slowly Beginning Shift	125	111	752	AE	reportage (excerpt)	changes in the conditions of blacks in the Southern states	Segregation and desegregation	ethnic minorities; poverty; regions; social mobility

Chapter VI: Religion and Education

Text	Titel	SB, S.	LB, S.	Wortzahl	Sprach-variante	Textform/-variante	Inhalt/landeskundliche Thematik	Semantic and collocational field	Weitere thematische Verknüpfungen
1	Berton Rouecké: Our People Take Religion Very Seriously	139	121	128	AE	report (excerpt)	religious diversity in the USA	Religion	American values; conservatism
2	C. Malcolm Watkins: God's Chosen People	140	122	880	AE	historical study (excerpt)	the Puritans' concept of life and their search for an ideal society	Puritans and society	religion and politics; colonial times; work; American values
3	Jonathan Raban: Pleasant Hill Missionary Baptist Church	144	124	736	BE/AE	memoirs (excerpt)	a political rally / religious service in a black church	–	religion and politics; Civil Rights Movement; human rights
4	Year of the Bible – A Proclamation	147	127	517	AE	proclamation	the position of the bible in American society	American values	religion and politics; Founding Fathers, colonial times; national identity
5	America's Catholics: Who They Are, What They Think	149	128	–	AE	diagram and explanatory text	the social position and opinions of American Catholics	Morality	religion and politics; American values
6	Nicholas Ashford: Jerry Falwell's Moral Majority	150	130	815	BE	feature story	a well-known evangelist's thoughts and his political and educational activities	Religion	religion and politics; American values; conservatism; education
7	Lucia Solorzano et al.: A Tough School Pays Off	153	132	564	AE	reportage	changes undertaken in a school formerly known for its low standard of discipline	Education	growing up; crime and violence; immigration; class system

Chapter VII: Social Security and Civil Rights

Text	Titel	SB, S.	LB, S.	Wortzahl	Sprach-variante	Textform/-variante	Inhalt/landeskundliche Thematik	Semantic and collocational field	Weitere thematische Verknüpfungen
1	Studs Terkel: A Ford Assembly Line Worker	163	141	990	AE	interview (excerpt)	working conditions at an assembly plant	Assembly line work	world of work; technology
2	Raymond Barrio: The Miscalculation	165	143	872	AE	novel (excerpt)	a conflict between Mexican fruit pickers and their Mexican overseer	Exploitation	world of work; poverty; immigration; ethnic minorities; industrial relations
3	Carey W. English: Women and Organized Labor	168	146	487	AE	interpretive news story (excerpt)	the increasing involvement of working women in unionism	Women and unionism	world of work; industrial relations; women's movement
4	Betty Friedan: The 100 Percent Perfect Superwoman	170	148	1002	AE	speech (excerpt)	the problems facing women in today's world of work	Women and career	world of work; family; women's movement
5	Frank Trippett: The Anguish of the Jobless	172	150	1073	AE	essay (excerpt)	the psychological consequences of unemployment	Unemployment	world of work; poverty; individual in society; economics; work ethic
6	Some Voices in the American Social Welfare Debate	177	152	a) 231 b) 193 c) 371	AE	a) report (excerpt) b) book review (excerpt) c) proclamation (excerpt)	the pros and cons of welfare and social security	Welfare	poverty; economics; individual in society; American values
7	Alice Walker: Freedom March	179	154	986	AE	novel (excerpt)	the fight against racial segregation from a young black woman's point of view	Demonstration	Civil Rights Movement; individual in society; ethnic minorities

Chapter VIII: Constitutional History and Political Reality

Text	Titel	SB, S.	LB, S.	Wortzahl	Sprach-variante	Textform/-variante	Inhalt/landeskundliche Thematik	Semantic and collocational field	Weitere thematische Verknüpfungen
1	Excerpt from the Declaration of Independence (1776)	189	160	181	AE	legal document (excerpt)	the philosophical and political principles of the American Revolution	–	human rights; individual in society; American values
2	The Bill of Rights (1791)	192	162	481	AE	legal document	the constitutional rights of the citizens of the USA	The law	human rights; individual in society; American values
3	Maurice Cranston: Human Rights	194	164	573	AE	essay (excerpt)	the historical origins and and the development of the concept of human rights	Human rights	American values; individual in society
4	Ray Bradbury: The Happiness Boys	195	165	1107	AE	novel (excerpt)	a futuristic society's attempt to achieve mass happiness through thought control	–	human rights; individual in society; political and social (anti-) utopias; aggression, violence
5	Political Parties	199	168	581	AE	report (excerpt)	the US party system	Government and politics	system of government
6	John Steinbeck: Americans and Their President	201	169	663	AE	essay (excerpt)	Americans' conflicting attitudes towards the presidency	Public opinion	American values; national identity
7	Dick Pawelek: The Highest Judicial Power in the Land	203	171	638	AE	report (excerpt)	the Supreme Court's history and constitutional role	The law	system of government; human rights; civil rights

Chapter IX: Town and Country

Text	Titel	SB, S.	LB, S.	Wortzahl	Sprach-variante	Textform/-variante	Inhalt/landeskundliche Thematik	Semantic and collocational field	Weitere thematische Verknüpfungen
1	Michael Manser: The Nonsense of Conformity	215	181	505	BE	comment (excerpt)	contemporary architecture and the conflict between conformity and innovation	Architecture and design	art; architecture; environment
2	Brian Clark: Architectural Hindsight	218	183	491	BE	drama (excerpt)	Britain's "New Towns"	–	architecture; town planning; environment
3	Joyce Carol Oates: Dreaming America	220	185	203	AE	poem	the gradual displacement of nature and agriculture by urban growth	–	environment; American Dream
4	W.J. Weatherby: Apartment-Hunting in New York City	221	187	630	AE	feature story (excerpt)	the problems faced by an individual looking for an apartment	City housing	class system, social mobility; immigration; ethnic minorities; crime and violence
5	Edward I. Koch: Racial Integration in Housing	223	188	533	AE	comment (excerpt)	problems arising from racially and socially mixed areas	Class and race in housing	class system; poverty; social mobility; ethnic minorities
6	Saul Bellow: I Want to Report a Crime	224	190	482	AE	novel (excerpt)	crime in New York City	Crime	crime and violence
7	Stephen Gardiner: The Biggest Blunder of All	226	192	774	BE	comment (excerpt)	criticism of British town planning since the 1950s	City planning	architecture; town planning; environment

Chapter X: Language and the Media

Text	Titel	SB, S.	LB, S.	Wortzahl	Sprach-variante	Textform/-variante	Inhalt/ landeskundliche Thematik	Semantic and collocational field	Weitere thematische Verknüpfungen
1	Susanna McBee: English, the Language of Prestige	237	202	907	AE	report (excerpt)	the spread of English and its role as a world language today	The English language	language and society; English-speaking world; Empire; Commonwealth
2	Christopher Priest: American English and British English	240	204	819	BE	essay	the problems of translating from British into American English and vice versa	Varieties of English	English-speaking world
3	Peter Trudgill, Jean Hannah: Standard English	242	206	722	BE	linguistic study (excerpt)	varieties of the English language	English in foreign language teaching	English-speaking world
4	Alem Mezgebe: Language as a Tool of Racist Attitudes	245	208	779	BE	comment	racist terms in the English language	Racism in language	language and society; (hetero- and auto-) stereotypes; human rights
5	Casey Miller, Kate Swift: Sexist Bias in Language	248	210	784	BE	linguistic study (excerpt)	sexism in language and how to avoid it	Sexism in language	men and women; language and society; (hetero- and auto-) stereotypes; human rights
6	Truth and the Press – A Discussion	252	212	1326	AE	discussion	the role of the press in modern American society	The Media	mass media
7	David Anderson, Peter Benjaminson: The Classic Ethical Dilemma	255	216	626	AE	political study (excerpt)	problems and questions raised by investigative reporting	The Media	mass media; individual in society; human rights

Chapter XI: Literature and the Arts

Text	Titel	SB, S.	LB, S.	Wortzahl	Sprach-variante	Textform/-variante	Inhalt/landeskundliche Thematik	Semantic and collocational field	Weitere thematische Verknüpfungen
1	Thomas L. Wymer: Why Didn't He Come Right Out and Say It?	265	225	949	AE	textbook introduction (excerpt)	the purpose and meaning of literature	Literature	language; fiction: culture
2	Ted Hughes: The Thought-Fox	267	227	137	BE	poem	the creative process	–	fiction; poetry
3	Robert Penn Warren: A Poem You Can Feel to Your Toes	268	229	491	AE	interview (excerpt)	how to write and appreciate poetry	Poetry	language
4	S.I.Hayakawa: Poetry and Advertising	270	231	532	AE	linguistic study (excerpt)	similarities in the form and function of poetry and advertising	Poetry and advertising	language and society
5	Hiram Haydn: The Elizabethans and Modern Man	272	233	360	AE	literary study (excerpt)	some parallels between the Elizabethan age and our own	–	Elizabethan England; scientific and technological progress
6	Charles Lamb: Painful Reality on the Stage	274	235	289	BE	essay (excerpt)	the difference between reading Shakespeare and seeing his plays performed	Tragedy	–
7	Willy Russell: It's Fun, Tragedy, Isn't It?	275	236	972	BE	drama (excerpt)	a working-class woman's impressions of a Shakespeare performance	Tragedy	education; class system
8	Yet Another Version of Shakespeare	277	238	137 / 108	AE BE	comic (excerpt)	a comic strip version of Shakespeare's *Macbeth*	The performing arts	literary adaptions

Chapter XII: War and Peace

Text	Titel	SB, S.	LB, S.	Wortzahl	Sprachvariante	Textform/-variante	Inhalt/landeskundliche Thematik	Semantic and collocational field	Weitere thematische Verknüpfungen
1	Aldous Huxley: Bokanovsky's Process	291	247	431	BE	novel (excerpt)	large-scale in vitro fertilization to produce artificial human beings	Genetic engineering	individual in society; political/social (anti-)utopias; science and technology: advances in medicine; human rights
2	Spencer Reiss et al.: High-Tech Babies	294	250	623	AE	feature story (excerpt)	contemporary reproductive science and the ethical questions raised by it	Ethics and procreation	family; men and women; science and technology: advances in medicine; human rights
3	Varindra Tarzie Vittachi: The Sorcerer's Apprentice	296	252	548	AE	comment (excerpt)	scientific and technological progress and the question of responsibility	Science and responsibility	science and technology; human rights
4	John Scott of Amwell: The Drum	299	254	101	BE	poem	an 18th century critical view of the glorification of war	–	individual in society; war and peace
5	Ambrose Bierce: The Ingenious Patriot	300	256	305	AE	parable	technological progress and the arms race	Armaments	science and technology; war and peace
6	Robert Waithman: Force of Nature Harnessed	301	258	581	BE	interpretive news story	the development and first use of the atom bomb	The atomic bomb	science and technology; war and peace
7	Nevil Shute: Deadly Winds	304	261	776	BE	novel (excerpt)	a conversation between two people in Australia after a nuclear war has wiped out life in the northern hemisphere	Radiation	science and technology; political/social (anti-)utopias; war and peace

Chapter I: Commonwealth and Common Market

Das erste der vier Kapitel über Großbritannien beschäftigt sich mit der Stellung Großbritanniens in der Welt, ihrer Veränderung und den Folgen, die sich daraus für die Gegenwart und Zukunft ergeben. In der "Info-Box" (SB, S. 21 f.) wird das zum Verständnis nötige historische Hintergrundwissen vermittelt.

Bei der Wahl der Texte mußte notwendigerweise getrennt werden, was in der Realität verzahnt ist. So lassen sich Verbindungslinien sowohl zu den Kapiteln II bis IV ziehen, z.B. im Bereich der Themen „Erziehung", „Arbeitslosigkeit", „Bedeutung der Monarchie", „Parteien", als auch zu Teilen der "Universal Topics", wie sie in den Kapiteln IX bis XII behandelt werden, z.B. im Bereich der Themen „Stadtentwicklung", „Sprache". Vergleiche bieten sich insbesondere mit Problemstellungen in den Kapiteln V, VII und VIII, d.h. dem den USA gewidmeten Teil, an, z.B. im Bereich der Themen „Einwanderung", „Ethnische Gruppen", „Arbeit und Arbeitslosigkeit", „Stellung der Frau", „Verhältnis zu Europa", „weltpolitische Bedeutung".

Der für Kap. I gewählte inhaltliche Rahmen wird exemplarisch anhand von Texten erschlossen, die wichtige Akzente setzen. Die Auswahl erfolgte mit dem Ziel, das Verständnis der Schüler/innen für das gegenwärtige Großbritannien zu fördern, was jedoch ohne geschichtliche Kenntnisse nicht zu erreichen ist. Bei der Vermittlung dieser Kenntnisse sollte die "Info-Box" (SB, S. 21f.) herangezogen werden. Auch die "Background information" zu den einzelnen Texten kann vollständig oder in Teilen in den Unterricht integriert werden.

1 The British Empire at Its Greatest Extent, 1920

Didaktische Hinweise

Diese Karte dokumentiert das Britische Empire zur Zeit seiner größten Ausdehnung und veranschaulicht den ersten Teil der "Info-Box" (SB, S. 21). Bei der Auswertung sollte den Schülern/Schülerinnen zunächst Gelegenheit gegeben werden, ungesteuerte bzw. durch die vorangestellte "Note" nur wenig gelenkte Wahrnehmungen und daraus resultierende Probleme zu versprachlichen. Ergänzende oder stimulierende Lehrerfragen könnten sich beziehen auf die geographische Ausdehnung (Schwerpunkte, relative Leerstellen), auf die unterschiedlichen Abhängigkeitsverhältnisse (in ihrer Verteilung), auf die Größe des „Mutterlands" im Vergleich zu einzelnen oder allen abhängigen Gebieten sowie auf die politischen, ökonomischen, kulturellen und ethnischen Probleme. Von besonderer Wichtigkeit ist die Frage nach der Bedeutung der englischen Sprache für das Empire. Zum einen bildete das Empire die Voraussetzung dafür, daß Englisch zur Weltsprache werden konnte; zum anderen resultieren Probleme der Identitätsfindung in manchen der ehemaligen Kolonien auch aus der Tatsache, daß Englisch in ihnen, wenn nicht Amtssprache, so doch Zweitsprache ist (vgl. zum Thema „Sprache" u.a. Text 10 und besonders Kap. X, Text 1 bis 4). Schließlich böte sich – eventuell als Arbeitshypothese – die Frage an nach dem möglichen Einfluß des Empire auf die

Briten (positiv etwa im Sinne von Weltoffenheit, negativ etwa im Sinne eines
generellen Überlegenheitsgefühls) und auf die Angehörigen der abhängigen Gebiete
(Gefühl der Unterdrückung, Gefühl der Zusammengehörigkeit).

2 Louis Fischer: Gandhi, the Salt Criminal

Didaktische Hinweise

Historischer Hintergrund von Text 2 ist die Zeit des Übergangs vom Empire zum
Commonwealth, hier anhand eines Beispiels, an dem die innere Notwendigkeit der
Veränderung besonders deutlich wird. Dabei wurde mit Indien eine Kolonie
gewählt, die sowohl unter einem eher unwägbaren emotionalen Gesichtspunkt
(*Königin* Victoria war *Kaiserin* von Indien) als auch unter ökonomischem Aspekt
(Indien als größter Handelspartner, d.h. Abnehmer britischer Produkte) von
besonderer Bedeutung war. Gandhi und sein gewaltloser bürgerlicher Ungehorsam
wurden weit über das Britische Empire bzw. Commonwealth hinaus bekannt und
vorbildhaft für andere Unabhängigkeits- und Bürgerrechtsbewegungen (vgl. Kap.
VII, Text 7 und 8).

Der lange und nicht ganz einfache Text hat den Vorteil, eine in sich abgeschlossene Episode darzustellen und Gandhi selbst zu Wort kommen zu lassen.
Unterrichtsmethodisch ist er darüber hinaus geeignet für andere als die sich bei
kürzeren Texten anbietenden Formen der Erschließung.

Background information

Louis Fischer (1896–1970): American journalist, who, from 1921 onwards, reported on
events in Russia, Spain and India in particular. Apart from his reports on current
affairs, he wrote more than twenty books on political topics. He was a member of
the Institute for Advanced Study, Princeton, and a member of the faculty of
Princeton University.

Mohandas Karamchand Gandhi (1869–1948): usually referred to as Mahatma
Gandhi (Mahatma means "Great Soul", a title which was probably conferred on
him by Rabindranath Tagore). He came from a Hindu family which taught him
pacifism and respect for all living things as part of its religious belief. In 1888 he
went to England to study law. From 1893 to 1914 he worked in South Africa, where
he started his political career as an advocate for his fellow Indians who had to
endure racial discrimination. It was while in a South African prison that he read
Thoreau's essay "On the Duty of Civil Disobedience", which, according to Gandhi's
biographer Louis Fischer, concurred with his own view.

Back in India, Gandhi soon became the leader of the Indian national movement
against British subjugation. His struggle for Indian independence lasted for 28 years.
His policy of nonviolence and non-cooperation earned him world-wide respect. As
head of the Indian National Congress he finally saw independence obtained in
August 1947 – at the expense of partitioning the country into India and Pakistan. He
was shot by a fanatic in January 1948.

Britain and India: The relationship between Britain and India was established in the seventeenth century when the British Government granted the East India Company the right to an unlimited British trade monopoly in Asia. Gradual expansion of its power in India led to an interest in colonialism, which, aided by the lack of homogeneity among the Indian states, eventually resulted in various forms of direct and indirect rule over most of the subcontinent.

Following the Indian Mutiny of 1857, control over India was assumed by the British Government. India's new status and Prime Minister Disraeli's (cf. SB, Ch. III, Text 7, and "Background information", p. 64 f. of this book) proclamation of Queen Victoria as empress of India in 1876 did little to relieve the aspiration of Indians for political participation and self-government. In 1885 the Indian National Congress party was founded, the leaders of which were instrumental in the process of gaining independence. Growing agitation and frustration, particularly at Britain's failure to reward India's loyalty and participation in World War I, culminated in the 1919 protest at Amritsar, a protest which turned into a massacre when British troops fired on the crowd, killing and wounding hundreds of protestors. It was then that Gandhi started his struggle for Indian independence. Success was partial, in that reforms were put forward by the British Government, but these met with criticism in both countries for being either too liberal or not liberal enough. The most important reforms were laid down in the Government of India Acts of 1919 and 1935, the latter of which was drafted after several Round Table Conferences, two of which were attended by Gandhi.

With the outbreak of World War II, considerations of India's independence were put to one side by Britain. Therefore, it was not until August 15, 1947, that Dominion status was finally granted. However, contrary to Gandhi's hopes, the country was divided into two states: India (predominantly Hindu) with Nehru as its first prime minister and Lord Mountbatten (who had been viceroy since 1946) as governor-general, and Pakistan (predominantly Moslem), which originally consisted of East Pakistan (Bangladesh since 1971) and West Pakistan (now Pakistan). In 1949 India became a republic within the Commonwealth. After its separation from West Pakistan, Bangladesh stayed in the Commonwealth, whereas Pakistan left in 1972.

Semantic and collocational field "Repression and subjugation"

a system of progressive exploitation, organized violence ✧ (to) impoverish sb., (to) reduce sb. (e.g. a people) politically to serfdom, (to) sap the foundations of a culture, (to) crush the life out of sb., (to) make the burden fall on sb., (to) arrest sb.

Semantic and collocational field "Forms of protest"

an armed rebellion, (to) explode into nationwide violence ✧ organized nonviolence, (to) embark on civil disobedience ✧ publicized defiance (to) disregard the provisions of a law, (to) march, (to) exhort sb. to do sth., (to) break a/the law ✧ (to) convert sb. through nonviolence, (to) make sb. see the wrong they have done

Talking about the text – Suggested answers

1. Gandhi wants political serfdom to be replaced by political self-determination, he wants exploitation to end and Indian culture to be restored to its old strength (cf. ll. 21–24). In short, his main objective is independence for India, i.e. at least Dominion status (cf. l. 25). In his 1930 activities he focuses on exploitation and, in particular, on the injustice of the British salt tax, esp. for the poor (cf. ll. 27–37).

2. As far as Britain and the British are concerned, he distinguishes between British rule in India and the British as individuals. British rule, in his view, is a curse (cf. ll. 19–20). He speaks of "the organized violence of the British government" (ll. 51–52). As to individual Englishmen, he does not intend harm to them or to any legitimate interest they may have in India (cf. ll. 20–21). His letter to the British Viceroy Lord Irwin, which, incidentally, starts with the words *"Dear Friend"* (l. 15), bears witness of his attitude towards the individual Englishman, even if he is the representative of the British government; Gandhi writes: "I have too great a regard for you *as a man* to wish to hurt your feelings" (ll. 46–47). Although he wants the evils caused by the British rule removed (cf. l. 56), his attitude is free of hate and revenge. The words that he chooses when stating his ambition in his letter to Irwin have strong moral and religious connotations (cf. ll. 53–54).

3. As he says in his letter to Irwin, he decides "to disregard the provisions of the Salt Laws" (ll. 60–61). He puts his plan into practice when, after dipping into the Arabian Sea at Dandi, he picks up some of the salt left behind by the waves (cf. ll. 95–96). This means – though rather symbolically – that he is in possession of salt which has not been bought from the government salt monopoly which, according to British law in India, is a punishable crime (cf. ll. 98–99).

4. First and foremost his choice of nonviolent action stems from his religious beliefs, which forbid him to "intentionally hurt anything that lives" (l. 18). In addition, moral superiority, of whose eventual effectiveness he seems to be convinced, can only be gained through nonviolent action (cf. ll. 53–54). [Cf. also question 5.]

5. If effectiveness is equated with immediate success, Gandhi's method is not effective at all. The fact, however, that Gandhi attracts so many supporters who are willing to risk their lives speaks for the man and his method. This method is effective indeed, for it paves the way for India's independence: it makes the Indians aware of their strength while it undermines British power by pointing out its moral deficiency.

6. In l. 11 the reader is told that Gandhi has come to a decision, but instead of being informed about its contents immediately, the reader is presented with Gandhi's letter to the viceroy, which – some 50 lines further down – contains Gandhi's plan "to disregard the provisions of the Salt Laws" (ll. 60–61) on a certain day. Before this plan can be put into practice, Gandhi has to wait for Irwin's reaction, and the reader is informed at length about the situation in India. After that the reader follows Gandhi on his march for 24 days (or 22 lines respectively). Only then does the reader learn the details of Gandhi's plan: Gandhi becomes a salt criminal by picking up salt left behind by the waves of the sea. Thus the writer – and with him the reader – follows the course of events in the way the people of India experience it. Fischer provides the reader with extensive quotations from Gandhi's letter to Irwin, so it could also be argued that the reader is kept slightly better informed than people in India were at the time. But since the letter does not give away any details, it adds – together with other quotations – to the vividness of the text and increases the reader's suspense by interrupting the actual narration.

7. – –

● 8. *Report to the class on Gandhi's life (based on Louis Fischer's "The Life of Mahatma Gandhi").*
   – –

● 9. *Compare and contrast Gandhi's Salt March and Martin Luther King's March on Washington (including his "I have a dream" speech).*
   – –

3 Bernard Porter: The Emperor's New Clothes – A Sham

Didaktische Hinweise

Während Text 2 den inneren Zwang zum Umbruch im Empire verdeutlicht, widmet sich Text 3 der Einschätzung des Commonwealth als der „Nachfolgeorganisation" des Empire. Es wurde bewußt ein Text gewählt, der zwei einseitige Sichtweisen gegenüberstellt und so die grundsätzliche Frage nach der Bedeutung des Commonwealth provoziert. Die als Text 4 abgedruckte Karte (SB, S. 16) sollte bei der Arbeit mit diesem Text zur Verdeutlichung herangezogen werden.

Literaturhinweise: Dennis Judd, Peter Slinn: *The Evolution of the Modern Commonwealth, 1902 – 1980*. London, MacMillan 1982. – Bernard Porter: *The Lion's Share. A Short History of British Imperialism 1850 – 1983*. London, Longman [2]1985.

Background information

Commonwealth: For information on the Commonwealth in general, cf. "Info-Box" (SB, pp. 21 f.) and "Background information", pp. 6 f. of this book.

"In the 1950s the fact that so many ex-colonies had elected to stay within the Commonwealth ..." (ll. 1–2): Actually, fewer than ten colonies or dependent territories became independent in the 1950s or shortly before. It must have been the importance of the colonies that counted. Among the colonies that decided to stay within the Commonwealth after independence were India and Pakistan. (Pakistan left in 1972.) Already in the Commonwealth were the "settler" countries such as Australia and Canada. (For the dates concerning the members of the so-called "Old Commonwealth", cf. "Info-Box", SB, pp. 21 f.)

"But by the 'sixties ..." (l. 15): In the 1960s about 25 colonies/dependent territories became independent, most of which remained within the Commonwealth.

"British nationality" (l. 12): *"Common citizenship"* (l. 14): Common citizenship was finally abolished when the 1981 British Nationality Act came into effect on January 1, 1983. It restricted British citizenship – together with the right to settle in Britain – severely. It may be seen as a continuation of the earlier (Commonwealth) Immigration Acts of 1962, 1968 and 1971.

"Commonwealth conference" (ll. 25–26) is another term for the Heads of Government conference (cf. "Background information", p. 7 of this book).

Semantic and collocational field "Empire – Commonwealth"

an imperialist, loss of empire ✧ an empire-substitute, a substitute for empire, an ex-colony, a dominion ✧ an extended family, a mother country ✧ filial gratitude, tradition, friendship, a common/mutual interest, loyalty ✧ a continuing unity, a substantive continuity, (to) be cemented by common bonds, (to) be united ✧ (to) stay within the Commonwealth, (to) join sth. ✧ trade preferences, the right to enter Britain freely, a common citizenship ✧ (to) air one's grievances, (to) force sb./sth., out, (to) break off diplomatic relations with a country

Talking about the text – Suggested answers

1. In the first paragraph (and the first sentence of the second paragraph) the writer describes the imperialists' view of the Commonwealth. It is indiscriminately positive.
The second paragraph seems to reflect the frustrations of the imperialists, their wishful thinking and unrealistic ideas now being replaced by rejection and disillusionment. But it is not so much the Commonwealth that was changing, for "the Commonwealth was never united at all" (ll. 21–22). The indiscriminately negative view at the end of the second paragraph is the writer's own, which he uses to mock the imperialists' false expectations. The views in the two paragraphs do share one characteristic: they are both one-sided.
2. The imperialists' real intention was selfish rather than altruistic. They wanted to use the Commonwealth as an instrument of British power and influence (cf. ll. 27–29), seeing it more or less as their old Empire under a new name.
3. The old imperialists can hardly be expected to favour a modern view of the family as a unit of equals. Thus, the family metaphor would have to be seen in the context of something like the Victorian family structure, in which there was a clear head of the family (i.e. the father in Victorian times, the "mother country" in this case), with a body of dependent members (i.e. the Commonwealth countries).
4. [In terms of figures, such a definition implies that a substantial part of the world's population (about 20 percent) would be legally entitled to settle in Britain. Even if only a fraction of the potential immigrants actually arrived, overpopulation (with all its social and financial consequences) as well as a clash of cultures would be among the problems.]
● 5. *Give a short report on the functioning of the Commonwealth today.*
[One good source for students to use is "Britain. An Official Handbook". For the most important points of the 1989 edition, cf. "Background information", below.]

4 The Commonwealth, 1988

Didaktische Hinweise

Diese Karte veranschaulicht die Ausdehnung des Commonwealth im Jahre 1988, nachdem die meisten der vormals abhängigen Gebiete ihre Unabhängigkeit erlangt hatten. Sie stellt insofern eine didaktische Progression dar, als auch Informationen über das Empire und die aus dem Commonwealth ausgetretenen Staaten integriert wurden. Bei ihrer Versprachlichung bietet sich daher in erster Linie ein Vergleich mit dem Empire an. Hinweise zum Commonwealth allgemein und zu einzelnen Gebieten und Aspekten finden sich in der "Background information" (vgl. unten), im ersten Teil der "Info-Box" (SB, S. 21 f.) und in den "Background information" zu den Texten 2 und 3 dieses Kapitels (vgl. S. 2 f. und S. 5).

Diese Karte kann auch bei der Erörterung der in den weiteren Texten dieses Kapitels angesprochenen Probleme zur Verdeutlichung herangezogen werden, etwa bei den Texten 5, 6, 8 bis 11 mit den Themen „Commonwealth und EG", „Einwanderung und Minoritäten", „Großbritanniens Vergangenheit, Gegenwart und Zukunft".

Background information

The Commonwealth is a voluntary association of independent states, all of which recognize the British monarch, Queen Elizabeth II, as "Head of the Commonwealth" – this non-functional title is not hereditary. All the member states previously formed part of the British Empire.

In 1989 the Commonwealth comprised 48 member states with a population of more than 1,100 million, among them republics, national monarchies and 17 countries of which the Queen is head of state. According to the 1971 Declaration of Commonwealth Principles the Commonwealth exists as a means of "consulting and co-operating in the common interests of their peoples and in the promotion of international understanding and world peace". It has no formal constitutional structure. High commissioners in each member country – equal in status to ambassadors – are responsible for permanent or immediate consultation.

Heads of government meet every two years. Consultation at ministerial level takes place either annually (finance ministers) or every two or three years (health, education, law ministers). The meetings are organized through the Commonwealth Secretariat in London, which was established in 1965. The Secretariat is also involved in promoting cooperation, e.g. through the Commonwealth Fund for Technical Co-operation, which is administered by the Secretariat.

For further information cf. *Britain 1989. An Official Handbook.* Her Majesty's Stationery Office, London, 1989.

5 Britain and the EC

Didaktische Hinweise

Die Entscheidung, den Texten und Karten zur Entwicklung vom Empire zum Commonwealth eine Textgruppe zur EG-Problematik folgen zu lassen, wurde getroffen, um zunächst Großbritanniens gegenwärtige Außenpolitik weiterverfolgen zu können, ehe mit den Texten 8 bis 11 innenpolitische Probleme angesprochen werden. Das schließt jedoch nicht aus, daß die Behandlung der Texte 8 bis 11 – abweichend von der im SB gewählten Reihenfolge – auch im unmittelbaren Anschluß an Text 4 (Commonwealth–Karte) erfolgen kann.

Die Texte 5 bis 7 bilden eine geschlossene Textgruppe. Dabei behandeln die Texte 5 und 6 die von vielen Seiten als problematisch erachtete Eingliederung Großbritanniens in die EG (vgl. auch "Background information", unten, und die "Info-Box", SB, S. 22), Text 7 hat dagegen eher eine *Comic relief*-Funktion.

Während sich in der Bundesrepublik seit einigen Jahren immer mehr der Begriff „Europäische Gemeinschaft (EG)" durchsetzt, wird in Großbritannien bis heute überwiegend die Bezeichnung "European Economic Community (EEC)" bzw. "Common Market" verwandt. In den Lösungsvorschlägen wird die im jeweiligen Text stehende Abkürzung benutzt; fehlt sie, findet sich "EEC" bei der Behandlung historischer Fakten, "EC" bei der Beschäftigung mit der gegenwärtigen Problematik.

Background information

The two texts are taken from two of the three brochures that were delivered to every British household at the time of the referendum on Britain's further membership of the EEC in 1975.

Text 5a) is an excerpt from the official government brochure with the title "Britain's New Deal in Europe". Text 5 b) is part of the brochure "Why you should vote NO", published by the National Referendum Campaign.

Britain and the EC: Britain's relations with the EEC have been difficult from the start. In 1961, four years after the Treaty of Rome, the Conservative government of Harold Macmillan decided to apply for membership of the EEC. Negotiations, with Edward Heath as chief British negotiator, seemed to point to a successful conclusion, but in 1963 President Charles de Gaulle of France vetoed British membership because of Britain's Commonwealth ties. He feared that the relatively free trade of the Common Market would be open to all the countries of the Commonwealth. Britain's application was renewed in 1967 under the Labour government of Harold Wilson – despite the Labour party's opposition to the original application – and was again turned down by de Gaulle, this time his reason being Britain's poor economic situation.

A third attempt was started after de Gaulle retired in 1969. Negotiations began in June 1970, and these proved successful. In July 1972 the relevant bill was passed in the House of Commons by the Conservative government of Edward Heath, though by a narrow majority, due to the opposition Labour party's dissatisfaction with the terms of entry.

On January 1, 1973, Britain joined the EEC. A transition period was to last until 1979. In the 1974 election campaign Harold Wilson promised to hold a referendum on the question of Britain's further membership of the EEC – the first referendum ever to be held in Britain. After winning the elections, Harold Wilson reopened negotiations with the EEC on the terms of continued membership. Once these were improved, he recommended the British public to vote in favour of continued membership in the referendum of June 5, 1975, which they did by a large majority (67.2 % in favour).

However, at the end of the transition period in 1979/80, the Conservatives as well as Labour seemed to be ready to withdraw. Margaret Thatcher implied such a move in a fierce dispute with EEC member states over Britain's financial contributions. In its 1980 conference, the Labour Party voted in favour of a British withdrawal, which was, incidentally, one of the reasons for the founding of the SDP (cf. Ch. IV, Text 4).

Since then Britain has remained an uneasy partner within the EC. Although there seems no likelihood of a British withdrawal at present, Britain is quick to criticize the deficiencies of the EC as well as some of its more idealistic aims. It will be interesting to see how Britain's view of the EC changes after the introduction of the single European market in 1992.

Semantic and collocational field "EC membership"

a trade bloc, the Common Market, the European Community, a rigid/flexible organization ✧ Common Market policy, a loan, a grant, (to) decide/change policies, (to) enact laws, (to) raise taxes, (to) make rules ✧ (to) join sb./sth., (to) stay inside sth., (to) remain part of sth., (to) merge into a single nation ✧ (to) face the future, (to) affect the future, (to) be tough going, (to) adapt to changing world conditions, (to) respond to differing needs ✧ (to) be in a strange position, (to) benefit from sth., (to) play a major part in sth., (to) fix the terms of sth., (to) obtain sth., (to) hold down prices, (to) bring down the price of sth. ✧ an independent future, more/less control over one's own life, (to) rule oneself, (to) remain free to do sth., (to) be on one's own ✧ a bad bargain, (to) take away a right, (to) take precedence over sb./sth., (to) be wholly contrary to

Talking about the text – Suggested answers

1. Text a) emphasizes the financial aspect, i.e. Britain's share of the money from various European Funds. It also mentions a political aspect as a secondary argument, i.e. Britain's chance to exercise power within the EEC as an organization of worldwide consequence.

    Text b), on the other hand, concentrates exclusively on the political and legal aspects of Britain's membership of the EEC, which is portrayed as a loss of some of her independence.

2. Text a) provides precise figures as far as the financial aspect is concerned. The phrases covering the political aspect, however, remain fairly vague.

    Text b) with its exclusively political and legal argument refrains from giving concrete examples, although the problems referred to rather summarily cannot be completely denied. The opening statement is a mere contention which lacks proof. Sentences two and three refer to original intentions of the EEC, which although they are long-term goals, are presented in the text as imminent dangers to Britain's political status. Generally speaking, the lack of concrete examples and the tendency towards increasingly unspecific expressions (intentionally or unintentionally) further misunderstandings (e.g. the use of the terms "laws" and "policies").

3. The purpose of Text a) is to convince voters of the advantages of Britain's continued membership of the EEC. The overall layout – short paragraphs of one or two sentences for easy reading – is not unusual for an argumentative text meant to reach a wide audience. More specifically, the writer and layouter have taken care to emphasize two significant words in the argumentation, "inside" and "more". Both words are stressed through repetition, and both are used anaphorically for further emphasis. At a glance and even without reading the text properly, the reader sees that "inside" (the Common Market) there is "more" to be had.

4. Apart from the sentence that leads over from the descriptive to the prescriptive part of the text ("Your vote will affect ... to come.") the three sentences of the last paragraph are the shortest of the whole text. Unlike the rest of the text – with its fairly complicated sentence structures – they consist of straightforward demands (the sub-clause of the first being cumbersome rather than helpful from the rhetorical point of view) each introduced by "We say". The repetitive (anaphorical) element and the increasing shortness of the following demands ending with the precise advice, "Vote No", make the passage easy to remember and thus a powerful piece of (propaganda) rhetoric.

5. Text a) reflects a realistic view in acknowledging Britain's reduced importance in the world. The text admits that Britain on her own lacks strength and is in need of money. Like the British Empire previously, the EEC is now the "world's most powerful trade bloc", exercising influence even on non-member states. Membership of the EEC enables Britain to retain more influence on world affairs than she would otherwise have and to exert a major influence within the community itself.

    Text b) refers more indirectly to Britain's actual position after losing her Empire. "The right to rule ourselves which we have enjoyed for centuries" refers to the indisputable fact that there has not been a successful invasion of Britain since 1066. But the demand for independence "by ordinary people ... everywhere" could be a reference to Britain's imperial past and changed status: the British do not want to lose what their former colonies have only recently gained – and what Britain was forced to give them. The idea of an "independent future" for Britain, i.e. outside the EEC, however, seems to be a somewhat unrealistic assessment of Britain's current position in the world.

6. *How convincing do you, personally, find these two pieces of political propaganda? Explain your answer.*

    – –

6 Shirley Williams: Britain and Europe

Didaktische Hinweise

Wird dieser Text im Anschluß an die Texte 5 a) und 5 b) behandelt, so eignet er sich einerseits zur Verdeutlichung der anhaltend problematischen Haltung Großbritanniens gegenüber der EG, andererseits geht er in seiner sowohl ausführlichen und aspektreichen als auch sorgfältigen und verständnisvollen Begründung weit über die einer Art Abstimmungspropaganda verhafteten Texte 5 a) und 5 b) hinaus.

Da Shirley Williams zu den Gründungsmitgliedern (vgl. "Background information", unten) der SDP gehört, bietet sich die Behandlung dieses Textes auch bei der Besprechung der britischen Parteien an (vgl. Kap. IV, Text 4).

Background information

Shirley Williams (1930 –   ) was a Labour MP from 1964 to 1979. She held various party and government positions, among them Secretary of State for Prices and Consumer Protection (1974–1976), Secretary of State for Education and Science (1976–1979) and Paymaster General (1976–1979). In March 1981 she was one of the founding members of the Social Democratic Party (cf. SB, Ch. IV, Text 4), for which she won a seat in Parliament in the Crosby by-election in the same year. After six years as an SDP MP she lost her seat in the 1987 general election. Since 1987 she has been a member of the newly-formed Alliance Party, which was formed from the SDP and the Liberal Party.

Semantic and collocational field "EC membership"

an interdependent world, trade balance, balance of power ✧ a European federation, a vehicle for ideas and policies, the Common Agricultural Policy ✧ international investment, main beneficiary, trading preferences, (to) influence sb./sth. in favour of sb./sth. else, (to) have more weight, (to) involve oneself in sth. ✧ a levy on imports, higher food prices, increased energy costs, rising inflation, a deepening recession, economic discontent, sb.'s/sth.'s significance diminishes ✧ a reluctant partner, (to) weaken sb.'s ties with sb./sth. else, (to) remain isolated from sth., (to) opt out, (to) sour sb.'s attitude to sth. ✧ (to) be held responsible for sth., (to) be ill-adapted for sth.

Talking about the text – Suggested answers

1. All her specific reasons result from her basic conviction (cf. ll. 1–2) that the concept of independence has necessarily been replaced by global *inter*dependence. According to Williams, opting out of the EC would have negative financial and political consequences for Britain (cf. ll. 2–7). Secondly, she believes that Britain's international relations would be negatively affected (cf. ll. 8–16). Above all, she considers it very important that Britain should keep its role as a mediator between the United States and the EC on the one hand (a role that is particularly profitable to Britain) and the Commonwealth countries and the EC on the other (which is equally or even more profitable to developing countries). Last but not least, Williams does not want Britain to renounce voluntarily and rashly any political potential latently inherent in the EC (cf. ll. 49–54).
2. She shows herself to be realistic (cf. paragraphs 1 and 2) as to Britain's position in the world, responsible (cf. paragraph 2) with regard to Commonwealth obligations and optimistic (cf. paragraph 5) as far as the future possibilities of the EC are concerned.

3. She distinguishes between historical and economic reasons. Historical reasons, particularly the fact of Britain's isolation and the consequent lack of invasions, hamper Britain's true understanding of the basic value of the European Community. Among the economic reasons, Shirley Williams considers British dissatisfaction with the Common Agricultural Policy (CAP) legitimate but exaggerated (cf. ll. 19–21, 25–33, 44–48). All the other attempts at blaming the EC for Britain's economic situation (cf. ll. 18–19, 43–44) are, according to Williams, either unfounded (cf. ll. 22–24) or a sign of Britain lacking insight into general economic development since 1973 (cf. ll. 41–44).

4. [One might assume that Britain will remain reluctant or even hostile towards the EC in the near future. The fact that withdrawal was still being debated only five years after the British electorate had overwhelmingly voted *for* Britain's continued membership (cf. Ch. I, Text 5 a) indicates a certain instability in Britain's attitude. It might be argued that Europe will have a better chance in Britain when the next generation of politicians, who will definitely be without personal experience of the Empire, come into power and the single European Market is introduced.]

5. Although both texts are pleas for Britain's continued membership of the EC, Shirley Williams opens up a much wider historical and political perspective. She deals with many more specific problems, and mentions disadvantages as well as advantages. Altogether, there is a stringent logic in her argumentation. She is not bound to the rules of propaganda, which ask for simplification rather than differentiation.

6. *Assess Britain's present attitude towards the EC. For up-to-date information consult English and/or German news (paper) reports on the most recent EC events.*
   – –

7. *What concrete advantages can you see for young people in being "European" (i.e. belonging to a member state of the European Community)?*
   – –

7   Gillman Noonan: Pensionskuhhaltung

Didaktische Hinweise

Bestimmend für die Wahl des dritten und letzten Textes zur EG-Problematik war die Überlegung, die Schüler/innen in einer Weise anzusprechen, die sich von den Möglichkeiten der beiden anderen Texte deutlich unterscheidet (vgl. S. 7 und S. 10). „Pensionskuhhaltung" ist in doppelter Weise als Kontrapunkt zu sehen: Der fiktionale Text präsentiert – im Gegensatz zu den vorangegangenen Sachtexten – kein politisches Thema. Statt dessen wird den Schülern/Schülerinnen mit einem kräftigen Schuß Humor und Satire eine schwierige Situation aus dem Arbeitsalltag eines kleinen EG-Angestellten nahegebracht. Da es sich um ein Problem der Übersetzung aus dem Deutschen ins Englische handelt, ist der Text für Schüler/innen besonders geeignet. Sie können vermutlich auch eigene Erfahrungen dazu beitragen, welche Auswirkungen die ständige Beschäftigung mit einem Themenkomplex und die Unlösbarkeit eines Übersetzungsproblems in diesem Bereich haben können.

Dieser Text soll den Schülern/Schülerinnen Lesevergnügen bereiten, über dessen Gründe sie auch Auskunft geben sollten. Um den individuellen Zugang nicht zu verstellen, wurde der Aufgabenapparat – wie auch bei einer Reihe anderer Texte – im LB untergebracht. Dem SB wurden jedoch umfangreiche Annotationen beigegeben, um Verständnisschwierigkeiten vorzubeugen.

Background information

Gillman Noonan (1937–   ) was born in County Cork, Ireland. At present he lives in Scotland. He has also spent time working in Germany and in Switzerland. His short story collection *A Sexual Relationship*, which included the story "Dear Parents, I'm Working for the EEC", was published in 1976.

Talking about the text – Suggested answers

1. *What sort of information on Peter's position within the European Economic Community administration can the reader derive from the text?*

   Peter has worked as a translator (cf. l. 16) for two years, but apparently he does not rank very high. His office is merely a cubicle – worse than other cubicles because it connects two open-plan sections, and there is no possibility of working in peace and quiet. The cubicle is not even situated in the main EEC complex but in the building next to it (cf. ll. 11–14). The speech he has to translate is ten months old and of no immediate interest to anybody (cf. ll. 44–45); instead, like all his work, it belongs to what is called "documentary afterbirth" (l. 51), which will rightly be forgotten in the end (cf. ll. 51–52).

2. *In what way does the point of view from which the text is presented affect the reader's involvement?*

   Although the text is a third-person narrative, it reflects the main character's – Peter's – mind and not an omniscient narrator's view. Thus the reader is encouraged, to a certain extent, to identify with Peter and share his experience. The technique does, though, make the reader feel inclined to set up a certain distance, in a way a first-person narrative would not.

3. *Describe in plain English Peter's difficulties with the word "Pensionskuhhaltung".*

   Some of the difficulties that Peter experiences with the word "Pensionskuhhaltung" are well-known to any translator – and therefore independent of this particular word. There is a word that seems to be vaguely familiar – at least its parts are known – but he cannot find its equivalent in his own language. His mind is a blank. The more he tries to concentrate on the word, the more inaccessible it seems to become. Finally, the originally unobtrusive word affects the translator's perception and creates what might well be called hallucinations.

4. *Why is the word "Pensionskuhhaltung" repeated several times?*

   On the one hand, the repetition of the word "Pensionskuhhaltung" can be seen as a structural element. It reflects Peter's involvement and, for him as well as for the reader, it functions as a constant reminder of the apparently unsolvable problem. On the other hand, each repetition, in the changing context of Peter's thoughts and ideas, seems to make the word – and Peter's job – more obscure and more absurd.

5. *How are readers likely to react to this text, and for what reasons?*

   Although the readers may feel sorry for Peter to begin with, they will most probably end up laughing when they try to feel with Peter in the way his thoughts are put into words, and to actually visualize the scene.

   The following lines may be most likely to provoke their laughter: ll. 22–27; 31–34; 41–43; 52–55. The last line seems to suggest that thinking about cattle so intensely has finally caused Peter to identify with the animals. The vision that may provoke laughter is only hinted at by his uttering "Moo".

6. *What impression of this EEC department does the text create?*

   The impression the text creates is anything but flattering. It is by no means the incompetence of the employees that either amuses or infuriates the reader, but the very idea that (out-)dated material should be translated for the files or "the channels of documentary afterbirth" (l. 51). It would seem that this EEC department is an utter waste of money and ought to be done away with.

[Further interpretation will probably differ: This institution may be seen as symptomatic of the EEC, or it could be seen as a dispensable addition (cf. ll. 12–13) that is no reflection of what is going on in the "main EEC complex" (l. 13).]

7. *Which characteristic of the German language does the term "Pensionskuh-haltung" illustrate?*

   It is a typical example of the German tendency to express complex facts by compounds of more than two noun parts and spell them together in one word.

8. *When translating from German into English or vice versa, what problems have you been confronted with that related either to structural differences between the two languages or to cultural differences? Give examples.*
   – –

8 Katharine Whitehorn: New People Produce New Ideas

Didaktische Hinweise

Die Problembereiche „Einwanderung" und „Ethnische Minoritäten" sind, insbesondere zu Zeiten wirtschaftlicher Krisen, in Großbritannien kaum voneinander trennbar. Beide sind in enger Verbindung zu Empire und Commonwealth zu sehen (vgl. auch den zweiten Teil der "Info-Box", SB, S. 22). Daher können die Texte 8 bis 10 als Grundlage für eine Unterrichtsreihe dienen, die gegebenenfalls erweitert, in anderer Reihenfolge und schließlich auch unmittelbar im Anschluß an die Texte und Karten 1 bis 4 durchgeführt werden kann.

Mit Katharine Whitehorns Beitrag wurde ein informeller, in persönlichem Ton gehaltener Text ausgewählt, der neue Perspektiven eröffnet für eine vorurteilsfreie Sicht des Themas „Immigration". Die Verfasserin setzt sich ab von den beiden begrenzten Sichtweisen, die sie gegen Schluß ihrer Ausführungen benennt und die – nicht nur in Lehrbüchern – nicht selten mit erhobenem Zeigefinger gegenübergestellt werden. Dabei geht es auch ihr ohne Zweifel um die Bewältigung aktueller Probleme der Immigration (und ihrer Folgen). Dieser Ansatz kann Schülern/Schülerinnen Mut zu neuen Wegen im Umgang mit Konflikten machen, denen sich auch ihre Generation stellen muß. In diesem Sinne ist der Ansatz über Großbritannien hinaus von Bedeutung und übertragbar.

Sowohl von der grundsätzlichen Thematik her als auch durch die konkrete Ausprägung des Textes (vgl. den expliziten Hinweis auf die USA, Z. 33–38) bietet sich der Vergleich mit den USA an (vgl. Kap. V, Text 3, 7 bis 12). Auch eine Verknüpfung mit den Texten 10 und 11 dieses Kapitels liegt nahe.

Background information

Katharine Whitehorn has been a columnist for *The Observer* since 1960. She is active in various social causes. She served, for example, on the BBC Advisory Group on Social Effects of Television in 1971 and 1972 and was rector of St Andrews University (Scotland's oldest, founded in 1411) from 1982 to 1985. She has written several books, including some on "How to Survive ...".

"anyone who is poor, black and harried by the immigration officials ..." (ll. 56–58): Black immigrants from the West Indies, who were excluded from immigration to the United States by the 1952 McCarren-Walter Act, have suffered most from the 1962 Commonwealth Immigration Act, which demanded that immigrants to Britain should have either private means of support, educational qualifications, particular skills useful for Britain or a job to come to. For information on further Immigration Acts cf. pp. 5, 15 f. of this book.

Semantic and collocational field "Immigration"

an incomer, an outsider, an immigrant ✧ an immigration official ✧ one's original culture, (to) see things from a different slant, (to) be outside existing hierarchies, (to) join an alien group, (to) start at the bottom of the pecking order, (to) fight one's way up, (to) be number two, (to) try harder, (to) produce new ideas ✧ (to) restrict the number of incomers, (to) treat sb. with hostility, (to) harry sb.

Talking about the text – Suggested answers

1. She speaks on behalf of black immigrants, that is: already successful applicants (cf. ll. 66–67) and those who are still in the process of applying (cf. ll. 56–58). The term "black" would seem to refer here to any "coloured" immigrant, thus including the so-called "brown" immigrants from the Indian sub-continent.
2. Instead of considering what immigrants stand to gain (= the conventional starting point for any dispute on immigration), she emphasizes the fact that they bring with them new ideas and views which could well be beneficial for Great Britain (cf. esp. ll. 72–75, but also ll. 41–48).
3. She may have wanted to draw attention to the fact that so many well-known and generally highly respected people connected with important British "institutions" (l. 1) were immigrants. Starting the text in this way makes her readers more inclined to listen to her subsequent argumentation.
4. In part 1 (ll. 1–33) she lists famous immigrants to Britain along with their achievements. Part 2 (ll. 33–55) presents conclusions in increasingly wider contexts. The reference to the United States, for example (ll. 33–38), suggests an interdependence of the number of immigrants and the country's inventiveness. The conclusion that the unbiased view of the outsider can be particulary effective (cf. ll. 39–48) seems, then, to be applicable to any place and time. The findings of the scientist are derived from animal behaviour, but the idea of working harder at the bottom of the pecking order (cf. ll. 49–55) can undoubtedly be transferred to human behaviour, too.
   In part 3 she applies her conclusions to those immigrants she speaks up for (cf. ll. 56–67). In part 4 she replaces the two existing views of immigrants with her new perspective.
5. Her plea for a change in attitude towards black (i.e. coloured) immigrants follows as a logical consequence of the ever-widening context in which she places the initial positive aspects of immigration. The structure of her argumentation excludes discrimination as untenable and enables her to define her new perspective on immigration in general as a third position that replaces the two previously mentioned mutually exclusive views.
6. It might be considered a weakness that the immigrants she refers to in part 1 were all white and, therefore, somehow different from the ones she supports at the end of the text. And, of course, there were many more immigrants who did not make it for every one that did.
7. **Would you agree with Whitehorn's suggestion that there might be a causal connection between the number of immigrants to any one country and the "upsurge**

of ideas" in that country (cf. ll. 33–38 and ll. 61–64)? Give reasons for your opinion.
– –

8. *Would you think that Whitehorn's new perspective might help us to cope with immigrants in Germany (i.e. people from various countries asking for political asylum)? Explain.*
– –

9. *Have you ever been an outsider in a group such as a class, school, club etc.? Try to relate your initial experience and your efforts to become one of the group. Discuss what might or should have been different.*
– –

9 Lindsay Cook: Rubeena's Double Life

Didaktische Hinweise

Ähnlich wie Katharine Whitehorn (Text 8) erweitert auch Lindsay Cook mit ihrem Beitrag das herkömmliche Spektrum zum Thema „Immigration/Ethnische Minoritäten". Im Gegensatz aber zu Katharine Whitehorn stellt sie den konkreten Einzelfall dar. Sie wählt die *"Asians"*, beschäftigt sich speziell mit der Situation der Frau und beschreibt eine weitgehend positive Möglichkeit der Verbindung zweier Kulturen.

Inwieweit die Kompromiß- und Eingliederungsbereitschaft auf der einen und die Annahme durch die (weiße) britische Gesellschaft auf der anderen Seite generalisiert werden können, sollten die Schüler/innen in eigenen Recherchen herauszufinden versuchen (vgl. unten, Aufgabe 6). Dabei sollte auf Hinweise zum Verhältnis der *Asian Community* zur *Black Community* geachtet werden. Eine solche Untersuchung könnte auch für die USA interessant sein und zu weiteren Vergleichsmöglichkeiten führen (vgl. Kap. V, Text 10 bis 12).

Literaturhinweis: Bei speziellem Interesse für die Situation der Frau bieten sich Ausschnitte an aus Beverley Bryan, Stella Dadzie, Suzanne Scafe: *The Heart of the Race: Black Women's Lives in Britain.* London, Virago Ltd 1985 (Virago Paperback Original)

Background information

Asian immigrants: Asian immigration became relevant in the 1960s. Immigrants came either directly from the Indian sub-continent or from East Africa (Kenya, Uganda, Tanzania), where a considerable number of Asians had lived and worked – mostly in commerce – since the middle of the 19th century.

The 1968 Commonwealth Immigration Act was specially devised to control, and/or stop, the entry of British passport holders of Asian origin coming from East Africa (Kenya in particular), where the policy of Africanization made them unwelcome. The Africans expected them to emigrate either to the home-country of their ancestors, i.e. India or Pakistan, or, more likely, to Britain. These British passport holders were only allowed into the country if they had substantial connections with Britain. Thus, the number of prospective immigrants of Asian origin was drastically reduced.

A new wave of Asian immigrants was expected when Ugandan President Idi
Amin expelled the Asians from his country in 1972. It was assumed that up to 60,000
Asians would seek admission to Britain; after lengthy debates it was decided to
grant admission to all those who applied for entry. In the end, only about 28,000
actually came.

In the 1980s new disputes arose on the question of whether and under what
conditions to admit husbands, wives or fiancées from the Indian sub-continent. The
rules concerning their admission still seem to be fairly complicated and therefore
open to interpretation, but there is reasonable hope that this problem will soon be
solved satisfactorily.

The 1981 British Census did not include any questions that asked explicitly about
ethnicity. Nevertheless, the heads of household birthplaces, together with other
statistical material, give fairly valid information on the ethnic minority population in Britain. Roughly speaking, in 1981 there were 2.2 million people of New
Commonwealth (cf. "Info-Box", SB, pp. 21 f. and "Background information", pp. 6 f.
of this book) and Pakistani origin, of whom about 40 % were born in Britain. 55 % of
those 2.2 million were of Asian origin (47 % – 1 million – from the Indian sub-
continent, about 8 % – 0.2 million – from East Africa). About 25 % (0.5 million, or
possibly slightly more) were of Afro-Caribbean origin. For up-to-date statistical
information cf. material prepared by the Commission for Racial Equality (Information Department, Elliot House, 10–12 Allington Street, London SW1E 5EH).

Semantic and collocational field "Asians in Britain"

a victim of arranged marriage, a domestic slave ❖ a dutiful daughter, traditional clothes, (to)
stick to soft drinks, (to) follow the Moslem way of life, (to) observe Ramadan, (to) fit in with
sb.'s religion ❖ a change in outlook, a question of choosing East or West, a double life, a
mixture of traditional and Western, (to) transform sb.`s life, (to) bridge the gap between two
cultures, (to) make a compromise between sth. and sth. else, (to) come to terms with sth. ❖
(to) appear thoroughly western, (to) carry on as normal, (to) encourage women to leave the
home, (to) choose one's own fiancé

Talking about the text – Suggested answers

1. In her life as a secretary the eastern influence can still be seen in her choice of clothes (cf.
   ll. 25 and 41–44), in her eating and drinking habits during office hours and when she
   spends time with her colleagues in the evening (cf. ll. 39–41, 63–74).
   Her overall status within the family, on the other hand, is distinctly western; it is reflected
   in her job (cf. ll. 48–49 and 59–62), her money (cf. ll. 49–50 and 101–102) and in her
   freedom to choose her future husband (cf. ll. 90–92).
2. She has presumably received a better education than she would have had as a girl in
   Pakistan. She also has a very good command of the English language, financial
   independence because of her own job, property, higher status within the family and the
   right to choose her future husband herself.
3. [In their discussion, students should consider the question of cultural roots and identity
   and whether Rubeena can fully belong to either culture while living her compromise.]
4. The greatest danger is to be seen in the immigration regulations that might not allow her
   fiancé to join her in Britain in the near future (cf. ll. 95 ff.). Another danger, which is only
   implied, is the possibility that either her colleagues' or her parents' attitudes might some
   day turn away from tolerance, although this does not seem likely at the moment (cf. ll. 40
   ff., 57 ff.).

5. *Lindsay Cook's findings are derived from interviews. Point out the difference between the supposed original form of the interview and the chosen form of the interpretive news story, and discuss whether you see them as advantages or disadvantages.*

Basic difference: processed material versus original material; subsequent differences obvious in this text: shorter; direct speech reserved for some of the interviewee's characteristic answers; fairly long summarizing passages written by the interviewer; interviewer's additional interpretation (most obvious in the term "philosophically", l. 99).

● 6. *Find additional material on Asian immigrants and their British-born descendants in the British press, and report your findings to the class.*

– –

7. *If you know people from a different cultural background living in Germany, compare their difficulties, attitudes and lifestyle with Rubeena's.*

– –

ᴘᴘ 10 Rhodri Jones: They Killin' 'im, They Killin' 'im

Didaktische Hinweise

Als Romanausschnitt unterscheidet sich Text 10 grundsätzlich von den beiden vorausgegangenen nicht-fiktionalen Texten zu den Themenbereichen „Immigration"und „Ethnische Minoritäten". Inhaltlich knüpft der Autor jedoch an einen in Text 8 erwähnten Teilaspekt an: die Probleme der *Black Community*, und hier besonders ihr Selbstverständnis gegenüber der weißen Polizei. Gleichzeitig wird damit ein Thema angeschlagen, das Ausdruck eines noch nicht bewältigten Teils des Empire-Erbes ist, die Tatsache nämlich, daß es farbige Bürger Großbritanniens gibt, die nicht eingewandert sind, sondern bereits in der zweiten oder dritten Generation im Vereinigten Königreich leben. Vergleiche mit Stationen der jüngsten amerikanischen Geschichte bieten sich an (vgl. Kap. VII, Text 7 bis 9b). Dabei ist zu beachten, daß es in Großbritannien seit 1976 keinen Bereich mehr gibt, in dem – auch indirekte – (Rassen-)Diskriminierung nicht gesetzlich untersagt wäre. Daß sie dennoch stattfindet, beschreibt u.a. Lord Scarman: *The Scarman Report: The Brixton Disorders, 10–12 April 1981*. Harmondsworth, Penguin Books Ltd 1981, von deren Ausgangssituation sich Rhodri Jones, wie ein Vergleich mit dem *Scarman Report* zeigt, bis in die Formulierungen hinein anregen ließ.

Erfahrungsgemäß vermag der fiktionale Text die Schüler/innen unmittelbar anzusprechen: *"Fiction derives its power from its presentation of experience as lived"* (Th. L. Wymer et al.: *Intersections*. Bowling Green, Ohio, The Popular Press 1978; vgl. Kap. X, Text 1, Z. 54–55). Beim vorliegenden Text kommt eine weitgehende Altersgleichheit von Hauptperson(en) und Schülern/Schülerinnen noch unterstützend hinzu. Aus diesen Gründen wurde auch hier der Aufgabenapparat im LB untergebracht.

Abgesehen von der im SB gewählten Abfolge der Texte 8 bis 10 gäbe es auch die Möglichkeit, die Auseinandersetzung mit den Themenbereichen „Immigration" und „Ethnische Minoritäten" mit diesem Text zu beginnen und das weitere Sachwissen im Anschluß daran zu erarbeiten. In jedem Fall ist *Hillsden Riots* (London, André Deutsch 1985) auch als Ganzschrift im Anschluß an die Lektüre des hier vorgelegten Exzerpts (S. 28–31 der Buchausgabe) zu empfehlen. Bei Zeitmangel käme statt dessen die Behandlung eines weiteren Textausschnitts in Frage, etwa S. 111–114 des

Romans (thematischer Schwerpunkt ist die Identitätsproblematik), der von Egon Werlich interpretiert wurde (*Sammlung Lensing 2*, Jahrg. 16, 4. Lfg., No. 318. Dortmund, Lambert Lensing 1987).

Background information

Rhodri Jones was formerly the headmaster of John Kelly Boys' High School, Brent, a state school in London. He has published a number of English language teaching books and several fictional works. In his fiction he focuses on young people and their problems in contemporary Britain. *Delroy is here* (1983) was his first novel, his second being *Hillsden Riots* (1985). In 1987 he published two more novels, *So Far to Go* and *Different Friends*.

Racial riots in Britain: The first – relatively speaking – minor post-war racial disturbances occurred in Nottingham and Notting Hill, London, in 1958. More than twenty years later there were outbreaks of violence in Southall, London, and St Paul's, Bristol (1980). However, it was not until the major disturbances of 1981, which extended throughout the country, that an official inquiry was set up to investigate the causes. The Brixton disorders (April 1981) are generally considered to have been the most serious. However, Southall in London, Toxteth and Moss Side in Liverpool, and various other cities such as Manchester, Wolverhampton and Birmingham were also affected by the disorders in 1981. Since then there have been further disturbances, the worst being those in Liverpool in 1982 and in London and Birmingham in 1985; these involved primarily black youth, but also members of other ethnic minorities and white youths as well.

The Brixton riots of April 1981, on whose beginnings, at least, Jones's novel *Hillsden Riots* seems to be based, took place on three successive days: from April 10 to 12, with minor incidents still happening on April 13. The immediate cause of the Friday (April 10) riots was an incident involving an injured black youth the police wanted to help. A crowd of black youths arrived on the scene, and they were not willing to appreciate the police's intentions and, in their view, rescued the youth from the police. The crowd then attacked the police (who had followed them) with bricks, bottles, etc.

When rioting was over two days later, 253 people had been arrested, 450 police officers and at least 48 members of the public had been injured, 121 police and 87 private vehicles had been damaged or destroyed, and 145 premises had been damaged, 28 by fire. (Based on: Lord Scarman: *The Scarman Report*, which, however, does not include either Lord Scarman's investigation into the deeper reasons for the riots, or his recommendations concerning the police in particular.)

Semantic and collocational field "Rioting"

a jostling crowd, a screaming mob ✧ a frenzied voice, an excited roar, a squeal of delight, a cheer of triumph, a rumble, (to) yell one's head off, (to) shriek out sth., (to) roar, (to) scream hysterically, (to) accuse, (to) demand ✧ a surge, (to) feel impelled to move, (to) be carried along with the tide, (to) try to stem the rush, (to) storm, (to) follow sb./sth., (to) be pressed along, (to) scurry along, (to) pound down the street, (to) lead the chase, (to) slow down, (to) push one's way forward, (to) be pushed forward, (to) stream, (to) spill over, (to) weave in and out ✧ (a) horror, an affront, rage, exhilaration, disbelief, angry, dazed, (to) feel oneself go cold, (to) grow wild, to be full of murderous hatred for sb./sth., (to) be high with pride ✧ (to) do sth.

about sth. else, (to) burst into frantic action, (to) grab sb./sth., (to) yank sth. open, (to) lift sb./sth., (to) bounce sth., (to) drag sb./sth. out, (to) cast sb./sth. to one side, (to) shove sb./sth. aside, (to) throw sb./sth. to the ground, (to) attack sb./sth. ✧ (to) stand up for oneself, (to) stand up for one's own ✧ the police, (to) harrass sb., (to) arrest sb., (to) get away with sth., (to) survey sb./sth. apprehensively, (to) try to pacify sb.

Talking about the text – Suggested answers

1. *How would you characterize black people's relations with the police in this text?*
   The feelings and actions of the black crowd with regard to the police seem to indicate pent-up anger (cf. ll. 11, 19, 35) and thirst for revenge (cf. ll. 20–21), fundamental distrust (cf. ll. 43, 52–54), verbal aggressiveness (cf. ll. 36–37, 50–55) culminating in apparently unfounded accusations (cf. ll. 38, 44, 54–55, 70), physical aggression (cf. ll. 56–57, 59–60) and growing hysteria directed at the police (cf. ll. 8–9, 38, 49, 55).

2. *What are the policemen like in this passage?*
   What they say seems quite reasonable (cf. ll. 39–41, 46–48); when attacked they do not seem to react in self-defence (cf. ll. 56–60). The use of "pale and tense" (l. 39), "apprehensively" (l. 42), "defensively" (l. 46), "to try to pacify" (ll. 46–47) implies that they feel intimidated and attempt to respond diplomatically (which may, of course, result from their being in the minority).

3. *How would you explain the striking difference in the behaviour of the opponents?*
   The reason for black people's behaviour can probably be traced back to their more frequent experience of a different kind in the past (cf. ll. 19–21, 71–72). The behaviour of the police could either be explained as resulting from fear (cf. answer to question 2), or it could be seen as an indication that policemen are not all alike, i.e. that not all of them harass black people.

4. *How much does the crowd help Leroy?*
   Their "frantic action" (l. 55) goes against any medical rules concerning persons injured in an accident. Professional medical treatment is most probably delayed. Leroy himself is beyond caring (cf. ll. 60–64); his condition is, in fact, worse in the end (cf. ll. 84–85).

5. *What does the event mean for the crowd?*
   For them it is a completely new experience of self-assertion (cf. esp. ll. 71–72) which gives birth to feelings of pride, satisfaction and joy (cf. ll. 75 ff., 86, 88).

6. *In l. 74 Desmond asks Wayne: "But what 'appen next?" Wayne does not answer this question. What* will *happen next, in your view?*
   – –

7. *From what point of view is the story told?*
   The story is told from a third-person, apparently omniscient, point of view, although at times the narrator's words seem to reflect Wayne's feelings, thoughts and observations (cf. ll. 19–21, 31–34).

8. *How is the reader affected by the narrator's point of view?*
   The reader is not allowed to identify fully with either the narrator nor any of the characters and thus become biased in his or her interpretation of the goings-on.

9. *How would you characterize the language used in the direct-speech passages?*
   There is a marked difference between the language of the (presumably white) policeman (neutral standard spoken English, with many short forms) and the language used by the black people. The deviations from standard English, particulary as regards pronunciation and syntax, seem to be systematic and not arbitrary, e.g.
   pronunciation: omission of [h] at the beginning of a word (cf. ll. 37, 50, 51, 74, 86), omission of [t] in the short form of "not" (cf. ll. 23, 50), changing [ɪ ŋ] to [-ɪ n] in all *-ing* forms (cf. ll. 16, 36, 38,);

syntax: omission of auxiliaries and the main verb "(to) be" (cf. ll. 7–8, 16, 23, 24, 36, 38, 54, 55, 73, 74, 86), third person singular simple present tense without -s (cf. ll. 25, 50), in one instance first person plural simple present tense with additional -s (l. 51, but cf. also ll. 86, 87), double negation (cf. ll. 51, 52).

The forms listed above are characteristic of the West Indian English Creole.

10. ***What does the direct speech used in the passage contribute to the reader's impression of the text and to his or her understanding?***

    Apart from immediacy and vividness, which are always brought about by the use of direct speech, the two language varieties (one of them with distinct features of Black English with relics of Creole) help to establish the ethnic conflict by showing the cultural and educational differences. (The social relevance of these differences can be seen in the difficulty black people often have finding jobs.)

11. ***The text conveys the impression of being a structural unit. How is this unity achieved?***

    The text starts when there is a break in the preceding activity of dancing. The usual relaxation in between dances is disturbed (cf. "disturbance", l. 5) by the entrance of someone who can hardly be seen because of the darkness. What the people in the club are able to understand is the sentence in ll. 7–8: "Rass, man. Leroy been drill up by the police." All the ensuing activities are connected with Leroy, and it is when the car with Leroy disappears that the unit ends. Whatever is to follow, it will definitely be a new phase in the action, as the crowd can no longer follow Leroy.

12. ***By what means is the dramatic intensity of this scene brought about?***

    The dramatic effect of the passage is based largely on the choice of words, esp. the verbs. Movement, haste and excitement are conveyed by verb forms and phrases like "flopped" (l. 2), "carried along with the tide" (l. 14), "stormed" (l. 17), "followed" (ll. 17, 29, 67), "pressed along" (l. 19), "scurrying along" (l. 22), etc.

    The idea of movement as well as excitement is continued in the choice of words relating to the pigeons and the car: "clapping of wings" (l. 81), "rose in a swirling cloud" (l. 82), "leaped out" (l. 89).

    Excitement and even hysteria are also conveyed by the expressions which describe how things are said: "yelling his head off" (ll. 5–6), "shrieked" (l. 8), "in a frenzied voice" (l. 8), "panted" (l. 22), "exasperated" (l. 25), "screamed hysterically" (l. 38), etc.

    Note that even the noise of the cars and pigeons is in tune with the atmosphere of excitement and hysteria: "shrieked to a halt" (l. 77), "clapping of wings and clucking protests" (l. 81), "a violent screeching of gears" (l. 89).

13. ***How does the narrator describe the people involved in the incident? To what effect?***

    Although the narrator singles out Leroy, Wayne, Mr Fernandez and Desmond, he generally talks about an anonymous mass of people. He achieves this by the extensive use of the word "crowd" (ll. 17, 26, 29, 35, etc.; cf. also "mob", ll. 55, 57), more or less generic terms like "man/men" (ll. 15, 17, 27, 63, 86, 88), "(black) boy" (ll. 32, 70), "(black) youth" (l. 31), "girl" (ll. 38, 44), "people" (ll. 13, 57, 65, 75), and "police/policeman/policemen" (ll. 8, 30, 32, 39, etc.), "passers-by" (l. 26), "drivers" (l. 28), "friends" (l. 79), indefinite terms like "someone" (ll. 5, 36, 43), "everyone" (l. 6), "no one" (l. 16), "some" (l. 58), "another" (ll. 37, 87), "the other(s)" (ll. 45, 87). The impression is intensified by the use of "bodies" (ll. 1, 12; cf. also "puppets", l. 2) and terms for parts of the body ("faces", ll. 12, 42; "hands", ll. 56, 59; "arms and legs", ll. 60), which allows for no individuality at all.

14. ***What sort of reaction would you foresee in the event of Leroy's death?***

    [1. His death would serve as a sobering shock to the revellers; 2. His death would be like dynamite, prompting further rioting.]

11 R.W. Apple, Jr.: A Nation in Decline?

Didaktische Hinweise

R.W. Apples Bilanz nach mehr als achtjähriger Korrespondententätigkeit in Großbritannien ist in besonderer Weise geeignet, den Abschluß dieses Kapitels zu bilden. In seinem notwendigerweise summarischen Rückblick und seinem die Grenzen zur Prophetie nicht überschreitenden Ausblick beschreibt er für die Gegenwart vor allem die bisherigen Ergebnisse der Veränderung, die sich in Großbritannien – einst Zentrum des Empire, nun *"just another medium-sized Western European power"* (Z. 14–16) – vollzogen hat, sowie die weitere, derzeit beobachtbare Entwicklung, aber auch das in aller Veränderung erhalten Gebliebene.

Insgesamt zeichnet Apple ein verständnisvolles, ausgewogenes und zutreffend liebenswürdiges Bild Großbritanniens. Seine Sicht erschien der *New York Times* so wichtig, daß sie den Beitrag auf der Titelseite beginnen ließ, eröffnet er doch auch eine Reihe von Vergleichs- und Bezugsmöglichkeiten zu den USA (vgl. Aufg. 8 und 9 unten).

Die Fülle der Aspekte, die unterschiedlich ausführlich behandelt werden, ermöglicht am Ende des Kapitels eine integrierte Wiederholung und Zusammenfassung. Apples breitgefächerte Thematik spricht den unmittelbaren Interessen- und Erfahrungsbereich der Schüler/innen an und bietet daher besonderen Anreiz zur Stellungnahme und/oder Ergänzung (vgl. Aufg. 10 und 11 unten). Der Hinweis des Journalisten auf in Großbritannien nach wie vor gültige nicht-materielle Werte und sein persönliches Bekenntnis zu einer Reihe von ihnen können abschließend auch unter den Schülern/Schülerinnen eine Diskussion über Wertvorstellungen (jenseits von wandelbarer politischer und wirtschaftlicher Macht) initiieren.

Background information

Dr. R.W. Apple has worked as a journalist for the *New York Times* since 1963. From 1977 to 1985 he was based in London. Since 1985 he has been chief Washington correspondent.

Semantic and collocational field "Time of change"

per-capita income, gross national product, political debate ✧ national unity, social cohesion, a sense of identity, class structure ✧ a nation of shopkeepers, memories of past glories, a stiff upper lip, stoicism, humour, a gentlemanly sport, an unarmed bobby, proud of Britain ✧ (to) muddle through, (to) make sth. tick ✧ a social evil, economic disadvantage, unemployment ✧ shabbiness of dress, a reluctance to work ✧ a young hooligan, a brawl, a decaying inner city, amounting incidence of violence, picket-line strife ✧ a nation in decline, a medium-sized power, a time of adversity, a sign of strain ✧ (to) become accustomed to sb./sth., (to) accept one's lot, (to) adjust to new/harsh realities, (to) buckle, (to) erode, (to) cling to sb./sth. ✧ a success story, a sign of success, a new work ethic, a sense of innovation

Talking about the text – Suggested answers

1. The text explicitly mentions the shrinking size of the army (cf. ll. 9–10), the position of Britain as "just another medium-sized western European power" (ll. 14–16), the economic situation showing in a standard of living below that of other European nations (cf. ll. 29–30, 76–79), high unemployment (cf. ll. 178–179), street violence (cf. ll. 79–80), squalor (cf. l. 80),

drug-taking (cf. l. 81), the poverty of service institutions (cf. ll. 81–85), signs of strain in the social cohesion showing in all kinds and degrees of violence (cf. ll. 107–158).

2. Two reasons account for Britain's economically unjustifiable status in the world. On the one hand, money is not the only thing that counts (cf. esp. ll. 237 – 242, but also ll. 39–41). Values such as friendship (cf. ll. 36–39), loyalty (cf. l. 37), civility (cf. ll. 91–92, 100), courtesy (cf. ll. 92–95, 100) and coziness (cf. ll. 95–99, 101) play an important part in human relations, and intellectual achievements are still highly appreciated (cf. ll. 42–47, 50–53). On the other hand, Britons also have "memories of past glories" (l. 70), and can look back on a long tradition of successfully handling precarious situations (cf. ll. 70, 86–90, 105–106).

   Together, the two strands have guaranteed social cohesion (cf. ll. 87, 107) and helped to establish the "British myth" (l. 103), which also includes the natural beauties of Britain (cf. ll. 62–63, 104–105) and the animals (dogs and horses, cf. l. 104) that are frequently associated with Britain.

3. In ll. 48–63 the writer uses the same overall structural pattern (minor variations are of no importance) in three successive complex sentences. They all start with "If Britain is a country ...", followed by a basically negative feature, however cautiously expressed. In the second parts of the sentences, all of which start with "it is also a country ...", positive traits are enumerated. This stylistic device (contrast) – all the more effective through repetition – could be interpreted as the reflection of the writer's attempts at balancing his attitude towards Britain and his intention to be fair. On the other hand, because the positive traits come last, they tend to carry more weight. This might be taken as a sign of Apple's favourable attitude towards the British.

4. First of all, their "poverty of desire" (l. 219) helps Britons to adjust to new realities (cf. ll. 26–30 and the use of expressions like "to become accustomed" in ll. 8, 13, 19–20 and "to accept" in l. 26). But "poverty of desire" is no favourable predisposition – let alone incentive – to overcome the economic crisis (cf. ll. 202–219). It leaves room, though, for particular groups of immigrants (cf. ll. 220–230 and Ch. I, Text 8, ll. 1–38) to assert themselves.

5. There are fewer instances of individual violence than cases of violence which involve groups (or at least many individuals). Apple names murder and rape (cf. ll. 111–112) as examples of the first category, and politically motivated violence in Ireland (cf. ll. 119–120), violence accompanying the miners' strike (cf. ll. 120–122), inner city riots (cf. ll. 19–25, 122–130) and hooliganism (cf. l. 158) as the most obvious examples of the second category. The idea of group violence can be expanded to include verbal aggression (cf. ll. 135–136), potential physical aggression as expressed in driving habits (cf. ll. 135–137) and various degrees of violence and its precursors (i.e. dying sportsmanship, cf. l. 138) in the realm of sports (cf. ll. 139–158).

6. In a general sense, he interprets violence as a sign of economic disadvantage (cf. ll. 73, 81). Yet, it seems unlikely that the forms of violence he enumerates (cf. ll. 108–158) all stem from economic disadvantage only – a conclusion that he himself does not explicitly suggest, although his remarks on Margaret Thatcher's way of dealing with unemployment (cf. ll. 177–202) do imply certain connections. Thus, the specific forms of violence are not explained conclusively.

7. As far as the future is concerned, he refers to the view of the unspecified "many" who, hesitatingly (cf. "might", l. 246) see a desirable place for Britain "in a strong and unified Europe" (ll. 246–247) (an expression which may well imply political unity). For the time being this is unrealistic for two reasons: 1. British people in general have not yet even become aware of the fact that they are Europeans (cf. ll. 248–251). 2. British journalists and politicians cannot function as (positive) opinion leaders because of their own lack of knowledge and interest concerning Europe (cf. ll. 251–256).

8. ***How does the American journalist try to capture and hold the attention of his American readers when writing about Britain?***

Most obvious are his explicit references to and comparisons with the United States and Americans, which cover a wide range of aspects: politics (cf. ll. 16–18, 50–53), crime and violence (cf. ll. 110–113, 130–134), sports (cf. ll. 140–146), commerce (cf. ll. 224—230), attitudes and values (cf. ll. 235–242). Apart from these explicit means, many of the aspects mentioned in his text (cf. also task 2) might appeal to American readers, because they touch upon often cherished views about the so-called "old world".

9. *"I don't think it's a linguistic accident that Americans run for office and the English stand for office" (ll. 232–234). What do you think the woman quoted means by this statement?*

According to the speaker, the two verbs which mark the difference between the AE and BE expressions do not indicate a latent mistake in either case. Instead, they adequately describe two different attitudes. There is much more eagerness involved in the American strife for a position ("(to) run" is a dynamic verb) than in the English way ("(to) stand" is a static verb).

10. *On the basis of what you have read in this chapter, do you consider this text to be a fairly adequate account of what Britain is like at present and, possibly, in the future? Give reasons for your answer.*

[On the whole Apple's observations do not contradict those of the other texts. Students could point out a particular correspondence of views concerning the role and status of immigrants and, at least partly, the inner city problems.]

11. *If you have had any personal experience of Britain or the British, which of Apple's observations would you tend to agree with, and which would you contradict?*

– –

Chapter II: Education and Class

Das zweite der vier Kapitel über Großbritannien stellt das Land aus der Perspektive sozio-kultureller Gegebenheiten vor, die das Leben der Briten nach wie vor stark beeinflussen in einer Gemeinschaft, in der traditionelles Klassendenken noch alle gesellschaftlichen Bereiche durchzieht.

Die ausgewählten Texte demonstrieren exemplarisch das enge Beziehungsgeflecht zwischen sozialer Herkunft, Schulbildung, Berufsaussichten und sogar den Chancen, allseits beliebte Sportarten wie Fußball oder Kricket zu betreiben. Eingeschlossen in die Betrachtung ist die Rolle von Mädchen und Frauen in den genannten Bereichen, die sich, wie die kontrastierenden Texte 1 und 8 zeigen, in den Jahrzehnten nach dem Zweiten Weltkrieg erst allmählich zu wandeln begonnen hat. Vergleiche mit den Vereinigten Staaten bieten sich an; auf Verknüpfungsmöglichkeiten mit Texten aus Kap. VI und Kap. VII wird bei der Kommentierung hingewiesen.

1 Arnold Wesker: Education – It's Asking Questions, All the Time

Didaktische Hinweise

Dieser erste Text, ein Exzerpt aus Weskers wohl bekanntestem Drama *Roots* (1959), kann in zweierlei Hinsicht als grundlegend für das gesamte Kapitel II betrachtet werden. Der durch Beatie heraufbeschworene Konflikt in der Familie veranschaulicht zum einen, wie eng in Großbritannien soziale Herkunft, Schulbildung, Artikulationsvermögen und die Fähigkeit, kritisch zu denken, miteinander verknüpft waren und bis zu einem gewissen Grad noch immer sind – hier aufgezeigt am Beispiel englischer Landarbeiter, die in keinem dieser Bereiche begünstigt waren. Kontrastierend wird in dieser Szene auf die Möglichkeiten und Einstellungen der "really talented people in the country" (Z. 56) verwiesen. Aus dieser Perspektive der Kritik an den unterschiedlichen gesellschaftlichen Chancen ergeben sich thematische Anknüpfungsmöglichkeiten vor allem an die Texte 4, 6, 7, 9 und 11 dieses Kapitels. Zum anderen läßt sich aus Beaties Definition von "education" eine erste Orientierung für das Hauptthema dieses Kapitels gewinnen. Beaties Verständnis von "education" (Z. 42 ff.) als Wille zu einer weltoffenen kritischen Fragehaltung kann verglichen werden mit abweichenden oder auch ergänzenden Positionen, wie sie etwa in den Texten 5, 7, 10 und 11 vermittelt werden.

Weskers Drama, Teil der *Wesker Trilogy,* eignet sich durchaus als Klassenlektüre. Sowohl *Roots* als auch die Trilogie sind in Paperback-Ausgaben erhältlich (London, Methuen; Harmondsworth, Penguin Books).

Literaturhinweise: Zu Weskers Stellung in der zeitgenössischen englischen Literatur vgl. John Elsom: *Post-War British Theatre.* (London, Routledge 1976), zur Wesker-Trilogie Rüdiger Hillgärtner: "Arnold Wesker: The Chicken Soup Trilogy. Die Frage nach der individuellen Lebensperspektive." In: Heinrich F. Plett (Hrsg.): *Englisches Drama von Beckett bis Bond.* München, W. Fink 1982, S. 118 ff.(UTB 1116); Hermann J. Weiand: "Arnold Wesker: The Chicken Soup Trilogy: Roots."In:

H. J. Weiand (Ed.): *Insight IV. Analyses of Modern British and American Drama.* Frankfurt, Cornelsen Verlag Hirschgraben ³ 1979, pp. 168 ff. (Best.-Nr. 127408).

Background information

Arnold Wesker (1932–   ) was born in Stepney, London, the son of Russian-Jewish immigrants. He was educated at Upton House School, and then worked in a variety of jobs before becoming successful as a politically-committed dramatist. His plays deal with the problems of the British working class in the twentieth century. He has aptly been called a "social realist" and a working-class dramatist, in contrast to contemporaries such as Samuel Beckett (*Waiting for Godot,* 1953) or Harold Pinter (*The Birthday Party,* 1958), who were concerned with the "absurdity" of existence (cf. Martin Esslin: *The Theatre of the Absurd.* Penguin Books, Harmondsworth, 1983).

Wesker's first play, *The Kitchen* (1956), was used to characterize a large section of the new naturalistic British drama of the 50s and 60s as "kitchen-sink drama", which substituted the pleasant drawing room settings of the previous decades. *Roots,* one of his most successful plays, was first performed in 1959.

The scene from Wesker's play *Roots* can serve as an example of the dramatic revival that characterized the period from 1956–1960. The year 1956 was marked both by John Osborne's play *Look Back in Anger* and Arnold Wesker's first play *The Kitchen.* Both Osborne and Wesker used working-class heroes to voice their generation's dissatisfaction with the values held by the establishment and the injustices arising from Britain's fossilized division into different classes. Writing at the time of the post-Suez years of Conservative rule and the years of prosperity under Prime Minister Harold Macmillan, writers such as Osborne and Wesker took a Leftist stance. In his *Chicken Soup Trilogy,* in which *Roots* is the second play, Wesker tries to describe the situation of the working class. He shows the development of British socialism as reflected in the life of one family. Its members experience a phase of pre-war enthusiasm, which is followed by post-war disenchantment and ends in a phase of resignation. Beatie's friend Ronnie Kahn, the main character in the trilogy, can be seen as voicing Wesker's own ideas about his particular brand of socialism. His great concern is the question how to educate the working class so that they come alive and gain access to the main-stream culture.

Semantic and collocational field "Approaches to life"

education, (to) ask for sth., (to) ask questions, (to) be alive, (to) be interested, (to) do sth. about sth. else, to know how to do sth., (to) make an effort, (to) think ✧ (to) appreciate, (to) be proud of oneself, (to) improve (oneself) ✧ (to) be bored with sb./sth., not (to) care a damn, (to) grumble, (to) take the easiest way out, empty, mentally lazy, one can't be bothered ✧ (to) be one's own fault, (to) count for nothing, (to) serve one right, one might as well be dead

Talking about the text – Suggested answers

1. *How does Beatie's reaction to her family change in the course of their argument?*
At the beginning, Beatie (still) responds to her mother's command to "answer" her and "talk" (ll. 2–3) with "I can't, Mother, you're right" (l. 4). However, she then does go on

talking, until, at the end, she realizes that she has been voicing more and more of her own views. She has become "articulate at last" (l. 82).

2. *What is the immediate cause of this change?*

   What starts Beatie's almost spontaneous flow of speech and ideas is her deep anger and disappointment at what appears to characterize herself, her family and the working class in general. In her view, they are "Stubborn, empty, wi' no tools for livin' " (l. 5), "just a mass o' nothin' " (l. 7). They do not know what their position in life is, nor what can keep their life strong (like a plant's "strong roots", l. 27) in a world that is rich with things happening, being discovered and improved (cf. ll. 15–17). In short, what Beatie holds against the working classes is that they are not interested in learning more about the world around them.

3. *What in particular does Beatie hold against her family and class?*

   For one thing, that they do not care about the larger political and historical context in which they live and which they might influence if they only took an active part in the decisions that others are making (e.g. the decision to drop "that ole atom bomb", ll. 33–34). They "can't be bothered" (l. 36). Beatie also resents the fact that they play no active part in the community because they are "mentally lazy" (l. 46) and shrink from any "effort" (ll. 36, 61) to get involved in influencing and changing things.

4. *What reasons does Beatie give for this state of affairs when Mrs Bryant rejects her criticism?*

   When they come together in groups, as in the present family gathering, they do not talk seriously with each other in the sense of discussing the world in which they live: "Hev you said anythin' ? I mean really said or done anything to show you're alive?" (ll. 31–32).

   They tend to mistake their passive consumption of radio, television and "the pictures" (l. 40) for being intellectually alive.

   They allow themselves to be exploited by the commercial interests of those who "know where the money lie" (l. 65): "The slop singers and the pop writers and the film makers and women's magazines and the Sunday papers and the picture strip love stories" (ll. 62–64). These people even adapt their use of language to the easy "words of one syllable" (l. 67) they believe typical of Beatie's class.

   They are gullible, believing the "squit" (l. 56) being spread by the papers "about the workers bein' all important these days" (l. 55). The "really talented people in the country" (l. 56), Beatie realizes, work only for themselves, securing their own power and furthering their own interests.

5. *How does Beatie compare with her family in this scene?*

   Unlike her family, Beatie does not yield to her despair and suffer in silence. She *talks,* whereas the members of her family merely briefly repeat her words (see the many questions and exclamations). Moreover, as Beatie begins to talk, she is increasingly able to outline the problems of her family in British society. Her use of language enables her to gain new insights. And thirdly, she is not only able to forget Ronnie's jilting her, but, through this experience, becomes able to free herself from him and see the potential in her own self: "I'm talking. Jenny, Frankie, Mother – I'm not quoting no more" (ll. 73–74), "on my own two feet" (l. 80).

6. *In ll. 42–43 Beatie comments "Education ent only books and music – it's asking questions, all the time." Why, then, is Beatie doomed to failure in her attempt to educate her family?*

   Beatie's attempt at educating her family by means of speech fails because "education" is possible only if certain conditions are fulfilled. As Beatie herself says, education is not primarily knowledge and good taste ("books and music", l. 43), but a process of continued interaction with people and the world in which we live ("it's asking questions, *all the time*", l. 43). In other words, individuals have to make the mental effort of using language to find out things about themselves and the world around them. Furthermore, an individual needs someone who can also ask questions and is equally alive intellectually, like Ronnie in Beatie's life (cf. l. 79: "God in heaven, Ronnie! It does work, it's happening to me …"). For education to take place, the individual needs someone who can open up his or her mind to the world and other people.

7. **To understand further what is happening to Beatie in this scene, compare her manner of speaking in ll. 45–46 and in ll. 52 ff. How does her language change?**
In ll. 45–46, Beatie makes an important general comment on her class, namely that they "don't fight for anything". For a supportive reason, however, Beatie still draws on someone else's ideas. She quotes her friend Ronnie ("That's what he say …", l. 47).
In ll. 52 ff., we see Beatie thinking aloud, as it were, and coming up first with a question and then an answer that differs from Ronnie's. While Ronnie thinks the farm labourers "count all right – living in mystic communion with nature" (l. 52), Beatie doubts this: "But us count? Count, Mother. *I wonder.* Do we? …" (ll. 53–54). As she continues talking, she gradually arrives at her own distinctive answer. Here, Beatie is "not quoting" (l. 74) anymore, but, for the first time, she has developed a view of her own. She is able to do so now because there was and is someone, i.e. Ronnie, who thinks differently. She now needs him only as an opposing position for her mind and language to interact with.

8. **Does Beatie's definition of education cover what you associate with the term? Give reasons for your answer.**
– –

9. **Would you say that speaking a dialect is an obstacle to education? Discuss.**
– –

2 Jilly Cooper: Everyone Has an Accent

Didaktische Hinweise

Text 2 und 3 beleuchten unterschiedliche Aspekte eines Klassendenkens, das auch heute noch in Großbritannien existiert. Am Beispiel der humorvoll vorgetragenen Beobachtungen Jilly Coopers läßt sich vor allem zeigen, wie eng für einen Briten die Aussprache eines Menschen mit Schlußfolgerungen über dessen soziale Herkunft verknüpft sein können. Zugleich jedoch wird deutlich, welches Umdenken seit den sechziger Jahren eingesetzt hat. Die ablehnenden Reaktionen vieler Briten nicht nur auf eine "affected gentility", sondern ebenso auf eine "deliberate anti-gentility" (ll. 29–30) einerseits und Jilly Coopers Bemerkung "people no longer despise you if you have an accent as long as you're successful and amusing" (ll. 21–22) andererseits lassen erkennen, daß sich Veränderungen in der Einstellung zu traditionellen Sehweisen abzeichnen (vgl. aber "Background information", unten).

Background information

Jilly Cooper (1937–   ) has been a columnist for *The Mail on Sunday*, a popular paper, since the paper's foundation in 1982. She has published numerous books, among them *How to Stay Married* (1969), *Super Jilly* (1977), *Class* (1979) and *The British in Love* (1980).

"the egalitarian revolution" (ll. 2–3), *"the revolution of the 'sixties"* (l. 17): These are references to the intellectual and social upheavals of the 1960s, in which traditional forms and attitudes were overturned, and the previously rigid class

structure was loosened. This movement was greatly influenced by students who subscribed to the egalitarian tenets of the New Left, and was also reflected in the replacement of the postwar tripartite system with the comprehensive system of education (cf. "Info-Box", SB, p. 49).

"Thus I think the word 'luncheon' is pedantic, but the word 'phone' is vulgar" (l. 39): Here Jilly Cooper points out a further linguistic difference, besides accent, that divides the classes in Britain: the choice of words. Systematic attention was first given to the difference of usage between the upper classes and everyone else in a learned article by Alan S. C. Ross, "Linguistic class-indicators in present-day English" (in the Finnish *Neuphilologische Mitteilungen*, 1954, reprinted as a popular essay in *Noblesse Oblige*, 1956). Ross, for instance, groups "wealthy" as "non-U" (= not Upper Class) and "rich" as "U" (= Upper Class); similarly, non-U "serviette" was grouped with U "napkin". When asked in the late 1970s whether matters had changed since his essay appeared, Professor Ross replied: "The answer is that the antitheses between U and non-U have *not* changed. To pronounce 'forehead' almost as if it were two words is just as non-U today as it was in 1956 or 1926; the U make – and made – it rhyme with 'horrid', and that old favourite non-U 'serviette'/U 'napkin' is still in full force." (Richard Buckle, ed.: *U and Non-U Revisited.* Debrett's Peerage Ltd, London, 1978, pp. 28f.)

Semantic and collocational field "Language and class"

pronunciation, an accent, (to) enunciate, (to) be pronounced with (a long/short 'a') ✧ the upper/middle classes, upper-middle class/middle-class/lower-middle class/crypto-working-class/regional accent, BBC English ✧ (to) determine sb.'s class ✧ (to) be accepted, (to) communicate with sb. ✧ (to) be mocked, (to) reduce sb. to fits of laughter, (to) mimick sb., (to) despise sb. ✧ an elocution lesson, affected gentility, deliberate anti-gentility, (to) change one's voice, (to) iron out one's accent ✧ out-dated, vulgar, barbarous, pedantic

Talking about the text – Suggested answers

1. They associate it with a particular class. Broadly speaking, accents place a speaker in one of three classes: working, middle or upper. However, for a finer distinction, the qualifiers "lower", and "upper" can be added, so that "middle and lower middle" (l. 18) can be distinguished.
2. Cooper first uses the sound of the letter "a" to illustrate certain typical accents: "bath" and "class" are pronounced with a long "a" [ɑː] by the "upper-middle" class (cf. l. 11); a short "a" [ʌ] in words such as "Africa" or "bank balances" is characteristic of the "middle and lower middle" classes (cf. ll. 18–20). She mentions in passing the "matey", i.e. nearly working class, pronunciation "luv" [lʊv] for [lʌv], then goes on to deal with the phenomenon of "affected gentility" (l. 29) of Edward Heath, who supposedly says "e-out" [ɪaʊt] for "yacht" [jɒt], and Margaret Thatcher, who is reputed to say "invole-ved" [ɪnˈvəʊlvd] instead of "involved" [ɪnˈvɒlvd] (cf. l. 28). The opposite phenomenon, "deliberate anti-gentility" by members of the aristocracy, in this case by Tony Benn, is treated equally unkindly (cf. ll. 32–35).
3. While she has observed an increasing tolerance in some speakers (cf. ll. 21–22) and even at the BBC (cf. ll. 17–20), she also notes a persistent attitude of derision or contempt towards accents other than one's own: "a person is still mocked because of the way he speaks" (l. 4). As a possible cause of the spreading tolerance she cites "the egalitarian revolution" (ll. 2–3) of the 1960s (cf. l. 17).

4. The example of the "two youths in anoraks" who were "reduced ... to fits of laughter" (ll. 5–6) shows that accents can at least be found humorous by some, but contempt (cf. l. 8) and suspicion (cf. l. 25) are still common. Mr Heath and Mrs Thatcher are said to lose votes because of the way they speak (cf. ll. 23–29). Just as bad, at least to Jilly Cooper, is the case of Tony Benn, an aristocrat by birth, pretending to be working-class. According to the writer, the electorate recognizes that Benn is not really one of them, but talking down to them. The obtrusive "r" in "yer know-ing" (ll. 32–33) betrays him as upper-class, and when Benn called an "unfortunate Labour supporter in a pub" (ll. 34–35) "my good man", that person was, no doubt, slightly intimidated. He would normally expect a member of his class to call him "mate". So, despite an improvement in the general perception of accents, people of the lower classes are truly accepted only if they are "succesful and amusing" (l. 22).

5. [Since the Queen still represents the top of the social hierarchy, her use of language tends to serve as a model for many speakers, esp. those who wish to achieve prestige, wealth and influence. To some extent, the monarch's example counteracts the change towards a pluralistic, egalitarian society in which different accents and social backgrounds are entirely acceptable.]

6. *According to Shaw, the English react to an accent by despising the speaker. Cooper herself experienced being ridiculed and mimicked, apparently because of her upper-middle-class voice. How, according to the text, have many English people tried to avoid such experiences – and with what success?*
   To avoid the experience of negative stereotyping on account of their accents, many English people have changed their voices (cf. l. 23). The writer mentions changes in both directions, upwards and downwards within the English class system. Traditionally, people from the working or lower-middle classes have striven to "iron out" their accents and to acquire the upper-middle-class accent of BBC speakers (cf. ll. 11–13). More recently, however, some people have tried to bring their voices down, "like the girl in the 'sixties who had elocution lessons to try and get her accent made less patrician" (ll. 30–31).
   Most such attempts, as Cooper's examples show, are unsuccessful, probably because people like Cooper listen and "gleefully wait for the first slip" (ll. 27–28). Logically, any change of accent is a waste of effort, since the classes above and below the class whose accent one assumes will still, according to the Shavian maxim, despise one.

7. *How would you explain the fact that people "shrink from affected gentility" (l. 29) as well as from "deliberate anti-gentility" (ll. 29–30)?*
   – –

8. *What is your opinion of people who try to make their accents more socially acceptable?*
   – –

9. *In your opinion, to what extent are accents of social importance in Germany?*
   – –

3 John Wain: Silly Notions of an Upper-Class Herrenvolk

Didaktische Hinweise

Ähnlich wie Text 2 veranschaulicht auch dieser Auszug aus John Wains Roman *Hurry On Down* (1953) Tradition und Wandel im Klassendenken Großbritanniens. Die Kritik, die der Held Charles Lumley in seiner Auseinandersetzung mit dem jungen Arzt Burge äußert, beleuchtet grell alle jene Faktoren, aus denen sich traditionell die Privilegien der gehobenen Mittel- und Oberschicht in England herleiteten: eine Privatschulerziehung und Universitätsausbildung in den Prestigeschulen und -universitäten des Landes, die ihrerseits wieder als Eintrittsqualifikation den Weg in die gehobenen Berufe und Positionen in der Gesellschaft freigaben. Mit Charles Lumley läßt John Wain zugleich eine neue, kritische Generation zu Worte kommen, die nach dem Zweiten Weltkrieg – u.a. als erste Auswirkung der durch den Education Act 1944 eröffneten Bildungschancen für eine "meritocracy" (vgl. die "Info-Box", SB, S. 49) – sowohl in der englischen Literatur (etwa mit John Osbornes *Look Back in Anger*, 1956, und Arnold Weskers *Roots*, 1959, vgl. Text 1) als auch in der Politik (etwa während der Labour-Regierung 1945–1951 und 1964–1970) engagiert für soziale Gerechtigkeit und Chancengleichheit zu kämpfen beginnt.

John Wains Technik, in die Auseinandersetzung zwischen Lumley und Burge Elemente des Cockney einfließen zu lassen, illustriert und ergänzt die Beobachtungen Jilly Coopers (vgl. Text 2) zum Status unterschiedlicher englischer Akzente. In Burges Wendung "let the side down" (l. 57) deutet sich darüber hinaus die enge Verbindung an zwischen bestimmten Sportarten (hier den Mannschaftsspielen Rugby und Kricket) und einer elitären Privatschul- und Universitätsausbildung einerseits sowie einem Klassendenken andererseits (vgl. auch Text 5, Z. 71–92). – Das Thema "Sport und Klassenzugehörigkeit" kann vertieft werden durch die Einbeziehung der Texte 5, 6, 7 und 8, auch ein Vergleich mit entsprechenden Phänomenen in den USA bietet sich an (Kap. VI, Text 8 und 10).

Background information

John Wain (1925–   ) was born in Stoke-on-Trent, Staffordshire, and educated at Oxford. He spent eight years as a lecturer in English Literature at Reading University before deciding in 1955 to devote himself entirely to writing. He has published novels, short stories, poetry, a book on Shakespeare and critical essays. His first novel, *Hurry On Down* (1953), from which this excerpt is taken, deals with a young graduate's unconventional search for his place in a society obsessed with rigid class distinctions. John Wain has travelled and lectured widely. In 1973 he was elected Professor of Poetry at Oxford University.

"that the nigger-driving sahib oughtn't to do anything that reveals he shares a common humanity with the niggers he drives" (ll. 67–68): Charles Lumley refers to the snobbish self-image which British colonial administrators cultured to distinguish themselves from the peoples they had subjugated. Writing as a former colonial police officer, George Orwell unmasked the injustice and hollowness of British imperial rule in his essay "Shooting an Elephant". (*Contemporary British Short Stories II*. Ed. by D. Becker. Cornelsen Verlag, Berlin. Best.-Nr. 5372).

Semantic and collocational field "Arguing"

(to) challenge sb. to say sth., (to) catch sb. out with a smart question, (to) shout, (to) snap, (to) say sth. in a dangerously cool voice/in a parody of sb.'s manner/in tones of (sincere and utter) loathing/in tones of cold hatred, (to) raise one's voice, (to) call sb. passionately, (to) say sth. outrageous, (to) throw in one's support on the side of sb./sth., (to) be liable to say (silly) things, with a hint of a choke in his voice ✧ (to) listen intently, (to) stare at sb., (to) look at sb. with cold contempt ✧ (to) brand oneself, (to) draw attention to oneself ✧ (to) advance towards sb., (to) hold oneself erect ✧ open hostility, (to) bear a grudge, (to) lose one's temper, (to) start trouble, (to) get serious, (to) be roused, one's heart pounds with rage, one's blood surges ✧ (to) hurt sb., (to) hit sb., (to) strike out, (to) raise one's fists, (to) throw up one's fists, (to) lay hands on sb. ✧ (to) break the tension, (to) check oneself, (to) indicate agreement

Talking about the text – Suggested answers

1. *What does Burge mean when he accuses Charles Lumley of "letting the side down" (l. 57)?*

   Burge, the young doctor, accuses Charles of having acted against the interests of the class into which their university education has raised them. By taking the lowly job of a hospital orderly instead of one in the professions for which his university degree has qualified him, Charles has threatened to undermine the distribution of privileges in society. The team games that both Charles and Burge have been brought up on (l. 14: "a decent game like rugger"; l. 85: "cricket") had been aimed at instilling the kind of team spirit in the individual that would later provide the type of class ideology that Charles attacks as the "notions of an upper-class Herrenvolk" (l. 66).

2. *How does Charles Lumley counter Burge's argument that "there are some classes of society that are born and bred to it", i.e. to "slop-emptying" and "emptying bloody dustbins", "and ours isn't" (ll. 54 –55)?*

   Charles counters Burge by saying that the latter's ideas are a relict of the past, when the British Empire still rested on a conviction of racist superiority which denied the "nigger" a "common humanity" with the ruling white "sahib" (ll. 67–68). Charles claims for himself "an education along humane lines that didn't leave me with any illusions about the division of human beings into cricket teams called Classes" (ll. 84–86). In terms of British education, Charles here also attacks as outdated the goals that have been pursued by British public schools. Although he apparently went to the same boarding school as Burge (Charles remembers Burge as a prefect; cf. l. 10), Charles drew a different lesson than Burge from this experience. What it taught Charles was an insight into how this kind of education tends to perpetuate an unjust "division of human beings" into privileged and underprivileged "Classes" (ll. 85–86).

3. *What do we learn about Burge through his calling Charles "a bloody socialist" (ll. 70–71) and through his association with a girl who reacts so hostily to Charles's "Red notions" (l. 76)?*

   When Burge calls Charles a "bloody Socialist" and the girl "who was evidently connected with Burge in some way" (l. 35) fears "more trouble with [Charles's] Red notions", Burge shows that he has a seriously limited view of society. His idea of social reality is restricted to wholly irrelevant stereotypes (Charles was at the same school and college as Burge and does not use the language of any political ideology). At the same time, Burge makes it clear that he opposes any ideas that would introduce a higher degree of social justice than that admitted by a class system based on privilege. His view may be described as highly conservative, self-centred and unjust.

4. *The novel from which this text has been taken was first published in 1953. What intention may Wain have had in drawing this contrast between Charles Lumley and Burge's group?*

   Wanted readers to side with Charles Lumley, to make them ask questions about the distribution of educational opportunity in the country.

   Wanted readers to look critically at the public-school élite in leading professional and political positions.

   Wanted to acquaint readers with questions concerning the traditional links between social class and educational and professional opportunities. To ask, for instance, whether being "brought up and educated for slop-emptying" (ll. 46–47) must be accepted as an inevitable fate or whether changes might be possible.

5. *What attitude to different accents is revealed by the youth "affecting a Cockney accent" (cf. ll. 1–2)? For background information, you can read Jilly Cooper's observations on accents (cf. Ch. II, Text 2).*

The Cockney accent, combined with a characteristic choice of words, is used by the "youth in a yellow pullover" to introduce comic relief in a tense atmosphere (cf. l. 3). That it can be used for this effect at this gathering of people with "some sort of education" (l. 40) shows that, judged by their own "educated" standards, Cockney is considered to be a "low" form of English. The intended effect ("One or two people tittered", l. 3) can be accounted for to some extent by Shaw's observation that "It is impossible for an Englishman to open his mouth without making some other Englishman despise him" (cf. Ch. II, Text 2, ll. 7-8).

6. *Burge has a liking for certain expressions, for instance, for adding "bloody" to his utterances. What does his use of this word reveal about his character?*
   The choice of this slang and somewhat rude word (cf. ll. 5, 6, 9, 26, 28, 37, 42, 45, etc.) cannot, in Burge's case, be understood as a sign of a linguistically deprived upbringing. Rather, it serves here to characterize him as a particular specimen of the public-school élite that the author holds up to criticism. It is a sign of his lack of respect for Charles, and also of his authoritarian ruthlessness in dealing with those he considers his inferiors. It may also be seen as an indication of his tendency to replace serious arguments with the repetition of suggestive stock phrases. Charles recognizes this when he observes Burge's "fumbl[ing] among his *small stock* of metaphors" (l. 56). Similarly, when Burge repeats the slogan "'Workers of the world, unite!'" (ll. 71 and 73), he has simply run out of arguments and refuses to listen to views questioning "the prime articles of all their faith" (ll. 50–51).

7. *In your view, are there any jobs that people need to feel ashamed of? Explain.*
   – –

4 School Fees Made Possible

Didaktische Hinweise

Die mit dieser Anzeige beginnende Textgruppe vermittelt Einblicke in Aspekte und Ziele der *private education* in England, die seit Jahrhunderten zur Herausbildung und Erhaltung einer privilegierten Machtelite beigetragen hat. Text 4 thematisiert die hohen Kosten, Text 5 wirft ein Schlaglicht auf die gruppenspezifische Ideologie, Text 6 lenkt die Aufmerksamkeit auf die Bevorzugung bestimmter Mannschaftsspiele im Sport, die noch heute ein wichtiges Band des Zusammenhalts im Commonwealth bilden (vgl. dazu im einzelnen auch Kap. I, Text 11).

Die hier wiedergegebene faksimilierte Anzeige vermittelt nicht nur einen Eindruck von der Höhe der (von Jahr zu Jahr steigenden) Kosten einer Privatschulerziehung, sondern zugleich auch von der offensichtlich ungebrochenen Attraktivität dieser Erziehung selbst für jene Eltern der Mittelschicht, die sich eine solche Erziehung für ihre Kinder nur unter langjährigen finanziellen Opfern erkaufen können. Daß Anmeldungen für die renommiertesten Privatschulen zum Teil bereits vor oder bei der Geburt eines Kindes vorgenommen werden (vgl. die diesbezügliche Anspielung in der Illustration), verdeutlicht, in welch geringem Maße die mögliche Begabungsrichtung und Neigungen des Kindes bei der Wahl der Schule den Ausschlag geben.

Für den Bereich der Universität setzen die Texte 7 und 9 das hier eingeführte Thema „Elternhaus und Bildungschancen" fort. Entsprechende Phänomene in der amerikanischen Gesellschaft werden in Kap. VI, Text 9 angesprochen.

Background information

On the expectations and attitudes that parents have when buying an education, the well-known writer on education Geoffrey Walford observes: "The fact of paying for schooling puts parents and pupils in a very different relationship with the school and its teachers. Parents are investing in a service; pupils investing in their futures. Both groups appear to take long-term and largely instrumental views of the schooling process. From the interviews with schoolmasters and from the questionnaires and interviews with pupils, it was apparent that the relationship between these two groups was increasingly that of buyer-bought and, with teaching staff now coming from a wide range of social backgrounds, the relationship could be frequently interpreted in class terms. It was as if the dominant class was simply buying an efficient, complete private tutor system for their offspring in the same way as the dominant class of the fifteenth century might have done. The schools acted not only as sites for cultural reproduction, but also acted as minor sites for social reproduction, reproducing the relationships between classes." (*Life in Public Schools.* Methuen, London, 1986, p. 240).

Semantic and collocational field "Specialist help"

a planning specialist ✧ (to) provide individual advice, tailored to sb.'s needs ✧ (to) make sth. possible, (to) secure sth., (to) stop sth. becoming a problem ✧ a major budget headache, a lump sum, (to) invest (money) ✧ (to) plan ahead, (to) save (money) on the overall costs ✧ (to) be recommended by sb.

Talking about the text – Suggested answers

1. The ad appeals to parents (cf. "family budget" and the accompanying illustration of children) who would like to buy a private education for their children but cannot easily afford the school fees of "thousands of pounds" per child per year (cf. "stop school fees becoming a problem"). Such parents are most likely to be found in the middle and upper-middle classes. The fact that the ad appeared in "The Observer", a weekly quality paper read largely by those groups, supports the theory.
2. The baby in the illustration with its rattle suggests that "planning ahead" for a private education often means starting at the time of the child's birth.
   Apparently the costs parents have to meet amount to a considerable portion of their income. There are, after all, "thousands of pounds" at stake, according to the ad.
3. The firm's customers are apparently convinced that their children will have the ability and the inclination to attend one of Britain's better independent schools. In case the parents show some healthy scepticism and are not entirely certain that things will develop that way, the ad offers reassurance, i.e. "the flexibility to use the benefits for whatever purpose you desire".
4. A private education is at least perceived of as being better than a state-financed education. And in the context of the British class system, parents apparently believe they are also investing in greater opportunity for their children in terms of career prospects.
5. It is implied that the lower ranks of British society cannot afford the "overall costs" of a private education for one or all of their children, even if these happen to be sufficiently gifted to receive the best kind of education. Low-income families are thus excluded from educational opportunities that more well-to-do parents can save for or afford to buy. In other words, fee-charging independent schools in Britain tend to be socially exclusive and to perpetuate traditional class divisions.
6. The advertisers use two strategies in order not to shock potential customers by referring directly to the high annual costs. One is their use of very vague and general terms when

talking about the necessary money, e.g. "a major family budget *headache*" "a *problem*", and "your *needs* ". The second is a stylistic strategy characteristic of all good advertising copy: they try to sound positive. The keynote is struck in the headline by "made *possible*", and later continued by "*save* thousands of pounds", "use the *benefits* for whatever purpose *you desire*", and "you can *secure* a private education *for your children*". This style is appreciatory. It relies on expressions with positive connotations.

7. *In the ad the insurance specialists say: "C. Howard & Partners are recommended by the Independent Schools Information Service as independent school fee specialists." Why, do you think, does "ISIS" recommend such firms ?*
   Insurers like C. Howard & Partners can help create a positive image of this socially controversial type of private education.They help secure a steady flow of new pupils for all independent schools, especially from the group of parents who may otherwise not be able to afford a private education for their children.They provide an information service that would cost an individual school a great deal of time and money.

8. *In your view, do the layout and wording serve the advertisers' purpose well? Explain your answer.*
   – –

5 William Trevor: The World in Miniature

Didaktische Hinweise

Dieser Auszug aus William Trevors Roman *The Old Boys* (London, The Bodley Head 1964) vermittelt einen Eindruck von der Atmosphäre und dem Miteinander von Lehrern und Schülern, wie sie in einer traditionellen englischen Privatschule zu finden waren – und mit geringen Veränderungen (etwa der, daß Schüler heute mit ihrem Vornamen angeredet werden) noch immer zu finden sind. Neben der Erläuterung der Zielsetzungen der Schule verdient das vom "Housemaster" verwendete Sprachregister besondere Aufmerksamkeit (vgl. unten, Aufg. 1, 2 und 6). Es ist ganz auf die häufig kritisierte Erziehung zu blinder Autoritätsgläubigkeit und Snobismus abgestellt. Obwohl seit der massiven Bedrohung ihrer Existenz durch die Labour Party ab Mitte der sechziger Jahre in bestimmten Bereichen der Privatschulerziehung ein Wandel eingetreten ist (insbesondere durch die Aufnahme von Mädchen und eine stärkere curriculare Verlagerung von sportlichen Aktivitäten hin zu zeitgemäßen naturwissenschaftlichen Angeboten), entsprechen die Grundmuster des von der Außenwelt isolierten Gemeinschaftslebens in den *boarding schools* und seiner Auswirkungen auf die Schüler noch immer William Trevors Darstellung. Für den Bereich der Universität veranschaulichen Text 8 und 9 exemplarisch, zu welchen Ergebnissen ein solches Elitedenken und die Überbetonung von Gemeinschaftssinn und Mannschaftssport auf der fortgeschrittenen Ebene der Erziehung führen können.

Background information

William Trevor (1929–   ) is the pen-name of William Trevor Cox. He was born in County Cork, Ireland, and went to Trinity College, Dublin. He is noted for his output of short stories and novels, but has also written radio and television plays. His novel *The Old Boys,* from which this excerpt is taken, received the Hawthornden Prize.

The Old Boys is the story of an old boys' committee acting out their school-day rivalries. It belongs to the minor literary genre of "the boys' school story". This genre began with Thomas Hughes's popular mid-nineteenth century novel, *Tom Brown's Schooldays* (1857), the story of an ordinary schoolboy at Rugby School, who experiences the cruelties and loyalties typical of public school life. These stories were generally didactic in nature, in that they sought to instil a particular set of values in the public schoolboy. In the classic examples of the genre, the stories supported the schools and the social structure of which they were a part. In the years between the two world wars, the life of the genre declined: "Now the genre was being used both to criticise the schools, their educational beliefs and their exclusiveness and to suggest or support alternative forms of educational organisation." P. W. Musgrave: *From Brown to Bunter. The Life and Death of the School Story*. Routledge & Kegan Paul, London, 1985, p. 239).

"Dowse's prowess on the sport fields" (l. 5): This attribute refers to the traditional emphasis on team games in public schools; sport, by encouraging team loyalty and healthy rivalry, as well as physical fitness, was considered an integral part of a schoolboy's general education. The justification for games was often drawn from observations such as the one attributed to the Duke of Wellington: "The battle of Waterloo was won on the playing fields of Eton". With reference to the present-day situation, Geoffrey Walford observes: "In sport ... there has been a move away from the dominance of team games towards more individual and socially exploitable sports. Ability and interest in golf, tennis or squash are far more of an advantage in terms of advancement in business or the professions than are football or rugby, for the squash or golf clubs are sites at which informal business discussions can be held. ... Public schools increasingly are providing these skills as a necessary component of their finished product." *(Life in Public Schools*. Methuen, London, 1986, pp. 241 f.).

"when you leave here you leave with the advantage of knowing what lies beyond" (ll. 46–47): Critics of the public school system usually take the opposite view: that public school pupils are kept separate from the rest of society during the most formative years of their lives, and consequently fail to learn how to deal with people who are not part to their social group. Until recently, girls were not per-mitted to attend boys' public schools; this tended to strain relations with the oppo-site sex. Once they left school, many students would never have occasion to move outside the charmed circle of privilege (cf. also task 5, below). Anthony Sampson (cf. p. 71 of this book) observed: "The old charge against Etonians was that they were confident, stupid and out of touch with the lives and needs of most of the country. The new charge is that they are confident, clever – but still out of touch." *(The Changing Anatomy of Britain*. Hodder & Stoughton, London, 1983, p. 144).

Semantic and collocational field "Secondary education" (public school)
a prep school, a housemaster, a study, the world in miniature, privileged ✧ (to) learn to do sth., (to) be taught sth., (to) absorb knowledge, (to) receive an education ✧ an ignoramus, ignorance ✧ (to) lose one's identity, (to) discover one's place/the extent of one's self ✧ (to) make the most of sth., (to) make a good job of sb./sth., (to) develop an interest in sth. ✧ (to) live in harmony with sb., (to) lead the way, (to) recognize superiority in sb., (to) bow to sb./sth.

✧ (to) abide by the rules, (to) smile on misfortune/triumph, (to) distribute/take punishment
✧ (to) leave a school, (to) know what lies beyond

Talking about the text – Suggested answers

1. *What do Dowse's words and his manner to Nox (up to l. 19) reveal about the attitude masters have to boys?*
   Dowse's manner is much more reminiscent of an authoritarian army officer to his troops than of a teacher to a pupil. He treats the 13-year-old boy like an inferior adult who is completely under his command. He denies the boy any polite forms of address, while he himself expects them (cf. "sir", l. 19). He does not ask Nox who he is – he tells him, then checks his list (cf. ll. 12–13). He shows no interest in the boy as an individual: Nox had "lost all other identity" (ll. 3–4). He disregards any identity the boy may have developed before (cf. ll. 13–14: " 'Well, Nox, you are about to begin *a new life.*' ").

2. *Show how characteristic forms of expression and style of Dowse's speech reflect the master's attitude.*
   An authoritarian impression is created by Dowse's constant use of short declarative sentences. Clear and simple, they leave no room for doubts or qualifications – and no opening for discussion. This is reinforced by the frequent use of "will" to indicate what Dowse expects of Nox (e.g. ll. 26–27, 41–45, 52–56, 68), the use in sequence of "must" to indicate a moral obligation (cf. ll. 47–50) and the use of short imperative sentences in rapid succession (cf. ll. 62–63).
   The phrasing and tone of Dowse's questions as well as their position in this authoritarian context do not give Nox the chance of answering honestly or as an equal. Dowse's first question, "Have you questions?" (l. 17) is so curt as to be intimidating. He ends two of his questions with the demeaning word "boy" (cf. ll. 32, 96), and he frightens the boy with his vague and euphemistic reference to masturbation and the subsequent question with its old-fashioned wording, "You know of what I speak?" (l. 64). Suggestive questions such as those in ll. 35–36 and 39 ensure that Dowse will get the answers he wants to hear, i.e. that Nox will submit to his authority.

3. *Dowse calls the education George Nox is about to receive "the finest form of education in the world" (l. 41). What educational goals set this particular education apart from all other kinds, in Dowse's opinion?*
   The principal feature is not preparation for academic achievement (cf. Dowse's references to Latin and mathematics in ll. 24–26, 51), but the intention of making the individual pupil conform to the requirements of the group: he is to learn to place himself in the service of the group's collective will and "live in harmony with your fellows" (l. 42); cf. also the emphasis on the *team* sports cricket and rugby; he is to learn self-control, "equanimity" in "misfortune" as in "triumph" (l. 53); he is to learn unquestioning subordination to authority (cf. ll. 43, 95–96).
   This kind of character-building within a close-knit group of peers is meant to release him into adult life as "one of the ones who lead the way" (l. 50). He will be shaped to enjoy the privileges of those who have travelled similar paths and already become leaders in various walks of life.

4. *Why is the Housemaster so confident that the school will successfully educate Nox in this way?*
   Nox appears to accept Dowse's authority and to be appropriately frightened by the Housemaster. And he has already learned to adopt his behaviour to the expectations of those in authority (cf. ll. 21–22). In other words, Nox appears to be suitably malleable. Dowse also knows from past experience of educating boys like Nox that peer pressure in the controlled environment of the school, nine months a year, from age 13 to 18, will help push the boy in the desired direction. The promise of success after their stay

in the public school and the knowledge that the "Old Boy network" will take care of them later provide boys like Nox with the additional motivation to conform.

5. *Dowse tells Nox, "You will find that our school is the world in miniature" (ll. 44–45). Considering what you know about the school's aims and environment, how would you assess this statement?*
   – –

6. *Dowse calls Nox a "privileged person" (ll. 45–46) and tells him that he "will be one of the ones who lead the way" (ll. 49–50). What long-term attitudes were public school teachers likely to produce in their pupils?*
   Apart from encouraging an uncritically favourable attitude towards the school and its masters, such comments were likely to make pupils think of themselves as the country's élite, with attendant feelings of superiority and arrogance.

6 Robert Holman: Cricket Snobbery Must End

Didaktische Hinweise

Obwohl allgemein als englischer Nationalsport etikettiert, ist Kricket – wie dieser Leserbrief exemplarisch verdeutlicht – eng mit einem Klassendenken verknüpft, das unter anderem auch Englands Privatschulsystem neben dem staatlichen Schulwesen in der Gesellschaft lebendig hält. Für die privilegierte Mittel- und Oberschicht mit einer Erziehung in Privatschulen und Elite-Universitäten (Oxford und Cambridge) ist Kricket, was Fußball für die breite Masse des Inselvolks ist. Wie das Privatschulwesen, das auf jahrhundertalte Traditionen zurückblicken kann, wahrt auch das Mannschaftsspiel Kricket (erstmals um 1550 erwähnt) noch heute die Verbindung der Oberschicht zu einer Reihe der ehemaligen Kolonien (vgl. "Background information", unten), deren Mannschaften sich alljährlich in den internationalen "test matches" messen. Für den Bereich der Elite-Universitäten illustriert Text 7, Z. 6 ff., wie nach elterlichem Vorverständnis jener Jugendliche eingeschätzt wird, der sportliche Aktivitäten unkonventionell durch Theaterspielen zu ersetzen versucht.

Als Lektüre zum Thema Fußball und *working class* empfehlen sich Barry Hines' Roman *The Blinder* (1966, Harmondsworth, Penguin Books 1966) und Peter Tersons Drama *Zigger Zagger* (1970, Harmondsworth, Penguin Books 1970). Zur Verknüpfung von Rugby und Kricket mit der Oberschicht vgl. u. a. Lawrence Durrells humorvoll-ironisches Kapitel "The Game's the Thing" in: *Stiff Upper Lip* (London, Faber & Faber 1958, S. 37–44).

Background information

"Scyld Berry is correct to assert" (l. 1): The *Observer* sports reporter wrote in an article that "England has fallen from its position of primacy in cricket as assuredly as Britain has lost its position at the head of Commonwealth or Empire" and gave two reasons for this state of affairs: the first being that several former colonies had simply become better at the game, and the second being "the lack of funding for the State schools and their cricket. Talent is surely being wasted in the London borough where only a single State school offers cricket on its curriculum, and in another where merely two do so." (*The Observer*, 17 August 1986, p. 8).

"the national side" (l. 25): a reference to the team that represents England at the international test matches. The first test match was played in Melbourne in 1877, when a team of Australia's best cricketers beat an English team. Lord's in London is the headquarters and home field of the Marylebone Cricket Club (founded in the 18th century), the world's leading cricket organization, and is the headquarters of the International Cricket Conference, the world governing body.

The test countries are Australia, South Africa (excluded from partaking since the 1970s, due to its adherence to apartheid), the West Indies, New Zealand, India and Pakistan. The matches last 30 hours, that is six days in Australia and the West Indies, and five days elsewhere.

Semantic and collocational field "Cricket"

a cricketer, a county player, a pitch, a recreation ground, (to) play (cricket), to possess the basic skills ✧ (to) run a cricket team, (to) organize cricket ✧ a pool for recruiting into the national side, (to) make use of one's resources ✧ (to) be afforded the same access, (to) be given experience, (to) be promoted, (to) give priority to sth., open to all

Talking about the text – Suggested answers

1. He wants to draw attention to two aspects of cricket he finds troubling:
   Because of its close links with the middle class (cf. ll. 2–3), "English cricket" (l. 31) does not recruit enough talent from all strata of British society. In international matches against countries such as the West Indies or Australia (cf. ll. 3–4), English cricket teams may be at a permanent disadvantage, since those countries' teams are "open to all" (l. 3).
   English cricket administrators discriminate against talent from state schools (cf. ll. 8, 34) and from provincial (Redbrick) universities (cf. ll. 25–30).
   In other words, Dr Holman highlights English cricket as an élitist game of the socially and educationally privileged strata of society.
2. It indicates that cricket is a game characteristically played in former English colonies. Although independent now, countries such as the West Indies, Australia, New Zealand, India and Pakistan are still closely linked with England through this game. [The bond among these countries is renewed every year during the international test match season.]
3. Obviously, cricket is a preserve of independent (public) schools (cf. *"State schools* give little priority to cricket", ll. 8–9; cf. also Ch. II, Text 5, ll. 80 ff.), and "outside of schools", fees for the use of a cricket pitch are prohibitive to less well-off teams if the pitch is available at all (cf. ll. 10–14). At the same time, football is considered a game for the lower classes: while there are several football teams on the (working-class) council estate where Dr Holman works, he helps "to run the *only* cricket team" (ll. 5–6). Cricket is perceived – perhaps falsely (cf. ll. 22–28) – to be best at the old, élitist universities of Oxford and Cambridge, which consist largely of middle-class students. Thus cricket "remains middle class, not open" (ll. 2–3).
4. He claims that the administrators select players for teams (cf. ll. 20–21) and set up matches between teams (cf. ll. 22–25, 28–30) not on the basis of talent but because of their membership of the country's élitist educational institutions. According to Holman, cricket and social privilege are unjustifiably linked.
5. In his concluding paragraph, the writer switches from his argumentative manner of speaking to instruction, i.e. a different text type, in the form of recommendations for action. The tone for subjective argumentation in ll. 1–30 is set by his opening confirmation of Scyld Berry's view: "Scyld Berry *is correct* to assert that ..." (l. 1). After giving evidence (cf. ll. 5–30) for the thesis (cf. ll. 2–3) that cricket in England remains unjustifiably "middle class", he switches to instruction (cf. the action-demanding sentences "two steps *are* necessary...", "the game *must* be more fully promoted in ..." and "the snobbery of the

game's administrators *must* go", ll. 33–36. Moreover, he chooses the order of numerical listing of "First" and "Second", which are typical of instructive texts). The intention is not to leave readers alone with a potentially convincing argumentation, but to show them where action can be taken to bring about a change.

6. *How might one explain Scyld Berry's observation that "in the West Indies and Australia" cricket is "open to all" (ll. 3–4)?*
   These and other countries are able to select the best players from all walks of life because they do not have England's dual education system of private vs. state schools and Oxbridge vs. Redbrick universities. Their societies are, therefore, less class- and privilege-oriented than England's is traditionally.

■ 7 Peter Shaffer: How Are You Settling Down at Cambridge?

Didaktische Hinweise

Die mit diesem Dramenauszug beginnende Textgruppe (Text 7, 8 und 9) verdeutlicht gesellschaftspolitische Aspekte der beiden Universitäten Oxford und Cambridge und erlaubt damit, die Diskussion über eine aus dem Privatschulbereich hervorgegangene Führungselite fortzuführen. Die Texte werden vermutlich besonderes Interesse wecken, weil sie mit ihrer Kritik an den bestehenden Verhältnissen nicht zurückhalten. In ihnen spiegelt sich der tiefe Interessenkonflikt wider, der die englische Gesellschaft infolge des Fortbestehens eines privilegierten Erziehungssystems durchzieht.

Was die zur Investition einer Privatschulerziehung verlockende Anzeige (Text 4) unterschwellig verspricht, das illustriert die Unterhaltung zwischen dem nichtakademischen Vater Stanley und seinem Sohn Clive. Clive hat einen Studienplatz in Cambridge erhalten und soll die Studienzeit für jene Zwecke nutzen, für die sie traditionell und nach allgemeiner Auffassung (noch immer) steht: Verbindungen zu Studienkollegen zu knüpfen, die später im Berufsleben weitertragen und den beruflichen und gesellschaftlichen Aufstieg, abgesichert durch *the old boy network*, erleichtern. Der erfolgreiche mittelständische Kaufmann möchte sich in seinem Sohn den Weg in die akademische Machtelite erkaufen. Clives Ansicht darüber, was Cambridge ihm statt dessen bieten und bedeuten könnte, kann mit Beaties Verständnis von *education* (Text 1) oder Charles Lumleys Überzeugungen (Text 3) verglichen und so das zentrale Thema dieses Kapitels weiter vertieft werden.

Five Finger Exercise (1958) ist in einer Paperback-Ausgabe erhältlich (Harmondsworth, Penguin Plays 1981). Eine Analyse von Peter Shaffers Bühnenwerk bietet Rainer Lengeler: „Peter Shaffer: Equus. Der Mythos vom ursprünglichen Leben". In: H.F. Plett (Hrsg.): *Englisches Drama von Beckett bis Bond*. München, W. Fink 1982, S. 272 ff. (UTB 1116), eine Interpretation von *Five Finger Exercise* von H. Wulf findet sich in *Das zeitgenössische englische Drama. Einführung, Interpretation, Dokumentation*. Hrsg. von K.-D. Fehse und N. H. Platz. Frankfurt, Athenäum Fischer Taschenbuch Verlag 1975, S. 71 ff.

Background information

Peter Shaffer (1926 –   ) and his twin brother, Anthony, author of the successful crime play *Sleuth* (1970), were born in Liverpool into a middle-class family. Peter attended the well-known London public school St Paul's. Then, after working as a miner in Kent and Yorkshire, which he did as an alternative to national service, he went to Trinity College, Cambridge, to study history. He then worked in New York City Library and for a London music publisher's before starting his writing career. He published literary and music criticism, and in 1958 produced his first stage play, *Five Finger Exercise*. Since then he has written several plays, his most sucessful being *Equus* (1973) and *Amadeus* (1979), which were both made into films. In 1989 he was awarded the Shakespeare prize of the F.V.S. Stiftung Hamburg for his contribution to English literature.

Like John Osborne's *Look Back in Anger*, which was produced two years earlier, Peter Shaffer's *Five Finger Exercise* is a family drama. Written in a seemingly conventional style, both plays voice the discontents and questions about life of the postwar generation. Osborne's play, with its working-class "angry young man", Jimmy Porter, and his rough colloquial language, proved to be more revolutionary than Shaffer's. Shaffer is mainly concerned with 19-year-old Clive's rebellion against his father Stanley and his fascination with Walter, an attractive young German tutor who tries to escape from his family's Nazi background by attaching himself to a respectable English family.

Semantic and collocational field "University education"

a good brain, (to) send sb. to university ✧ a privileged position, (to) play games, (to) join a club/society, (to) belong to a club/society, (to) take up fencing ✧ (to) make use of sth., (to) take advantage of sth. ✧ (to) make contacts with the right people, (to) get in with sb., (to) judge a man by the company he keeps ✧ (to) influence the rest of sb.'s life

Talking about the text – Suggested answers

1. The exchanges between father and son lead up to a climax – the father's attitude towards his son becomes increasingly critical and authoritarian. At the beginning (cf. ll. 1–16), Stanley politely asks his son about his new experience of university life at Cambridge. Clive briefly explains what changes he has experienced with regard to friends (l. 3), "clubs and societies" (l. 5) and "games" (ll. 12–14). Then, during the second stage (cf. ll. 17–36), Stanley begins to express doubts as to whether Clive is making the right "use"(l. 18) of Cambridge. Clive is challenged to criticize his father's view by explaining his own view of "education – being educated" (l. 29). The climax is reached during the third stage (cf. ll. 38–63), when the father brushes aside as irrelevant his son's talk about education and, without admitting further arguments from Clive (l. 50: "cuts him off immediately"), gives him instructions on how to use Cambridge for "making contacts with the right people" (cf. ll. 53–56).
2. As Clive starts to tell his father about the culturally oriented choices he has made so far in his first term at Cambridge, it becomes increasingly clear that these have nothing to do with the "use" (l. 18) Stanley expects him to make of the university. As his contempt for the "arty boys" (l. 48) and "fancy la-de-da people" (l. 55) later reveals, Stanley considers Clive joining a "Dramatic Society" (l. 7) to be just as wrong as his preference for fencing (cf. ll. 12–13) instead of team games such as cricket and football. In short, father and son have opposing ideas of what "Cambridge" should mean in a young man's life.
3. Clive's father is a self-made businessman (cf. "the contacts I made I had to work up myself", ll. 57–58), and he apparently has achieved some degree of success (cf. "I'll see to it you've got enough money", l. 60). He obviously has no experience of Cambridge (cf. "I never had your opportunities", l. 57) or of any other university, as his inappropriate choice of words shows when he talks about university life in terms of school life (e.g. "the other boys", l. 1; "lessons", ll. 4, 39). His lack of education shows further in his limited

understanding of Clive's references to the university Dramatic Society (cf. ll. 7–8) and to "coordination" (cf. ll. 13–15). Like most parents, Stanley wants his son to have a better life than he himself had, so he encourages Clive to make use of his stay at Cambridge in the best way he knows how. His idea of Cambridge is second-hand, reflecting what middle-class people associate with that university: "a privileged position" (l. 40) for a young man to become part of the social network that will lead to power and influence (cf. ll. 53–57).

4. Clive's view is quite the opposite of his father's concept. He sees Cambridge as a place for the student to be confronted with a highly attractive choice of people and cultural activities. At university he is not exposed to the group pressure of prep school – he can now "pick [his] own friends" (l. 3) and freely pursue his cultural interests (cf. l. 7, "I joined a Dramatic Society"). He desires exposure to intellectual stimulation and challenge (cf. ll. 34–35, "I think education is simply the process of being taken by surprise"). As opposed to his father's emphasis on the opportunities for social advancement and "contacts", Clive talks about educational benefits in terms of individual growth.

5. [It would seem that Clive agrees with his father's statement only because he links the words with a completely different area of reference. While his father links the words with expectations of social privilege and contacts, Clive understands it in terms of his "being educated" as an individual. So he outwardly agrees with his father to placate him and end this unpleasant conversation.]

6. *In ll. 29–35, Clive begins to explain what he understands by "education – being educated". What language does he use and what does it tell us about him?*
He uses both explicit comparisons, i.e. similes (ll. 30–31, "*like* setting off on an expedition into the jungle"; ll. 33–34, "*like* the nave of Wells Cathedral"), and implicit comparisons, i.e. metaphors (ll. 31–32, "The *old birds* fly out of the sky, new ones fly in …"; ll. 32–33, "*Trees* you expected to be a few feet high …"). He apparently chooses this comparative language because he is speaking about his new experiences at Cambridge, experiences for which both his father's and his own vocabulary prove to be inadequate. His emphasis is on the opportunity to discover novel systems of thought (e.g. "the jungle" where "gradually all the things you know disappear", ll. 30–31) and novel ideas (cf. his reference to "old birds" and "new ones"), in surprising order, depth and complexity (cf. his reference to the growth of "trees", "right up overhead", ll. 32–33). Apart from serving the purpose of exposition, all these comparisons carry positive connotations about Clive's experience of "being educated": a "process" (l. 35) of fascinating and awe-inspiring adventure.

7. a) *In your view, who does the dramatist want the reader or spectator to side with in this conversation? Justify your answer.*
– –

   b) *Are you still able to feel sympathy for the other character? Explain.*
– –

8. *What aspects of school or universiy education do you personally consider most important?*
– –

8 Catherine Blond: Macho College Falls to Women's Lure

Didaktische Hinweise

Während in Text 7 das Phänomen Cambridge aus der Perspektive eines jungen Mannes (Clive) dargestellt wird, der seine Selbstverwirklichung durch die intellektuelle Herausforderung anstrebt, wird in Text 8 die Frage nach vergleichbaren Chancen für junge Frauen gestellt. Am Beispiel von Magdalene College,

Cambridge, kann veranschaulicht werden, welche tradierten Einstellungen und Erwartungen kennzeichnend für junge Männer in der Universität waren, aber auch, welcher Wandel sich in der Mehrzahl der Colleges bereits in Richtung auf Chancengleichheit für junge Frauen vollzogen hat. Dieser Wandel verändert die traditionell enge Verbindung zwischen Reichtum, Privatschulerziehung und Privilegien für den Aufstieg in die Machtelite des Inselreichs. Insbesondere erfaßt der Wandel auch die traditionell gestörte Beziehung zum weiblichen Geschlecht – mit einem Abbau an Vorurteilen auf dem Weg zu einem natürlichen, gleichberechtigten Miteinander. Soll die Rolle der Frau in der britischen Gesellschaft eingehender untersucht werden, kann der Beitrag von Katharine Whitehorn (Kap. III, Text 5) im Anschluß an diesen Text behandelt werden.

Background information

"the governing body's decision ... to amend the college statutes" (ll. 8–10): Universities are self-governing institutions, and, as such, are responsible for all academic appointments, the university curriculum and student admissions. There are 47 universities in Britain, most of which were established by royal charters. Universities depend upon the State for much of their income. Recent government cutbacks have, however, forced universities to look further afield for sponsorship.

At present, most of the 295,000 university students receive student grants from their local education authority; however, the Conservative government of Mrs Thatcher has announced plans to introduce student loans.

"monstrous regiment" (l. 12): sarcastic allusion to *The First Blast of the Trumpet against the Monstrous Regiment of Women*, a 1558 pamphlet by John Knox (1505–1572), the founder of the Scottish Presbyterian Church, directed against Queen Mary Tudor of England and Queen Mary Stuart of Scotland, both of whom sought to promote Catholicism in the British Isles.

Semantic and collocational field "University education"

an undergraduate, a member, a fellow ✧ a(n) sporting/women's/Oxbridge college, the governing body, (to) amend the college statutes, (to) go co-educational, (to) let in/admit women, (to) exclude men ✧ an academic league-table, academic standards ✧ a rugby team, sport, a Blue, a Half Blue, (to) choose a team from (a number of people) ✧ an atmosphere, a sense of camaraderie, (to) dictate the tone of (college) life, a good feeling exists in college ✧ an exclusive drinking club, (to) initiate members

Talking about the text – Suggested answers

1. Most of the aspects mentioned here tend to confirm the popular stereotype of Magdalene as an élitist institution for the rich and stupid, e.g. its strong "passion for games" (ll. 22–23 and 62–63); the high percentage of "Old Etonians who dictate the tone" (ll. 20–21) and create " 'an atmosphere of sweaty public-school heartiness' " (ll. 58–59); its adherence to "hard drinking and fast driving" (l. 23) and other forms of "brutish jocularity" (ll. 24–25); its being " 'notable for the number of upper-class twits' " (ll. 56–57) and being " 'not for the poor' " (l. 60); its disregard for "academic" achievement (cf. ll. 63–65); its subjection of the individual to the dictates of a male community (cf. ll. 34–35, 59); its snobbishness (cf. ll. 35–37); and its distorted view of women, with treatment alternating between "old-fashioned chivalry" (l. 25) and "obscene suggestions" (l. 47).

All these factors would appear to be directly or indirectly related to the college's "444 years" (l. 14) of upper-class male exclusiveness.

2. It is considered backward or downright "archaic" (l. 24) because, in the meantime, other aspects have assumed greater importance at most, or all, of the other Oxford and Cambridge colleges. All colleges have by now gone "co-educational" as a result of "the tide of feminism" (ll. 15–16); the achievement of outstanding "academic standards" (ll. 67–68) is now considered at least as important as sporting prowess (cf. "the academic *league-tables*", l. 64); exclusiveness based on social privilege and the displaying of macho prowess are looked upon with contempt (ll. 56–57, " 'upper-class *twits*' "); the relationship with women has been normalized by admitting them as members and fellows into the former male bastions (cf. ll. 16–17).

3. Their wearing "mourning" (l. 2) and black armbands (l. 4), as well as the black flag they have hoisted "over the porters' lodge" (ll. 3–4), all point to their liking for ritual, especially if this helps them to demonstrate that they are something "special". They are prepared to spend a lot of money for what may appear as an adolescent hoax to most readers (cf. "More than £300 has been collected to place *In Memoriam* notices in the newspapers", ll. 5–7).

4. Blond's attitude is critical, disapproving, even contemptuous. It is not communicated directly – there are no first-person statements or explicit condemnations by Blond herself. Instead, her choice of language and descriptive detail as well as her use of selective quotation combine to produce a savagely ironic tone.
The serious, factual description of mourning which begins the article invites the reader to expect that someone important has died. The anticlimax which follows when this assumption is corrected (not a real death, only a change in the statutes to admit women) suggests that the undergraduates' reaction is excessive and ridiculous. This is heightened by Blond's ironic use of extravagant, exaggerated terms the undergraduates might well employ themselves, e.g. "grief" (l. 8), "the monstrous regiment" (ll. 11–12). Similarly ironic is her adoption of an insider's register in the fourth paragraph (e.g. "bloods", l. 20; "hard drinking and fast driving", l. 23).
Blond's quotations highlight only Magdalene's negative aspects (cf. her selection of damning phrases from the "Varsity Handbook", ll. 56–61). Further, she quotes only those Magdalene members who oppose co-education, picking out single remarks which neatly illustrate her negative characterization (cf. ll. 30–37, 39–44, 67–70, 72–74).
Again, Blond employs irony to ridicule these details and invite the reader to criticize them. In ll. 45 ff. Somerowski's apparently innocent "good times" are made to seem ironic and deplorable by the factual details with which Blond associates them, e.g. "obscene suggestions to female customers", "vomit". In l. 71, Blond's sarcastic introduction of Rich's remark as "a graver objection" provides a final pointer to the chauvinistic stupidity of Magdalene members.

5. ***Considering the message of the text itself, what view do you take of the headline's reference to a college falling "to women's lure"?***
[The headline is an example of the ironical use of sexist language and is thus in keeping with the tone of the whole article. The wording reflects the traditional view that women win all their victories by playing on their sexual attractions for men. Considering what the text actually says about the impending change, i.e. that it has been decided on "to increase academic standards" (ll. 67–68), "falls" is somewhat misleading and little more than a good eye-catcher.]

9 Richard Hoggart: Gilded Youth at Oxbridge

Didaktische Hinweise

Hoggarts Brief an den Herausgeber des *Observer* kann in mehrfacher Hinsicht als Abrundung der Problembereiche betrachtet werden, die in diesem Kapitel angesprochen werden: zum einen durch die Textgruppe 4 bis 6 (Ziele und gesellschaftliche Auswirkungen des englischen Privatschulwesens), zum anderen durch die Texte 7 und 8 (Oxford und Cambridge als gesellschaftliches Phänomen).

Ähnlich wie in den beiden Texten über Cambridge (vgl. Text 7 und 8) zeigt auch Hoggarts Kritik, daß für Oxford nach wie vor das Netz von Verbindungen der wohlhabenden Mittel- und Oberschicht zumindest ebenso stark zählt wie die Begabung des Einzelnen. Nach Hoggart wiegt dies um so schwerer, als die konservative Regierung unter Margaret Thatcher die Chancen für begabte Jugendliche aus den sozial schwächeren Schichten durch eine Beschränkung von Stipendien und Mitteln der Studentenförderung *(grants)* generell stark eingeschränkt hat. Hoggart entläßt daher seine Leser/innen mit der unausgesprochenen Frage, wie lange sich eine demokratische Industriegesellschaft noch eine solche Ungleichheit der Chancen leisten kann.

Die umfassendere Frage, welche Aufgaben die Regierung und der Staat für die Mehrzahl jener Heranwachsenden zu erfüllen haben, die den traditionellen Erwartungen an Begabung nicht entsprechen, stellt Hoggart hier nicht; sie wird in den dieses Kapitel abschließenden Texten 10 und 11 thematisiert.

Background information

Richard Hoggart (1918 –   ) was Professor of English and Director of the Centre for Contemporary Cultural Studies at Birmingham University from 1962 to 1973. He wrote the seminal work on the British working class, *The Uses of Literacy*. First published in 1957, it was reprinted as a Penguin book 13 times.

"The correlations between family background, school, the right sorts of connections and admissions" (ll. 22–24): In an article called "Class Bias in British Education", Hoggart summed up the situation like this: "The connections between social class and opportunity [in England] remain so tenacious that there is still virtually no more chance for working class people than there was thirty-five years ago." (Richard Hoggart: *An English Temper*. Chatto, London, 1982, p. 45).

Semantic and collocational field "University admissions procedures"

higher education, an admissions tutor, (to) accept sb., (to) obtain/be denied entry to a university ✧ a great university, a less fashionable provincial institution ✧ ability, a bright youngster, a brilliant/devoted student, (to) win one's way on merit ✧ a member of a set, a privileged person, the iniquities/distortions of (Oxbridge) admissions procedures, a family's connections, the correlations between family background and admissions, (to) owe one's place to the fact that …, (to) put a word in the right ear, (to) have a special relationship with sb./sth. ✧ (to) be sent down for (bad) behaviour

Talking about the text – Suggested answers

1. Hoggart suggests that, since Olivia Channon was herself well-connected and belonged to a particular "set" (l. 10) of people, a case can be made for the assertion that she – and

others – did not get into the prestigious university of Oxford "on merit" (l. 13). Indeed, their sometimes "loutish" (l. 29) behaviour suggests the contrary. According to the writer, only "some of them are bright" (ll. 13–14), so what channelled the rest past the admissions tutor must have been "family background, school, the right sorts of connections" (ll. 22–24, cf. also ll. 14–21).

2. The headline is possibly misleading in that it does not qualify the expression "gilded youth" in any way; instead, it sounds all-inclusive, a general comment on all Oxbridge students. The letter writer, on the other hand, is careful not to generalize unjustifiably about privilege at Oxford. He speaks specifically of "the set to which Miss Channon belonged" (ll. 10–11), and he further distinguishes between "some" who are no doubt "bright" and "others" who "clearly owe their places" to some sort of nepotism or favouritism (cf. ll. 13–21). Later in his letter he makes a point of recalling these qualifications: "a minority, no doubt" (ll. 27–28); "one can find there brilliant and devoted students" (ll. 66–67).

3. Hoggart's views can be summed up as follows:
At Oxford and Cambridge, educational opportunity should be offered strictly "on merit" (l. 13), i.e. to the intellectually most able candidates (cf. l. 25: "actual ability"; ll. 51, 57–58). Educational opportunity should be withheld or withdrawn on the basis of an unbiased form of justice for all, irrespective of class, in case of students' misconduct (cf. ll. 45–49, 68–75).
The government ought to increase, not cut down on spending for education, i.e. support "the State system" and "comprehensives" (ll. 41–43) and give those children "with no useful connections and no wealthy Daddy", but who are "bright and hard-working" (ll. 56–58), a fair chance in their competition with the wealthy. This is all the more urgent since the former grammar schools, which allowed such children to rise to the top, have been all but abolished since 1976. The competition is now between comprehensives and the costly private schools. It tends to widen the gulf between the classes if the government's policies aim at a reduction of spending on students' grants (cf. ll. 50–55).

4. It is true that the Tutor's letter points out a slight inaccuracy in Hoggart's argumentation: Hoggart ignores the part played by subject tutors in the admissions procedures. However, Hoggart's suggestion that the right family connections could "make the admissions tutor have no doubt about accepting" a candidate (ll. 19–20) is by no means refuted by the Tutor's letter. In fact, the Tutor highlights his own decisive role when he says that his job is "to act as public relations officer and to coordinate and administer admissions procedures". In his own subject, he is also involved in "the actual selection".

5. The questions serve a double purpose. As self-answering rhetorical questions they are intended to persuade the reader to share the writer's view of "Oxbridge admissions procedures" (l. 7): "Can it be seriously argued that …?" (ll. 9–13) and: "So why … have Mrs Thatcher and Sir Keith Joseph …, why have they not …?" (ll. 38–49). Even the question in ll. 68–70 ("But why do the members of those universities not …?") is rhetorical in intent, suggesting the answer that they apparently do not want to change the procedures.
All three questions occupy an important compositional slot in the body of the letter. The first is placed at the opening of the argumentation (ll. 9–12), and the second forms practically a whole paragraph. Both of them dominate long sections of the letter (ll. 9–37 and 38–62), thus helping to give them thematic unity. The third question (ll. 68–70) serves more or less as a summation or conclusion. All that has been said about "Oxbridge admissions procedures" is wrapped up in one tidy little package: "this particularly smelly bit of [the universities'] domain".

6. *A fairly long newspaper article on the "Oxford tragedy" quoted some of the students outside the privileged ranks: " 'Students are sickened by the smart set. How easy they have it and how they flaunt it sticks in our gullets,' said one undergraduate. A young woman with an invalid, unemployed father said: 'I'm going to live out of college next year, and I really don't know how I'm going to*

survive' " ("The Observer", 15 June 1986, p. 5). Which of Hoggart's arguments is supported by these comments, particularly the second one?
These comments can be linked with Hoggart's criticism of the policy of thrift pursued by Thatcher's conservative government (cf. ll. 50–62). If grants and student benefits are cut, even fewer "bright youngsters" (l. 51) who have "no useful connections and no wealthy Daddy" (ll. 56–57) will manage to get into, or stay at, Oxbridge.

10 Susan Crosland: What Is a Comprehensive?

Didaktische Hinweise

Die beiden letzten Texte dieses Kapitels stellen mit der "comprehensive school" exemplarisch jenen Schultyp vor, den die große Mehrzahl der englischen Schulpflichtigen gegenwärtig als weiterführende Schule besucht (zu ihrer Position in der Geschichte und zur Gliederung des englischen Schulsystems vgl. "Background information", unten, und die "Info-Box", SB, S. 49).

Dieses Exzerpt aus Susan Croslands Biographie *Tony Crosland.* (London, Jonathan Cape 1982) führt in die Mitte der sechziger Jahre, als der neue Schultyp erstmals von der Labour Party als sozialintegrative Schule der Zukunft propagiert und mit Tony Croslands *Circular 10/65* zur Einführung empfohlen wurde. Der Text gewährt am Beispiel der Gegensätze in der Familie des verantwortlichen Erziehungsministers Einblick in die grundsätzlichen Fragen von Erziehung, Gesellschaft, Klassenprivilegien und Demokratieverständnis: Susan Crosland bevorzugt für ihre Töchter zunächst die Privatschule, und zwar vor dem Hintergrund ihrer Erfahrungen mit amerikanischen "high schools" und eigener Privatschulerziehung in den USA (vgl. "Info-Box", SB, S. 159 f., und LB, S. 132, S. 136); Tony Crosland dagegen ist als einer der führenden ideologischen Väter des neuen Schultyps öffentlich und privat dem Prinzip "comprehensiveness" verpflichtet.

Zur Orientierung über Grundlagen, Geschichte und Probleme der "comprehensive school" empfiehlt sich Alan Weeks: *Comprehensive Schools: Past, Present and Future.* London, Methuen 1986 (insbes. S. 1–28 und S. 66–159).

Background information

Susan Crosland was born in Baltimore, Maryland. She went to a private day school for girls in Baltimore and at seventeen went to Vassar (New York State), America's most renowned women's college. She took her degree after three instead of the usual four years, married an Anglo-Irish journalist and joined him when he was posted to report from London in 1956. There she met Tony Crosland. They were married seven years later. In 1989, her first novel, *Ruling Passions* (Weidenfeld & Nicholson, London), was published.

(Charles) Anthony Crosland (1918–1977) studied at Trinity College, Oxford, served actively in World War II, and lectured at Oxford from 1947 until 1950, when he became a Labour Member of Parliament. He made his name as a political philosopher, with *The Future of Socialism* (1956) being his most influential treatise. He held five high offices of State, among them that of Secretary of State for Education and Science from 1965 to 1967. Only ten months after becoming Secretary of State for Foreign and Commonwealth Affairs, he died as a result of a stroke.

Of the 3,239,800 pupils in England's maintained (i. e. publicly financed) secondary schools in 1987, 85.6 per cent went to comprehensive schools (based on *Whitaker's Almanack 1989,* 121st edition. Whitaker & Sons, London, 1988, p. 438). Although the first comprehensive schools had already been introduced in the 1950s (the West Riding comprehensive was opened by the local Conservatives in 1956), the ideology of comprehensive secondary education did not become politically powerful until 1965.

"legislation on comprehensives" (l. 39): Comprehensive reorganization was introduced by a sequence of advisory circulars before it became statutory in 1976 through an Act of Parliament. The short history of circulars and acts of Parliament dealing with postwar educational reorganization in England strongly reflects the conflict of educational aims pursued by the Labour Party and the Conservative Party:

1965   The Labour Government (1964–1970) issues Circular 10/65, informing local education authorities that Government policy is in favour of non-selective secondary schools and asks them to send in plans for comprehensive reorganization in their areas.

1970   The new Conservative Education Secretary, Margaret Thatcher, issues *Circular 10/70,* cancelling Labour's *Circulars 10/65* and *10/66.* It recommends a binary system of comprehensive schools and tripartite schools.

1974   With the return of Labour to office (1974–1979), Margaret Thatcher's *10/70* is withdrawn and replaced by Labour's *4/74,* requesting local authorities to submit plans for comprehensive reorganization by the end of the year. The 171 selective direct grant schools of the state sector are asked to join the comprehensive system or go independent (119 decide to become independent fee-paying schools).

1976   Comprehensive education is made statutory by an Act of Parliament. Local education authorities are now "required" to submit proposals for comprehensive reorganization, which can be realized within five years of the proposals.

1979   The Conservative Government under Margaret Thatcher repeals the 1976 Act, and passes the 1980 Education Act, which emphasizes parents' right to send their children to a secondary school of their choice.

1988   Under Thatcher's government, the Education Reform Act is passed. It secures parental choice of school and provides for the introduction of a national curriculum of compulsory core subjects (English, maths and science) and seven foundation subjects, to be taught from 1989 onwards. Testing is proposed for all children at 7 (or there-abouts), 11, 14 and 16.

Semantic and collocational field "Secondary education" (comprehensive school)

a child's education, (to) be brought up, (to) give sb. a good academic education, (to) go to/attend a grammar/secondary modern/comprehensive/private day school, (to) start secondary school, (to) be content in one's school ✧ academic potential, a privileged child, a grammar school ethos ✧ the purpose of comprehensives, (to) offer preparation for the real world, egalitarian ✧ postwar educational policy, (to) discuss educational policy, (to) contemplate legislation on comprehensives, (to) amalgate a grammar school and a secondary modern school, (to) create a genuinely new school, (to) go comprehensive, (to) preach comprehensives

Talking about the text – Suggested answers

1. It is a new type of school, introduced in the mid-1960s and intended to be quite distinct both from the previous types of state school (cf. l. 3, "not the grammar schools or the secondary modern schools") and from private day or boarding schools (ll. 16, 27–33). Distinguishing aspects mentioned in the text are that it is "egalitarian" (l. 54), i.e. non-selective and open to all children above elementary school age; less academically oriented (cf. l. 27); and a "better preparation for the real world" (ll. 31–32). It is also implied that the new type of school is intended to give more children the opportunity to stay on into the sixth form (cf. Anthony Crosland's emphasis on the importance of buildings with "the physical requirements for a sixth form", l. 50). In all these respects, the comprehensive is to be a "genuinely new school" (l. 52), offering broadly based opportunities for the development of the nation's talent.

2. With humorous exaggeration (cf. l. 10, "for a thousand years", an instance of hyperbolic style), she (the American) is telling her British husband that Britain is extremely late in introducing a school type that fully acknowledges the individual's right to equal educational opportunity. The American high school fully corresponds to the ideal of democratic education in being free, co-educational and compulsory for all the children of the nation. The indirectly expressed suggestion of this sentence is that Britain, with its élite-oriented schools and strong resistance to change, is a rather backward country in terms of education.

3. Surprisingly, Susan Crosland at first takes a stance directly opposed to her husband's "ideals" (l. 16), asking why her children shouldn't go to "a private day school" as she had done (l. 16). The "compromise" husband and wife reach is that the children should not be "shuffled about" (l. 15), but that Ellen-Craig, once she reaches secondary school age, "would go to a comprehensive" (l. 20). So, despite the mother's familiarity with the American high school, the "comprehensive" still seems to be a controversial, or at least somewhat unfamiliar, institution. Her willingness to accept the compromise appears to derive from a desire to support her husband's position in public. As (Labour) Secretary of State for Education and Science (and thus an advocate of the new school), he does not wish to be one of those "people who preach comprehensives and always find very moving reasons why their own children do not attend one" (ll. 17–19).

4. Sheila's decision came about as a result of Anthony Crosland's tactic of "persuasion" instead of "coercion" (l. 21). He was, as his wife says, "a good teacher" (l. 25), and his discussions of democratic socialist principles "at family meals" (l. 22) with Sheila eventually persuaded her to the rightness of the comprehensive system.
    There is no direct indication that Susan Crosland's views were affected by her older daughter's decision, but it is strongly implied. Her curt portrayal of her talk with the headmistress at St Paul's implies a certain disbelief as regards that school's philosophy. She creates the impression that she does not take kindly to this woman calling her daughter "rather wet" – and for such a superficial reason. In the final paragraph, the reader senses the proud tone she uses when talking about her husband's decision, which, she says, "was *notable* for its *realism* and *flexibility* as he came down *firmly* on the *egalitarian* side" (ll. 53–54). This sentence is full of words with positive connotations and shows that Susan Crosland, like her daughter Sheila, has been converted.

5. The education secretary anticipated two different reactions. The "move to comprehensives" (ll. 43–44) was likely to be a success with the non-privileged strata of society, but local authorities with a Conservative majority would drag their feet, and many schools – though comprehensive in name – would uphold "the grammar school ethos" (l. 52) among headmasters and staff.

6. ***At the time of publication of her book in 1982, what may have made Susan Crosland refer to the debate about comprehensives as "the major argument in post-war educational policy" (l. 54)?***

Two possible reasons spring to mind. First, in 1982, when about 90 % of British children attended comprehensives and considered it their normal choice, Susan Crosland may have felt a need to remind people that the creation of the comprehensives was really quite recent and revolutionary. Second, she no doubt wanted to emphasize her husband's role in this revolution. He had, after all, laid the foundations for an "egalitarian" (l. 54) educational policy and thus opened the road to a more democratic society, a society that distributes educational opportunity more justly than the previous, privilege-dominated society had done.

11 Barrie Keeffe: Something for Everyone

Didaktische Hinweise

Der Monolog des sechzehnjährigen "Kid" aus Keeffes Einakter *Gotcha* (1976) kann als eine fiktional gestaltete kritische Bestandsaufnahme der bildungspolitischen Vorstellungen über *comprehensive education* und ihrer Umsetzung in die Praxis verstanden werden. Kernzonen der ideologischen Begründung – non-selectiveness, social integration through 'social engineering', size for a wider range of curricula and resources, widening of occupational chances, caring for individual talent through individualized teaching, equal chances to 'acquire intelligence' – werden hier aus der Schülererfahrung beurteilt, auch mit dem Blick auf die Leistung der Lehrer, der neuen Organisationsform und der sie tragenden Politiker (vgl. "the mayor", ll. 7 ff.).

Die Erwähnung des älteren Bruders (Z. 13) macht zugleich noch einmal die Folie des dreigliedrigen Schulsystems nach 1944 im Vergleich sichtbar (Z. 14–18). In Ergänzung zu Text 10 (der die politischen Ideale des Anfangs und die einer *comprehensive education* zugrundeliegenden Prinzipien verdeutlicht), gewährt Text 11 (in einem fiktionalen Sinnentwurf) Einblicke in die Verwirklichung einer sozialen Idee und ihr erzieherisches Ergebnis. Beide Texte erlauben einen Blick hinter die Kulissen auf die handelnden und verantwortlichen Menschen: Text 10 in das Zentrum der sprachlich-gedanklichen Gestaltung durch einen amtierenden Erziehungsminister, Text 11 in das Zentrum der gelebten und durchlittenen Erfahrungen, die in der nun realisierten Institution aus Gebäude, Lehrern und Schülern gewonnen wurden.

Gotcha, 1977 zusammen mit *Gem* und *Getaway* unter dem Titel *Gimme Shelter* uraufgeführt, ist als Paperback-Ausgabe erhältlich (London, Methuen). Als Hintergrundinformation über die Leistung einer "comprehensive school" empfiehlt sich die grundlegende Untersuchung von Stephen J. Ball: *Beachside Comprehensive: A Case-Study of Secondary Schooling*. Cambridge, Cambridge University Press 1981.

Background information

Barrie Keeffe [ki:f] (1945 –   ) was born in East London. He became an actor with the National Youth Theatre and got his first writing experience as a journalist. He made his name as a dramatist, writing prolifically for radio, television, film and the theatre. In *Gotcha,* the second of the trio of plays published under the collective title of *Gimme Shelter* (1977), he concentrates on the injustices resulting from different educational opportunities in a class-oriented society. Among his other publications are *Bastard Angel* (1980), *No Excuses* (1983) and *Better Times* (1985); he also wrote the screenplay of the film *Long Good Friday.*

The Government stated in *Circular 10/65* (cf. "Background information", p. 47 of this book) that they wanted to "preserve all that is valuable in grammar school education of the children who now receive it and make it available for more children". This has tended to perpetuate the values and attitudes of selective schooling within comprehensives. Early selection by the 11-plus examination (cf. below) was replaced by "delayed selection" through ability groupings, i.e. by "streaming" into individual subjects or by "setting" into different classes. Assessments by teachers were to be used as the basis for movement between streams of different ability and aptitude, resulting in "internal selection" and the separation of "remedial pupils" ("the no-hopers ... relegate them", ll. 4–5).

Due to "the absence of formulations that encompass the *practice* of comprehensive education" (S.J. Ball, op.cit., p. 3), the majority of comprehensives have been conceived of as grammar schools for all, with selective and academic sixth forms, and an emphasis on O and A levels in order to secure university entrance. There is, however, a major difference in method. Subscribing to egalitarian principles, comprehensive schools replaced the belief in segregation (in the tripartite system) by a belief in integration. Yet schools which strongly pursued egalitarian objectives would come into conflict with the merit criteria of success (and vice versa).

Eleven-plus examination: The concept of selecting those who have "merit" to receive a more intensive schooling at a grammar school was severely attacked and further discredited in the late 1970s when it was discovered that Professor Cyril Burt, an influential figure behind the 1944 Education Act, which established the examination, had falsified much of his statistics on which the Eleven-plus was based.

Semantic and collocational field "Secondary education" (comprehensive school)

a headmaster, a teacher, a subject, an O level, an A level, a report, (to) go to a secondary (modern)/comprehensive school/to university, (to) do O levels/A levels ✧ achievement, success, a no-hoper, (to) decide who's doing what/who's going where, (to) be judged by achievement, (to) relegate sb. ✧ a glittering prize, sb.'s big chance, sth. for everyone

Talking about the text – Suggested answers

1. The Kid's hope and expectations were based on encouragement from his brother and public speeches by the headmaster and the mayor, i.e. the promise of different social backgrounds being disregarded in order to form an integrated society (ll. 8–9, "everyone all together"); the promise of equal opportunities for everybody (l. 9, "all chances"); the promise of chances for a much wider range of aptitudes and interests than is served at traditional schools (ll. 9–10, "hundreds of subjects, something for everyone, put out your hand and take what you want"; and ll. 15–16, "this comprehensive! Paradise.").

2. All of the teachers, from the headmaster down, still judged pupils on the basis of their (assumed) social backgrounds and placed them in different streams of slower and faster learners, with corresponding expectations as to the level they would achieve (l. 3, "deciding who's doing what, who's going where"). The boy also had it figured out that the headmaster was insincere when he talked about comprehensive schooling, and that he was only humouring the politicians (cf. 11). In fact, he claims to have seen that the headmaster was sorting out "no-hopers" on the first day of school (cf. l. 5). One teacher, "Farty", apparently even went so far as to say so (cf. ll. 4–5).

The Kid also saw that academic achievement was valued over non-academic achievement. The brightest pupils were good for the school's public image, as the "glittering prizes" (l. 21) clearly demonstrated. He saw that "achievement … successes" were the "only way it's judged" (l. 22), and that "this new school" (l. 18) was really "just the same" (l. 20).

3. The boy's brother experienced two unpleasant aspects of the pre-comprehensive era. First, the eleven-plus examination was used to sort pupils into three ability groups. Only the best were allowed to go to grammar schools, while the rest were relegated to secondary modern schools (the majority) or secondary technical schools. The boy's brother apparently was sent to one of the latter two (ll. 14–15, "secondary school he went to"). Secondly, once pupils were assigned to either secondary modern or secondary technical schools, they were considered "factory fodder" (l. 15), i.e. an army of future industrial workers, with no chance of advancing beyond the class for which the eleven-plus examination had cut them out. Those who made it to grammar schools, however, got the opportunity to go to university and perhaps join the ranks of the nation's élite.

4. The headmaster and his teachers had themselves been formed by the old competitive and selective system and were filled with the old ideals. So it is likely that they, on the one hand, simply found it difficult to change their ways from one day to the next. On the other hand, they may have actively resisted the change, thinking that the old methods were in fact better for their pupils, some of whom would some day be competing with pupils from independent, fee-paying schools for places at a university.

[It is also worth noting that the government "request" (cf. Ch. II, Text 10) for local authorities to convert their schools to comprehensives was rather vague. Susan Crosland writes that her husband's *Circular 10/65* was flexible (cf. l. 53), which means that, apart from outlining the lofty goals of social integration and equality of opportunity, it contained no concrete guidelines or curricula for putting these ideals into practice. The boy's headmaster, then, simply applied the familiar values and attitudes of selective schooling to fill a vacuum.]

5. The boy's manner of speaking is characterized by a lack of fluency (cf. the frequent pauses within sentences, indicated by three dots or by the stage directions in ll. 12, 19), many incomplete or chopped-up sentences (e.g. ll. 7, 8–10, 13, 20–23) and by the use of nonstandard, informal or vulgar expressions (e.g. "sod", l. 10; "me brother", l. 13; "chucked in", l. 15). All these characteristics are what one would expect of a person of low social standing. However, what the Kid says reveals a highly perceptive, critical mind. He is intelligent, but the system – or rather the headmaster's way of implementing the system – has deprived him of the education his mind deserved, because of his "low" social background.

6. [Some aspects students should consider in their discussion: *Positive* – large number of students necessary for integration of social groupings; concentration of facilities, esp. of costly technical equipment, allows teaching at up-to-date standards; large numbers of pupils and teachers makes wide range of subjects possible at different ability levels. *Negative* – individual pupils and individual initiative get lost in the crowd; personal relationships between pupils or between pupils and teachers difficult; discipline problems; anonymity.]

7. *In his book "Clever Children in Comprehensive Schools" (Penguin, London, 1980, p. 42), Auriol Stevens observes that comprehensives live "with an unresolved, and possibly unresolvable, conflict between egalitarianism and élitism. It is a conflict which divides members of staff as much as it divides outsiders." Against the background of this chapter on British education, would you say that the presence of fee-paying private schools aggravates this conflict? Why or why not?*

– –

Chapter III: Work and Welfare

Kapitel III konzentriert sich auf soziale Probleme Großbritanniens. Es beginnt mit der sprachlich und inhaltlich leichten fiktiven Darstellung eines Einzelschicksals, des jugendlichen Arbeitslosen Mick. Die Schilderung der schwierigen Beschäftigungslage im Großbritannien der Gegenwart wird durch Text 2, einen geographischen und historischen Überblick, angereichert und vertieft. Die Überleitung zum britischen Wohlfahrtsstaat heutiger Prägung geschieht durch die faksimilierte Reproduktion eines Faltblatts (Text 3), das zur Inanspruchnahme sozialer Leistungen auffordert. Dieses Bild wird ergänzt und erweitert durch die nachfolgende "Info-Box" (SB, S. 68) und schließlich relativiert durch die Wiedergabe der Erfahrungen einer bedürftigen jungen Mutter (Text 4). Mit Temperament, Ironie und pointierten Verkürzungen argumentiert in Text 5 eine Journalistin für mehr Wettbewerbs- und Leistungsbewußtsein und mehr Selbstvertrauen der berufstätigen Frau. Damit fügt sich eine weitere Façette in das Bild der heutigen britischen Gesellschaft. Der anschließende Blick in die Zukunft, ein Auszug aus einer Science Fiction-Story (Text 6), dient in erster Linie dem Lesevergnügen, soll jedoch auch den Blick schärfen für die problematische Ambivalenz einer hochtechnologisierten Welt. Kontrapunktisch hierzu führen die nächsten vier Texte (Text 7 bis 9 b) in die Geschichte zurück. Der Auszug aus Disraelis Roman schildert bewegt-pathetisch Kinderschicksale aus einer Zeit, die hinreichenden Schutz vor Ausbeutung nicht kannte, und eröffnet damit den thematischen Einstieg in die Geschichte und Entwicklung der britischen Gewerkschaftsbewegung. Anthony Sampsons fast impressionistische Beschreibung des britischen Gewerkschaftskongresses (Text 10) leitet zur Gegenwart über; Text 11 faßt mit seiner Thematisierung eines demokratischen Grundrechts Teilaspekte der Texte 7 bis 10 zusammen und lenkt den Blick auf die künftige Entwicklung. Die dazwischengeschaltete zweite "Info-Box" dieses Kapitels (SB, S. 81 ff.) vermittelt Grundkenntnisse über die Zeit der Industriellen Revolution sowie über die Entstehung und gegenwärtige Situation der britischen Gewerkschaften, die zum vertieften Verständnis der angesprochenen Thematik beitragen. Diese Thematik wird also anhand unterschiedlicher Textformen dargestellt und von konträren Standpunkten aus diskutiert. Die Kürze der Texte und die Heranführung an die Jetztzeit erlauben es, diesen Jugendliche vielleicht nicht ohne weiteres ansprechenden Themenbereich, dessen Behandlung die Lehrpläne zu Recht fordern, sprachlich und inhaltlich zu bewältigen.

1 Barry Hines : At the Careers Office

Didaktische Hinweise

Der fast szenenhaft geschlossene Auszug aus dem Roman *Looks and Smiles* des britischen Autors Barry Hines (vgl. "Background information", unten) dient als Einstieg in dieses Kapitel. Anhand dieses konkreten Beispiels für den in diesem Kapitel behandelten Themenbereich „Arbeitswelt" sollen die Schüler/innen sowohl für die Gesamtproblematik motiviert als auch auf Text 2 vorbereitet werden, der sich auf abstrakterem Niveau mit der allgemeinen Wirtschafts- und Beschäftigungslage Großbritanniens befaßt. "At the Careers Office" veranschaulicht die Schwierigkeiten und Frustrationen eines englischen Schulabgängers, der sich vergebens bei der Berufsberatung um einen Arbeitsplatz bemüht.

Der Roman ist als Penguin Book erhältlich und eignet sich sowohl inhaltlich als auch sprachlich für die Verwendung als Ganzlektüre. Bei entsprechendem Interesse für die Thematik könnte er daher ergänzend im Unterricht behandelt oder auch einzelnen Schülern/Schülerinnen zum häuslichen Lesen empfohlen werden. Danach böte sich ein kurzer Bericht über die Hauptinhalte vor der Klasse an.

Background information

Barry Hines (1939 –   ) was born in a mining village near Barnsley, Yorkshire. After leaving grammar school, he worked as an apprentice mining surveyor and played football for Barnsley. He then entered Loughborough Training College to study physical education. For several years he worked as a teacher in London and Yorkshire before becoming a full-time novelist and TV playwright. Since 1966 he has published several books, including the bestseller *Kes* (cf. annotated version edited by L. Hermes. Cornelsen Verlag Hirschgraben, Frankfurt, 1983. TAGS, SB Best.-Nr. 666000, LH 666651), which originally appeared as *A Kestrel for a Knave* (1968), and *Looks and Smiles* (1981; cf. also SB, Ch. IX, Text 8); both novels have been made into successful films.

Looks and Smiles is about the lives of three youngsters in northern Britain, set against the background of economic recession. Mick Walsh, his friend Alan and girl-friend Karen have left school and are looking for work. Much of their time is spent purposelessly, and occasionally they are on the wrong side of the law. At the end Mick is faced with the decision whether to join the army and go to Northern Ireland with Alan or to remain in Sheffield with Karen and face the prospect of long-term unemployment.

For information on the general employment situation in Britain cf. p. 55 of this book.

Unemployment among the young reached about 20 % in the late 1980s. The fact that in the UK only about 63 % of 16- to 18-year-olds go through proper education and training schemes as compared with about 85 % in the Federal Republic of Germany shows that Britain has not paid much attention to the education of its labour force. Nevertheless, successive governments have become increasingly aware of their responsibility for career guidance.

The Department of Employment, which is responsible for employment policy and for the payment of benefits, provides, among other things, a whole range of employment and training measures, particularly for the long-term unemployed and the young.

Local education authorities are required to set up careers advisory offices that provide career guidance and an employment service to all who are attending or leaving educational institutions, below university level.

The Youth Training Scheme (YTS), introduced in 1983, has, since 1986, been offering two years of training for 16-year-old and one year for 17-year-old school-leavers, with 20 and 7 weeks off-the-job training respectively. Participants get vocational qualifications or credit towards them, and a certificate.

Unemployment benefit is payable for up to 12 months in any spell of unemployment. Those who claim it must be available for employment. If the beneficiary is single and under pension age, his or her weekly rate (in April 1989) is £ 32.75 (based on *Britain 1989. An Official Handbook.* Her Majesty's Stationery Office, London, 1989, pp. 157–166).

"exams and ... qualifications" (ll. 47–48): for information cf. SB, Ch. II, "Info-Box", p. 49.

Semantic and collocational field "Looking for work"

(to) take an exam, (to) get qualifications, (to) leave school ✧ a career office, an interview room, a record card, (to) catalogue sth., (to) fill in/check a card ✧ an unemployed youth, a Social Security Office, (to) sign on ✧ (to) look for a job, (to) look in the paper, (to) write in for a job , (to) advertise ✧ a requirement, (to) be suitable ✧ a vacancy, an interviewer, a reply, (to) take sb. on, (to) find a job ✧ a working life, a trade, a craft apprenticeship, a dead-end job ✧ a firm, a warehouse

Talking about the text – Suggested answers

1. One may take it that the unemployment rate among young people is very high. School-leavers, even if they have qualifications (cf. l. 50), find themselves faced with great difficulties in getting jobs through newspaper ads (cf. ll. 22–25). Even careers offices [set up for all school-leavers by local authorities] are unable to channel young people into prospective jobs (cf. ll. 33–35). All they can do is register them, keep in touch and help them get their unemployment benefits (cf. ll. 55–64).
2. On the one hand, he waits patiently at the beginning, shows a sense of humour (cf. ll. 12–16) and a certain amount of self-confidence (cf. l. 49) and leaves with a smile. On the other hand, he is unconcentrated at times (cf. ll. 29–30), gets angry and is determined not to accept just any job because he thinks he is qualified for a trade rather than unskilled labour (cf. ll. 49–51). He obviously has little experience of job-hunting and its frustrations.
3. She tries not to discourage Mick too much and to make him realize that she is genuinely interested in his particular case. So she keeps up a personal, friendly tone, tries not to betray her own frustration, but rather to cover it up by pretences (cf. ll. 41–47, 60–69). She offers him one job, though hardly suitable, but also appeals to his own initiative (cf. ll. 56–57) and helps him with the appointment card (cf. ll. 57–64).
4. It is drab and frustrating. It is created by a number of references to the physical setting – "shrivelled house-plant" (l. 6), "empty office block" (ll. 6–7), the "stains" on the desk (l. 31) – and intensified by the posters referring to unemployment, the noises of similar interviews in adjoining rooms and Mrs Reid's behaviour after Mick has left the room (cf. ll. 68–70).
5. ***What effect may the novelist have intended in choosing a form reminiscent of a dramatic scene?***
   Hines may have chosen this scenic mode of presentation in order to show this part of the plot in concrete, dramatic detail. In this way the reader is challenged to participate more directly and to rely on his or her own observations and interpretations rather than on the novelist's telling.
6. ***What else might Mick possibly do to find a job, independent of the careers office?***
   – –
7. ***What opportunities are available to you as a pupil to get information on a possible career, its qualifications and prospects, and the job market in general? Have you ever tried any of them? If so, what were your experiences?***
   – –

2 Bill Hewitt et al.: The Haves and the Have-Nots

Didaktische Hinweise

Auf die personalisierte, fiktionale Präsentation eines Teilaspekts des Themas „Arbeitswelt" in Text 1 folgt nun eine umfassendere allgemeine Darstellung der wirtschaftlichen Situation in Großbritannien. Da diese *interpretive news story* verschiedene Teilthemen des Kapitels – z.B. Industrielle Revolution, Wohlfahrtsstaat, Arbeitswelt und Arbeitsmarkt, Veränderungen der Industrie- und Wirtschaftsstruktur – in ihren historischen und gegenwärtigen Zusammenhängen aufzeigt, kommt ihr im Rahmen dieser Textsequenz eine Schlüsselrolle zu. Nach der Behandlung dieses Textes im Unterricht kann man sich daher – je nach didaktischer Schwerpunktsetzung und Interesse des Kurses – von der im SB gewählten Reihenfolge der Texte lösen und andere Textverknüpfungen herstellen. So liegt z.B. insbesondere der unmittelbare Bezug zu Disraeli (Text 7) und den anderen historischen Texten (Text 8, 9a, 9b) nahe. Auch zum Teilthema „Klassengesellschaft" (Kap. II, Text 1 bis 3) bestehen direkte Verbindungslinien. Und schließlich bietet es sich an, diesen Text mit R.W. Apples Bestandsaufnahme "A Nation in Decline?" (Kap. I, Text 11) zu kombinieren, in der die positiven Aspekte stärker herausgearbeitet wurden.

Background information

As a pioneer in the Industrial Revolution Britain has traditionally been strong in the manufacturing industries. However, in the 1970s and 80s industrial production fell, particularly in the coal, steel, shipbuilding and textile industries. The reasons usually given for this decline include growing competition in the world market, decreasing exports to the Commonwealth countries, a lack of structural improvements and investment in industry, failure to modernize production and marketing methods, a badly educated labour force (cf. p. 53 of this book), relatively high pay rises, overstaffing and a high inflation rate. The regions hardest hit have been the traditional industrial areas in Scotland, the north of England, the Midlands, Wales and Northern Ireland.

Growth has been taking place in the service sector, especially in tourism, the retail trades and financial and business services. In recent years there has been a considerable expansion in high-tech industries such as biotechnology, computers and telecommunications. It is mainly the south that has benefited from these developments, thus widening the gap between the two parts of the country – the so-called "North-South Divide".

Semantic and collocational field "Britain's economic situation"

living costs ✧ heavy industry, a high-tech venture, industrial cooperation ✧ a nationalization campaign/programme, competitive market forces, (to) rebuild an industry ✧ the welfare state, the national health system, free medical care ✧ the world of finance, the Big Bang, deregulation ✧ new prosperity, a boom, a burst of entrepreneurial activity, prospects for a better life, (to) blossom, (to) thrum with activity ✧ a new breed, energetic, forward-looking ✧ industrial decline, a bleak future, hard times, a deepening and lasting crisis, Britain's crippled industrial heartland ✧ the haves and have-nots, a class system, the privileged, an impoverished urban underclass, (to) be out of work, (to) live on government assistance, unemployed

Talking about the text – Suggested answers

1. In Dickens's and Disraeli's times the Industrial Revolution brought prosperity to the middle classes all over Britain, but poverty to the lower classes, esp. those in urban areas. The people were thus divided into two vastly different social blocks. These days there is again a wide gap between rich and poor, aggravated by mass unemployment, especially amongst the young. What is different now is that the gap also moves along geographical lines, dividing the stagnant north from the newly prosperous south.

2. The costs of the post-war welfare state, particularly in the fields of health and public housing and the nationalization of heavy industries, which both resulted in heavy taxation; the protection of obsolescent manufacturing and production methods from competitive free market forces; traditional class antagonism and unwillingness of labour to cooperate with management; the trend of upper-middle class talents to shun industry for the sake of law, commerce and banking. The north especially suffered from the decline of its characteristic industries whereas the south prospered from the new technologies and its proximity to London.

3. They intended not only to give facts, events and verifiable statistical data but also background information, even historical references, interpretations of different aspects and their interrelations as they see them. Thus they produced an interpretive news story with more depth and reader appeal than a straight report.

4. By using a large number of emotive words and expressions, e.g. "demarcation line" (l. 15), "venture", "burst" (l. 18), "revolution" (l. 21), "Big Bang" (ll. 22–23); by working with metaphors, esp. from the field of human life and nature, e.g. "blossoming" (l. 21), "windfall" (l. 25), "breed" (l. 26), "crippled" (l. 27), "idle" (l. 31), "born" (l. 38), "seeds", "agony" (l. 69), "plant" (l. 70); by the paradox "two Britains" (ll. 65–66), imitating Disraeli's "Two nations" (l. 1); by the reference to Horatio Alger (l. 129) and the allusion to Dickens's "Hard Times" (l. 37); by employing contrasts throughout (e.g. present – past, north – south, middle class – underclass, rich – poor) and thus simplifying to a certain extent.

5. It introduces the central topic; perhaps startles the reader, in particular through the repeated, contrastive generalizations; functions as a motto; prepares for the historical and literary perspective taken in the text.

6. The references and allusions to Disraeli and Dickens (ll. 1–13, 37–43, 65–66) as parts of a common Anglo-American literary heritage, the knowledge of the Industrial Revolution (ll. 38–39), Margaret Thatcher (ll. 122–123) as well as the role of the City of London and the Big Bang (ll. 22–27), the reference to the Great Divide (l. 14) and to Horatio Alger (l. 129).

7. *Compare "At the Careers Office" (Ch. III, Text 1) and "The Haves and the Have-Nots" with regard to their intentions and effects.*
   "At the Careers Office", as a fictional text, personalizes, emotionalizes, creates its own atmosphere, dramatizes, enables the reader to identify with the protagonist. "The Haves and the Have-Nots" gives facts and information, generalizes, rationalizes, analyses, explains and systematizes.

● 8. *Prepare notes or a short paper on British industries, e.g. computer technology, coal mining, shipbuilding or steel production, and report to the class.*
   [The student may use a geography book, an encyclopedia, "Britain. An Official Handbook" (Her Majesty's Stationery Office, London), „Großbritannien" (Informationen zur politischen Bildung, H. 214, 1987).]

3 Family Income Supplement

Didaktische Hinweise

Dieser Teil eines vom Department of Health and Social Security verteilten Faltblatts zeigt, wie der britische Wohlfahrtsstaat sich auf konkrete und direkte Weise bemüht, die Bedürftigen durch verschiedene Maßnahmen finanzieller und nicht-finanzieller Art anzusprechen und zu unterstützen.

Da der Text je nach didaktischer Intention entweder zur Illustration herangezogen oder aber im Detail auf Inhalt, sprachliche Form und Layout hin untersucht werden kann, wurde der Aufgabenapparat im LB untergebracht. Notwendige Grundkenntnisse über den Wohlfahrtsstaat vermittelt die "Info-Box" (SB, S. 68). Eine Problematisierung einiger Teilaspekte dieser für das moderne Großbritannien so charakteristischen Institution bietet Text 4.

Background information

For information on different theories concerning the welfare state and for further details of the main sectors of public welfare activities and expenditures in Britain cf. p. 58 of this book.

Semantic and collocational field "Income Supplement"

a family on low earnings, total weekly income, earnings before tax, income limits ✧ full time work, (to) work full time ✧ child/one parent benefit, maintenance payments, Family Income Supplement ✧ national insurance ✧ a free prescription, free dental treatment, (to) get help with rent and rates, tax-free ✧ a social security office, (to) deal with a claim, (to) claim sth., (to) fill in a claim form

Talking about the text – Suggested answers

1. *What helps the reader to grasp the information at a glance and to understand its essentials?*
   The layout in boxes, each with its own heading, and in narrow columns; the use of different sizes and types of letters; the drawing; the numbering of questions and answers; the repetition of "free"; syntactical condensations, relatively simple vocabulary and sentence structure throughout; the model calculations.

2. *How is the reader encouraged to make use of the benefits?*
   By offering money and help free of charge, by addressing him or her directly with the word "you", by the use of imperatives, by promising privacy and confidentiality, by facilitating the procedures of application.

3. *Many people are hesitant about claiming benefits from the Welfare State. What do you think their reasons might be?*
   [In their discussion, students should mention reasons such as pride, shame, resignation and a general fear of contacts with authorities and bureaucracy.]

● 4. *Find out how people on a lower income in the Federal Republic of Germany are supported by the state. Report your findings to the class.*
   – –

🎧 4 Paul Harrison: Adding Insult to Injury

Didaktische Hinweise

Dieser Text ist ein Auszug aus einer Auswertung von Hunderten von Interviews sowie von dokumentarischem Material über das Leben der sozial Schwachen im Londoner Stadtteil Hackney am Rande des Wohlfahrtsstaats in Zeiten der Rezession, Ausgabendrosselung und des Verfalls von Bausubstanz und Lebenswert. Die Studie wurde in Buchform unter dem Titel *Inside the Inner City. Life under the Cutting Edge*. (Penguin, Harmondsworth 1983, rev. ed. 1985) veröffentlicht.

Während Text 3 am Beispiel eines Faltblatts einige konkrete Hilfsmaßnahmen des Staates veranschaulicht, vermittelt Text 4 in Form eines persönlichen Berichts einen Einblick in einige negative Begleiterscheinungen des staatlich gesteuerten Wohlfahrtssystems, etwa Bürokratisierung, Starrheit der Vergabemethoden, Unwirtschaftlichkeit, mangelnde Flexibilität und Fehlverhalten der Beamten und Mitarbeiter, Verärgerung, Frustration und Entwürdigung der Bedürftigen. Auch zu diesem Text bietet die "Info-Box" (SB, S. 68) das notwendige Basiswissen. – Ist eine vertiefende Behandlung des Themas vorgesehen, lassen sich Vergleiche mit entsprechenden Problembereichen in den USA anschließen, etwa anhand von Kap. VII, Text 5, 6a) –6c).

Background information

Paul Harrison is a freelance journalist and writer living in London. He went to school in Manchester and then studied at Cambridge and the London School of Economics. Among his publications are *Inside the Third World* (Penguin, London, 1979) and *The Third World Tomorrow* (Penguin, London, 1983).

The Welfare State: There are various opinions in Britain about the role of the welfare state in society. Libertarian Conservative opinion holds that most needs should be met by the family, voluntary organizations, self-help or commercial insurance in the first place, and that the government should only fill the gaps and provide a secondary safety net. Only those who cannot provide for themselves should be assisted, and state provision should be related to the country's economic wealth.

A Labour-Socialist view sees social services as an integral part of social politics, and that it is the duty of the state to provide for its citizens. If hardship is created by the modern industrial society, then society must be reformed and its resources redistributed from the better-off to the worse-off. Existing inequalities should be levelled out through the operation of the social services.

Since 1945 none of the political parties has undertaken more than marginal reforms of the National Health Service (NHS) and of social security.

"Planned spending on social welfare in 1988–89 is: health £ 21,000 million and personal social services £ 3,700 million (together representing 13 per cent of general government expenditure); and social security nearly £ 46,000 million (30 per cent)" (*Britain 1989. An Official Handbook.* Her Majesty's Stationery Office, London, 1989, p. 137).

Hospitals often complain to the NHS these days that their staff are overworked and cannot keep up services as they would want to. Others, however, claim that the public has constantly rising expectations and that the health of the general public, particularly of the elderly, has significantly improved.

Semantic and collocational field "Social Security support"

a social security office/official, a visiting official ✧ a clothing/food voucher, money for clothes, a grant ✧ a bill, money for the rent, (to) save for sth., (to) scrimp, (to) heat sth. (e.g. a flat) ✧ (to) stop money towards sth., (to) ask sb. for money, the money runs out ✧ (to) get money out of sb., (to) live on an estate ✧ (to) be in work, (to) be out of work ✧ (to) care about sb./sth. ✧ (to) feel degraded/stupid, (to) be in rage, poor, meagre

Talking about the text – Suggested answers

1. Mainly about the behaviour and methods of the social-security officials. They humiliate her, do not trust her, take too long to react, and they intimidate those who complain. Their methods include impractical, even paradoxical advice (cf. ll. 35–36), the reduction of claims to a petty minimum, the issue of vouchers instead of cash, although this may mean higher expenses for the welfare service.
2. Obviously, the general recession in Britain and problems of high unemployment have been major factors contributing to her situation. In her case, early marriage to a man without steady employment and no particular job skills started her on a path to poverty. When she got divorced, she was left alone with three children to take care of, and so she had virtually no chance of getting a job herself.
3. Most of the text consists of Jean Clements's own report in direct speech. Thus it gains a documentary quality and becomes more vivid. The reader is challenged to form his or her own opinion. Responsibility for the truth of the statements is left with the woman. Her report is only interrupted three times to allow the journalist to verify (cf. ll. 27–28) or annotate (cf. ll. 36–37, 38) some of her statements. At the beginning (cf. ll. 1–9) and end (cf. ll. 41–46) of the excerpt, Paul Harrison also summarizes Jean Clements's background and clarifies the overall situation. This prepares and rounds off the reader's understanding of the woman's story, condenses parts of the original recording and gives the writer a chance to voice his own impressions.
4. [Some possibilities: child-care facilities, job skills training, help in learning to budget.]
5. – –
6. *What might be the reasoning behind the voucher policy Jean Clements complains about? What disadvantages can you see in such a policy?*
    [Probably designed to prevent abuse and to control expenditure; only more expensive shops willing to accept vouchers because of the time needed to deal with the necessary bureaucracy; recipient might never learn to budget.]
7. *Considering her experience, how would Jean Clements most likely react to the leaflet distributed by the Department of Health and Social Security (cf. Ch. III, Text 3)? Discuss.*
    – –

5 Katharine Whitehorn: The Paula Principle

Didaktische Hinweise

In diesem 1986 im *Observer* erschienenen Artikel befaßt sich die erfolgreiche Kolumnistin Katharine Whitehorn auf etwas ungewöhnliche Weise mit dem Thema „Frau im Arbeitsleben". Ausgehend vom *"Peter Principle"* (vgl. "Background information", unten), das nach Aussage des Textes für berufstätige Frauen – nicht nur infolge ihrer Diskriminierung am Arbeitsplatz, sondern auch ihrer eigenen Einstellung zu beruflicher Tätigkeit – keine Gültigkeit habe, entwickelt sie in einer Art *light argumentative essay* das *"Paula Principle"*. Ihm zufolge tragen auf Grund von Tradition und Erziehung und den daraus resultierenden Verhaltensweisen die Frauen selbst dazu bei, daß sie in höheren Positionen zahlenmäßig unterrepräsentiert sind. Der persönliche Ton, die Namen, Bezüge und Anspielungen, vor allem das ironische, ja sarkastische Spiel mit den Begriffen *"Peter Principle"*, *competence* und *incompetence* sind konstituierende Merkmale dieses Textes, werden aber von den Schülern/Schülerinnen u.U. nicht gleich erkannt (vgl. Aufg. 5).

Bei entsprechendem Interesse könnte das Thema durch die Erörterung der wirt–schaftlichen, sozialen, politischen und rechtlichen Situation der Frau in Vergan–genheit und Gegenwart vertieft werden (vgl. "Background information", unten), auch durch die Einbeziehung von Kap. VII, Texte 3 und 4 (die Frau in der amerikanischen Gesellschaft), Kap. II, Text 8 ("Oxbridge" und ihre Einstellung zur Frau), Kap. I, Text 9 (die Frau als Angehörige einer ethnischen Minorität in Großbritannien).

Background information

Katharine Whitehorn: cf. p. 13 of this book.

Although in the 19th century women formed an important part of the factory workforce, they were barred from various jobs which were either of a dangerous nature or were better-paid. In the competition for jobs it was the women who normally lost out; however, many women needed to work to supplement their family's income. They even organized themselves into trade unions – the most important being the Women's Trade Union League, founded in 1874, and the National Federation of Women Workers, founded in 1906. Since the turn of the century more and more unions have accepted women as members.

Though women's careers are still handicapped by tradition and prejudice, there have been considerable changes in our century, which have been aided by new legislation. The Equal Pay Act of 1970, amended in 1984, entitles women in Britain to equal pay with men for the same or similar work, and under the Sex Discrimination Act of 1975, it is illegal to discrimate between men and women in employment, education or job training. The Equal Opportunities Commission was set up in 1975 in order to enforce these two Acts.

Today about 43 % of Britain's total workforce are women; about 26 % of the labour force are married women as compared with only 4 % in 1921. However, 47 % of working women have only part-time jobs, compared with 5 % of men. Women's earnings are still lower than men's, and women are more often employed in the lower-paid sectors of the economy. The average weekly earnings for full-time adult employees was £ 224 for men and £ 148.10 for women in April 1987.

Most women work in three main areas: clerical, educational and social work. Men, on the other hand, are involved in all sectors of employment, with manual manufacturing work ranking first. 58 % of women in manual jobs do service work such as cleaning and catering, many of them working part-time. 55 % of women in non-manual jobs are typists or do general clerical work. When employed in the same area of work, men are more often in a better grade; for example, although there are more women in the teaching profession than men, there are significantly more male than female secondary school headteachers.

The image women have of themselves is responsible for steering many of them away from technical work. Statistics of school examination entries reveal that among girls there is still a bias away from science and towards art subjects – for example, well under a quarter of all girls entering 16+ examinations in 1984 took science subjects as compared with between a third and a half of all boys (based on: *Working Women*. Trades Union Congress, London 1983, pp. 10–15; *The Education and Training of Girls and Women. A TUC Report*. Trades Union Congress, London, Feb. 1987, pp. 2, 4; *Britain 1989. An Official Handbook*. Her Majesty's Stationery Office, London, 1989, pp. 351).

"The Peter Principle" (l. 1): This is one of a number of so-called principles or laws, especially popular in English-speaking countries, formulated to provide a brief, ironical criticism of various defects in human nature or in society. The Peter Principle claims that "in a hierarchy every employee tends to rise to his level of incompetence". It was made up by Professor Laurence J. Peter, a Canadian. His book *The Peter Principle*, written together with Raymond Hull (William Morrow and Co., New York, 1969) became a bestseller and is available in English and German paperback editions. In 1985 Professor Peter published *Why Things Go Wrong or the Peter Principle Revisited* (William Morrow and Co., New York).

Semantic and collocational field "Career"

(to) do a job well, (to) do something one likes, to run sth. (e.g. an organization), (to) administer sth. ✧ pay [U], a salary ✧ responsibility, a challenge, a job prospect, outside the range of one's experience ✧ an application, (to) apply, (to) get the job ✧ a promotion, (to) get/be promoted, (to) be driven by ambition, (to) hold back from promotion ✧ a head office, the upper echelons, management ✧ (in)competence

Talking about the text – Suggested answers

1. She thought that the Peter Principle did not apply to women, that women rated job satisfaction higher than pay and position, considered intact social relations essential, were less ambitious, and preferred sticking to the jobs they were doing and were capable of filling.
2. According to the theory, women tend to shy away from greater responsibility and untried work, they often do not apply for promotions in order to avoid competition. This all goes back to the way women have been brought up.
3. The advantages are that a principle sounds attractive, is easy to grasp, remember and pass on. The disadvantages lie in the danger of over-generalization, over-simplification, possibly even distortion of rather complex matters.
4. The alliterations and identical rhythm; the familiarity of first names; the generalizations through the use of the formulation "any man" and the plural "women"; the paradoxical parallelism in "any man is promoted to the level of his incompetence" (ll. 2–3) and "women stay below the level of their competence" (ll. 40–41), which produces an ironic, even sarcastic effect.
5. ***What does the writer do to arouse the readers' interest in this somewhat complex matter and to help them understand her intention?***
   She uses the first-person point of view; short forms and informal expressions, e.g. "dither" (ll. 49–50), "numbskull" (l. 59), "bloke" (l. 69); irony , e.g. "Assistant Under Director in charge of Quality Control" (ll. 15–16); intensifying and attitudinal adverbs that reflect the writer's personality, e.g. "widely" (l. 1), "only" (ll. 5, 24, 50), "much" (ll. 9, 17) –

"rather" (l. 13), "doubtless" (l. 46), "simply" (l. 60); breaks the text up into short paragraphs; paraphrases and illustrates the "Principles" and uses a playful tone.

6. **In a part of the original article not reproduced here, Whitehorn claims, "... if we do want Paula promoted, ... we have to start at the bottom. Giving girls soft options is the worst thing we can do to them." Discuss.**
   – –

7. **Examine the position of the girls or women in different fields at your school. What conclusions can you draw from your study?**
   – –

6 John Wyndham: No Ordinary Robot

Didaktische Hinweise

Dieser Auszug aus John Wyndhams Science Fiction-Story "Compassion Circuit" präsentiert eine durch den technologischen Fortschritt veränderte künftige Welt. Dienstleistungen im Haushalt werden hier von einem Roboter übernommen, der Wunsch nach einem Heinzelmännchen ist erfüllbar geworden, die alte Idee der Schaffung eines künstlichen Menschen ist verwirklicht.

Die Erörterung dieses Textes im Rahmen dieses Kapitels kann an die Vorstellung zukünftiger Veränderungen im Arbeitsleben durch die technologische Entwicklung anknüpfen (vgl. "Background information", unten). Darüber hinaus aber wird die hier mit hintergründigem Humor gezeigte ambivalente Haltung des Menschen zur Maschine Jugendliche sicher interessieren. Schließlich lassen sich an diesem Text auch einige der für die Gattung Science Fiction typischen Elemente aufzeigen. Um den Schülern/Schülerinnen die Möglichkeit zu geben, sich von diesem sprachlich und gedanklich leicht verständlichen Text unmittelbar ansprechen zu lassen, wurde der Aufgabenapparat im LB untergebracht. – Den vollständigen Text der Erzählung bieten u.a. John Wyndham: *The Seeds of Time.* Harmondsworth, Penguin 1972; *Science Fiction Stories.* Ed. and annot. by F. and J. Poziemski. Frankfurt, Diesterweg 1985; *Science Fiction Stories.* Chosen by J. L Forster. London, Ward Lock Educational, No. 2.

Literaturhinweise: *Die Utopie in der angloamerikanischen Literatur. Inter-pretationen.* Hrsg. von H. Heuermann, B.-P. Lange. Düsseldorf, Cornelsen Verlag Schwann-Girardet 1984, Best.-Nr. 74531; *Der Science-Fiction-Roman in der anglo-amerikanischen Literatur. Interpretationen.* Hrsg. von H. Heuermann. Düsseldorf, Cornelsen Verlag Schwann-Girardet 1986, Best.-Nr. 74540; E. Barmeyer: *Science Fiction. Theorie und Geschichte.* München, Wilhelm Fink 1972; P. Bruck: „Die Vergangenheit der Zukunft: Amerikanische science fiction stories von William Tenn bis Damon Knight." In: *Die Short Story im Englischunterricht der Sekundarstufe II. Theorie und Praxis.* Hrsg. von P. Freese, H. Groene und L. Hermes. Paderborn, Schöningh 1979, S. 179 ff.

Background information

John Wyndham ['wɪndəm](*Parkes Lucas Beynon Harris*) (1903–1969) was born near Birmingham and tried several careers before he started writing in 1925. He published various detective and science fiction stories under the pen-name John Wyndham until the outbreak of World War II. After serving in the war, he continued to write science fiction stories, which are usually set in the present time and involve a foreign force disrupting comfortable English society and threatening human life; in many of the stories children play an important role. *The Seeds of Time* (1956) is a collection of short stories, in which "Compassion Circuit" first appeared. Amongst his novels are *The Day of the Triffids* (1951), *The Kraken Wakes* (1953), *The Chrysalids* (1955), *The Midwich Cuckoos* (1957, filmed as *The Village of the Damned*), *The Trouble with Lichen* (1960) and *Chocky* (1968).

Compassion Circuit, the short story from which this excerpt is taken, concerns an invalid woman, Janet, who reluctantly buys a domestic robot to do the housework for her. The robot pities human beings for their weakness and their liability to illness. One day the robot takes Janet to hospital. When she comes home, her husband discovers she has a robot's body.

"robot" (l. 11): The word was coined by the Czech dramatist Karel Capek (1890–1938) to mean a worker automaton in human form. In his play *R.U.R.*, i.e. Rossum's Universal Robots (1920), mechanical men and women, the products of scientists, develop emotions and rise against their masters.

Semantic and collocational field "An electric mechanism"

a contraption, a mechanism, a robot, a battery-driven model ✧ an electronic circuit, a control switch, the mains, a knob, a panel ✧ (to) be fitted with a battery, (to) be designed to do sth., (to) consume electricity

Talking about the text – Suggested answers

1. *The robot has been bought to serve as a parlourmaid. In what respects is it different from a human servant?*
   It is fitted with a battery, set to work by turning a knob, is untiring in its work, is repaired by a mechanic when it breaks down.

2. *Where in the text do the robot's linguistic responses seem to be pre-programmed and where not?*
   It seems programmed where it introduces itself using set formulas (cf. l. 35); it seems spontaneous and human where it voices its opinion and passes judgment (cf. ll. 52–53). [One may ask, however, why a robot with these linguistic abilities could not be expected to use euphemism in certain communicative situations as claimed in l. 51.]

3. *How does George seem to treat the robot?*
   Without emotions, as one would treat any technical apparatus.

4. *How does Janet's attitude to her new maid differ from her husband's? What development does it undergo within the first four months?*
   She is, at first, baffled, excited and even a little disturbed by that doll-like "contraption" (l. 1), but she soon looks upon it as a person with female qualities (cf. her embarrassment when her husband unbuttons the robot's dress, ll. 16–17), gives it a name and addresses her as a social equal, regards her as a friend and finally as a trustworthy companion whom she looks up to.

5. *What in the author's choice of words when referring to the robot reflects its puzzling, ambiguous nature?*
   The frequent change between "it/its" and "she/her" in the first half of the text, ending up with the feminine pronouns only; the almost synonymous use of nouns like "doll" (l. 1), "contraption" (ll. 1–3), "person" (l. 7), "model" (l. 8), "figure" (l. 16), "robot", (ll. 11, 28, 33),

"mechanism" (l. 28), "friend" (l. 40), "company" (l. 48); the implication of sexuality in ll. 16–28. [Paradoxically, both Janet and Hester apply the term "poor, weak *thing*" to human beings (ll. 49–50, 52).]

6. *How does Wyndham establish a relationship between the present and the future in this science fiction story?*
He presents the future on the basis and as a comprehensible development of present-day scientific, technical and social realities. His domestic servant of the future is a robot which can be set to work by activating a simple circuit; it fulfils the same duties as a parlourmaid of our time, expresses feelings, makes judgments and converses appropriately in 20th-century English.

7. *Do you agree that people would "find it harsh or grotesque" (ll. 3–4) if robots did not look like human beings? Discuss.*
– –

8. *Why is it difficult to design and manufacture a robot to do the large variety of duties in a household? Discuss.*
– –

7 Benjamin Disraeli: Children's Work

Didaktische Hinweise

Dieses Exzerpt aus Disraelis vielleicht bekanntestem politischem Roman (vgl. "Background information", unten) ist der erste der historischen Texte dieses Kapitels. In einer Sequenz von vier Einzeltexten (Texte 7 bis 9b) werden den Schülern/Schülerinnen nicht nur drei wichtige britische Repräsentanten des späten 18. und des 19. Jahrhunderts vorgestellt, sondern auch zentrale ökonomische und soziale Aspekte dieser von der Industriellen Revolution geprägten Epoche veranschaulicht. Der fiktionale Text 7, charakteristisch für den Literaten und Politiker Disraeli, vermittelt einen Eindruck von den schwierigen, geradezu unmenschlichen Arbeitsbedingungen im britischen Bergbau in jener Zeit, insbesondere vom Elend der Kinder und Jugendlichen, einen Eindruck, der geschichtlicher Nachprüfung standhält. Für eine vertiefende Behandlung des Themas können Kap. 6 "Charlotte Bronte: Shirley" und Kap. 7 "Charles Dickens: Hard Times" aus U. Schulz: *British Literature as a Mirror of British Life* (Berlin, Cornelsen Verlag 1986; Best.-Nr. 7812, LH 7820) herangezogen werden. – Basisinformationen über das Zeitalter der Industriellen Revolution enthält die "Info-Box" (SB, S. 81 f.).

Background information

Benjamin Disraeli [dɪsˈreɪlɪ], *first Earl of Beaconsfield* (1804–1881) was a novelist and Conservative statesman. Well-read, ambitious and a brilliant speaker, he entered Parliament as a Tory member in 1837 and eventually became Prime Minister in 1868, and then again from 1874 to 1880. This government passed many reform bills, which, among other measures, encouraged slum clearance, codified public health laws, reduced working hours and clarified the position of trade unions, but the most noticeable feature of his premiership was his policy of imperialism. He published many political writings and several novels, the best known being *Coningsby, or The New Generation* (1844) and *Sybil, or The Two Nations* (1845), which reflect the political and social attitudes of the day.

Sybil, or The Two Nations is set in the fictional industrial town of Mowbray and the splendid Abbey of Marney, both in the north of England. It reflects the living conditions of the early Victorian Age (1837–1844), which was characterized by low wages, mass poverty and overcrowding in miserable tenements for the workers and large profits for the employers. Agitation against these conditions and the gap between "The Two Nations", i.e. the rich and the poor (cf. Ch. III, Text 2), led to the emergence of Chartism (1837–1848), a working-class movement which drew up and presented a charter to Parliament, demanding universal adult suffrage, and electoral reform. Parliament rejected the demands of the Chartists on two occasions, the first of which in 1839 sparked off the Chartist riots in various parts of the country. Against this background and among a bewildering number of topics in *Sybil*, there is a central romantic plot between the heroine of the title, who is the poor daughter of a militant Chartist leader, and Charles Egremont, brother of a mean industrialist. The novel ends with a vision of hope for the future.

Child labour: Although children had always been employed in agriculture and home manufacturing, it was the factory system that introduced them to long working days and monotonous, often dangerous work. Parishes, the workhouse management and impoverished parents often felt that children had to contribute to their livelihood. Working life for many began at the age of six or seven, with hours from 5 a.m. to 8 p.m. being quite common.

Factory legislation became a necessity, and many acts were passed in the 19th century (cf. "Info-Box", SB, p. 82) dealing with conditions and hours of work, sanitary provisions and safety in factories and workshops.

The Health and Morals of Apprentices Act of 1802 and the 1819 Cotton Mills Act both banned work for children under the age of 9 altogether and reduced working hours for those under 16 to 72 per week, but they were not enforced. In 1842 it was made illegal to employ children under the age of 10 and women in work underground, but again it took years to be put into practice. An act of 1844 enforced the use of safety guards around the moving parts of machinery.

In 1847 the Ten-Hours Act reduced the working hours of women and children aged between 13 and 18 in textile factories to 10 hours on weekdays and 8 on Saturdays.

Legislation was repeatedly extended, but enforcement remained a problem. Child labour for those under the age of 10 was abolished after the introduction of obligatory schooling by the Education Act of 1870. Under Disraeli's second government working hours were limited to 56 per week for everyone.

"Society for the Abolition of Negro Slavery" (l. 18): ironic attack against the Whigs, who, under the inspiration of William Wilberforce (1759–1833), enacted the abolition of slavery throughout the British Empire in 1833.

Semantic and collocational field "Work in a mine"

a mine, a pit, a subterranean road ✧ a miner, a collier ✧ a forge, an engine, a coal-waggon, a tub of coal ✧ labour, toil, (to) haul sth., (to) be in sb.'s employ ✧ naked to the waist ✧ the safety of the mine

Talking about the text – Suggested answers

1. Poor clothing; low, steep, dark and wet galleries; long working hours; hard, dirty work; "the savage rudeness of their lives" (l. 14); and in addition, with the youngest, solitude and burdensome responsibility.
2. He regards them as hypocrites, who favour the abolition of negro slavery but close their eyes to the horrible conditions of work in England, the more so since these abolitionists support the system for their own profits.
3. He can expect to reach a large audience because a novel is more entertaining than an essay or a report; he is able to appeal to the imagination and emotions of his readers even more since he can personalize his message. With less responsibility for exact detail and objectivity, he is at liberty to deal with his topic more freely and to better effect.
4. It begins with a glimpse of the evening hour in exotic countries, peaceful and given to religious devotion. This is contrasted with a detailed description of the end of a workday in England, with its misery, squalor and exhaustion. It first describes the men, continues with the youngsters and widens into a picture of their working conditions, to end up with a commiserate look at the small, tender children and their fate.
5. *Explain how the narrator gives more than just an objective description.*
    The description is highly impressionistic and emotive through the use of metaphors, e.g. "the bowels of the earth" (l. 22); personifications, e.g. "the hour ... announces ... and sends forth" (ll. 4–5), "the mine delivers its gang and the pit its bondsmen" (l. 7); a change to the narrative present (l. 7); comments containing bitter sarcasm (ll. 17–21, 26–28); exclamations (ll. 10, 12–13, 22); a rhetorical question (ll. 13–14) and direct address of the reader (l. 22).
6. *Give a short report on Disraeli's role as a politician or on one of his novels.*
    – –
7. *Study the mass media for instances of the exploitation of children in various parts of the world. Report your findings to the class.*
    – –

8 Henry Brougham: Address to Labourers on Destroying Machinery (1830)

Didaktische Hinweise

Ähnlich wie unser gegenwärtiges „nachindustrielles" Zeitalter besonders durch Entwicklungen im Bereich der Computertechnik und der Kommunikationstechnologie einschneidend verändert wird (vgl. Text 6), führten wichtige Erfindungen vor allem im Großbritannien des 18. und 19. Jahrhunderts bereits damals zu folgenreichen ökonomischen und sozialen Umwälzungen großen Ausmaßes, zur Industriellen Revolution (vgl. "Info-Box", SB, S. 81 f.). Ebenso wie heute der rasche technische Fortschritt infolge seiner Auswirkungen auf den wirtschaftlichen und gesellschaftlichen Bereich nicht nur auf Zustimmung trifft, kam es auch damals unter den betroffenen Arbeitern und Handwerkern zu heftigen Reaktionen. Diese auffallende Parallelität kann für den Einstieg in die Erarbeitung dieses Textes genutzt werden, gegebenenfalls vertieft durch Hinweise auf weitere historische Fakten (vgl. "Background information", unten). In interessierten Klassen bieten sich Vergleiche mit ähnlichen Vorkommnissen in anderen, an der Schwelle zur Industrialisierung stehenden Staaten an (vgl. unten, Aufg. 5).

Background information

Henry Peter Lord Brougham [bruːm] (1778–1868), a British lawyer and Whig states-man of many talents, was an MP from 1810 to 1812 and from 1816 onwards. He supported the course of reform in politics, education and law with his untiring activities and became Lord Chancellor in 1830. As such he was influential in passing through the Reform Bill of 1832. In 1802, together with Francis Jeffrey and Sydney Smith, he founded the *Edinburgh Review,* which in 1808 published a contemptuous criticism, probably by Brougham himself, of Byron's *Hours of Idleness*, a collection of poems (1807); Byron replied to this article with his satirical poem "English Bards and Scotch Reviewers" (1809).

Mechanization was introduced early into textile manufacturing, and revolutionized spinning and weaving. The Spinning Jenny, invented in 1776 by James Hargreaves (1720–1778) could spin wool through many spindles and needed only one operator. Sir Richard Arkwright (1732–1792) developed a complicated spinning frame for cotton in 1768, which was, however, still driven by horse or water power.

Early experiments with steam power came close to perfection with James Watt (cf. Text 9a). Richard Trevithick (1771–1833) made the first steam-propelled vehicle in 1801. The first transport railway was laid out in 1825 by George Stephenson (1781–1848) between Stockton and Darlington (ca. 40 km), and the first passenger railway, using Stephenson's "Rocket", was opened in 1830 between Liverpool and Manchester, marking the beginning of the modern railway system. The first steamboat was built in 1802 in Britain by William Symington (1763–1831), while Henry Bell (1767–1830) initiated steam navigation in Europe with the regular service of his "Comet" in 1812.

It was many years after the application of steam power to transport and manufacturing that British agriculture made use of this form of energy to intensify farming and raise yields to meet the needs of the growing population. The Scottish millwright Andrew Meikle (1719–1811) constructed the first threshing-machine in 1787, but it was still drawn by horse power. The farm-hands' opposition to thresh-ing-machines culminated in the agricultural riots of 1830, when many machines were damaged or wrecked. Then, around 1840, locomotive-type steam engines came into use. These developed into the agricultural traction engine and were combined with the threshing-machine into self-moving and self-working units around 1859. The first harvesting-machine was patented by the American Cyrus H. McCormick (1809–1884) in 1834, and was later mass-produced in Chicago. Combine-harvesters, which not only harvested, but also threshed and bagged the grain, were constructed in California in 1875. The tractor, invented at the turn of the century, and the combine-harvester eventually made the threshing-machine obsolete.

For further reading cf. L.T.C. Rolt: *Victorian Engineering.* Penguin, Harmonds-worth, 1970.

"The breaking of Machinery" (l. 34): The general effects of mechanization and the ban on forming trade unions (under the Combination Laws of 1799–1800) drove embittered workers to lawlessness. In Nottinghamshire and Yorkshire, unemployed hand operatives and their friends went about attacking mills and destroying machinery. They were called Luddites in 1811 because their organizer was rumoured

to be a certain Ned Ludd. They destroyed property and were finally suppressed, with some bloodshed, when soldiers were called in. Byron wrote an apotheosis of "King Ludd" in his "Song for the Luddites" (1812).

Semantic and collocational field "Introduction of new machinery"

a machine, a tool, an instrument ✧ an invention, the introduction (into use) of sth., an improvement, (to) be a gainer ✧ (to) spare human labour, (to) throw sb. out of employment, (to) prevent sb. from being employed ✧ (to) do sth. at the least cost, (to) be sold at the lowest price, (to) depend upon sb./sth. for sth. else ✧ a demand for labour, (to) dislike sb./sth., (to) destroy sth.

Talking about the text – Suggested answers

1. Technical progress begins at the moment any – even the simplest – instrument is used. Work done exclusively by hand is possible but strenuous and much less productive because more people then have to do more work to produce the same amount or, quite likely, even less. Consumers must pay the higher prices of low productivity, whereas they could otherwise enjoy the lower prices of high productivity. Mechanization brings about some unemployment initially and forces workers to seek occupation in other, perhaps new fields of work.
2. He tries to reason with the workers to explain the necessity of technical progress, to convince them of the benefits of mechanization, to calm them in their anxiety, to give them new hope, also to warn them of short-sighted destructiveness that would only be to their own disadvantage.
3. By adapting his argumentation to his audience of simple farm labourers, e.g. he defines the primary meaning of "machine" (ll. 5–8) and uses illustrations and analogies from their sphere of life (cf. ll. 7–8, 11–24); by appealing to their moral responsibility (cf. ll. 9–14, 30–33, 34–36); by striking a patient, serious, admonishing tone consistently; by directly addressing his listeners throughout; by employing a number of rhetorical means such as anaphora and parallelism (cf. ll. 1–4, 9–11), contrast (cf. ll. 5–7, 23–24, 25–30), concession (cf. ll. 25–28), a rhetorical question (cf. ll. 17–20), intensifying and attitudinal adverbs and adverbial expressions (e.g. ll. 2, 3, 5, 6, 8, 15–16).
4. – –

● 5. *Collect material for a report on other instances of workers struggling against new technologies, such as weavers in France and Germany around the same time the text was written, or printers in the British newspaper industry in the 1980s. Report your findings to the class.*
     – –

● 6. *Prepare a talk on the steamboat or the railway, two inventions that revolutionized transport and also contributed greatly to the growth of Britain as a technical, economic and political world power.*
     – –

9 a James Watt: On Worker Organization – A Letter (1796)

Didaktische Hinweise

Dieser Auszug aus einem Brief James Watts an den ihm bekannten Ingenieur John Rennie (vgl. "Background information", unten) wirft ein Schlaglicht auf die Folgen der beginnenden technisch-industriellen Revolution. Hier wie in den folgenden drei Texten (Text 9b, 10, 11) werden die sich ausprägenden und verändernden Beziehungen zwischen Unternehmern und Arbeitern *(industrial relations)* thematisiert. Auf Grund dieser inhaltlichen Verbindungen, insbesondere auch wegen der didaktisch fruchtbaren Kontrastierung mit Text 9b, wurde hier die chronologische Reihenfolge durchbrochen und diese Briefpassage erst hinter den Auszug aus Disraelis Roman (Text 7) und Broughams Rede (Text 8) plaziert.

Background information

James Watt (1736–1819), born in Scotland, started his technical career as a mathematical-instrument maker to Glasgow University. From 1763 to 1774 he acted as a civil engineer making surveys of canals and harbours. He improved the efficiency of steam engines by the addition of an exterior condenser that eliminated loss of power. Patented in 1769, this invention was applied to the first commercially used steam engines, which Watt and the factory owner M. Boulton started manufacturing near Birmingham in 1775. Watt devised a variety of other mechanical appliances including a letter-copying press (1780) and established the mechanical unit of "horse power". He is regarded as one of Britain's greatest inventors. In his honour the unit of electrical power was named the "watt" (the unit necessary to maintain a current of one ampere under a pressure of a potential of one volt).

John Rennie (1761–1821), to whom Watt addressed this letter, was born in Scotland and became a civil engineer. He worked under the millwright Andrew Meikle (cf. p. 67 of this book) and was later employed by Boulton and Watt in Birmingham. Then he went to London, where he planned and constructed Southwark Bridge, Westminster Bridge, London Bridge (of late taken down and reconstructed in the USA) and Waterloo Bridge. The construction or improvement of canals, docks and harbours all over Britain made him the leading British engineer in these areas.

Semantic and collocational field "Employment in the late 18th century"

a journeyman, a master, a servant, a carpenter, a cabinet maker, a joiner ✧ (to) employ sb., (to) engage sb., (to) engage with sb., (to) learn a trade ✧ (to) become a member of sth. (e.g. a society), (to) attend a meeting ✧ a rebellion, (to) give way to sb./sth., (to) prosecute sb.

Talking about the text – Suggested answers

1. Journeymen are rebelling against conditions of work and employment, joining in some form of trade union and attending its meetings.
2. Not to tolerate the workers' activities, to employ workers in jobs for which they are not trained, to give work only to those who agree not to join trade unions, and to hire men who have not finished their apprenticeship because they are cheaper and more compliant.
3. They see it as a pure master-servant relationship, exploitative, restrictive, even oppressive.
4. *Why would methods such as those suggested in this letter be unlikely or at least hard to practise nowadays? Discuss.*
   [The student may think of the protection of labour laws, the watchfulness of the authorities, the trade unions and the mass media.]
● 5. *Gather material for a brief summary of James Watt's life and achievements. Report your findings to the class.*
   – –

9 b Workers, Unite! (1892)

Didaktische Hinweise

Nach dem der "possessing Master Class" (l. 4) zuzurechnenden Erfinder und Unternehmer James Watt (Text 9a) kommt hier die andere Seite, der Arbeiter, zu Wort. Dieser Aufruf der National Union of Gasworkers and General Labourers vermittelt den Schülern/Schülerinnen einen Eindruck von der klassenkämpferischen Entschlossenheit britischer Gewerkschaften am Ende des 19. Jahrhunderts, die inzwischen – fast hundert Jahre nach Watts Brief – ihre gesetzliche Anerkennung gefunden haben (vgl. "Info-Box", SB, S. 82, "Background information", unten, und LB, S. 72 f.) und nun um eine stärkere Machtposition ringen.

Background information

Trade unionism originated in Great Britain as a product of the Industrial Revolution. However, increasingly repressive legislation culminated in the passing of the Combination Acts of 1799 and 1800, which made trade unionism illegal as possible centres of political unrest. The unions survived, however, under the guise of "friendly societies" or by going underground. Members were often introduced and initiated into underground unions with secret rites and were made to swear to accept the directives of the union. After the repeal of these acts in 1824/25, the unions were granted the right to engage in collective bargaining but were otherwise still subject to legal restrictions. Attempts were made by the unions in the following decades to establish a mass-consolidated movement, but this failed. The story of British trade unionism then became the history of many smaller societies developing simultaneously. A series of trade union acts from 1871 to 1876 provided for the protection of union funds against liability charges and charges of criminal conspiracy, and, at the same time, lifted other restrictions. For information on later developments cf. pp. 72 f. of this book.

Semantic and collocational field "Trade unionism"

a worker, the working class, unskilled labour, (to) form a union, (to) organise, (to) unite, (to) embrace sb./sth., (to) admit all workers on an equal footing ✧ an immediate object, an ultimate goal, an aim ✧ hope for the future, an improvement of the material conditions, the emancipation of the working class ✧ the interests of sb./sth., (to) protect oneself, (to) expect no help from sb./sth. ✧ (to) be opposed to sth.

Talking about the text – Suggested answers

1. The text shows society as being deeply divided into two classes, "Masters" (l. 5) and "Workers" (l. 6), with the former being unwilling to share profits with those who produce them. The text is antagonistic, written in the rhetoric of class warfare.
2. On the basis of unfailing solidarity it is ready to accept "every kind of 'unskilled' labour" (ll. 12–13), strives for better protection of its members, material improvement by the sharing of profits, a better present and future for their children, more human dignity and happiness, more equal sharing of the quality of life between the classes, in general, "the Emancipation of the Working Class" (l. 25).
3. The text begins with a positive picture of the trade unions' achievements so far, which is then contrasted with the utterly negative portrait of a traditional two-class society of exploiters and exploited, thus rather over-simplifying matters. It then outlines the

necessity of union organization in general and the foundation of this union in particular. The second half continues with details of the union's "immediate objects" (l. 14) and solicits the workers' understanding, solidarity and militancy (cf. the metaphors of warfare in ll. 23–25). It finally points to the ultimate goal and ends with a climax, a passionate appeal to the workers to unite.

4. *In what way does the tone of the text reflect the purpose of the preamble?*
   It is self-confident, resolute, impatient, passionate, aggressive, even militant.

5. *Discuss the advantages and the limits of group solidarity in such fields as politics, work, sport or school.*
   – –

10 Anthony Sampson: Trades Union Congress

Didaktische Hinweise

Dieser Auszug aus Anthony Sampsons in mehreren Auflagen erschienenem Standardwerk *The Changing Anatomy of Britain* (London, Hodder and Stoughton; erste Auflage 1962 unter dem Titel *Anatomy of Britain*) führt die im historischen Text 9a begonnene Diskussion des Teilthemas „Gewerkschaften" an die Gegenwart heran. Der Text bietet über die in der "Info-Box" (SB, S. 82 f.) vermittelten Grundkenntnisse hinaus weitere Informationen zur britischen Gewerkschaftsbewegung, besonders zum Trades Union Congress. Die Passagen fast impressionistischer Beschreibung von Ort und Atmosphäre dieser Kongresse und die eine Reihe von Paradoxa enthaltenden prinzipiellen Schlußfragen eines nachdenklichen Beobachters sollen den Schülern/Schülerinnen den Zugang zu dem etwas spröden Thema „Britische Gewerkschaften" erleichtern. Eine Erweiterung des Themas unter dem Aspekt „Frauen in der Gewerkschaftsbewegung" läßt sich durch die Einbeziehung von Carey W. Englishs Artikel "Women and Organized Labor" (Kap. VII, Text 3) erreichen.

Background information

Anthony Sampson, (1926–   ) started his career by publishing a magazine in South Africa. In 1955 he became a columnist for *The Observer.* He is best known for his book *Anatomy of Britain* (Hodder and Stoughton, London, 1962; revised edition under the title *The Changing Anatomy of Britain*), now also available in a paperback edition (1983). Written in a highly personal style, this "sociogram" describes and analyses British institutions and the people who wield power in them.

For information on the development of trade unionism cf. pp. 70 and 72 f. of this book.

Semantic and collocational field "Trade unionism"

the trade union movement, the Trades Union Congress, a fixed institution, an organisation ◇ an annual meeting, a conference, an assembly, an audience, a delegate, an orator, (to) assemble, (to) meet ◇ a formalised pageant, a rigmarole ◇ (to) represent sb./sth., (to) give a voice to sb. ◇ a trade, organised labour ◇ working-class, a proletarian character, a cross-section of life, a range of accents and intonations ◇ a sentimental reference to sth., emotional, long-winded, legalistic ◇ division, unity, a compromise, a paradox ◇ (to) sway sb., (to) bring down sb./sth., (to) set up sth.

Talking about the text – Suggested answers

1. Its size, age and diversity, the character of its membership and meeting grounds, the atmosphere and procedures of the meetings, the power of the TUC. His purpose is to give a balanced picture of the Congress as a venerable British institution of long standing by conveying knowledge as well as passing on impressions.

2. The solid, elegant Victorian look and atmosphere have faded and been largely replaced by a modern, more working-class life-style and a cheap architecture. The signs of middle-class rule are thus disappearing, although the "old-fashioned jollity" (l. 11) of the seaside resort remains. Both of these facts are likely to appeal to the TUC.

3. They might get first-hand knowledge of the mood of an important section of Britain's working population, their aims and strategies, as well as their possible future leaders.

4. They remind delegates and observers of the movement's roots, preserve long-established traditions and help in the smooth running of the conference. They strengthen the feeling of camaraderie and solidarity and conceal controversies.

5. He adds illustrations and examples to the relatively abstract notions "working-class" (l. 12), "cross-section" (l. 18), "distractions" (l. 23), "interests" (l. 29), "paradoxes" (l. 35); gives brief statistical information; uses only a limited number of technical terms, and even emphasizes three of these by using quotation marks; describes Blackpool's atmosphere; stimulates the reader with a question (cf. l. 34).

6. *Discuss possible reasons for some of the paradoxes mentioned in the final paragraph.*

– –

11 Jimmy Reid: A Basic Democratic Right

Didaktische Hinweise

Obwohl *secondary picketing* inzwischen infolge gesetzlicher Maßnahmen der Thatcher-Regierung kaum noch möglich ist (vgl. "Background information", unten), bleibt das allgemeine Anliegen dieses Zeitungsartikels dennoch auch weiterhin aktuell, kontrovers und bedeutungsvoll. Reid stellt in seiner Argumentation einen Bezug her zwischen dem Recht der Arbeiter auf Streik und generellen Grundrechten des Menschen. Die in diesem Kapitel insgesamt angesprochenen Probleme werden damit auf eine allgemeinere Ebene gehoben.

Background information

Around 1900, successive acts of Parliament broadened the unions' field of action and allowed them to engage in political activity. Originally trade unions had represented only craftsmen, but around the turn of the century the organization of unskilled labour spread and a trend set in towards general unions. Unionism also expanded to include professional and clerical workers as well as women. The restrictive Trade Disputes and Trade Unions Act, passed one year after the general strike of 1926, was repealed after World War II. The Wilson Labour governments shied away from legislative reforms in 1969 and later, in 1974, repealed the Industrial Relations Act (1971) of the Conservatives, who had tried to put more restrictions on the unions, e.g. legal enforcement of collective agreements, compulsory "cooling-off" periods and strike ballots.

The Conservative Thatcher governments passed four Employment Acts (1980, 1982, 1984, 1988), which restricted the "closed shop" (a practice whereby only members of a certain trade union may be employed by a firm), picketing and "secondary action" (i.e. when a trade union not involved in a dispute goes on strike in sympathy with another union which is already on strike following a dispute), defined "unlawful" trade disputes more clearly and enforced more democratic procedures on the unions. The TUC and most unions remain opposed to these measures.

Between 1893 and 1940 there were about 1,000 and 1,300 trade unions in Britain. Since then the numbers have dropped. Membership, on the other hand, rose gradually to reach 11.7 million in 1974. During the 1980s the membership declined and in 1987 stood at about 9 million.

The TUC is a nationwide organization with about 82 affiliated unions, comprising nearly 83 % of all British trade union members. The TUC's General Council is responsible for carrying out the annual Congresses' decisions; it provides educational and advisory services to unions and presents the trade unions' viewpoint to the government. It works through influence rather than sanctions and plays an active international role (mainly based on H. Pelling: *A History of British Trade Unionism* [Penguin, Hamondsworth, 1976] and *Britain 1989. An Official Handbook* [Her Majesty's Stationery Office, London, 1989]).

Semantic and collocational field "Workers' rights"

a worker, an employee, an employer ✧ an inalienable right, a democratic right, freedom of speech/the press/assembly, the right to withdraw one's labour ✧ a collective bargaining procedure, (to) organize, (to) negotiate with sb. ✧ industrial relations/peace, a confrontation/difference with sb., (to) challenge sb./sth., (to) defend sb./sth. ✧ (to) persuade sb. of sth., (to) assert sth. ✧ the justice of one's cause, (to) merit support ✧ a strike, on strike, secondary picketing, supportive action ✧ intimidation, obstruction, (to) coerce sb. ✧ (to) outlaw sth., (to) impose a legal ban on sb./sth. ✧ at the mercy of sb./sth., powerless, forced labour

Talking about the text – Suggested answers

1. *What basic democratic rights have the unions secured so far, according to Reid, and what is the new issue under discussion here?*
   The unions have secured the right to organize themselves and to negotiate collectively, the right to withhold their labour, the right to persuade others of the rightness of their cause. The new issue is secondary picketing, i.e. actions meant to support strikes by stopping workers in other industries not directly involved from getting to work.

2. *What arguments does the writer offer in support of his opinion?*
   He sees secondary picketing as a traditional democratic right that needs to be defended. He interprets it as an inseparable part of other well-established rights and sees it as an act of justifiable persuasion. He also reminds his readers of the warning examples of totalitarian governments that regularly suppressed democratic trade unionism.

3. *Which actions of workers would Reid not tolerate in a democratic society?*
   Actions beyond accepted "norms of behaviour" (l. 35) and endangering the rights of others, coercion, physical intimidation and obstruction.

4. *What behaviour would you consider to be within or beyond the norm in a private or public conflict? Discuss.*
   – –

5. *Secondary picketing has been generally declared illegal in Britain in the meantime. Do you think this weakens the democratic rights of labour decisively? Discuss.*
   – –

Chapter IV: Constitutional History and Present Politics

Kapitel IV, das letzte der ausschließlich Großbritannien gewidmeten Kapitel, beschäftigt sich mit der Entwicklung des Landes vom mittelalterlichen, absolutistisch regierten Königreich zur modernen konstitutionellen Monarchie in ihrer gegenwärtigen Ausprägung, mit ihren politischen Erscheinungsformen und Problemen. Die Texte 1a und 1b bieten Ausschnitte aus historischen Dokumenten und dienen der exemplarischen Veranschaulichung der in der "Info-Box" (SB, S. 88 ff.) genannten "Constitutional Landmarks". Die Texte 2 bis 4 und die zweite "Info-Box" dieses Kapitels (SB, S. 94 f.) thematisieren die wichtigsten, historisch gewachsenen Elemente der britischen Verfassungswirklichkeit und erörtern sie aus heutiger Sicht. Die anglikanische Kirche und ihr von Anfang an besonderes Verhältnis zum Staat bilden das Thema der Texte 5 und 6. Und schließlich wird in der dritten "Info-Box" (SB, S. 106 f.) und in den Texten 7 bis 9 der Nordirland-Konflikt angesprochen mit Auszügen aus fiktionalen und nicht-fiktionalen Darstellungen aus der Sicht der unmittelbar und mittelbar Betroffenen.

Vergleiche mit den Vereinigten Staaten – etwa im Bereich der Verfassungsgeschichte, der Parteien oder der Menschenrechtsproblematik – bieten sich an. Auf Verknüpfungsmöglichkeiten wird bei der Kommentierung der einzelnen Texte hingewiesen.

1a Excerpts from the Magna Carta (1215)

Didaktische Hinweise

Obwohl die *Magna Carta* noch kein Dokument einer demokratischen Staatsauffassung ist und zur Zeit ihrer Entstehung niemand elementare bürgerliche Rechte im Auge hatte (sie wurden im 17. Jahrhundert nachträglich hineininterpretiert), ist sie doch das erste Dokument, in dem Beschränkungen der absoluten Macht des Königs festgehalten und dem Adel, der Geistlichkeit und den Städten bestimmte Rechte und Privilegien zugestanden wurden. In diesem, Feudalrechte garantierenden Vertrag fand die mittelalterliche Vorstellung, daß Recht und Gesetz dem König übergeordnet sind und Widerstand gegen einen Unrecht übenden Herrscher erlaubt ist, erstmals ihren staatsrechtlich verbindlichen Niederschlag. Damit kann die *Magna Carta* als ein Grundstein der englischen Verfassung angesehen werden. Als solcher spielt sie auch heute noch – nicht nur im Bewußtsein der Briten – eine große Rolle (vgl. auch "Background information", unten). Die Kenntnisse der Schüler/innen über die Verfassung der Bundesrepublik (eventuell auch die anderer Nationen) können für den Einstieg in die Arbeit mit diesem Text genutzt werden.

Background information

Henry II (1154–1189) decided that after his death his "dominions" (which included England, Ireland and half of France) should be divided between his three eldest sons, leaving nothing for John, which seems to have led to his nickname "Lackland". In 1199, however, John succeeded to the English throne, following the death of his brother, Richard I ("the Lionheart"). Shortly afterwards, King Philip Augustus of

France overran most of the Angevin Empire, which was part of the English Crown's inheritance, and in 1203 John was left with England, Ireland and Gascony as his sole possessions.

In order to finance his attempts to recover his lost lands on the Continent, John levied exorbitant taxes on the country, which, together with an unusually high rate of inflation, caused financial hardship and resentment among the barons.

John also quarrelled with the Church. In 1205 he refused to recognize the election of Stephen Langton, the Pope's choice, as Archbishop of Canterbury. Pope Innocent III then laid an interdict on England and Wales, which suspended all church services, and excommunicated John in 1209. After several years John, faced with a baronial rebellion and an invasion by the French king, gave in to the Pope, realizing that an excommunicated king was particularly vulnerable. In an act of humiliation he offered to hold England as a fief of the papacy, thereby completely winning the support of Innocent III.

John's defeat by Philip Augustus in 1214 resulted in a rebellion of the English barons. They centered their revolt around a programme of reform, which was written down in a document which later, due to its size, was to be known as the "Magna Carta". John saw it as an infringement of royal power, and, faced by the strength of the oppositon, signed it at Runnymede only in order to buy time. As a peace treaty, the *Magna Carta* was a failure, since fighting was to continue until John's death. As a statement of law, however, it has always been taken seriously.

The *Magna Carta* was, in fact, a treaty between the king and the barons, who were acting essentially in the interests of their own class. Not a single line refers to the people, the serfs.

However, a conception was formed that there is a law above the king, independent of regal power, controlling the monarch. Although the Common Law owed quite a lot to feudal custom, and the Common Counsel was a feudal assembly, they have nevertheless been considered steps towards the principles of parliamentary control and political participation, towards "no taxation without representation", towards the *Declaration of Independence* (cf. Ch. VIII, Text 1 and pp. 160 ff. of this book).

The Latin document, which was not translated into English before the 16th century and which editors have divided into 63 clauses, can be described as a comprehensive survey of specific wrongs the king had committed and of rights he had undermined, rather than as a coherent constitutional plan. Its importance lies in the fact that it names specific remedies for these evils. It guarantees the privileges of the Church, limits monarchical power, prevents the king from manipulating the law, defines the relationship between the king and the barons, outlaws the misuse of administrative powers, protects against the king's officers, guarantees the right to a fair trial for all freemen and provides for a council of 25 barons to watch over the law and to receive complaints.

During the 13th century the *Magna Carta* continued to be of great importance as a document restricting royal power; it was appealed to on numerous occasions and was constantly revised in the 14th and 15th centuries. However, when the Parliaments of Edward I were established, it became obsolete in parts and fell into oblivion (e.g., Shakespeare's King John is not concerned with the charter at all). In the 17th century, when the battle for Parliament flared up again, the *Magna Carta* was revived; its role as a narrow programme of a small social minority was ignored and it was used as a legal weapon against James I and Charles I. And, although, in centuries to come, historians were to point out that the original meaning of a number of terms had been lost – e. g., "freeman" (ll. 22, 26, 35) was not the same as a "free man" –, the *Magna Carta* became a constitutional symbol for the predominance of the law over the king.

Four copies of the *Magna Carta* survive; two copies are in the British Museum, one is in Lincoln Cathedral and one is in Salisbury.

Talking about the text – Suggested answers

1. Article 12 implies that taxes were imposed by the king arbitrarily. He also seems to have undermined the special rights – particularly the important right of levying taxes upon import and export – of the city of London, as can be concluded from Article 13.

    Of course, the King's absolutist conviction that he was Prince by the Grace of God made it completely unacceptable for him to take advice from anyone (14). Article 15 shows that the barons apparently extorted from the lower classes of the population what the King had extorted from them. The King's despotic rule naturally also applied to his administering of the law; punishment frequently seems not to have been in accordance with the offence and must have included cases where an offender's livelihood was destroyed (20).

    Article 38 shows that the King's officers must have carried on in the same manner and it is only consistent that there was corruption and that justice was frequently sold or refused.

2. The most important principle is that there is a law which is above the king, i.e. that even kings/rulers were subject to the law.

    The institution of a "common counsel" (l. 18) served as a basis for the democratic principle of parliamentary control.

    As far as law and justice are concerned, one certainly has to consider rights such as the protection against the king's officers and the guaranteed right to a fair trial by equals and according to the law of the land. These were significant steps in the direction of future rights and liberties.

1b Excerpts from the Bill of Rights (1689)

Didaktische Hinweise

Die aus 13 Artikeln bestehende *Bill of Rights* (1689) ging aus der im gleichen Jahr von einer formlos zusammengerufenen Parlamentsversammlung verkündeten *Declaration of Rights* hervor. Sie richtet sich, ähnlich wie fast vierhundert Jahre früher die *Magna Carta* (vgl. SB, S. 85 f.), gegen den absolutistischen Machtmißbrauch, jetzt durch den katholischen Stuartkönig James II. (vgl. "Background information", unten) und fordert unter anderem parlamentarische Kontrolle der Gesetzgebung und der Steuererhebung, freie Wahl der Parlamentsmitglieder, Redefreiheit, Abschaffung der geistlichen Gerichtshöfe und regelmäßige Geschworenengerichte, das Petitionsrecht und die Zustimmung des Parlaments zum Unterhalt eines stehenden Heers in Friedenszeiten. Die *Bill of Rights* gilt als eines der großen verfassungsrechtlichen Dokumente Englands auf dem Weg zu einer parlamentarischen Demokratie. Entstanden in einer Zeit, in der unter dem Einfluß Ludwig XIV. auf dem Kontinent der Absolutismus in höchster Blüte stand, darf sie jedoch nicht mißverstanden werden als ein Gesetz, das bürgerliche Freiheitsrechte garantiert wie etwa rund hundert Jahre später die 10 Ergänzungen zur amerikanischen Verfassung, die unter dem gleichen Namen bekannt wurden (vgl. Kap. VIII, Text 2).

Immer wieder wurde im britischen Parlament versucht, eine Bill of Rights zu verabschieden, die allgemeine Menschenrechte, wie sie unter anderem auch die *Universal Declaration of Human Rights* formuliert, zum Inhalt hat. Die jüngste, 1987 im Unterhaus debatierte Gesetzesvorlage umfaßte auf der Basis der Euro-päischen Konvention der Menschenrechte z.B. "the right to freedom of association and expression, the right to privacy and a fair trial". Die derzeitigen Aussichten für die Verabschiedung einer solchen Gesetzesvorlage sind jedoch gering, da sie die Doktrin von der Souveränität des Parlaments ungültig machen würde. Einer Bill of Rights, die die Menschenrechte verbindlich proklamiert, müßten sich auch das Parlament und die Krone unterordnen. Dafür gibt es in Großbritannien heute noch keine parlamentarische Mehrheit.

Literaturhinweise: Eine knappe Darstellung der Diskussion um eine moderne Bill of Rights findet sich in Philip Norton: *The Constitution in Flux.* Oxford, Basil Blackwell 1984.

Background information

When James II (1633–1701), who had become a Catholic in 1668, succeeded to the throne after his brother's death in 1685, he established religious equality for his Catholic subjects, hoping for a mass conversion to the Roman faith. The Tory-Anglican nobility were extremely offended by his extension of religious toleration to Roman Catholics; their anger was further increased when James II produced a male heir, who would have succeeded to the throne instead of his Protestant daughter, Mary, making the institution of a Catholic dynasty a strong possibility.

The loyalty of the English to their Church proved greater than to their king. In 1688 seven leading figures invited William of Orange and his wife, Mary (James II's daughter), to England to protect the Anglican Church and the ancient liberties. James II fled to France; Parliament declared that the throne was vacant and offered the Crown jointly to William and Mary. With French aid and money James tried to defend Ireland against William, but he was defeated at the Battle of the Boyne (cf. "Info-Box", SB, p. 106).

Possibly one of the most important results of the "Glorious Revolution" of 1688 was the acceptance of parliamentary monarchy. The *Bill of Rights* clearly overrode the royal prerogative, which was replaced by the will of the people as expressed through Parliament. The *Bill of Rights* was not a new constitution, but it was certainly a decisive turning point in the understanding of the concept of government. This was all the more important since absolutism was on the rise on the Continent. The *Bill of Rights* enumerated a number of infringements and abuses of the rights and liberties of his subjects by King James II and declared them illegal, and also made royal decisions and actions dependent on the consent of Parliament. It also prohibited a Catholic from becoming a monarch and a monarch from marrying a Catholic, thus paving the way for the establishment of the Protestant succession to the throne of England.

Semantic and collocational field "Law"

(to) execute/amend/preserve/strengthen/suspend a law, (to) dispense with a law ✧ (to) be against the law, illegal ✧ prerogative, (to) petition sb., ✧ (to) impeach sb., (to) question sb. in a court, (to) require bail, (to) impose a fine, (to) inflict punishment on sb.

Talking about the text – Suggested answers

1. He must have suspended laws at will and distorted justice, denying offenders the right to a fair trial. Fines and punishment seem to have been imposed accordingly; it is only consistent that the sums people had to pay to get out of prison while waiting for their trial to come up were excessive and unfair. People apparently were prosecuted when they petitioned the king. He also demanded excessive sums of money from his subjects – very likely in order to maintain a standing army. Parliament must have been seriously crippled by the king's denial of free speech.
2. That the consent of Parliament should be necessary in cases of suspending the law or of dispensing with the law (1, 2), for levying taxes and for maintaining an army in times of peace (4, 6). It also demanded free elections for members of Parliament, frequent parliamentary sessions, and also the sovereignty of Parliament as far as free speech and free proceedings were concerned (8, 9, 13).

2 James Callaghan: The Fixed Centre

Didaktische Hinweise

Text 2 ist der erste in einer Gruppe von Texten, die sich mit den staatstragenden Institutionen in Großbritannien beschäftigen. Thema des vorliegenden Exzerpts ist die Krone, Text 3 lenkt den Blick auf die gegenwärtige Situation des Oberhauses und damit auf das Parlament, in Text 4 erörtert Anthony Sampson die Chancen einer dritten Partei im Rahmen des britischen Wahlsystems. Bei der Erarbeitung dieser Texte empfiehlt es sich, die "Info-Box" (SB, S. 94 f.) heranzuziehen.

Die Tatsache, daß Elizabeth II von einem Labour-Politiker und ehemaligen Gewerkschaftler (vgl. "Background information", unten) charakterisiert wird, verleiht dem hier gezeichneten Bild einen hohen Anschein von Objektivität. Besonders interessant ist das menschliche Engagement, mit dem die Monarchin in Callaghans Augen ihre Rolle erfüllt (vgl. Aufg. 2), ohne Zweifel ein Grund für das noch immer ungebrochene Verhältnis vieler Briten zu ihrem Königshaus.

Background information

James Callaghan [ˈkæləhæn] (1912–   ): British Labour politician and trade unionist and an MP from 1945 till 1987 when he was made a life peer. He has held all the important cabinet posts in various Labour governments, and from 1976 till 1979 he was Prime Minister. He now sits in the House of Lords.

Elizabeth II (1926–   ): Since 1952 Queen of the United Kingdom of Great Britain and Northern Ireland and head of state of several Commonwealth countries, e.g. Australia, Canada, and New Zealand (cf. "Background information", pp. 6 f. of this book). She is the official head of state, the head of the legal system of Britain, the commander-in-chief of the armed forces and the head of the Church of England. However great the Queen's power may be theoretically, the actual legislative power resides in Parliament. Nonetheless many important political steps require the monarch's participation, e.g. the opening, proroguing and dissolving of Parliament and the approval to Acts of Parliament before they become law (royal assent). The Queen bestows honours and awards such as the Order of the Garter or the Order of Merit. After a general election she invites the leader of the strongest party to form a government. She also appoints government ministers, judges, diplomats and bishops. She has the power to reduce or suspend sentences imposed on criminals (royal pardon). All these functions are part of the "royal prerogative", but with few exceptions they are carried out following the Prime Minister's advice.

Semantic and collocational field "The Monarchy"

a head of state, the Queen, the Crown, the Head of the Commonwealth, an institution, the Palace, (to) reign ✧ a focal point, continuity, stability, (to) project oneself as head of the nation ✧ a sense of duty, a high and conscientious regard for one's responsibility, (to) fulfil one's responsibilities, (to) care about one's duties, (to) convey a genuine sense of social caring, (to) command loyalty, (to) win loyalty/admiration/affection, (to) strengthen one's hold on a country ✧ a public appearance, (to) go to (immense) trouble with a speech ✧ a modification, (to) adapt oneself (to sth.)

Talking about the text – Suggested answers

1. There are several reasons. First there is the historical aspect. The system, consisting of Parliament and the Crown, has grown continually over the centuries and has become a characteristic feature of the national character. Then, as a result of this historical process, there is the structure of the system, with Parliament and the Crown as separate institutions, but at the same time dependent on one another; this, he says, "gives rise to least controversy" (l. 14). Comparing Parliament to a flywheel and the Crown to its fixed centre, he indicates two further important reasons: stability and continuity. These result from the fact that the monarch is head of state by right of birth and for life, and that the elected representatives of the state continually reflect the mood of the country.
2. According to Callaghan, Elizabeth II has a "high and conscientious regard for her responsibility as head of state" (ll. 27–29). She is a hard worker, with a "sense of social caring" (l. 36) and a sense of fairness, and she also shares the ordinary British citizen's "commonsense view of things" (l. 69).
3. What is probably most important is the fact that she reflects on her role as head of state, that she thinks about the function of the monarchy and the impact of the monarch, that she has come to a "true understanding of the significance of her role in the daily lives of the people" (ll. 71–72). Therefore she does not interfere in political events and decisions, but sticks to the monarch's function as an official figure-head; this is why she does not decline to fulfil duties which seem to be dull or routine but which may be important to the ordinary people. Her understanding of her role causes her to stand above current affairs, not to favour any one person or to support any one party, but to treat every Prime Minister with the same consideration. The prestige she has gained in this way, her knowledge of the problems of former British colonies, and her self-confidence have helped her to exercise considerable influence as Head of the Commonwealth.
4. Stability and continuity are ensured by adaptability. The monarchy, like any system, will survive if it shows itself capable of finding new answers to new questions, of coping with the changing times. In the Prince of Wales, the heir apparent to the throne, Callaghan sees all the personal qualities that are characteristic of his mother.
5. Callaghan's personal attitude towards the Queen is characterized by respect and admiration. This becomes obvious through his use of emotive language, culminating in "her sterling character" (l. 86) and "womanly intuition" (l. 87), when he does not hesitate

to use sentimental clichés. It also shows from the nouns that he associates with the Queen, e.g. "loyalty", "admiration", "affection" (ll. 25–26) or even "gratitude" (l. 75). The impression that James Callaghan really admires the Queen also arises from some of the phrases that he uses to describe the way she is doing her job, e.g. "She goes to immense trouble" (l. 31), "She has a splendid capacity for ..." (ll. 43–44), she "cares deeply about ..." (l. 46), she "has a keen eye and ear" (l. 66), "she has a true understanding of ..." (ll. 70–71), "She has grown immensely in confidence and understanding" (l. 75–77), she fulfils "her responsibilities so admirably" (ll. 88–89). All this makes Callaghan's final wish "Long may she reign" (l. 90) a genuinely personal variation of the regal formula "long live the Queen".

6. *James Callaghan alludes to the past, when Crown and Parliament were "bitter historical rivals" (l. 5). Summarize some historic events that are considered of great importance for the development of the British political system.*
[For answers cf. "Info-Box", SB, pp. 88 ff.]

7. *How does Callaghan's use of metaphors help to describe the relationship between Parliament and the Crown?*
Describing Parliament as the flywheel and the Crown as the fixed centre, he first of all stresses the interdependence of the two institutions. He also shows how they support each other, with the Crown particularly responsible for stability and continuity and Parliament for perpetual mobility and political change. These metaphors mean that the political lives of prime ministers depend on election results, while "the Queen remains on stage" (ll. 20–21), independent of all political changes, although the Crown must constantly adapt to these.

8. *Discuss the importance of a country having a head of state. Do you prefer having an elected head of state to the British system? Give reasons for your answer.*
[The teacher may want to add the US system with its combined head of state and head of government to the discussion. When discussing this question, students should not neglect the different historical backgrounds of the UK and the Federal Republic of Germany and should pay attention to the fact that political structures cannot simply be transferred from one country to another.]

9. *West Germany's popular press offers quite a lot of coverage of the British monarchy. Why do you suppose the British monarchy fascinates so many people in this country?*
– –

3 Spencer Reiss, Donna Foote: New Life in the House of Lords

Didaktische Hinweise

Auch dieser Text beschäftigt sich mit einer der staatstragenden Institutionen und bildet daher mit dem vorausgehenden Text 2 und dem folgenden Text 4 eine inhaltliche Sequenz. Abgesehen davon, daß das House of Lords als eine Klammer, die Geschichte und Gegenwart verbindet, verstanden werden kann, rechtfertigt sich die Aufnahme dieser *interpretive news story* auch dadurch, daß in den letzten Jahren über kaum eine Institution so heftig diskutiert wurde wie über das House of Lords. Hinzu kommt, daß seine auf Ausgleich und Mäßigung angelegte Funktion besonders an Bedeutung gewinnt, wenn im House of Commons eine Regierung die Mehrheit hat, die bei ihren Entscheidungen auf einen breiten gesellschaftlichen Konsens verzichtet, den Kompromiß eher als Schwäche ansieht und die Konfrontation nicht scheut.

Background information

The House of Lords consists of almost 1,200 members who can be divided into four main categories: bishops, Lords who have inherited their titles, Lords who have been given their titles for life, and Law Lords. The reason for the existence and composition of the House of Lords is historical: it goes back to the medieval King's Council, to which the great nobles and churchmen were summoned. The ancient Council was also the highest court of justice in the kingdom.

The Lords Spiritual, as the bishops are called, consist of the Archbishops of Canterbury and York, the Bishops of London, Durham and Winchester and the twenty-one most senior bishops of the Church of England. All the other peers are known as Lords Temporal. About 800 of them are hereditary peers, many of whose titles go back far in history. In 1963 they were allowed to renounce their titles, if they so wished, thus enabling them to sit in the House of Commons. The two most prominent examples are Tony Benn, formerly Lord Stansgate, and Sir Alex Douglas-Home ['dʌgləs 'hjuːm], formerly Lord Home, who was then able to become prime minister (1963–1964). Although it was assumed that no hereditary peers would ever again be created, Margaret Thatcher made William Whitelaw a hereditary viscount in 1983 and Harold Macmillan a hereditary earl in 1987.

Life peerages, created in 1958 by Harold Macmillan, have been given to several hundred people, including a few women, and have helped change the tone of the House of Lords. Life peerages are given by the Queen, who follows the Prime Minister's selection. They are considered a means of rewarding political or personal friends, of "promoting" members of the House of Commons to the House of Lords, and of honouring distinguished people from the world of art, business, trade unions, academic institutions, etc.

There are 28 Law Lords. Nine of them are judges who have been given a life peerage in order to enable them to sit on the highest court of appeal in England. The Lord Chancellor, who presides over the debates as the "speaker" of the Lords, is the highest legal officer in England, as well as being a member of the Cabinet and of the monarch's private council, the Privy Council.

Not all members attend the House. On average there are about 300 Lords who choose to take part in the work of the House. The large number of Lords who do not attend the House are known as "backwoodsmen". The Lords receive no salary but are paid small expenses.

The work of the House of Lords is complementary to the work of the House of Commons. It reviews, examines and revises bills from the Commons. The debates are often more thoughtful than in the Commons, as the Lords are not pressed for time to such an extent as MPs in the Commons are, nor are they answerable to political masters. They can make amendments to bills or delay bills for one year (except for financial bills, which can be delayed for only four weeks). The Lords, like the Commons, has the duty to control the Government, and to make government ministers answer for their decisions and actions.

A very important function of the Lords is its legal work. Cases of public importance where a point of law is in question are heard by the Law Lords. Their decision is final, as they form the highest court of appeal. The Lords also plays an important role in the law-making process of the European Community (cf. p. 8 of this book). All European proposals are closely reviewed in a special committee; its reports on the effects of a proposed law are considered by the government to be an important factor in the process of reaching a decision as to whether a proposal should become law or not.

"reports of the death of the House of Lords are greatly exaggerated" (ll. 7–9): This is a reference to one of Mark Twain's most quoted remarks, "The report of my death was an exaggeration." He wrote these words to a newspaper which had published his obituary slightly prematurely.

"the lower house" (l. 39): the House of Commons consisting of 650 members (MPs) who are elected by universal suffrage in constituencies throughout the UK. There are 523 seats for England, 72 for Scotland, 38 for Wales and 17 for Northern Ireland. All British citizens, and Irish and Commonwealth citizens resident in the UK, are eligible to vote and stand in a general election. Between 1978 and 1987 the salaries of MPs nearly doubled to stand at £ 18,500; MPs may also receive allowances for secretaries, travel and overnight accommodation.

As the supreme legislative authority in the UK, Parliament's main function is to pass laws, to carry out the work of government and to scrutinize government policy. In practice virtually all the power is concentrated in the Commons and more specifically in the government of the day (especially when it has a large majority). Most bills are introduced in the House of Commons by the government, but private member bills may also be introduced. The procedure is as follows: An MP proposes a motion, the Speaker proposes the motion as a subject of debate, and at the end of the debate, a vote is taken. If the majority of the MPs vote in favour of the bill becoming law, it is passed to the House of Lords; if not, it is rejected.

Semantic and collocational field "Parliament"
a legislative body, an unwritten constitution ✧ a prime minister, a powerful head of government ✧ the House of Lords, the Lords, the upper chamber/house, an unelected institution, the world's oldest legislative body, a life peer, (to) hold a hereditary title ✧ the Commons, the lower house, "the other place", a leader of a party, a majority in the Commons ✧ legislation, a defeat for the government, (to) defeat/scotch a bill, (to) reject a government plan, (to) reform the upper house ✧ a Labor-backed move, a lopsided Tory majority ✧ a debate, (to) trample democratic freedoms

Talking about the text – Suggested answers
1. The House of Lords consists of nearly 1,200 non-elected peers, about 800 of whom are hereditary peers (Royal Dukes, Dukes, Earls, Viscounts, etc.). In addition there are the two archbishops and the 24 most senior bishops of the Church of England. Some 350 members have been given their seats by receiving a life peerage. They are usually people near the end of a distinguished career in their professional or political lives. So the House of Lords does look somewhat like an old people's home, with the average age on the increase.
2. In 1215 the barons and bishops enumerated a number of abuses of rights by the king and declared them illegal. Royal decisions were made dependent on the consent of Parliament. When Margaret Thatcher's Government decided to abolish the Greater London Council and to cancel local elections, the Lords stepped in. They rejected the Government's plan, in which they saw nothing but an abuse of democratic power. They delayed the bill, convinced that "they have a duty to guard our unwritten Constitution" (ll. 27–29), as Lord Bethell put it.

3. The larger the majority of the Government in the Commons, the greater the temptation to rush legislation through the House of Lords and to disregard the proposals or resistance of the Opposition – the Tories' apparent abuse of power and the introduction of highly controversial bills have given the Lords the chance to act as a kind of balancing counterforce, compelling the Government to compromise. This is made clear by the three examples given in the text: the Lords were able to avert the proposed sale of council houses which would have been a severe social injustice; they were also successful in their fight against violations of human rights such as the use of telephone taps by the government or the stop-and-search powers of the police.

4. Lord Mowbray is right when he puts forward the view that the members of the House of Lords do not depend on demands or claims of a constituency, do not constantly have to consider the question of re-election, but are able to discuss important matters in all objectivity. Party discipline in the House of Lords is not as strong as in the House of Commons. On the other hand, considering the hereditary and rather conservative background of most of them, the Lords are not free from special interests either. And of course, there is the age problem, with most of the life peers in their 60s, and as one consequence, the irregular attendance and large-scale absenteeism.

5. The introductory pun "living proof of life after death" (ll. 2–3) is used to catch the readers' attention at this point. The mention of others who have described the House of Lords as a "geriatric day-care center" (l. 4) is similarly intended to build up interest in a topic which is normally not of great interest to foreign readers. Quoting Jeremy Thorpe, the authors might also have speculated on their readers' recollection of a spectacular murder case he was involved in a few years ago.
   The two quotations in ll. 27–30 and ll. 71–77 clearly counteract the laughable effect made at the beginning. Two Lords, aged 46 and 61, who take an active part in the political work of the House of Lords, show where the importance of the upper chamber lies today, thus supporting the message of the article as a whole.

6. Certain facts and explanations are given that would not be necessary in a text for a predominantly British readership, e.g. giving London as the place of publication for the "Times" (l. 11), explaining the term "life peers" (ll. 52–54), mentioning "former coal miners" or "a card-carrying Communist" (ll. 55–56) as members, describing the ritualistic way of speaking (cf. ll. 58–60).

7. *What other, non-legislative function does the House of Lords have?*
   The House of Lords also acts as the highest court of appeal. There are only 28 Lords, the so-called Law Lords, engaged in this work. They include the Lord Chancellor and distinguished judges who have held high judicial office.

4 Anthony Sampson: A Disaster for the Middle

Didaktische Hinweise

Text 4 beschäftigt sich mit den im House of Commons vertretenen Parteien und mit dem britischen Mehrheitswahlrecht. Zwar stehen die Situation der Social Democratic Party und die Chancen einer dritten Partei, die politisch zwischen den beiden großen Parteien angesiedelt ist, im Mittelpunkt der Ausführungen von Anthony Sampson, doch werden auch die politischen Grundsätze und Ziele der Konservativen und der Labour Party in Umrissen deutlich (vgl. "Background information", unten). Thematisch bestehen enge Bezüge zu Text 2 und 3 dieses Kapitels, aber auch zu Bill Hewitts et al. Beitrag über Großbritannien als eine "divided nation" (Kap. III, Text 2). Sampsons Bemerkung "The American parallels are becoming closer" (Z. 130–

131) kann darüber hinaus zum Anlaß genommen werden, auf die Parteien in den USA einzugehen (vgl. Kap. VIII, Text 5).

Ohne Frage befindet sich das britische Zwei-Parteien-System im ausgehenden 20. Jahrhundert in einer instabilen Phase, die noch deutlicher würde, wenn das von den Liberalen – und von der SDP – immer wieder geforderte Verhältniswahlrecht eingeführt würde. Die Ergebnisse der beiden Parlamentswahlen 1983 und 1987 zeigen, daß es zumindest im Bereich des Möglichen lag, daß das traditionelle Zwei-Parteien-System abgelöst würde durch ein Mehrparteienspektrum. Auch eine Umkehr des Kräfteverhältnisses zwischen den seit 1918 aus der Regierungsverant-wortung entlassenen Liberalen und Labour war vorstellbar.

Background information

Anthony Sampson: cf. p. 71 of this book.

Britain's present party system can be dated back to the 17th century, when two political parties arose from the political groupings of the "Cavaliers" (supporting the king) and the "Roundheads" (opposing the king). But it was only after the restoration of the monarchy in 1660 that a parliamentary party system came into being, one group being called Tories and the other being called Whigs. The Tories supported the interests of the Monarchy and the Church, while the Whigs represented the interests of the upper nobility and the wealthy merchants, demanded religious and political tolerance and emphasized the role of Parliament. Over the centuries the two parties developed into the modern Conservative and Liberal parties.

The *Conservative Party* is one of the two large parties in Britain, being the major right-wing party. It received its present name in the 1830s. Throughout the 19th century it pursued a strict imperialist policy and was responsible for the formation and development of the Empire.

The Conservatives' political identity has always been determined by the conflict between two ideological positions: a humane capitalism (enterprise without selfishness, property-owning democracy and partnership in industry) on the one hand and an aggressively competitive free enterprise on the other. In the 1970s and 1980s this conflict was decided in favour of the latter doctrine when Margaret Thatcher pursued the political and economic policies now known as Thatcherism, marked by increased private enterprise, the cutting of public expenditure, denationalization, the curbing of trade union power and the fight against inflation by controlling the flow of money. Present-day Conservative government ideology is determined by two groups: the libertarian and organic Conservatives. The former believe that the state should have minimum control over industry and enterprise and that individuals should be responsible for ordering their own lives, while the latter accepts the free market economy but believes that government should be politically authoritarian, regulating various aspects of its citizens' lives.

The Labour Party is the other large party in Britain. It supports the interests of the working classes as opposed to those of the employers, and describes itself as a "democratic socialist" party. It draws its support mainly from the highly urban centres and industrialized areas in the North of England and the Midlands, and has also strongholds in Wales and Scotland. Although it is predominantly the party of the working classes, it is also supported by middle-class workers, particularly by intellectuals.

The origins of the Labour Party go back to the end of the 19th century when, following the Reform Bill of 1867, urban working men were given the right to vote. They organized themselves in trade unions, and tried to get representatives into the House of Commons. In 1900 the Labour Representation Committee was founded as a merger of four labour movements – among them the Fabian Society (with its prominent member George Bernard Shaw), a group founded by intellectuals, which still has some influence on the party's policy. In 1906 the Labour Party first took its name, and in that year returned 29 members to the House of Commons. During the following years it continued to gain in strength, while the Liberals declined in importance. By 1918 it had become the official Opposition representing 57 constituencies. Since 1923, when Labour formed a minority government, the party has alternated fairly regularly with the Conservatives in governing Britain.

The Labour Party's policies are closely connected with those of the trade union movement. It introduced the National Health Service in 1946 (cf. pp. 58 f. of this book), the Comprehensive School System in 1965 (cf. p. 47 of this book) and favours the nationalization of important industries, unilateral disarmament and the abolition of nuclear weapons. Fierce political struggles within the party, together with a drift towards the left in the 1970s, caused four prominent Labour politicians – the "Gang of Four" (l. 75, cf. also below) – to leave the party and found the SDP.

The Liberal Party ceased to exist in 1988, when it merged with the Social Democratic Party to form the Social and Liberal Democratic Party (for information on both these parties cf. below). The Liberal Party went back to the Whig Party, which changed its name to the Liberal Party in 1839. It became the party of reform, of freedom of thought and action and brought about many political changes while in government. With the rise of the Labour Party it lost its influence. Although the party's support in the country was much greater than reflected by its representation in the House of Commons, it became paralyzed by the British electoral system. In order to overcome this disadvantage it joined forces with the newly formed SDP in the so-called Alliance.

The *Social Democratic Party* (SDP) was formed in 1981 when it seemed as though the Conservatives under Margaret Thatcher were moving to the right, while Labour was moving to the left, leaving a political vacuum in the centre. Some dissatisfied members of the Labour Party – Shirley Williams, Roy Jenkins, David Owen and Bill Rodgers were the most prominent among them – left the Labour Party and founded the SDP to offer a moderate and pragmatic political platform between the two extremes to the voter. In all, 14 Labour MPs left the party and gave the SDP a flying start in Parliament. Influenced by the German SPD, a party platform was drawn up that gained considerable support from middle-class voters. One of the main issues was, of course, to replace the British first-past-the-post electoral system with proportional representation. In order to overcome the handicaps of the present system and to concentrate the opposition forces, the SDP and the Liberals formed the Alliance in 1981. The 1987 election, however, made it quite clear that the two leaders, David Owen and David Steele, did not succeed in convincing the voter of their common political goals and a common strategy. The failure of the Alliance in the 1987 election caused a majority of the SDP party members to ballot for a merger with the Liberal Party (cf. below). David Owen refused to accept the merger and with a few supporters has formed a new SDP around him.

The *Social and Liberal Democratic Party* is Britain's newest party, founded in 1988, from a merger between the Liberal Party and the SDP. It seeks to occupy the centre ground of British politics. As yet, its future is uncertain, having failed, in the form of the Alliance, to have made a significant impact in the general elections of 1983 and 1987.

Among the other minor parties only two need be mentioned here: The Scottish National Party and Plaid Cymru (the Welsh national party).
    Plaid Cymru was originally a Welsh cultural organization, but became a political force in the 1960s and won its first seat in 1966. It campaigns for cultural, political and economic independence, i.e. the separation of Wales from the United Kingdom
    The Scottish National Party (SNP) advocates the separation of Scotland from the United Kingdom for nearly the same reasons. It was founded in 1928 and reached its climax in the 1970s when the cry for devolution was loudest and when in the 1974 general election they won 30 % of the Scottish vote and returned 11 MPs. As devolution is no longer a political issue, the nationalist parties have lost their influence.
    Northern Ireland has different political parties unrelated to those in Great Britain (cf. "Background information", p. 94 of this book).

"Breaking the Mould": allusion to the title of a book by Ian Bradley, *Breaking the Mould?: Birth and Prospects of the Social Democratic Party*. (Martin Robertson, Oxford, 1981). It describes the birth of the SDP in the context of the political situation of the 1970s, which is characterized by an ideological split between the right and the left in the Labour Party and by the economic and geographical division of Britain into two nations, into one of affluence and one of poverty, into South and North (cf. also p. 55 of this book).

"the polarization between right and left" (ll. 19–20): Unlike other European democracies, the British system of government is very much a two-party system, in which power is concentrated almost exclusively in the House of Commons. The arrival of the SDP in 1981 and the formation of the Alliance effectively split the opposition vote, and gave the Conservatives a large majority in the Commons. This state of affairs caused Lord Hailsham (cf. p. 92 of this book) to warn of an "elective dictatorship" and Francis Pym, a former Conservative Cabinet minister, to describe the lack of a strong opposition as unhealthy. In a country without checks and balances, with no written constitution or a modern bill of rights, the legislative power of the Commons has increased, and accordingly the power of central government, as the strong party organization ensures that virtually all legislation introduced into the Commons by the government is "ramrodded through" (l. 39).
    To counteract this, a group of liberal intellectuals drew up a manifesto called Charter 88 (which takes its name from the Czech human rights movement Charter 77) and launched a campaign to change the way Britain is governed,

through the introduction of proportional representation, a written constitution and a bill of rights. The Charter 88 campaign coincided with the third centenary of the Glorious Revolution, when the absolutist monarch James II was removed from the throne. It is unlikely, however, that Parliament will introduce any reform measures, but nevertheless Charter 88 is one more statement against the presumed inadequacies of the British parliamentary system.

"the 'Gang of Four'" (l. 75): This term has its origins in Chinese politics. After Mao Zedung's death in 1976, his widow and three other Maoists attempted to return China to the political doctrines of Mao. They were referred to as the "Gang of Four". The term was given to David Owen, Shirley Williams (cf. p. 10 of this book), Roy Jenkins and Bill Rodgers, who desired a return to more moderate Labour policies.

Semantic and collocational field "Party system"

a victory in the general election, an electoral system, a credible party of government, (to) begin another term ✧ (to) gain a quarter of the total vote, (to) take 23 percent of the vote, (to) attract voters ✧ a traditional voter, a supporter, an opponent ✧ a strong leader, a parliamentary seat ✧ the traditional alternation between Conservative and Labour, the two-party mould of British politics, (to) be stuck with a two-party system, the electoral system works against (a party), to split the vote ✧ a realignment/reform of the British political system, a place/strong case for a third party, (to) break the mould of British politics, (to) support/launch a new political grouping, to promote/maintain a third force/party, (to) found a party, (to) move a party closer to the middle ground ✧ a polarization between right and left, (to) become more militant, the opposition is divided ✧ the left wing of the Labour Party, Labour's policies, the dogmas of the left, (to) be realistic about defence/the economy ✧ a party's future, the future looks bleak

Talking about the text – Suggested answers

1. Sampson states that the "mold" (l. 16), i.e. the British two-party system, has not yet been broken. At least this is what the 1987 election results show. It is therefore doubtful whether there is still a place for a third party (the SDP has been turned into a factor of such minor importance that he speaks of humiliation). He feels, however, that there is still a strong need for a third force in British politics. The situation that originally led Anthony Sampson to support the SDP has remained the same or even got worse. This means that, as Sampson says, "the argument for some kind of realignment, and reform of the British political system, is now stronger than ever" (ll. 91–93).
2. He was hoping for a change in British politics, for an alternative to the "traditional alternation between Conservatives and Labor" (ll. 17–18), i.e. for the end of the two-party system. He was supporting a third political force in order to overcome the polarization which, according to him, has become a dangerous feature of the British political, social and geographical landscape.
3. First of all he thinks the polarization between the Conservatives and Labour damaging to the real interests of Britain. As the economic and social problems of the country become more and more serious he has become convinced that the Labour Party would not be able to solve them. In his eyes the Labour Party has been drifting too far to the left, thus increasing the polarization between left and right, rich and poor, north and south, instead of bridging the gap. Labour under its leader Michael Foot had become unrealistic about defence and the economy. Even with Neil Kinnock as its leader, the Labour Party does not seem to be the party to oppose Thatcherism effectively. In Sampson's view, the

militant left wing of the Labour Party will cause trouble that may even result in a split in the party. A Labour Party that is holding on to its "old dogmas of the left" (l. 147) does not seem able to find new answers for a new generation of workers.

4. The British electoral system works best when there are no more than two major political parties competing for power. It becomes unfair and its outcome no longer represents the views of the electorate the moment a third political grouping takes up the fight for parliamentary seats. The reason for this is quite simple. Each constituency returns only one MP. The winning candidate is the candidate who gets the most votes. All the other votes given to the other candidates – which may add up to over 50 % – are lost. Nationwide this can – and frequently does – mean that a party has a majority of seats in Parliament without having won a majority of votes in the election (cf. also diagram, SB, p. 98). It could even mean that a party might win, say, 20 % of the votes and not get a seat in Parliament at all. The reason for this is the geographical distribution of the votes or the voters' residence pattern.

   In the 1987 election not a single constituency in the South of England was won by Labour, just as the Tories are hardly represented in the industrial North of England or in Scotland. The votes for the Alliance on the other hand were scattered all over the country. This shows that the two big parties are supported by different social groups who live in distinctly different parts of the country and who make up the safe seats of their respective party. For a party like the Alliance, which cuts across all social groups instead of finding its voters concentrated in one area, it is therefore impossible to win one of the safe Labour or Tory seats. It is very difficult for them to win even one of the marginal seats.

5. Italy is known for political instability. Governments there are toppled quite frequently, due to factionalism. Political violence – terrorism – is often the result. Sampson foresees such consequences in Britain, and he uses Neil Kinnock's words "abyss of division" (l. 94) to describe the state of affairs. The writer sees Britain already as a divided nation – even to the point of saying that different regions have their own prime minister in spirit if not in fact. There is the danger of separatism – not only in Scotland or Wales – and there is the danger of violence and terrorism – not only in Northern Ireland.

6. **What, according to Sampson, is the lesson the opposition should learn from parties in the USA?**

   They must – as new American parties already do – learn to work "within the existing structure" (ll. 137–138), i.e. accept the realities of a two-party system. That means that all the opposition forces must unite to defeat the Tories. In order to do this, extreme views, "the old dogmas of the left" (l. 147), will have to be abandoned. Individuals and groups with very diverse views must "come together in a broader coalition" (ll. 151–152). The result would be less like a typical European political party, but rather like the loosely structured Democratic Party in the US.

7. **How is the opposition's problem of gaining a majority dealt with in the Federal Republic of Germany?**

   In the Federal Republic of Germany, the electoral system gives smaller parties a better chance of getting into Parliament. Once in Parliament, political parties may form coalition governments or unite in opposition, usually without having to give up their own identity.

● 8. *Find out about the history of the other major parties in Britain: when and under what circumstances they were founded, major turning points, etc. Report your findings to the class.*
   – –

5 Jasper Ridley: The Birth of the Established Church

Didaktische Hinweise

Die Texte 5 und 6 behandeln das Thema „Kirche und Staat". Während sich Text 5 unter historischem Aspekt mit der Gründung der englischen Staatskirche beschäftigt und verdeutlicht, wie stark Henry VIII. in Belange Roms eingriff und sich schließlich zum weltlichen Haupt der Anglikanischen Kirche ernannte, greift Text 6 anhand eines aktuellen Ereignisses die Frage auf, wie weit die Kirche zu politischen Tagesereignissen, hier den Wahlaussagen der Konservativen anläßlich der Parlamentswahlen von 1987, Stellung nehmen darf. Sie rührt an ein grundsätzliches, nicht nur für Großbritannien geltendes Problem, und so liegt es nahe, Vergleiche mit der Bundesrepublik (vgl. Aufg. 7 zu Text 6, LB, S. 93) und den Vereinigten Staaten (vgl. Kap. VI, Text 1–6; Kap. VII, Text 6 c) zu ziehen.

Background information

In 1509, Henry VIII succeeded to the throne, not quite 18 years of age. Soon after his accession, he married his elder brother's widow, Catherine of Aragon. This marriage was made possible by a papal dispensation which had been obtained by Henry's father, Henry VII.

It was this dispensation which caused problems when Henry VIII decided to divorce Catherine some twenty years later. She had only produced one heir, the Princess Mary. Henry, however, wanted a male heir to the Tudor throne, and felt that God was punishing him for having married his sister-in-law. His strategy was to prove to Pope Clement IV that the dispensation obtained from Pope Julius II was invalid and consequently he had, in theory, never been married. This would have enabled him to marry Anne Boleyn, his mistress. However Clement IV, who was, in the first place, reluctant to declare an earlier exercise of papal power illegal, was also the prisoner of Emperor Charles V, Catherine of Aragon's nephew. For personal and political reasons Charles was opposed to an annulment and prevented the Pope from acting.

When the divorce proceedings reached a standstill, Henry dismissed his Lord Chancellor, Cardinal Wolsey, and summoned Parliament. He appointed Thomas Cranmer, a man of Protestant leanings, Archbishop of Canterbury, who then declared Henry's marriage to Catherine null and void. To protect the annulment, Parliament, which for the first time in English history worked together with the king, passed legislation which separated England from Rome. Among other bills, they passed the Act of Supremacy, which declared that the king of England was the Head of the Church of England. Dignitaries who denied the royal supremacy, such as Sir Thomas More, were executed. The monasteries were destroyed, which made the Crown immensely rich, but did not indicate a sympathy for Protestantism. Royal supremacy was not the basis of a development towards religious reformation, but rather a convenience for the king. He always believed in Catholicism – without a Pope.

Semantic and collocational field "The church"

the Pope, papal supremacy, the Bishop of Rome ✧ royal supremacy, the Established Church, the head of the Church ✧ a bishop, a parish priest, a preacher, a reformer, a parishioner ✧ a parish church, a churchyard, a prayer book, a holy day, (to) attend Mass, (to) go on a pilgrimage ✧ a pulpit, the power of the sermon, (to) preach to sb. (e.g. the people), (to) preach with/without a licence ✧ a doctrine, the Word of God, justification by faith, a miracle, the threat of hellfire and eternal damnation ✧ a religious revolution, a vehicle for political propaganda, a heretic, (to) spread sedition and heresy, (to) attack an established doctrine, (to) denounce sb./sth. ✧ (to) have authority (in a country), (to) obey sb.

Talking about the text – Suggested answers

1. By censorship: every trace of the Pope had to be erased from the prayer books.
    By indoctrination: the clergy had to convince the people that from now on the king was the Supreme Head of the Church, and to make the people accept the new situation without questioning.
    By intimidation: the clergy were in trouble and even physical danger if they did not comply with the king's wishes.
2. The power and the influence preachers had in those days were considerable. As people were obliged to attend church, the preachers had a unique platform from which to reach the people. As representatives of God they were at the same time agents of ultimate punishment. Those who were not impressed by the threat of hell-fire or eternal damnation could normally be influenced by the threat of worldly punishment. Thus a parish priest had always to be considered by the government as a potential seducer or agitator of the masses. And as there were no mass media in those times, the government or the king had nothing to counterbalance the clergy's influence.
3. In 1534 Henry was primarily interested in establishing a new church and not in theological revolution. In order to accustom people to the new situation it was necessary to avoid theological controversy. Besides, too much unrest could have been a threat to Henry's control.
● 4. *Find out from a biography to what extent Henry's private life influenced his official decision to break with Rome.*
        – –
● 5. *Read Shakespeare's "King Henry VIII" and describe how the royal divorce is treated in the play.*
        – –

6 Colin Hughes: The Bishop and the Lord

Didaktische Hinweise

Auch Text 6 beschäftigt sich mit dem Thema „Kirche und Staat". Der in Text 5 angesprochene Fragenkomplex – das Verhältnis von weltlicher und kirchlicher Macht – hat nichts von seiner Brisanz verloren und wird hier aus heutiger Sicht und anhand eines konkreten Einzelfalls erörtert. Eine Vertiefung der behandelten Problematik läßt sich durch einen Vergleich mit der Situation in der Bundesrepublik (vgl. Aufg. 7, unten) und den Vereinigten Staaten (vgl. Kap. VI, Text 2, 4, 5) erreichen.

Der streitbare, sozial engagierte Bischof von Durham hat seine Gegner nicht zur Ruhe kommen lassen. Ende 1988 erschienen seine Bücher *God, Politics and the Future.*

God, Jesus and Life in the Spirit. God, Miracle and the Church of England. (London, SCM Press), in der Öffentlichkeit als "confounding the critics" angekündigt.

Background information

In Britain everyone has the right of religious freedom without interference. Whether or not one belongs to a denomination does not matter for the holding of public office. Only the Sovereign must be a member of the Church of England.

There are two established churches, that is, churches legally recognized as official churches of the State: in England it is the Church of England (Anglican), in Scotland it is the Church of Scotland (Presbyterian). About one-sixth of the adult population of Britain are members of a Christian church: England 13 %, Wales 23 %, Scotland 37 % and Northern Ireland 80 %. There has been a decline in recent years in the recorded adult membership of the larger Christian denominations, accompanied by a significant growth of new religious movements.

Churches and religious societies may run schools that are partly or wholly maintained with public money. Clergymen who work in the armed forces, national hospitals and prisons are normally members of the established churches and are paid by the State. The State does not directly fund the churches. There is no church-tax as in Germany, so churches rely mostly on donations and returns on investments.

The Church of England: It was created in the 16th century as a Protestant church by the Act of Supremacy, when Henry VIII broke with Rome and made the Sovereign the only Supreme Head of the Church (cf. also p. 89 of this book). Archbishops, bishops and deans are appointed by the Sovereign on the Prime Minister's advice. The two Archbishops (Canterbury as the head of the Church, and York as the deputy religious head), the bishops of London, Durham and Winchester, and 21 other bishops sit in the House of Lords.

The Church of Scotland: It is completely free to control its own spiritual matters. It is governed by elders who are all of equal rank. Its status as the national church goes back to the early 18th century and to the Church of Scotland Act of 1921, which confirmed its complete freedom in all spiritual questions. Both men and women are admitted to the ministry, without interference by the State.

The Roman Catholic Church: After the break with Rome, the Catholic Church was outlawed and only restored in 1850. Today it is the second largest denomination in the United Kingdom.

The Free Churches: All the Protestant churches which are not established are called Free Churches. Among them are the Methodists, Baptists, United Reformed and Salvation Army. They are totally independent of the State. There are also other denominations which serve the West Indian community.

For decades cooperation between the Church of England and the Conservative Party was so close that the Anglican Church was sometimes called the "Tory Party at prayer". This has changed in recent years, since the Church has become more active in social and political matters; for example, several bishops have questioned the uncompromising free market conservatism of Prime Minister Thatcher. In 1983 the

Archbishop of Canterbury, Dr. Robert Runcie, appointed a commission which was to examine "the strengths, insights, problems and needs of the Church's life and mission in Urban Priority Areas and ... to reflect on the challenge which God may be making to Church and Nation: and to make recommendations to appropriate bodies". The outcome was the commission's publication *Faith in the City*. (Central Board of Finance of the Church of England, 1985), one of the most important and controversial documents in modern Britain.

"Lord Hailsham ... as a former Lord Chancellor" (ll. 1–2): Quintin McGarel Hogg, Lord Hailsham of Saint Marylebone (1907–   ), Lord High Chancellor 1970–1974 and 1979–1987.

The Lord (High) Chancellor is the chief legal officer in England and Wales; he is responsible for the administration of justice. Besides being a member of the Cabinet and of the Privy Council, he is also the Speaker of the House of Lords.

"The Bishop of Durham" (l. 3): The Rt. Rev. David E. Jenkins (1925 –   ) has been a controversial figure since his appointment in 1984. He is a liberal theologian who has questioned several tenets of the Christian faith and criticized various policies of the Conservative government, making him unpopular with both High Churchmen and right-wing politicians.

Semantic and collocational field "Religion and politics"

a clergyman, the clergy, a layman, the laity, a Christian ✧ the relations between politics, law and morality ✧ a secular subject, a moral issue/principle, a belief ✧ (to) pontificate to the laity, (to) be better informed than sb. on sth., (to) require instruction on sth. ✧ a wide range of political views or affications, (to) have a/no place in politics, (to) have a/no special standing in politics

Talking about the text – Suggested answers

1. The Bishop had criticized Tory policy as a free market policy that shows no regard for the poor and had described the motives of people who voted for the Conservatives as self-interest.
2. Lord Hailsham calls the Bishop of Durham "stupid" (l. 3) and of "intellectual limitations" (cf. ll. 35–36). He accuses him of treating laymen in the same way medieval bishops treated illiterate peasants (cf. ll. 14–16; ll. 43–45). He considers him unable to understand how free market policies work (cf. ll. 66–84) and he implies that the Bishop is using his office to give his words an authority they are actually lacking.
3. Lord Hailsham does not believe members of the clergy have any special authority when talking about politics; in fact, he feels they know even less than the average person about secular matters (cf. ll. 30–31). In his view, there is no "evidence that the intelligent laity require instruction on moral principles, from persons of the intellectual limitations of the Bishop of Durham" (ll. 33–36).
4. In the Bishop's opinion, the impact of free market forces is disadvantageous for the less fortunate and poor people. These forces work in favour of the strong, the fortunate and the rich, who then become stronger and richer than ever before. It is therefore clear that people who vote Tory do so out of self-interest, hoping to install a government that will not put restraints on their attempts to follow their interests and improve their lot – at the cost of the poor.
   Lord Hailsham rejects this view and contradicts the Bishop. According to the Lord, the Bishop has made mistakes in his analysis of the economic situation and does not really

understand how the free market works in Britain. It is not a totally free market ruled by the law of the jungle, where the strong push the weak out of the market to become stronger and stronger, but it is restrained by the regulatory powers of the government. People, including the poor, are protected by the law.

5. Only in the first paragraph does the writer put forward his own opinion, which he immediately backs up with supporting evidence in the second paragraph. Apart from the first paragraph, the whole article consists of direct or indirect quotations or of factual information. In order to make it clear to the reader what the Lord's criticism is all about the author mentions what the Bishop said after the election. Thus the writer avoids having to take sides in the controversy.

6. – –

7. **Compare the relationship between Church and State in England and in the Federal Republic of Germany.**
– –

7 Peter Carter: Things Weren't as Nice as They Had Been

Didaktische Hinweise

Die drei letzten Texte dieses Kapitels – und damit des ausschließlich Großbritannien gewidmeten Teils – lenken die Aufmerksamkeit auf die Nordirland-Problematik. Der fiktionale Text 7 schildert eine Episode aus dem Leben zweier Jugendlicher in Belfast, unmittelbar vor dem Ausbruch der Gewalttätigkeiten im Jahr 1968, und ihre Freundschaft, die über die Religionsgrenzen hinweg allen äußeren und inneren Bedrohungen standhält. Paul Theroux (Text 8) läßt in seiner zu Beginn der achtziger Jahre entstandenen impressionistischen Beschreibung der Stadt ein düsteres Bild der "awful city" entstehen. Drei Jahre später berichteten amerikanische Journalisten von ihren (gedämpft optimistischen) Eindrücken, die sie bei einem Besuch Belfasts gewonnen hatten (Text 9). Diese drei Texte, zu unterschiedlichen Zeiten entstanden und von unterschiedlicher Wirkungsabsicht, bilden eine thematische Einheit. Da gerade in der Nordirland-Frage historische Zusammenhänge von entscheidender Bedeutung sind, sollte bei der Arbeit mit diesen Texten die "Info-Box" (SB, S. 106 f.) herangezogen werden.

Peter Carters Roman *Under Goliath* (Oxford, Oxford University Press 1977), aus dem dieses Exzerpt stammt, ist als Paperback-Ausgabe erhältlich (Harmondsworth, Puffin Story Books 1980). Um den spontanen Zugang zu dem hier angebotenen Exzerpt zu gewährleisten, wurde der Aufgabenapparat wiederum im LB untergebracht.

Eine vertiefende Behandlung der Nordirland-Frage wird sowohl fiktionale als auch nicht-fiktionale Texte einschließen. Zahlreiche Text-Sammlungen sind auf dem Markt, von denen nur einige genannt seien, z.B. *Anglo-Irish Literature. A Reader*. Hrsg. von C. Althammer und R. Breuer. (Unterrichtsmodelle für die Sekundarstufe II, Textsammlung Best.-Nr. 661501, LH 662010); *Modern Irish Short Stories*. Hrsg. von K. Lubbers. (TAGS, Textsammlung Best.-Nr. 666902, LH 666953); *Irische Kurzdramen*. Hrsg. von H. Kosok. (TAGS, Textausgabe Best.-Nr. 667704, LH 667755), alle Frankfurt, Cornelsen Verlag Hirschgraben. *Northern Irish Images*. Hrsg. von S. Gutknecht, V. Hellmann und H. Reid. Berlin, Cornelsen Verlag (Cornelsen Senior English Library, SB Best.-Nr. 52125, LH 52133); *Ireland. Course material for advanced language study.* Ed. by D. Christie. Berlin, Cornelsen & Oxford University Press (The Centre for British Teachers, SB Best.-Nr. 43312, LH 43347).

Background information

Peter Carter (1929–   ) was born in Manchester. He worked on building sites before going to Oxford University to read literature; in 1972 he received his M.A. Since 1973 he has been a professional writer. His main field is the historical novel for teenagers. His works include *The Black Lamp* (1973), *Under Goliath* (1977), from which this excerpt is taken, *The Sentinels* (1980), *Children of the Book* (1982) and *Bury the Dead* (1986).

Belfast, the capital of Northern Ireland, has a population of 303,800 (1987). Situated at the entry of the River Lagan into the Belfast Lough, it was a site of settlement as early as the 12th century. It remained very small until the 17th century, when French Huguenots found refuge in the town and became engaged in the manufacture of linen. The Industrial Revolution made Belfast the most prosperous city in Ulster and one of Britain's leading shipbuilding and engineering centres. Approximately three quarters of the population is Protestant and a quarter is Catholic.

Like other large towns, Belfast is highly segregated. Segregation along religious lines existed before Partition in 1920, but it became firmly established afterwards, especially in the 1960s and 70s when Catholics and Protestants who formed a minority in their area were driven from their homes to areas where their faith was that of the majority. As a consequence West Belfast, centred around the Falls Road, became exclusively Catholic, while the Shankhill Road district became exclusively Protestant. This residential segregation has led to the development of two separate cultural spheres, in which people read different newspapers, attend different schools, and are taught different histories, so that the polarization between the two communities has become greater than ever.

Political parties: The Ulster Unionist Party is the largest and oldest party (founded in 1905) in Northern Ireland. It is a Protestant pro-British party, which from 1921 until 1972 controlled the Northern Irish parliament (Stormont).

The Democratic Unionist Party is a right-wing party in favour of union with Britain. It was founded in 1971, with the Rev. Ian Paisley as its leader. It is more outspoken and anti-Catholic than the Ulster Unionist party.

The Alliance Party was formed in 1970 to unite Catholics and Protestants. It is a moderate middle-of-the-road party.

The Social Democratic and Labour Party is a left-wing, Catholic party. It seeks the unification of Ireland through democratic and peaceful means.

Sinn Fein [ʃɪn'feɪn] was founded in 1905 to unite various competing nationalist bodies in the struggle to win Irish independence. Today it is the political wing of the Provisional IRA, and seeks to justify the use of force to unite Northern Ireland with the Republic of Ireland.

Irish Republican Army (IRA): A militant organization of Irish Catholic nationalists that was founded in 1919 to fight the British. Its significance decreased after

Partition and, although from 1956 to 1962 it waged a campaign of violence and terror against British rule in Northern Ireland, it had very little impact on life in the northern province until the late 1960s. In 1969 the IRA split into an Official and a Provisional wing, both of which wanted Britain to leave Northern Ireland. The Officials, though not giving up violence, took a socialist standpoint and thought change could be brought about in a democratic way, while the Provisionals committed themselves to guerilla warfare.

"Orangeman" (l. 17): member of the pro-Protestant Orange Order, founded by Protestant extremists in 1795 to maintain Protestant supremacy. The name derives from King William of Orange who defeated the Catholic King James II at the Battle of the Boyne (cf. also "Info-Box", SB, pp. 106 f.).

Talking about the text – Suggested answers

1. *What does the text tell us about the background of the two boys?*
   The two boys live in adjoining areas of Belfast. Alan's street is situated in a Protestant area, whereas Fergus Riley, his friend, comes from a Catholic area. Of course, they also belong to different denominations; Alan, the narrator, is Protestant, Fergus is Catholic. Both boys are still at school and both belong to different musical bands. Alan's father works in the shipyards where most of the employees are Protestants, while Fergus's father is employed in a typically "Catholic" firm. The fact that some of the women in Alan's street bought "special bowls so that they would look posh" (l. 3) when they go out of their houses to get water and the fact that some of the people live on social security (cf. ll. 26–28) indicate that the social background is working-class.

2. *Why is there no water in Alan's street?*
   The reservoir was blown up. It is not clear whether this was done by the Catholic I.R.A. or the Protestant U.D.F.

3. *Compare life in Alan's street before and after the bombing. What are the social effects of this act of terror?*
   Before the attack it was nice to live in this street. Catholic families lived next door to Protestants, even to militant Protestants. People looked after each others' houses if they went on holiday or after each others' children if someone had to go to hospital.
   After the bombing of the reservoir all this changed. Mrs Gannon and Mrs O'Keefe are discriminated against, they are socially isolated and even slandered because of their Catholic faith and because the Protestant inhabitants of the street blame the I.R.A. for the bombing.

4. *What does Alan think about these changes?*
   Alan says about Mrs Gannon's and Mrs O'Keefe's treatment by the Protestant women that "it was a pity actually" (l. 11) and "It seemed silly when you thought about it" (ll. 21–22). His comment on the change in general is that "it really was a shame" (l. 29). These somewhat naive comments show that he is very sad about the new situation, but that he is unable to anticipate the short-term development when social isolation could well be followed by physical violence, with Catholics being driven out of the street altogether and eventually seeking retaliation.

5. *If you consider the way the narrator describes the gun, what would you say his attitude towards violence is?*
   The gun is described as an instrument of violence and as a symbol of death. When Alan takes it into his hands after the bombings "it seemed heavier than it had been before" (ll. 33–34). He describes it as "nastier", "slippery", with "a slimy sweat" (ll. 34–35); he uses words that express physical disgust, revulsion and loathing. He creates a similar atmosphere when he describes the cellar where the gun seems to have "been buried"

(l. 36). Just like his friend Fergus he is glad when he can climb out "into the fresh air" (l. 39) again, leaving this atmosphere of discomfort and death behind.

6. *What other signs of division on religious grounds are there in the text?*

   Social discrimination (Mrs Gannon and Mrs O'Keefe versus Mrs Burns), cultural division (different band-practice), political division (different affiliations: I.R.A. – U.D.F.), occupational division and discrimination (different work places: Grady's, Mackies, the Yards), different views of personal future (going to England to find a job – staying in Northern Ireland).

7. *Describe the friendship between Alan and Fergus.*

   Alan and Fergus demonstrate that at that time, friendship across the religious demarcation line was still possible, at least among children and teenagers. They can naively talk about topics such as band-practice, topics that have completely different meanings for adults, since the parades the bands put on are group demonstrations and acts of defiance.

   The relief they both feel when leaving the cellar shows that they both share the same rejection of violence. It is also a very strong sign of friendship when Fergus, who has stolen two packets of cigarettes from his uncle, gives one of them to Alan.

8. *In spite of their friendship, what indications are there that the two boys belong to two different worlds and that they are already influenced by the adults in their worlds?*

   They do not live outside society but in different areas determined largely by religion. Fergus comes from a Catholic neighbourhood, Alan from a predominantly Protestant street, and it is therefore quite natural that they should take the prejudices of their adult worlds for granted and suspect the militants on the other side of having blown up the reservoirs. It becomes obvious that their friendship is susceptible to friction born of prejudice and ignorance if you consider that Alan does not understand Fergus's joke about the shortage of holy water, while Fergus is apparently too embarrassed to tell Alan how many brothers and sisters he has got. It is an open question whether their friendship will last until Fergus goes "over the water" (l. 83) one day.

ೋ 8 Paul Theroux: The Awful City

Didaktische Hinweise

Ebenso wie die Texte 7 und 9 behandelt auch dieser Auszug aus Therouxs Reiseerinnerungen *The Kingdom by the Sea* (1983) einen Aspekt der Nordirland-Problematik. Hier ist es ein amerikanischer Autor, der seine Belfast-Impressionen beschreibt und damit den didaktisch fruchtbaren Vergleich mit den in Text 9 wiedergegebenen Ansichten des Journalisten-Teams geradezu herausfordert (vgl. Text 9, Aufg. 1, SB, S. 111; Aufg. 7, LB, S. 100).

Background information

Paul Theroux [θəˈruː] (1941–   ) was born in Medford, Mass. He spent some years in Africa and then taught at the University of Singapore. Today he lives with his wife and children in London. His first novel, *Waldo,* was published in 1967. His novel *Picture Palace* (1978) won the Whitbread Literary Award, and *Mosquito Coast* (1982) was the *Yorkshire Post* novel of the year. In 1982 he published *London Embassy* which was followed by *The Kingdom by the Sea* in 1983, available as a paperback edition (Penguin Books, Harmondsworth, 1985).

For general information on Northern Ireland and on Belfast cf. "Info-Box" (SB, pp. 106 f.) and p. 94 of this book.

Semantic and collocational field "Terrorism"

an urban guerilla, a threat, a murder, a ruin, terrorist activities ✧ a (new) type of bomb, a fire-bomb, an explosion, a bomb-blast, a detonator, (to) explode, (to) spread fiery fluid, (to) be destroyed/burned/scorched, (to) be worth blowing up, made of explosive fluid ✧ security, a high steel fence, a turnstile for people, a barrier for cars, (to) pass through a checkpoint, (to) be guarded by sb. ✧ a bag search, a metal detector, to check/examine sb./sth., (to) frisk sb.

Talking about the text – Suggested answers

1. The buildings, the people, the smell, the fences. The buildings are mouldering, scorched, with broken windows. The people are tough-looking. There is a frightening routine of frisking and checking. The city's face is crudely distorted by the attempts to protect something which has already been destroyed.

2. He characterizes Belfast as a city that is mad with fear, and at the same time he quotes O'Faoláin, who described it as vulgar and proletarian, materialistic and given to shallow entertainment and quick satisfaction, a city inhabited by "these ... hate-driven poor" (l. 15).

3. First of all, there really *are* bombs. During the author's stay a new bomb has come into use, and ten people are killed. What is particularly nasty about this kind of bomb is the fact that it can hardly be detected and that when it explodes, it spreads its lethal fluid. Then there is the high steel fence around the centre of the city, which does not merely protect the people inside it but, by its very existence, shows how dangerous life is.

4. [Students might mention a kind of morbid motive, out of "horror-interest" (l. 17), a kind of threatening attraction. This view could be supported by describing how the writer rings up the Confidential Telephone number and says "Have a nice day" (l. 34) when he learns that there is only an answering machine. All this makes the writer look almost like a voyeur.]

5. He uses the technique of personification and treats the city as being synonymous with its inhabitants. The city has "a bad face" (l. 1). He calls it "demented" (l. 10), "sick" (l. 11) and describes the state it is in as a "desperate frenzy" (l. 11) and a "death agony" (l. 12). It is narrow-minded, in a sneaky way defiant, tricky and murderous (cf. l. 39). Using this technique, i.e. describing the city as human, the writer gives expression to his fascination, even if it seems to be a somewhat morbid fascination.

6. *Nouns:*; "bombs" (ll. 6, 9, 24, 25, 26, 34), "murder" (ll. 31, 34, 39), "threats" (ll. 30, 31), "explosions" (l. 31), "detonator" (l. 25), "decrepitude" (l. 18), "death agony" (l. 12), "Hell" (l. 29) – "fences" (ll. 2, 19), "checkpoint" (l. 21), "turnstile" (l. 21), "barrier" (l. 21), "barricade" (l. 40).
   Adjectives: "awful" (ll. 1, 10), "bad" (l. 1), "mouldering" (l. 1), "tough-looking" (l. 2), "frightening" (l. 6), "maddening" (ll. 6–7), "scorched" (l. 9), "broken" (l. 9), "demented" (l. 10), "sick" (l. 11), "desperate" (l. 11), "hated" (l. 12), "homeless" (l. 15), "hate-driven" (l. 15), "explosive" (l. 25), "fiery" (l. 25), "threadbare" (l. 37), "blackened" (l. 37), "dangerous" (l. 38), "bellicose" (l. 38), "sneaky" (l. 39), "boarded" (l. 40), "starved" (l. 41), "dirty-faced" (l. 41).
   Verbs: "blow up" (ll. 3, 5), "explode" (l. 25), "burn" (l. 28), "destroy" (l. 28), "guard" (l. 3), "frisk" (l. 3), "check" (l. 4).
   The dominating noun is "bomb". Together with "threat", "murder", "explosion", with "barrier", "barricade" and "checkpoint", it creates an atmosphere of danger, fear and threat. This atmosphere is enhanced by the adjectives and verbs that are used. The adjectives make the city look extremely hostile, almost uninhabitable, unfit for human beings. The main verbs, "blow up" and "check", correspond to the nouns used.

7. The crucifix and the Orange Lodge Widows' Fund badge. The crucifix is worn like a dagger by a brute and the Widows' Fund badge is, of course, also a sign of revenge, violence and death (cf. ll. 42–43). The Catholics who paint "God Save the Pope" (l. 44) on one ruin, and the Protestants who paint "God Save the Queen" (ll. 44–45) on another, oppose each other in a sneaky, defiant, narrow-minded and murderous way. It is the "bellicose religion" (l. 38) of Northern Ireland that causes this hatred and misery.

8. *Compare the descriptions of Belfast in Texts 7 and 8. What similarities and differences are there?*
Both writers use the first person singular point of view and create a very vivid and personal picture of the city. The main difference is, however, that in "The Awful City" Belfast is described from the outside, i. e. the narrator is an outsider who is attracted by and lured into the city, whereas in "Things Weren't as Nice as They Had Been" the narrator is part of the city and sees it from the inside. He is not fascinated by his city, but as an inhabitant he is a victim and, of course, part of the narrator's fascination in Text 8.

9 Robin Knight: Good Fences – Good Neighbors?

Didaktische Hinweise

Der Titel dieses Textes spielt – ebenso wie Robert Frost in seinem Gedicht "Mending Wall" (vgl. Kap. XII, Text 11) – auf das bekannte Sprichwort "Good fences make good neighbours" an, und so liegt es nahe, das Gedicht in die Besprechung der Nordirland-Problematik zu integrieren. Nicht minder interessant ist aber auch der Vergleich mit Paul Therouxs Nordirland-Impressionen (Text 8). Die Frage nach der Rolle von Zäunen, Mauern oder Eisernen Vorhängen bei der Friedenssicherung als Voraussetzung für gut nachbarliche Verhältnisse berührt ein weltweites Problem und ist gerade für deutsche Schüler/innen von hautnaher Realität. Die Nordirland-Frage unter diesem Aspekt zu betrachten (vgl. auch Kap. XII, Text 9–12), kann dazu beitragen, sich dem Problem unverstellteren Blicks zu nähern und damit zur Erreichung eines der fächerübergreifenden Lernziele, des Abbaus von Vorurteilen und der Erziehung zur Völkerverständigung, beizutragen.

Background information

For general information on Northern Ireland and Belfast cf. "Info-Box" (SB, pp. 106 f.) and p. 94 of this book.

"a grateful English monarch" (ll. 96–97): James I of England and VI of Scotland (1566–1625).

Semantic and collocational field "Terrorism"

the IRA, a Catholic/Protestant extremist, a gunman, a car bomber, the British Army, in camouflage green ✧ a troubled city/place, a longstanding sore, a violent past, the violent 1970s, terror, fear of bombings/arson/ riots, (to) be at war ✧ (to) stand abandoned, (to) be destroyed/damaged by explosions, (to) be wrecked ✧ periodic disturbances, anti-British graffiti, (to) force the British out ✧ greater security, (to) reduce violence, (to) subdue a rebellion, (to) protect sb./sth. from sb./sth. else.

Talking about the text – Suggested answers

1. The two faces are symbols of the city's future and of its past. The future is characterized by hope for a peaceful life, for peaceful cooperation and for an end to violence, murder and terrorism. It is just this terror, this violence, which makes up the city's past, so that memories can only cause fear and dread. The headquarters of the British Army stands as a symbol of the past (cf. ll. 6–10); it was from here that the Army was to *stop* violence. However, it was not long before the Army itself became an object of hatred to both sides (cf. l. 45) and that the headquarters were considered a seat of violence. Now, together with the building, a certain part of the past is to be demolished; and, with a view to the future, a new shopping centre is to be built in its place (cf. ll. 10–13).

2. The writer employs personification by the use of terms for the human body, e.g. "The heart of this Northern Ireland capital" (ll. 6–7), the city's "heart being ripped out by terror" (l. 36), "the heart of the city" (l. 83), "the city's … sores remain unhealed" (l. 63), "The troubled city of Belfast wears two faces" (ll. 1–2). The use of this metaphorical language makes the reader almost feel the pain that is so typical of life in this city. It is consistent with this figurative style to use "cosmetic" (l. 61) for the visible changes. "Cosmetic" refers to outward appearance, to the face rather than to the character of a person – or a city. It is not enough to soften the signs of terror by using "a dull green paint" (ll. 87–88).
    A lot remains to be done if the changes are no longer to be described as merely cosmetic. The hope for the future is that the sores will heal and that the murderous hatred will become weaker and will eventually be no more than a memory of the past.

3. The tensions between Protestants and Catholics go back centuries, the foundation of Belfast itself having been a reward for the defeat of a Catholic rebellion. Sectarian violence goes back a long way and has led to nothing. A comparison between these historical facts and the situation in the second half of the 20th century suggests very strongly that human beings indeed seem to be incapable of learning from history. There are still two extremist religious positions, Protestant and Catholic, locked up in civil warfare. Their "balance sheet" (l. 32) for the 1970s is particularly disastrous, with thousands of homes destroyed, hundreds of pubs and buses blown up, a dramatic decrease in population, entire streets abandoned (cf. ll. 46–52), tens of thousands of people changing houses, rigidly separated residential patterns, irreconcilable polarization between the two religious camps (cf. ll. 114–122), decline of the main industries, and, what is worse, with a terrible feeling of fear.

4. The walls and the concrete and metal barricades, officially known as "sectarian interfaces" (ll. 20–21), are there to keep the Catholic and Protestant communities apart. They were built to protect one religious community from being attacked by the other. Religious hatred, violence and death are walled in, aggression, religious war, and death are walled out.
    The comparison with the Berlin wall (cf. l. 24), however, shows that it is not only religious groupings that are kept apart, but also two different ideologies, two different political affiliations and objectives. The central shopping area in the city of Belfast shows that the high metal fence that is built round it has some positive effect. The protected area seems to be rather pacified and life appears to be almost normal (cf. ll. 82–94).

5. The British Army was originally called into Ulster to protect the Catholic minority from Protestant attacks and to keep the two parties apart. As they had to deal with extremist organizations such as the IRA and the UDF, which were not interested in peace as long as their political aims were not reached, the soldiers soon became a target of hate and had no support.

6. In 1985 there were no socially mixed areas. When about 60,000 people moved house, they did so according to a definite pattern. Catholics concentrated where a majority had always lived – in the Falls Road area. This is the area where it is still possible to find graffiti and murals glorifying IRA gunmen. It is here that police stations still look like "medieval

fortresses" (l. 68). The area associated with extremist Protestants is the Shankhill Road district, where the slogans on the walls demand that Northern Ireland should remain British. As one elderly lady says in the text, "things got so bad there was little point in mixing" (ll. 128–129).

This polarization is reflected additionally by the people's voting behaviour. Since political opinions are just as divided as the two religious camps, and since the dominant feeling of the population is fear and each side is afraid of being sold down the river, the majority of the votes in the 1985 local election went to political extremists such as the Catholic Sinn Fein organization or radical Protestant leaders. The Alliance, which as a middle-of-the-road party propagated reconciliation and compromise, suffered a devastating defeat.

7. *If you compare this description of Belfast with the picture that Paul Theroux draws of the city in Text 8, what appears to be the main difference?*

   – –

Chapter V: The Frontier and the American Dream

Mit Kapitel V beginnt der zweite Teil des Buches, in dessen insgesamt vier Kapiteln ein facettenreiches Bild der USA gegeben wird.

Die Begriffe "Frontier" und "American Dream" haben das amerikanische Denken und Handeln tief geprägt. Sie bilden die didaktische Klammer des vorliegenden Kapitels und spiegeln sich in unterschiedlicher Ausformung in den vorgestellten Texten und Materialien wider. Dabei erscheinen weitere Konzepte, wie z.B. "Melting Pot", "Manifest Destiny", "Westward Movement", "ethnicity" oder "ethnic minority", deren Erörterung von vielen Lehrplänen vorgeschlagen bzw. vorgeschrieben wird. Insbesondere die Vorstellung vom „amerikanischen Traum" läßt sich in den anschließenden drei Kapiteln weiterverfolgen.

Kapitel V befaßt sich vor allem mit Aspekten der Einwanderung und Besiedlung, gibt Einblicke in ausgewählte Regionen wie den Süden, den Südwesten und den Westen (zur regionalen Gliederung vgl. LB, S. 116 f.) und stellt einige wichtige Bevölkerungsgruppen mit ihren speziellen Problemen vor. Für die Behandlung der vorgesehenen Teilthemen steht außerdem illustrierendes und ergänzendes Material zur Verfügung. So können neben den Photos die physikalische Karte im hinteren Einband des SB, die Karte zur territorialen Entwicklung der Vereinigten Staaten (SB, S. 114), das Säulendiagramm zur Einwanderung (SB, S. 136) sowie die beiden "Info-Boxes" (SB, S. 121 f. und S. 135 f.) herangezogen werden.

Die in den Kapiteln V bis VIII behandelten Aspekte der amerikanischen Geschichte, Politik, Wirtschaft und Kultur lassen sich vertiefen und ergänzen. Material hierzu findet sich in den folgenden Veröffentlichungen: *Die Vereinigten Staaten von Amerika.*(Informationen zur politischen Bildung, Heft 21); *Die Vereinigten Staaten von Amerika. Geschichte, Probleme, Perspektiven (USA-Ploetz).* Würzburg, Ploetz-Verlag 1985; E. Fawcett, T. Thomas: *America and the Americans.* London, Fontana 1983; I. Friebel, H. Händel (Hrsg.): *Britain – USA Now: A Survey in Key Words.* Frankfurt, Diesterweg [5]1985; J. Garreau: *The Nine Nations of America.* Boston, Houghton Mifflin Company 1981; H. Kleinsteuber: *Die USA. Politik, Wirtschaft, Gesellschaft.* Hamburg, Verlag Hoffmann & Campe 1984; U. Klinge (Hrsg.): *The American Dream.* Düsseldorf, Cornelsen Verlag Schwann-Girardet 1986 (Courses in English, Bd. 6, Best.-Nr. 547065); C. Landauer: *Sozialgeschichte und Wirtschaftsgeschichte der Vereinigten Staaten von Amerika.* Stuttgart, Metzler 1981.

1 Archibald MacLeish: A Country of Extremes

Didaktische Hinweise

Als Einstimmung in dieses Kapitel dient ein Auszug aus einem Text des amerikanischen Dichters Archibald MacLeish, aus dem seine Begeisterung und Liebe für Amerika, für dessen Weiträumigkeit und Vielfalt sprechen. Auf Arbeitsaufträge im Schüler- oder Lehrerbuch zur Erschließung dieser Passage wurde bewußt verzichtet. Die impressionistische Darstellung soll die Schüler/innen dazu anregen, ihr Wissen und ihr Vorverständnis von den Vereinigten Staaten zu artikulieren. Im Verlauf der Arbeit mit den folgenden Texten können diese Vorstellungen überprüft, korrigiert und vertieft werden. MacLeishs Text kann aber auch zum Studium der beiden Karten (SB, S. 114 und hintere Umschlaginnenseite) überleiten, die wichtige allgemeine geographische Sachverhalte und bedeutsame Stadien der historischen Entwicklung der USA sichtbar machen und auf die im Verlauf der Behandlung der vier USA-Kapitel immer wieder zurückgegriffen werden kann. Auch die beiden "Info-Boxes" (SB, S. 121 f. und S. 135 f.) können hier bereits ergänzend und das Kapitel vorbereitend herangezogen werden.

Background information

Archibald MacLeish (1892–1982) was an American poet, novelist, playwright and critic. From 1923–1928 he lived in Europe. After his return to the USA, he turned his attention to the social and political problems of his country, and also to the growing menace of totalitarianism in the world. He won three Pulitzer Prizes and held important political and academic posts.

2 M.-G. Jean de Crèvecœur: The American - A New Man

Didaktische Hinweise

Diese berühmte Passage aus de Crèvecœurs *Letters from an American Farmer* (vgl. "Background information", unten) bietet Anlaß für intensivere Textbetrachtung. Der Autor zeichnet hier ein idealisiertes Bild Amerikas, das aus dem Denken dieser Zeit zu verstehen ist und auf damalige potentielle europäische Auswanderer eine stark werbende Wirkung ausübte. Es muß im weiteren Verlauf des Kapitels anhand verschiedener Texte problematisiert und relativiert werden (vgl. Text 3, 6 bis 12). De Crèvecœur stellt die USA als eine Art weltliches und religiöses Paradies dar, in dem sich aus dem Zusammenleben der verschiedensten, jedoch noch vorwiegend westeuropäischen Einwanderergruppen ein neuer Menschentyp entwickelt. Damit nimmt er Vorstellungen wie "Melting Pot" und "American Dream" vorweg, die erst später mit den entsprechenden Begriffen belegt wurden (vgl. LB, S. 118). Der Text charakterisiert den Amerikaner als den „neuen Menschen". Eine solche Kennzeichnung mag einem Bedürfnis jener Zeit entsprochen haben. Der Ausdruck "American" für den weißen Amerikaner ist zum ersten Mal für das Jahr 1765 belegt.

Background information

Michel-Guillaume Jean de Crèvecœur [krevˈkɛː ☆ –kɛːr] (1735–1813) was born in France. He emigrated to Canada, where he became a soldier and an explorer. In 1759 he travelled to New York State, where he later settled on a farm. During the Revolution, he was a Loyalist and was consequently forced to flee to France in 1780. He is best known for his *Letters from an American Farmer*, consisting of 12 essays written in the decade before the American Revolution. Published in London in 1782 under the pen name J. Hector St. John de Crèvecœur, they show him to be a theorist on a variety of topics; his ideas are clearly influenced by Rousseau and Montesquieu. The excerpt in this book is from the third letter. On his return to the USA at the end of the War of Independence, de Crèvecœur discovered that his wife was dead and his children had disappeared. After locating his children, he went to New York and there became the French consul. In 1790 he returned to France, where he died.

"the great circle" (l. 16): This is an early autostereotype of American history, which embodied and secularized the Puritan ideal of the "City on the Hill", the "New Jerusalem" and the "Promised Land". It held that historic processes proceed from east to west, from Europe to America, to come to fruition there as in a cycle. It was expected that material abundance and technical progress would be an integral part of American life. Growth towards freedom, culture and spirituality were anticipated as part of the idea of the millennium – a thousand years of happiness and peace brought to a climax with the return of Christ. The regeneration of the human race would take place amongst the "Chosen People" on American soil – a new Garden of Eden – and serve as a model for the rest of the world. This model society, so utterly different from the corrupted Old World, is also reflected in the preamble to the Declaration of Independence (cf. SB, p. 189 and pp. 161 f. of this book).

Talking about the text - Suggested answers

1. Because of the despotic rule of state and church (cf. l. 25), dependence and exploitation (cf. l. 29), poverty (cf. ll. 1–2, 22–23) and unemployment (cf. ll. 28–29), social inequality and prejudices (cf. ll. 9–10).

2. Material rewards in the form of land, labour, livelihood, health and security (cf. ll. 3–4, 20–21, 23–24, 30); spiritual rewards such as dignity and social equality (cf. ll. 4, 10–11, 17–18), liberal government (cf. l. 11), independence (cf. l. 25) and happiness (cf. ll. 22–23), in general a "new mode of life" (l. 10, cf. also ll. 27–28).

3. He sees the American as a mixture of different ethnic and national elements (cf. ll. 5–9, 12–13, 16–17). The American missionary spirit shows itself in his vision of the "new man" (l. 5, cf. also ll. 27–28) on his pilgrimage to the west, mastering a great future and playing a leading role for the world (cf. ll. 12–16).

4. The perpetual hopes to find a new identity, opportunity, success and material well-being, equality and independence, happiness and self-fulfilment.

5. It gives an exclusively positive, even idealistic picture of the country, its social and political system, its people and their way of life. At the same time it severely criticizes Europe by describing it as nearly the opposite. This is reflected in the structure of the text, which is dominated by contrastive order, e.g. "a country where he had nothing" (ll. 1–2) – "his country is now ..." (l. 3); "ancient" (l. 9) – "new" (l. 10); "scattered all over Europe" (l. 16) – "here ... incorporated" (l. 17); "this country" (l. 19) – "that wherein ... born" (ll. 19–20); "before" (l. 22) – "now" (l. 23); "From ...labor" (ll. 28–29) – "he has passed to ... subsistence" (l. 29–30).

   In addition, it appeals to the reader's emotions by illustrating daily family life (cf. ll. 2–3, 6–9, 22–27); by personifying America as a mother (cf. l. 12); by using a number of adjectives with positive denotations: "new" – 10 times, "great" – four times, "finest" (l. 17), "fat and frolicsome" (l. 23), "exuberant" (l. 24), "ample" (l. 30); by addressing the reader as "you" (ll. 6–7); by employing rhetorical questions (cf. ll. 1–2, 22, 27); by putting "here" repeatedly in front position for emphasis (cf. ll. 12, 17, 20, 26).

6. *This is an excerpt from de Crèvecœur's "Letters from an American Farmer". What seems to be the intellectual background of this letter-writer?*

   It does not quite seem to be what one would expect from an average farmer but rather somebody with some formal education and power of expression. There are, for example, two Latin expressions (cf. ll. 4, 12), a lot of formal and poetic words, quite a number of relatively complex sentences (cf. ll. 6–9, 9–11, 14–16, 22–25, 28–30) and a considerable amount of rhetorical accomplishment (cf. also question 5). In addition, the writer subscribes to certain views of history that were being discussed in his time (cf. ll. 14–16).

3 E. L. Doctorow: A Crazy Quilt of Humanity

Didaktische Hinweise

Dieser Auszug aus E.L. Doctorows Roman *Ragtime* (1974) vermittelt am Beispiel einer jüdischen Familie einen Eindruck von den Erfahrungen der Einwanderer zu Beginn des 20. Jahrhunderts, in der Spätzeit der "classical immigration" (vgl. "Info-Box", SB, S. 121 f.). Hier wird das von de Crèvecœur gezeichnete positive Bild Amerikas (Text 2) relativiert. Die Metapher "crazy quilt of humanity" verweist schon auf neuere Auffassungen von der Zusammensetzung der amerikanischen Gesellschaft, die die traditionelle Vorstellung vom "Melting Pot" in Frage stellen oder gänzlich ablehnen (vgl. Text 12) und statt dessen Begriffe wie "rainbow" und "Joseph's coat" verwenden (vgl. Text 11, Z. 89–90, 95).

Für Doctorow typisch ist die Mischung fiktionaler und nicht-fiktionaler Elemente, die eine sorgfältige Analyse erfordert (vgl. Aufg. 5, unten).

Der Roman ist als Taschenbuch-Ausgabe erhältlich (London, Pan Books 1985). Der Band H. Friedl, D. Schulz (Hrsg.): *E. L. Doctorow* (Essen, Verlag Die Blaue Eule 1988) bietet Material für eine Auseinandersetzung mit Doctorows Erzähltechnik.

Background information

E(dgar) L(awrence) Doctorow (1931–   ) was born in New York City, the son of second-generation Americans of Russian-Jewish descent. He was educated at Bronx High School and Kenyon College, Ohio. He worked as an editor at New American Library and Dial Press and taught at various American universities; he now teaches for the graduate writing programme at New York University. His books are widely sold, among them *Welcome to Hard Times* (1960), *The Book of Daniel* (1971) and *Ragtime* (1974), the story of three fictional families living in early 20th century America. Their lives are entwined with the lives of real people such as Henry Ford, Scott Joplin (who was the inspiration behind ragtime music) and Houdini. These novels were made into films. His seventh book, *World's Fair*, was published in 1985.

"Ellis Island" (l. 2): Situated in upper New York Bay, southwest of Manhattan, with an area of about 27 acres, this island used to serve as the chief immigration station in the USA. About 17 million immigrants landed there between 1892 and 1943, 300,000 of whom were deported as mentally or physically unfit to become Americans. In spite of all the bureaucracy, most newcomers passed through in a few hours. From 1943 to 1954 Ellis Island served as a detention centre for deportees and immigrants whose entry was questioned. President Johnson declared it a National Historic Site in 1965. The compound of 33 buildings has since been restored to its original turn of the century style – the main building is an ornate French neo-Renaissance structure – and is to contain a conference centre, a restaurant, a museum, theatres, space for exhibitions and other modern amenities.

"despised by New Yorkers" (l. 9): It is interesting to compare this picture of New York immigrants with what Henry James observed in the third chapter, "New York and the Hudson. A Spring Impression", of *The American Scene* (1907). After nearly 25 years' absence he felt like an "inquiring stranger" and was disturbed by the new

ethnic groups of Armenians, Serbs, Spaniards, Portuguese and especially Italians who populated the ghettos. He feared for American manners, culture and for the language, but was also fascinated by their exoticism.

Semantic and collocational field "Immigration"

an immigration official, the police, power ✧ the poor, a derelict, riffraff, indigent, illiterate ✧ an immigrant, an ethnic population, second-generation, (to) be absorbed into sth., (to) become accustomed to sb./sth. ✧ a tenement, a need of housing ✧ a pedlar's business, (to) make one's living, (to) sew, (to) make ends meet, (to) work for next to nothing, (to) roam the streets ✧ a disease, starvation, a rash, a cold, a running sore, a corpse, (to) die of sth. ✧ filth, (to) reek of sth., (to) stink of sth. ✧ sanitation, health ✧ moral degeneracy, (to) be guilty of sth., (to) kill sb./sth., (to) steal sth., (to) rape sb., (to) let sb. have their way, (to) knock sb./sth. down

Talking about the text – Suggested answers

1. Poverty, exploitation and even sexual abuse, prejudice, discrimination and violence, substandard living conditions, i.e. crowded housing, insufficient sanitation, disease.
2. As immigrants from eastern and southern Europe, they are not welcome, but rather are suspect, despised and often ill-treated by former immigrants, often from western and northern Europe. They tend to settle in distinct ethnic neighbourhoods, either because of external pressures and strains or for personal reasons such as a need for companionship and common cultural bonds. The "melting pot" does not seem to work for them.
3. There is, first of all, their wish to survive, their willingness to work hard (cf. ll. 24–26, 39–41), their vitality (cf. ll. 22–23) and toughness (cf. ll. 48–49) as well as their faith that their life will change, be transformed (cf. ll. 61–62).
4. The "human warehouse" suggests that the new arrivals on Ellis Island are not treated as people but rather as goods or even animals. This effect is enhanced by the repeated use of the passive voice (cf. ll. 1, 3).
   "People stitched themselves to the flag" implies that they grow active, take great pains to become part of the American nation and even begin to identify themselves with it.
   A "crazy quilt of humanity" means that they have managed to be recognized as human beings and accepted as a separate, identifiable segment of the nation as a whole.
   The words "stitch" and "quilt" are taken from the immigrants' sphere of daily work and thus add to the cohesion of this excerpt. The three metaphors in their sequence suggest the transition from passiveness to activeness, from reservation to acceptance and perhaps even to some gain in human status.
5. *Doctorow mixes fact and fiction in this excerpt. What are the advantages and disadvantages of this?*
   The advantages are that readers can fall back on their previous factual knowledge of history and thus have a basis for their historical orientation. The text also gains in suggestiveness and verisimilitude.
   The disadvantages, even dangers, are that it may be difficult to tell fact from fiction, which may mislead readers to take the fictional world for reality, that the factual elements impair the timelessness of the novel and may limit the interests of the non-informed readership of the novel.
6. *What contributes to the author's relatively high narrative speed? What effect does this have on the reader?*
   He does without proper scenic presentation, presents and mixes, in quick succession, flashes from different areas of New York life. He mostly uses the simple form of the verb and amasses facts in relatively short and simple sentences. All this jumping about tends to leave the reader breathless, giving him or her a good feel for the atmosphere of the scene being described, of this "crazy quilt of humanity" (l. 67).

7. **To what effect does the narrator use an unlimited point of view?**
   It not only allows the reader to identify and thus sympathize with the main figures, but also enables him or her to adopt other characters' views and follow their reactions at times.
8. **There is a tendency towards ethnic neighbourhoods in some German cities, too. Is this a good or a bad thing for those concerned? Discuss.**
   – –

4 Frederick Jackson Turner: The Frontiersman's Prophetic Dream

Didaktische Hinweise

In einem Kapitel, das sich mit der historischen Entwicklung der USA befaßt, dürfen die Darstellung und Auseinandersetzung mit der Besiedlung des amerikanischen Westens und dem Phänomen der "Frontier" nicht fehlen. Einen besonders nachhaltigen Einfluß auf das Selbstverständnis der Amerikaner hatte die Interpretation F.J. Turners, der – erstmals in seinem Vortrag "The Significance of the Frontier in American History" (1893) – die Auffassung vertrat, daß die Amerikaner und insbesondere der "Western man" des 19. Jahrhunderts wesentlich vom Erlebnis der Frontier geprägt worden seien. Turner erwähnt im vorliegenden, der Essaysammlung *The Frontier in American History* (1920) entnommenen Text eine Reihe von historischen Persönlichkeiten, Ereignissen und Begriffen, deren Erörterung und Kenntnis im Rahmen dieses Themas von Bedeutung sind, so z.B. "manifest destiny" (Z. 15) und "the purchase of Louisiana" (Z. 21–22). Notwendige Grund- und Zusatzinformationen lassen sich der "Info-Box" (SB, S. 121 f.) sowie der Karte "US Territorial Expansion" (SB, S. 114) entnehmen. Ob Turners Thesen intensiver, auch kritisch, diskutiert werden sollen, hängt von der gewählten didaktischen Schwerpunktsetzung ab. Soll das Frontier-Thema ausführlicher behandelt werden, lassen sich auch Romanauszüge von J.F. Cooper, Geschichten oder Auszüge von W. Irving, B. Harte, M. Twain, S. Crane, J. London oder Gedichte von W. Whitman heranziehen. Eine Auseinandersetzung mit dem "Frontier"-Begriff und seiner Bedeutung im Amerika des ausgehenden 20. Jahrhunderts bietet Text 5.

Background information

Frederick Jackson Turner (1861–1932) was an American historian. An address on "The Significance of the Frontier in American History" (1893), reprinted in 1920, was his pioneer work that opened new fields for historical study and inaugurated a new interpretation of the West. According to Turner's theory, the westward settlement created a frontier, which is to be understood as a zone of transition rather than a line. This frontier was a meeting-place of civilization and savagery and meant a return to primitive conditions for the frontiersman. According to Turner, continuous contact with the changing frontier throughout the nineteenth century shaped American democracy as well as the American national character. Successive frontiers had their folk heroes, too. However, Turner's theory has been attacked as "poetic", "oversimplified" and "contradictory" (cf. R.A. Billington, ed.: *The Frontier Thesis. Valid Interpretation of American History?* Robert E. Krieger Publishing Company, Huntington, 1977).

   The frontier can be said to have influenced many American writers and affected distinctive aspects of American literature, especially the ballad, the tall tale and the local colour movement.

The Westward Movement: By 1790 the Atlantic seaboard from Maine to South Carolina had been settled by whites to a depth of roughly 400 km inland. Within the next 60 years settlers had moved north-, south- and westwards to St. Louis, Kentucky, Tennessee, Alabama, Louisiana, Georgia and northern Florida.
   By 1880 a good deal of the Midwest and, to a lesser extent, the Southwest and Pacific Northwest had been colonized. This included the whole Pacific coast. Huge areas from Oklahoma to Montana were, however, only occupied after 1890.
   The settlers followed a few main trails west. There was the Overland Trail, from Kansas City through Nebraska and Wyoming, branching into the Oregon and California Trails; and the Santa Fe Trail, which led from Kansas City to Los Angeles via Santa Fe and Utah.
   Initially, the Pony Express was the only western postal route. In operation from April 1860 to October 1861, it went from St. Joseph, Missouri, to San Francisco via Salt Lake City. Five important transcontinental railroads, built between 1860 and 1890, were instrumental in the opening up of the far west. They were the Northern Pacific, the Union Central Pacific, the Atlantic Pacific, the Texas Pacific and the Southern Pacific, the latter two joining in El Paso.

"valleys to be preempted" (ll. 1–2): Numerous land acts, from 1796 onwards, were established to help settlers acquire their own property:
   The Pre-emption Act of 1830 authorized settlers who had cultivated land on the public domain before 1829 to claim as much as a quarter of a section, i.e. 160 acres (three miles by three miles), as their property at the minimum price of $ 1.25 per acre.
   The Distribution Pre-emption Act of 1841 made the pre-emption feature permanent and meant a victory for the western settler. It stipulated that settling before purchasing was not illegal. Actual settlement was given priority over financial concerns as part of the official policy.
   The Homestead Act (1862) gave a quarter of a section of unoccupied, surveyed land to the homesteader, i.e. any citizen or intending citizen who was the head of a family and over 21, for a nominal fee of about $ 30 after five years residence. Such land could also be bought after six months of residence at $ 1.25 per acre. These homesteads were exempt from attachment for debt.

"manifest destiny" (l.15): This phrase was first used in 1845 in connection with the annexation of Texas and became popular with mid-19th century politicians. It was the expression of a belief that the USA was a chosen land and that it had been allotted the entire North American continent by God. Under the guise of benevolence, it justified a policy of imperialistic expansion; "destiny" as an inevitable future event was used to excuse everything.

Semantic and collocational field "The opportunity of the West"

a pioneer, a frontiersman, an idealist, a vision, belief in one's destiny, (to) dream dreams ✧ a self-made man, (to) make one's dreams come true, (to) seek one's own ✧ opportunity, (an) open field, freedom of the individual, unchecked by restraints ❖ a natural resource, a mine, a fertile valley, a cornfield ❖ expansion, (to) seize sb./sth.

Talking about the text – Suggested answers

1. There were, on the one hand, hostile Indians, Spaniards and Englishmen, all with older claims to land, who blocked their advance (cf. ll. 15–16, 18–19, 23); on the other hand, there were the wilderness of the country and the hazards of a rather primitive frontier life (cf. ll. 24, 32–34).
2. An abundance of land, seemingly unlimited space (cf. ll. 27–30), natural resources promising economic opportunity and wealth (cf. ll. 1–2, 26–32), freedom from old social orders and from government regulation and bureaucracy (cf. ll. 4–5). All of these provided ample opportunity for self-fulfilment (cf. ll. 6–8).
3. Rudeness, grossness (cf. ll. 34–35) and shrewdness (cf. l. 2), but also boldness (cf. l. 2), even belligerence (cf. ll. 21–23); moreover, love of independence (cf. ll. 3–8), individuality (cf. ll. 6–8) and leadership qualities (cf. ll. 10–14), all carried by a democratic spirit (cf. ll. 3–5, 36) as well as self-confidence, optimism, idealism (cf. ll. 34–37) and vision (cf. ll. 15, 24–25, 35–38).
4. According to Turner, the Westerner was critical of the Easterner, who is said to have been indifferent and unsympathetic to certain interests of the West and governed by short-sighted pragmatism, even egoism (cf. ll. 16–21).
5. He makes use of another well-established authority to support his view of the frontiersman's vision as a motivating factor in American history. It enables him to contrast it with a foreigner's uninspired judgment of the chances of America's future. It also adds an element of enthusiasm, emotionalism and poetic rhetoric.
6. ***What may Turner mean when he writes that the conditions of the frontier experience "were exceptional and temporary" (ll. 8–9)?***
    The historical constellation may be understood as something singular, outstanding and not repeatable. Later generations can never again enjoy such a full range of challenges and opportunities for the individual and society for, once the frontier is settled, it will be that way forever.
7. ***Turner's concept of the West and the frontiersman helped to shape the self-image of many Americans. What problems can you see with his attempts to define the overall characteristics of life on the frontier?***
    Trying to characterize a period of almost a century, with all its variety of people with different backgrounds, on the move through an entire continent, not only results in a lack of differentiation (e.g. "the West", "the Western man") but, in this case, also in a certain amount of glorification, hero-worship and myth building.
8. ***The Westerner and frontier life have been favourite motifs for American media, entertainment and literature. Select an example and discuss it in class.***
    [The student may refer to advertising, numerous films and TV programmes, country and western music, and the whole range of literature from trivial to serious, even to western-style fashion.]

5 David Galloway: The American Frontier – The Line of Potential

Didaktische Hinweise

Dieser knappe und sprachlich einfache Auszug aus der Rede eines amerikanischen Professors vor deutschen Anglisten umreißt das amerikanische Verständnis von "frontier". Gleichzeitig macht D. Galloway das Fortbestehen verschiedener traditioneller Konzepte und Mythen im Denken der Amerikaner deutlich, etwa die Idee des "Manifest Destiny" (Z. 6) und implizit die des „Amerikanischen Traums", die in den folgenden Texten – aber auch in Joyce Carol Oates' Gedicht "Dreaming America" (Kap. IX, Text 3) – immer wieder aufgegriffen, mit neuer Bedeutung gefüllt, auf andere Gegebenheiten übertragen und variiert werden.

Background information

"Manifest Destiny" (l. 6): cf. "Background information" p. 107 of this book.

"a new frontier" (l. 8): This is a phrase used to refer to President Kennedy's political programme. The term "frontier" is also used today for any challenge to extend the limits of knowledge and exploration. It is interesting, in this connection, to note that four of the American unmanned lunar and interplanetary probes and spacecraft between 1958 and 1978 were named after types of frontiersmen – "Pioneer", "Ranger", "Surveyor", "Explorer" – and that two of the manned space shuttles were called "Challenger" and "Discovery".

Semantic and collocational field "The new frontier"

a border, a frontier, the line between the known and the unknown, the edge of the known world, a mythology, an impulse, a drive, (to) plunge into the unknown ✧ the realization of a dream, the conquest of outer space, a triumph of technology

Talking about the text – Suggested answers

1. *How has the concept of the "frontier" been adapted to modern American life, according to the speaker?*
   During the time of the Westward Movement it was the zone of transition between settled land and wilderness on the American continent. In modern times it has been applied to the bounds of the earth against the unknown universe around it. In a broader sense it is the border between the known and the unknown, in any sphere of life, which has always challenged the American mind to explore it.

2. *How does Galloway try to make the American concept of "frontier" under-standable to his European listeners?*
   He compares the American understanding of the word "frontier" with the European one (cf. ll. 10–14) and illustrates their differences (cf. ll. 14–20).

3. *Relative to the concept "frontier", what is the significance of naming a spaceship "Pioneer"?*
   Outer space might be considered a modern "frontier" and its conquest is similar to that of early America's. Such a name reaches back to these historical times and images and carries them into the present.

4. *Discuss some modern "frontiers" of knowledge or activity whose limits still need to be explored or pushed forward.*
   [The student may refer to the challenges of medicine, the sciences and technology, Third-World problems, etc.]

5. *Discuss whether this sort of "frontier spirit" can be considered uniquely American.*
   – –

6 Dave Martin Nez: New Way, Old Way

Didaktische Hinweise

Dieses Gedicht eines Indianers steht am Beginn einer Gruppe von Texten, in denen einige ethnische Minderheiten vorgestellt werden (vgl. auch Text 7 bis 9). Da der Behandlung der Ureinwohner Nordamerikas in den Englischlehrwerken für die Sekundarstufe I in der Regel ausreichend Raum gewährt wird, ist dieser Bevölkerungsgruppe hier ein literarischer Text gewidmet, der zentrale Probleme der "Native Americans" anspricht. Ausgehend von der Unterrichtssituation sollte entschieden werden, ob die Erörterung dieses Themas durch die Lektüre weiterer fiktionaler und nicht-fiktionaler Texte oder auch durch Kurzreferate ergänzt werden soll. Anregungen und Orientierungshilfen hierzu bietet die "Background information" (unten).

Background information

Dave Martin Nez [nez] is a member of the Navajo tribe and lives in Arizona. From 1962 to 1965 he studied at The Institute of American Indian Arts at Santa Fe, New Mexico.

American Indians: Until the arrival of European settlers, American Indians had lived in highly developed tribal societies, speaking a wide variety of languages. The encroachment of the white man eventually shattered the Indian culture and way of life. Indians were regarded as racially and culturally inferior and were relentlessly driven from their lands and persecuted. It seemed as though they were doomed to extinction.

The future looks brighter now, however, and their numbers are growing. In the 1980s there were about 1.5 million "Native Americans" in the USA, with about half of them living on or near one of the roughly 260 reservations. These reservations first came into existence in 1786; since 1824 they have been under the administration of the Bureau of Indian Affairs, which is part of the Department of the Interior. Originally the Bureau had jurisdiction over trade with Indians and was responsible for their removal to reservations in the West; it gradually developed into a land administration agency, but today is responsible for providing Indians with education and various forms of support. If they are lucky, reservation Indians can make a living from natural resources, such as coal, oil, natural gas or uranium, which can be found on some of the reservations. The Indians lease out exploitation rights to white companies. Others eke out a living from agriculture or tourism.

Nearly half of all Indians try their luck in the urban centres. Even if they have job skills and adequate education, they are often confronted with negative stereotype images and feel socially and culturally cut off.

Both tribal and urban Indians suffer from unemployment, alcoholism and frequent disease. These also reduce their life expectancy to far below the American average and may account for an alarmingly high suicide rate. Altogether they still rate as the poorest ethnic group in the USA.

Past efforts at forced assimilation ("termination policy") have largely failed. These days Indians are trying to keep their cultural roots and tribal identities alive, but for the foreseeable future they will not be able to do without government support in the form of health care, education, etc. Although Indians became US citizens in

1924, it was not until the 1960s that they began to make themselves clearly heard and started to gain political attention and influence. The militant American Indian Movement has employed such means as demonstrations and armed occupations to air their grievances.

Semantic and collocational field "Blending two American cultures"

a way of life, a tradition ✧ a dwelling, a drum, a costume ✧ a cowboy, a horse, a herd ✧ machinery, an invention, a hydro-electric plant, a microphone, (to) engineer sth. ✧ economics, planning, an enterprise ✧ (to) master sth., (to) learn from sb./sth., (to) learn sth., (to) listen to sb., (to) handle sth. ✧ (to) be equipped to do sth. ✧ tribal action, (to) clash ✧ (to) retain sth., (to) blend sth.

Talking about the text – Suggested answers

1. The aesthetic quality of life as represented by the decorations of the dwellings, music and dance, costumes (cf. ll. 1–3, 25, 29, 34); a joyful acceptance of life (cf. l. 4); respect for the old and their wisdom (cf. ll. 5–6, 20); the togetherness of generations (cf. l. 29); pride, vitality, strength and a life close to nature (cf. ll. 10–14).

2. Physical survival as a consequence of the occupation and cultivation of fertile land by the whites (cf. ll. 9, 11–12); inability to adapt themselves to new economic and technological demands (cf. ll. 15–22); identity problems caused by alienation and integration difficulties (cf. ll. 7–8, 12, 19–21, 35).

3. In retaining and revitalizing some of the old ways of life (cf. ll. 5–7, 25, 29, 34); learning from the whites and adopting their achievements (cf. ll. 30–33); emancipating themselves from white dominance (cf. ll. 21–22, 30–33); new confidence and tribal solidarity leading to assertive action (cf. ll. 26–35).

4. After the nearly verbless impressions of the first four lines he employs the timeless present tense (cf. ll. 5–9). Then he uses the past tense (cf. l. 10), the past perfect (cf. l. 11) and the past again (cf. ll. 12–22); he comes back to the present (cf. ll. 23–29) and finishes with the future (cf. ll. 30–35). Thus the use of tenses mirrors his occupation with the present, reflections on the past and outlook on the future.

5. By the combination of the following means in the last stanza: the "shall"-future expressing determination and confidence; combined parallelisms and anaphora; the gradation of "learn", "handle", "master"; and the exclamation mark at the very end.

6. *How are Indians often presented in films and on TV? Why do you suppose Indians are portrayed in this way? Discuss.*
– –

7. *Many Indians today prefer being called "Native Americans". What differences can you see between the two terms?*
– –

[♫] 7 Vern E. Smith: A Slowly Beginning Shift

Didaktische Hinweise

Ähnlich wie die Indianer nehmen auch die Schwarzen unter den ethnischen Gruppen Amerikas aufgrund der langen und leidvollen Geschichte ihres Verhältnisses zu den weißen Amerikanern eine Sonderstellung ein. Der schwarze *Newsweek*-Reporter Vern E. Smith berichtet hier über die Lage dieser größten amerikanischen Minderheit im tiefen Süden der USA, im Staat Mississippi. Damit wird gleichzeitig ein Einblick in eine bestimmte Region dieses Landes geboten. Die Beschäftigung mit weiteren Texten zur Situation der Schwarzen in den USA (etwa Kap. VI, Text 3, Kap. VII, Text 7, 8, 9a, 9b einschließlich der "Info-Box", SB, S. 182 f., Kap. IX, Text 5) sowie die Lektüre literarischer Texte schwarzer Autoren (z.B. R. Wright, L. Hughes, J. Baldwin, R. Ellison, A. Walker) können die hier gewonnenen Kenntnisse und Einsichten zu dieser Thematik erweitern und vertiefen. Auch ein Vergleich mit der Situation der Schwarzen in Großbritannien, etwa durch die Einbeziehung des Exzerpts aus Rhodri Jones' *Hillsden Riots* (Kap. I, Text 10), liegt nahe.

Background information

Blacks in the USA: Blacks make up approximately 12 % of the US population. They tend to be highly concentrated, living mostly in the South and in the cities of the North-East. Between 20 % and 40 % of the population of several Southern states is black, and blacks constitute a majority in many districts in Mississippi, Alabama, Georgia and South Carolina. As a consequence of northward "inland migration" since 1910, blacks form a majority in many cities further north, e.g. Washington, D.C. (70 %), Detroit (63 %), Newark (58 %), Baltimore (55 %). The birthrate of blacks has consistently exceeded that of whites.

Blacks throughout American history have suffered from discrimination, but a steady liberalization since the 1950s has taken place. The civil rights laws of the 1960s banned overt segregation: Title VII of the Civil Rights Acts of 1964 declared discrimination on the grounds of race, sex and national origin illegal. Attitudes and prejudices have, however, been slow to change: "In the first six months of 1988, racial incidents against blacks were recorded in at least 20 states, according to the Southern Poverty Law Center. There were 4,500 housing-discrimination complaints last year in the US, up from 3,000 in 1980." (*Time*, 17 Oct., 1988, p. 54). Blacks still lag behind and are afflicted with many social problems; for example 33.8 % of blacks live below the poverty line (cf. p. 189 of this book), compared with 28.4 % of Hispanics and 11.5 % of whites. In the American conscience blacks are becoming only one minority group amongst several.

For further information on America's blacks, cf. "Background information", pp. 152, 158 of this book.

Semantic and collocational field "Segregation and desegregration "

racial attitudes, segregation, white only, all-black, all-white, a segregated school, the Ku Klux Klan, ugly, restrictive, stifling, fearful ✧ a farm hand, (to) live in enduring poverty, (to) hoe cotton ✧ a metamorphosis, a transformation, (to) change, (to) change sb.'s lot ✧ desegregation, integrated housing, an integrated school ✧ a black voter, a black elected official, a candidate, in management position ✧ a civil-rights worker, (to) conduct a voter-registration drive, (to) register to vote ✧ an act of defiance, a public demonstration, (to) man a picket line

Talking about the text – Suggested answers

1. They lived under restrictive conditions. Public places and schools were segregated. The blacks were, as a rule, kept from voting and could not get any leading positions in administration or politics. Higher education hardly ever helped them to find well-paid jobs (cf. ll. 1–15). In rural areas they were mostly farm hands, who worked hard for little pay and lived under very poor conditions (cf. ll. 64–69, 95–97).
2. On the whole the atmosphere is less restrictive (cf. ll. 31–32, 41–43). Schools and public places have been desegregated by court order (cf. ll. 24–25). More blacks make use of

their voting rights and some advance to better-paid jobs, management and official positions (cf. ll. 19–20, 36–39). In rural areas there is a redundancy of farm hands caused by structural changes in agriculture (cf. ll. 69–77) thus perpetuating poverty in the countryside in spite of minimum wage laws (cf.ll. 64–69, 88–90). Political power there is still largely in the hands of the whites (cf. ll. 78–84, 107–109).

3. By the support of white civil-rights workers, who declared their solidarity with black people and joined them in demonstrations and campaigns to help blacks claim their voting rights (cf. ll. 48–51, 57–60); also by the enforcement of desegregation as required by law [Civil Rights Acts (cf. "Info-Box", p. 183; Ch. VII, Texts 7, 8)].

4. At first the whites upheld the system of segregation, even resorting to violence to do so (cf. ll. 1–5). Later they bowed to the law, but some still attempted to bypass it, e.g. by sending their children to private schools instead of to the integrated state schools (cf. ll. 21–27). In general, white people still cling to the old power structures, which only allows for slow changes (cf. ll. 107–113).

5. Smith revives the personal experiences of his childhood. In addition, he reviews the conditions of many different parts of Mississippi, quoting directly from interviews with the locals and utilizing statistical data.

6. **What does George Hooper mean when he states that blacks "weren't ready to go through" (l. 84) when civil rights workers came to help them in the 1960s?**
    He seems to be referring to the blacks' economic dependence on whites, their fear of repressions, their lack of a basic education as well as political awareness and experience. Blacks at the time also had to contend with problems of motivation resulting from lifelong habits.

● 7. **Prepare a short report on aspects of the South as a region, e.g. historical, economic, geographical, etc.**
    – –

● 8. **If you have read a literary work by a white Southern author, e.g. William Faulkner or Tennessee Williams, study the representation of the black characters and report on it in class.**
    – –

8 Richard Reeves: This Is the Land of Opportunity

Didaktische Hinweise

Dieser und der folgende Text lenken den Blick auf die zahlenmäßig bedeutendste Gruppe innerhalb der neueren Einwanderungsbewegung, die Immigranten aus Lateinamerika. Hier werden Aussagen einer mexikanischen Familie in Kalifornien wiedergegeben. Dabei werden ihre Gründe für das Verlassen des Heimatlands, ihre Erwartungen an die USA, ihre Schwierigkeiten bei der Eingliederung sowie ihre – in diesem Fall weitgehend erfüllten – Hoffnungen erkennbar. Durch die Einbeziehung des Gedichts von Abelardo Delgado (Text 9, vgl. auch Aufg. 5 und 6 zu diesem Text, LB, S. 116) und des fiktionalen Textes von Raimond Barrio (Kap. VII, Text 2) läßt sich die Diskussion über die hier beschriebenen Positionen vertiefen.

Background information

Hispanic and Asian Americans: There are approximately 19.4 million Hispanic Americans in the USA (US Census Bureau, 1989 announcement), i.e. 8 % of the total population. They constitute a majority in several US cities, e.g. San Antonio (53.7 %) and Miami (55.9 %). About 60 % come from Mexico, the rest from Puerto Rico, Cuba and other Latin-American countries. There are, in addition, estimated to be about five million illegal immigrants, also known as undocumented workers. In spite of a million apprehensions annually, mainly along the Mexican border, about 200,000 illegal immigrants are believed to make it across each year. With a higher birth rate than whites and blacks there is little doubt that Hispanics will become the largest American minority group by the end of the century.

Asians constitute about 2 % of the American population. They come mostly from the Philippines, China, Japan and India; the latter three ethnic groups have proved very adaptable and surpass the other new immigrants with their desire to learn and with their financial, professional and academic success. This creates some resentment and anger against them.

To ease the problem of illegal immigrants the Simpson-Rodino Bill or Immigration Reform and Control Act was passed in 1986. It gave those illegal immigrants who have lived and worked in the USA since 1981 the opportunity to apply for the status of permanent residents and eventually be granted American citizenship. The application period ended on 1 November, 1987, except for immigrants from Poland, Ethiopia, Afghanistan and Uganda.

Semantic and collocational field "Immigration"

a land of opportunity, a dream, an opportunity for sb., (to) go further ✧ middle-class values, the church, school, graduation, (to) graduate, (to) know the rules, (to) contribute to sth. ✧ a culture shock, (to) have difficulty with a language, (to) defend oneself (in English) ✧ discrimination in work, (to) discriminate against sb., (to) look down on sb. ✧ an illegal alien, (to) receive government benefits

Talking about the text – Suggested answers:

1. It was the idea of the USA being "the land of opportunity" (l. 85), where an immigrant could find work, make good money and satisfy his or her daily needs easily if he or she only had energy and ambition (cf. ll. 23–26, 85–86). It included the prospect that all peoples were given the chance of getting a good general and further education, which gave access to all sorts of careers (cf. ll. 31–34, 36–37, 49, 62–64).

2. Mr. Valenzuela found work, and even though his family did not become rich, they at least managed to reach a moderate standard of living (cf. ll. 4–9). The children received a good education and graduated with plenty of honours (cf. ll. 9–20). Beyond the parents' expectations Estevan even studied at Harvard, an elite university (cf. ll. 65–70), and became a businessman of at least some importance (cf. ll. 103–107). The older generation, however, suffered from language difficulties and problems of assimilation at the beginning (cf. ll. 28–30).

3. Their strong Catholic faith (cf. ll. 13, 35–36, 39–43), the use of Spanish at home (cf. ll. 22–23), their conservative ideas of a girl's education (cf. ll. 51–57), their pride (cf. ll. 116–118), and their strong family ties, which can also be seen in their understanding for the illegal Mexican immigrants (cf. ll. 90–99).

4. The Valenzuelas exhibit gratitude for the chances they were given (cf. ll. 78–84), general respect for, and faith in, America's political and humanitarian values (cf. ll. 62–64). They even identify quite strongly with their new country (cf. ll. 100–101).

5. *How does the description of the living-room help to characterize the family?*
   The smallness and the sparse furnishing of the room indicate that they live in moderate conditions; the decals and trophies on the walls are proof of the younger generation's ambition and pride in their educational success; the crucifix symbolizes their religiousness.

6. **Why do you think the reporter uses direct speech?**
   He may want to give the text a touch of liveliness and immediacy, an element of objective presentation, even documentation, e.g. of the individuals' speech, while at the same time keeping in the background.
7. **Discuss Estevan's opinion on illegal immigration (cf. ll. 90–99).**
   – –

9 Abelardo Delgado: stupid america

Didaktische Hinweise

Abelardo Delgados Gedicht aus dem Jahr 1969 spielt eine wichtige Rolle in der Chicano-Bewegung und gilt als Klassiker in der Literatur dieser ethnischen Minderheit. Das in vielen Anthologien erschienene Gedicht ist hier als Kontrapunkt zu Richard Reeves' Bericht (Text 8) zu verstehen (vgl. auch Aufg. 5 und 6, unten). Die Erfahrungen mexikanischer Einwanderer in ihrer Wahlheimat werden hier aus der Sicht des Künstlers dargestellt und literarisch verarbeitet. Die Erwartungen des Sprechers in diesem kritischen, ja aggressiven Gedicht sind weniger auf Integration in die amerikanische Gesellschaft und auf materiellen Erfolg gerichtet als auf das Recht zur Selbstverwirklichung und auf die künstlerische und kulturelle Anerkennung, die dieser ethnischen Minderheit – nach Aussage des Textes – bisher verweigert wurden.

Background information

Abelardo Delgado (1931–   ) was born in a Mexican village in the state of Chihuahua. He moved to Texas in 1943 and is now a US citizen. He studied at the University of Texas at El Paso and later taught at the University of Utah. Delgado has earned a national reputation as a Chicano activist, had a role in the founding of a number of Chicano institutions and served on various boards of cultural and social bodies on the state or national level. He has published 10 books of poetry and prose, including the autobiographical novel *Letters to Louise,* for which he received the Tonatiuh Prize for literature in 1977.

"carve christ figures" (l. 6): an allusion to the "santeros, the carvers of religious statues in the Spanish colonial area which included what is now the US Southwest. This folk art form is still practised in New Mexico according to aesthetic principles centuries old." (J.D. Bruce-Nova: *Chicano Poetry. A Response to Chaos.* University of Texas Press, Austin, 1984, p. 31).

For information on Hispanic Americans cf. "Background information", pp. 113 f. of this book.

Talking about the text – Suggested answers

1. *How does the speaker see the Chicanos' potential role in American culture?*
   He credits them with a lot of artistic talent, by which they could enrich American culture; however, the Chicanos are not given the proper chances to realize their creative potentials. This may result in anger, frustration, even violence or simply an unfulfilled life for them.

2. *Which concrete details of the poet's illustrations reflect his particular ethnic background?*

He employs the nouns "chicano" [from Span. "mejicano" = "Mexican"] and "chicanito" for the Mexican-American. The carving of Christ figures may remind the reader of the Mexican-Americans' Catholic faith and their way of worshipping. The Chicano painter is identified with Picasso, the outstanding representative of modern Spanish painting.

3. *According to the poem, what picture do Americans have of Chicanos?*

The poem suggests that Americans are afraid of Mexican-Americans, expecting to be knifed by them (cf. l. 4). They also apparently find Chicanos loud and abusive, "shouting curses on the street" (l. 9). Many seem to think that Hispanics are stupid, as they don't do well in school. Delgado attempts, in his poem, to set these images right.

4. *Show how Delgado uses certain techniques to give his poem structural unity and, at the same time, add emphasis to the points he is making.*

In each of the three parts of the poem, Delgado uses the example of an artist. Each part is introduced with parallel structures and identical words, i.e. by anaphora. In addition, each section follows the same pattern: the accusation "stupid america" followed by Americans' supposed and incorrect perceptions of the Chicano, then by the poet's correction of the picture.

5. *The Valenzuelas (cf. Ch. V, Text 8), as well as this speaker, have specific expectations of America. To what extent do they differ?*

The Valenzuelas hoped to find mainly economic and material success as well as integration by education. The speaker expects self-fulfilment and the recognition of his specific cultural potential, e.g. his contributions to painting, sculpture, music, etc.

6. *Compare this poem with the feature story on the Valenzuela family (cf. Ch. V, Text 8) with regard to the validity or reliability of the information or message.*

The feature story is a non-fictional text on an individual case and, as such, verifiable. It is, however, not necessarily representative of all cases. The artist in Delgado's poem serves, rather, a symbolic purpose and represents this ethnic group's potentials, claims and deprivations. Characteristically, the poet uses the timeless present tense, whereas the reporter basically employs the past tense. The reporter, therefore, is more careful to limit the bounds of his text's validity, whereas the poet makes a statement he believes to be valid for all time.

10 N. R. Peirce, J. Hagstrom: California - Still the Promised Land?

Didaktische Hinweise

Nachdem Kalifornien bereits den Hintergrund für das Interview mit einer mexikanischen Einwandererfamilie bildete (vgl. Text 8), informiert dieser expositorische Text gezielt über unterschiedliche Aspekte dieses bevölkerungsreichsten Staates der USA, der in vielfacher Hinsicht eine besondere Stellung einnimmt. Text 10 kann daher als Basistext für die in manchen Lehrplänen geforderte genauere Betrachtung einer bestimmten Region der USA dienen. Dabei kann Kalifornien, der traditionelleren Auffassung entsprechend, als Teil des "Far West" gesehen werden; man kann jedoch auch neueren regionalen Untergliederungsvorschlägen folgen und – wie im Text und der "Info-Box" (SB, S. 135 f.) angedeutet – Südkalifornien dem "Southwest" und Nordkalifornien dem "Pacific Northwest" zurechnen.

Neal R. Peirce und Jerry Hagstrom eröffneten mit ihrem Buch *The Book of America. Inside 50 States Today* (New York, Warner Books 1984), aus dem dieser Auszug stammt, ebenso wie Joel Garreau in seiner Veröffentlichung *The Nine*

Nations of North America (New York, Houghton Mifflin 1981) neue Aspekte einer sozio-ökonomischen Gliederung der Vereinigten Staaten, den "regional approach". Beide Bücher bieten eine Fülle von Informationen zu den in diesem Text ange– sprochenen Themen.

Semantic and collocational field "The lure of California"

a resident, a longtime Californian, a refugee, a flow of immigrants, a floodtide of immigration, (to) flood into somewhere ✧ the Promised Land, a power centre, a centre of decision making, second to none ✧ power, wealth, (to) challenge sb./sth., (to) command a salary ✧ aerospace/defence industries, motion pictures, tourism, hard-working ✧ high demand, a product, (to) create a market for sth., (to) produce sth., (to) invest sth. in sth. else ✧ a life in the sun, a leisure culture, environmental protection, a beneficent climate ✧ rapid revolutionary change, an idea, independent ✧ in search of sth., (to) offer sth., (to) attract sb./sth., (to) arrest one's attention, (to) seek sth.

Talking about the text – Suggested answers

1. Geographically, its position on the Pacific coast with its pleasant climate; its size and extent from north to south; its economic power based on modern manufacturing and high-tech industries as well as a high agricultural standard with its specialized produce crops; its large population with a considerable percentage of Hispanics and Asians.

2. On the one hand, there is the feeling of independence derived from California's economic strength and its distance from the traditional power centres in the East. On the other hand, the state is tied into the federal system and largely dependent on government investments. Also it is commercially and financially interlocked with the East. Within its boundaries there is occasional tension over water (the south gets much of its water supply from the north). And, because of the state's vastness, operation and coordination are generally rather difficult.

3. Environmental problems such as pollution (cf. l. 3) and the density of surface and air traffic (cf. ll. 37–39), the fear of earth-quakes (cf. l. 43), the rising cost of living (cf. ll. 55–61), the increasing stress of competitiveness (cf. ll. 65–67), the growth of social tensions resulting from Latin American and Asian immigration and changes in the population structure (cf. ll. 74–75).

4. *How do the writers endeavour to make their main statements convincing?*
   They introduce each major passage with a general statement (cf. ll. 3–4, 13, 19–20, 29–31, 37, 43–45, 53) and then proceed to underpin it with a good deal of statistical data, comparisons, illustrations and other people's opinions.

5. *What might further strengthen the feeling of independence in the California of the future? Discuss.*
   [The student may consider the distance from the capital, the growing proportion of Asians and Hispanic immigrants, the latter strongly clinging to their language and culture, the easy access to Asian markets and the closer links with the economies and cultures of Asia, esp. Japan.]

11 Richard D. Lamm: The US at a Crossroads

Didaktische Hinweise

Die beiden letzten Texte dieses Kapitels behandeln abschließend und die zahlreichen Teilaspekte zusammenfassend die Bedeutung der Einwanderung für die USA
heute und ziehen, jetzt auf höherem Abstraktionsniveau, Schlußfolgerungen für die
zukünftige Entwicklung. Dabei unterscheiden sie sich grundsätzlich in ihrer Haltung
zur Eigenständigkeit ethnischer Minderheiten und verdeutlichen so zwei wichtige
Grundpositionen in der öffentlichen Debatte. Während Richard Lamm in seinem
Kommentar eine moderne Variante der traditionellen „Schmelztiegel"-Theorie
vertritt, setzt sich John Naisbitt (Text 12) für die Bewahrung kultureller Vielfalt
innerhalb der amerikanischen Gesellschaft ein. Beide Standpunkte sollen die
Schüler/innen zur eigenen Stellungnahme herausfordern und sie zu Vergleichen mit
der Bevölkerungsstruktur und -politik in der Bundesrepublik Deutschland veran-
lassen (vgl. auch Aufg. 6 zu Text 12, LB, S. 120).

Background information

Richard D. Lamm was Democratic governor of Colorado from 1975 to 1987 and,
together with Gary Imhoff, published a book about the dangers of immigration,
called *The Immigration Time Bomb: The Fragmentation of America* (E.P. Dutton,
New York, 1989). Today he teaches at the University of Denver.

The Melting Pot: This phrase was made popular by the Jewish writer Israel
Zangwill (1864–1926) in his play of the same name (1908), which ran on Broadway
for months. The idea, however, was much older. De Crèvecœur expressed it in his
Letters from an American Farmer (1782, cf. p. 102 of this book); Emerson discussed it
and Henry James wrote of the "cauldron of the American character" (1907).

   Originally, the term meant the complete biological and cultural fusion of all
Americans. In the strict sense of the word the melting pot never functioned for the
Native Americans, blacks, Chinese and Japanese, but in a looser sense it worked in
the 19th century, when immigrants from Ireland and southern and eastern Europe
made themselves strongly felt. Today the melting-pot ideal is being superseded by
growing ethnic awareness ("ethnicity") and the recognition of cultural pluralism in
American society.

"minorities press for autonomy, if not independence" (ll. 59–60): The writer refers to
the Franco-Canadians in Canada, the Walloons in Belgium, the Chinese in
Malaysia and the Christians in Lebanon (cf. l. 57) who strive for recognition, greater
autonomy or even ascendancy in the state. In 1974, following a bloody civil war,
Pakistan (cf. l. 60) recognized the independence of East Pakistan, now called
Bangladesh. In 1975 Cyprus (cf. l. 60) was invaded by Turkey and divided into a
northern Turkish section and a southern Greek section. In Nigeria (cf. l. 61) the
Biafrans failed in their attempt to create a republic of their own in 1967, and many
became victims of genocide.

Semantic and collocational field "Assimilation of immigrants"

a newcomer, a legal/an illegal immigrant, a flood of immigrants, (to) accept sb./sth., (to)
welcome sb./sth. ✧ at a crossroads, (to) come to grips with a problem ✧ integration, a melting

pot, naturalization, assimilation, (to) assimilate into sth., (to) hold sth. together, (to) integrate into sth., linguistically cohesive ✧ economic and social success, a bright future, future success, (to) succeed ✧ nonassimilation, fragmentation, cultural divisiveness, alienation, autonomy, a bilingual society, (to) be separated from sb./sth. by sb./sth. else ✧ a high rate of poverty/illiteracy/illegitimacy, social agenda, a welfare recipient, a need for welfare, (to) provide sb. with sth. ✧ social crisis, turmoil, tension, a violent society, ethnic rebellion

Talking about the text – Suggested answers

1. The fragmentation of American society as a result of the separation of the largest immigrant group, which sticks to its own language, culture and traditions, concentrates in some southwestern and southern parts of the USA and constitutes a poverty class (cf. ll. 29–31, 64–70); the loss to the American economy and the burden on the public budget as a consequence of a high rate of illiteracy and low educational achievements of Hispanic students who face poor job prospects and may have to claim social benefits (cf. ll. 32–41, 76–81); social and political instability caused by tensions between different classes and ethnic groups, the increase of violence and crime and a potential desire for autonomy, even independence, on the part of the ethnic minorities (cf. ll. 41–42, 54–60, 71–73, 78–79).

2. He strongly pleads for the complete integration and assimilation of the newcomers to preserve the American nation as it is. This calls for English as the one common language, which means the prevention of a bilingual society (cf. ll. 48–50, 64–70, 87–100).

3. It must melt all immigrants into Americans, i.e. a people unified by the use of English as its common language but in which each ethnic group is allowed some cultural identity of its own (cf. ll. 48–50, 87–100).

4. By referring to expert studies of the problem (cf. ll. 21–31), by quoting Lipset, a sociologist, and using Lipset's findings as parallels to the American situation (cf. ll. 51–63), by comparing the fate of blacks with the possible future lot of the Hispanics (cf. ll. 75–76) and by making use of some statistical data (cf. ll. 4, 24–27, 34–38). He also tries to add a touch of objectivity by conceding the "success of many Indochinese immigrants" (ll. 44–45), though only in one passing reference.

5. *What, in the language and style of this comment, helps to influence its readers?*
   Its style is quite persuasive, in general. Within its emotive language, e.g. "destiny" (l. 9), "crisis" (l. 42), "ominous" (l. 47), "staggering" (l. 74), a number of metaphors stand out, which, in this context, particularly rouse the readers' feelings. On the one hand, there are those that signal warning or danger, e.g. "flood" (l. 13), "warning sign" (l. 46), "crossroads" (l. 64), "tide" (l. 78), "cacophony" (ll. 95–96). On the other hand, there are those that appeal to traditional American concepts expressed in such terms as "melting pot" (ll. 48–49), "Joseph's coat" (ll. 89–90), "color-blind" (l. 94) and "rainbow" (l. 95). The reader may also be influenced by intensifying adverbs such as "by far" (ll. 15–16), "increasingly" (l. 29), "closely" (l. 33) and attitudinal adverbs, e.g. "inevitably" (l. 66), "rightly" (l. 77), "startlingly" (l. 80) and "madly" (l. 83). It is finally quite characteristic that the text ends with a series of strong recommendations in the form of parallelisms and concessive contrasts set against each other by "but" (cf. ll. 87–100).

6. *Considering the history of American immigration, to what extent do you agree with Lamm's views on the need for and the functioning of the "melting pot"? Discuss.*
   [The student may want to consider the "Info-Box", pp. 121 f., and Texts 2, 3, 8 and 9 of this chapter.]

7. *Do you think it is possible to give up your native language and still retain your cultural identity? Discuss.*
   – –

12 John Naisbitt: Ethnic Diversity - Abandoning the Melting Pot

Didaktische Hinweise
Vgl. die Hinweise zu Text 11, LB, S. 118.

Semantic and collocational field "Cultural uniformity and diversity"
American culture, (the) national character, a country's general mood and values, a former heritage, a native tongue ✧ an immigrant, a newcomer, immigration policy, (to) enter (a country) ✧ (to) encourage uniformity/diversity, (to) accept sb./sth., (to) abandon sb./sth., to give up sth. ✧ a melting pot, a homogenized American, the Wasp ideal, (to) be in tune with sth., (to) emulate sb./sth. ✧ a multiple-option era, cultural/ethnic diversity, ethnically diverse, (to) be free to be oneself ✧ ethnic composition, ethnicity, a recognized ethnic group, a sizable minority, the Spanish-speaking population, a self-sufficient community ✧ (to) resent sb./sth., (to) encounter racial and ethnic prejudice

Talking about the text – Suggested answers
1. It was to blend, assimilate and "homogenize" immigrants to produce a population of a uniform character. It was to leave few identifiable ethnic features but to preserve the original white, basically western and northern European composition and culture. To this purpose, learning English was considered vital (cf. ll. 7–11, 18–21, 34–37).
2. He welcomes ethnic diversity, pleads for the freedom of immigrants to retain their cultural identities, including their native languages, wants to see large numbers of immigrants from non-Anglo and non-white backgrounds tolerated and believes in the ending of racial and ethnic prejudice.
3. Because the number of different ethnic groups is so large, and three of them, the blacks, Spanish and Asians, count so many millions that they cannot be absorbed. They need to be recognized as distinct groups. Also, whites have themselves discovered their own ethnicity and no longer adhere to the Wasp ideal as before.
4. He uses slogans and other generalizing statements that may appeal to the reader but, in fact, lack real proof (e.g. ll. 1–11). In addition he contrasts the two opposing views employing words with clearly positive or negative connotations, e.g. "celebrate" (l. 1), "free" (l. 2), "celebration" (l. 6), "a far cry" (l. 7), "enormous" (l. 15), "new dimension" (l. 22), "massive" (l. 25), "new game of diversity" (l. 40); "myth" (ll. 2, 6), "blender", "homogenized" (l. 8), "packed off" (l. 10), "either/or world" (l. 33), "over forever" (l. 34), "uniformity" (ll. 34–35, 39), "Wasp ideal" (l. 37). Finally, he tries to impress the reader by quoting "Newsweek" (cf. ll. 19–21) and the prestigious "Harvard Encyclopedia" (cf. ll. 23-26).
5. *Considering what you have learned about American immigration, how long and under what conditions did the "melting pot" really work?*
    [To some extent it worked from the early days of American settlement through the middle of the 19th century, i.e. as long as immigrants mainly came from northern, western and central Europe. Certain prejudices amongst them, however, did exist, and blacks, Native Americans and the Chinese were never integrated. When immigration from southern and eastern Europe increased at the end of the 19th and in the early 20th century, it threatened to upset the traditional ethnic balance. The "melting pot" ideal proved illusionary. The government felt compelled to introduce various restrictive measures in an attempt to preserve the predominantly Anglo-American character of the society as a whole (cf. "Info-Box", p. 122).]
6. *With regard to ethnic minorities in the Federal Republic of·Germany, which view would you sympathize with, Lamm's, Naisbitt's or some other one? Discuss.*
– –

Chapter VI: Religion and Education

Das zweite der insgesamt vier Kapitel über die Vereinigten Staaten beschäftigt sich mit grundlegenden amerikanischen Wertvorstellungen, die vor allem in den Bereichen Religion und Erziehung, aber auch im Sport zum Ausdruck kommen und zueinander in vielfältige Wechselbeziehungen treten.

Die ersten sechs Texte des Kapitels machen deutlich, wie stark das gesellschaftliche Leben in den USA von religiösen Vorstellungen und Ausdrucksformen geprägt ist. Neben einem historischen Rückblick auf den Puritanismus des 17. Jahrhunderts finden sich vor allem Darstellungen gegenwärtiger Erscheinungen und Entwicklungen. Eine "Info-Box" (SB, S. 143 f.) liefert grundlegende Informationen zum Thema. Weiterführendes Material findet sich in K. Carlson-Kreibohm (Hrsg.): *"One Nation under God." Religion in America.* Berlin, Cornelsen Verlag 1989 (Best.-Nr. 52141).

Der zweite Teil des Kapitels befaßt sich mit dem amerikanischen Erziehungssystem. Auch hierzu gibt eine "Info-Box" (SB, S. 159 f.) einen Überblick und erleichtert so den Schülern/Schülerinnen ein Verständnis des Gegenstands. Die Verhältnisse im staatlichen und im privaten Schulwesen werden in den Texten 7 und 9 näher untersucht.

Der Sport ist ein wichtiger Bestandteil sowohl der schulischen und universitären Ausbildung in den USA als auch der Freizeitgestaltung der meisten Amerikaner. Die Texte 8 und 10 wenden sich diesem Bereich zu.

1 Berton Roueché: Our People Take Religion Very Seriously

Didaktische Hinweise

Kapitel VI beginnt mit einem kurzen Text, der geeignet ist, die Schüler/innen auf das Thema "Religion in America" einzustimmen und ihnen einen ersten Eindruck von der Rolle der Religion in den USA zu vermitteln. Entsprechend wurde hier der Aufgabenapparat im LB untergebracht.

Berton Rouechés Text zeigt zum einen, welche große Bedeutung die Religion für den Einzelnen hat (vgl. Z. 9–10), zum anderen weist er auf die für Europäer verblüffende Zahl von christlichen Konfessionen hin (vgl. Z. 4–8 und "Info-Box", SB, S. 143 f.). Schließlich wird der konservative Grundcharakter vieler Religionsgemeinschaften angedeutet (vgl. Z. 10–11) – ein Aspekt, der im Verlauf des Kapitels noch vertieft wird (vgl. besonders Text 6).

Für das weitere Vorgehen im Unterricht eröffnet Rouechés Text eine Reihe von Möglichkeiten. So kann man sich entweder mit Text 2 der Frühzeit christlicher Religionsausübung in den USA (und damit den Ursachen für den konfessionellen Pluralismus) zuwenden, sich mit einer der bei Roueché genannten Konfessionen eingehender beschäftigen (Text 3: Baptisten, Text 5: Katholiken) oder anhand von Text 6 das Phänomen des christlichen Fundamentalismus behandeln.

Background information

Berton Roueché (1911–   ) was born in Kansas City, Mo. He first made his reputation with articles and books on medical subjects. Later he developed an interest in ecology and turned his attention to the description of unspoilt places in America and to small-town America, as for example in *Special Places: In Search of Small-Town America* (Little, Brown & Co, New York, 1982), from which this excerpt is taken.

Semantic and collocational field "Religion"

a church, a denomination, a God-fearing Christian, a Catholic, a Lutheran, a Baptist, a Methodist, a Presbyterian, a fundamentalist ✧ (to) be a part of sb.'s life, (to) take sth. (e.g. religion) seriously

Talking about the text – Suggested answers

1. *What can you conclude, from this short text, about religion in America?*
   Religion seems to play an important role in the lives of Americans, since there are so many churches in one county (cf. l. 4), and so many denominations (cf. ll. 5–8). People's beliefs tend to be conservative, favouring a literal interpretation of the Bible (cf. ll. 10–11).

● 2. *Find the church directory in your local newspaper. How many churches offer services? How many different denominations are listed there? If there isn't a church directory in your local newspaper, compare the number of churches in Harrison County with the number of churches listed in the telephone directory of your town.*
   – –

● 3. *Find out how many denominations there are altogether in America. How many members does each denomination roughly have? Which denominations can be seen as belonging to a larger group?*
   [Reference books for the teacher: *The World Almanac & Book of Facts.* Newspaper Enterprise Association, New York; Staatsinstitut für Schulpädagogik und Bildungsforschung München (Hrsg.): *Religion in America.* (Handreichungen zur Amerikakunde im Leistungskurs Englisch am Gymnasium, Band 2) Verlag Auer, Donauwörth, 1985.]

2 C. Malcolm Watkins: God's Chosen People

Didaktische Hinweise

Text 2 beschäftigt sich mit dem Puritanismus des 17. Jahrhunderts. Die religiösen und gesellschaftlichen Vorstellungen der englischen Siedler haben die Entwicklung der USA entscheidend geprägt. C. Malcolm Watkins' Text macht die historischen Wurzeln zahlreicher Erscheinungen der Gegenwart sichtbar. Die Analyse des Textes im Unterricht sollte ihr Augenmerk vor allem auf folgende Aspekte richten:
die zentrale Stellung der Bibel als einziger theologischer Autorität (vgl. Z. 6–8 und 38–39), die die Herausbildung einer der Kirchengemeinde übergeordneten Kirchenorganisation verhinderte und so die Entwicklung der für die USA typischen Vielfalt der Konfessionen begünstigte (vgl. Text 1; zur Rolle der Bibel heute vgl. auch Text 4); das puritanische Arbeitsethos (vgl. Z. 30–32 und 42–49 und "Info-Box", SB, S. 143);

die Bedeutung, die die Puritaner der Erziehung beimaßen (Z. 37–42; vgl. auch die
Abbildung, SB, S. 141), und die Tatsache, daß religiöse und erzieherische Ziele im
Puritanismus eng miteinander verknüpft waren;
das Verhältnis von Kirche und Staat (vgl. Text 4).
Unerwähnt bleiben in Watkins' Text die strengen Moralvorstellungen der Puritaner.
Die ergänzende Lektüre eines Textes von Nathaniel Hawthorne, etwa eines Auszugs
aus *The Scarlet Letter* oder seiner Kurzgeschichte "The Minister's Black Veil",
bietet sich hier an.

Background information

"Henry VIII" (l. 2): cf. p. 89 of this book.

"King James version" (l. 39): The Authorized Version of the Bible, commissioned by
King James I in 1611, became a major work of English literature. There have been two
revisions of the Authorized Version: the Revised Version (1885) and the Revised
Standard Version (1952).

"Hannah Adams" (ll. 54–55): A distant cousin of President John Adams, she lived
from 1755 to 1831 and was the author of several historical and religious books,
including *A Summary History of New England,* from which the quotation in the text
is taken, *Truth and Excellence of the Christian Religion, History of the Jews* and
Dictionary of Religion.

Semantic and collocational field "Puritans and society"

a self-governing congregation, a Puritan, a dissident member of the Church of England, a
Protestant critic, a religiously elect male, (to) appoint a minister ✧ (to) oppose sth., (to)
disagree with sb./sth., (to) regard sth. as an abomination ✧ a return to Roman Catholicism,
(to) dilute Puritanism ✧ an intensive personal seeking to learn God's will, (to) seek direct
communication with God, (to) search for an honest relationship with God, (to) look to sth. (e.g.
the Bible) as God's will ✧ (to) be dedicated to a goodly life, (to) be driven by religious
principles, (to) remain within the church ✧ (to) abhor toleration, (to) believe in toleration, (to)
be tolerated ✧ a self-governing community, a self-disciplined society, a meeting-house, the
electorate, (to) elect sb. as governor, (to) conduct local civil affairs, church and state are
inseparable ✧ (to) fear loss of one's freedoms, (to) harass sb. with impunity, (to) protect one's
rights

Talking about the text – Suggested answers

1. They opposed the formalism and ceremony of the Anglican Church and its organization
   (cf. ll. 2–4), the accretions of ritual (cf. l. 5), the intervening presence of authoritative
   bishops and a hierarchical priesthood (cf. ll. 7–8), as well as Mass and the Holy
   Sacraments (cf. ll. 8–9). They hoped to achieve the more direct communion with God the
   early Christians had, i.e. their simplicity of belief (cf. ll. 5–7).
2. The Puritans looked upon their political affairs as inseparable from their religious affairs,
   both of which were directed by annually elected leaders (cf. ll. 21–26). They also believed
   in hard work as God's will. The wealth that resulted from that hard work was seen as a
   recognition by God and therefore had to be used with social responsibility, especially for
   the church, the public and the poor (cf. ll. 30–36). Another important aspect is the Puritan
   belief in education, which meant everyone had to be able to read so that they could study
   the Bible (cf. ll. 37–42).

3. The basis of the Puritans' colonial and economic success was their religiously motivated work ethic. Work in itself was a sacred activity (cf. ll. 30–32). Material wealth, as a result of their hard work, was considered a sign of approval from God (cf. ll. 32–34). In addition, they were far-sighted enough to invest their productive energies in worthwhile economic activities such as maritime commerce, trade and craft industries (cf. ll. 43–46). As a consequence, a steady stream of new Puritan settlers was attracted, which led to rapid expansion of their colony (cf. ll. 47–51).

4. I.   The Puritans's theological dissent with the Church of England: a) opposition to its formalism and ceremony, b) opposition to the hierarchical order of priests and bishops, c) desire for direct communion with God by means of the Bible, d) revival of the religion of the early Christians

   II.   Emigration to America: a) dissolution of Parliament as their main reason for leaving, b) organization of the colony as chartered, self-governing company

  III.   Puritan beliefs: a) political and religious affairs inseparable, b) self-government, c) hard work, d) social responsibility of their wealth, e) education, f) economic endeavours

   IV.   Colonial and economic success: a) maintenance of self-government, b) establishment of churches, parsonages, prisons, housing etc., c) successful involvement in commerce, trade and crafts, d) attraction of new settlers, e) rapid geographical expansion

    V.   Decline of Puritanism in New England colonies: a) acceptance of religious toleration, b) revocation of royal charter, c) appointment of royal governor, d) establishment of Anglican churches

   VI.   The impact of Puritanism on present-day America

5. ***What hints in the text reveal the writer's attitude towards the Puritans?***
   The writer apparently has great respect for the power, strength and intelligence of the Puritans. He calls them "men of substance and influence" (l. 13) who could not be intimidated. And, although they were rebels, "dissidents" (l. 1), and "critics" (ll. 2–3), it was for a worthy cause: "remaining within the church" (ll. 1–2), they "sought … to 'purify'" (ll. 4–5), "intensive personal seeking to learn God's will " (l. 9), "search for an honest relationship with God" (l. 14). He describes them and their work most positively, e.g. "honest hard work" (l. 32), "vigorously and productively energetic" (l. 42), "self-disciplined" (l. 47).

👁 3 Jonathan Raban: Pleasant Hill Missionary Baptist Church

Didaktische Hinweise

Text 3 schildert aus der Perspektive eines britischen Beobachters eine politische Veranstaltung in einer schwarzen Baptistengemeinde, die die Form eines Gottesdiensts annimmt. Distanziert und fasziniert zugleich beschreibt Jonathan Raban das dialogische Wechselspiel zwischen dem Geistlichen und seiner Gemeinde. Die Darstellung trägt durchaus humoristische Züge, ohne jedoch etwa diskriminierend zu wirken.

Der Text, der auf der Textcassette *Selected Texts on Cassette* (Best.-Nr. 54861) zu finden ist, ist in zweierlei Hinsicht aufschlußreich. Zum einen erlaubt er einen Einblick in das Leben der schwarzen Kirchen in den USA mit ihrer besonders ausgeprägten Emotionalität, die sich gerade im gemeinsamen Gottesdienst und in der lebendigen Interaktion zwischen Prediger und Gemeinde ausdrückt. Zum anderen verdeutlicht er das enge Verhältnis zwischen Religion und Politik, das für die USA charakteristisch ist: Der Text der amerikanischen Unabhängigkeitserklärung (vgl. Kap. VIII, Text 1, Z. 6–8) wird zum hymnisch vorgetragenen Predigttext, politische und religiöse Befreiungsbotschaft sind eins.

Anknüpfend an Rabans Text ließe sich die Haltung anderer Konfessionen zu politisch-gesellschaftlichen Fragen untersuchen (etwa Text 5 und Kap. VII, Text 6c: Katholiken; Text 6: christliche Fundamentalisten). Die Schilderung kann jedoch ebenso als Einstieg in eine Unterrichtssequenz zur Situation der Schwarzen und zur amerikanischen Bürgerrechtsbewegung dienen (vgl. Kap. VII, Text 7 bis 9 sowie "Info-Box", SB, S. 182 f.).

Background information

Jonathan Raban [rəˈbæn](1942 –   ) is a British essayist and travel writer. He pursued a career as an academic, working as an assistant lecturer in English literature at various universities, before deciding, in 1969, to become a full-time writer. His books include *Arabia Through the Looking Glass* (1979) and *Foreign Land* (1985). *Old Glory: An American Voyage* (1981), from which this excerpt is taken, is the account of his journey down the Mississippi River. The journey had its origin in Raban's boyhood, when he read Mark Twain's *Huckleberry Finn*.

Since the days of slavery, black and white Protestants have tended to worship in separate churches. Even since the abolition of slavery and the civil rights movement in the 1960s there has been a reluctance on the part of the black churches to unite with the white churches. This is because the church has always been the centre of community for the blacks; it was the only institution where a black leadership which was able to express their religious and political aspirations existed. Many black political leaders, e.g. Martin Luther King and Jesse Jackson, were preachers before becoming political figures.

Black American worship has its roots in African worship, which involved dancing, moving in rhythm, chanting and entering into trances. There is a strong emotional tie between the preacher and his congregation, which interjects during the sermon. Many sermons are also chanted. Much of white American evangelism has been strongly influenced by the emotional nature of black worship.

Black denominations are often divided along social lines. Poorer blacks tend to belong to Baptist congregations, while middle-class blacks tend to belong to the more formal Presbyterian and Congregationalist denominations. In the 1960s many blacks converted to Islam, which they saw as being a non-white religion.

Talking about the text – Suggested answers

1. *The speaker, Otis Higgs, employs the stories of Rip Van Winkle and Gethsemane in a way that his audience can easily relate to. How does he do this and what is his purpose?*

   He speaks of the legendary story of Rip Van Winkle, who was asleep for 20 years (not a hundred as the preacher says), and the biblical story of Gethsemane, where the disciples of Jesus also fell asleep when Jesus was arrested and needed their help. By evoking these two stories he wants to draw a parallel to the situation in Memphis. In the same way Rip Van Winkle should have fought for American independence during the American Revolution, and the disciples of Jesus should have defended Jesus against those who arrested him, the people of Memphis should wake up at this crucial time and fight for their town (cf. "a spell … to cast out devils and city bosses", l. 83).

2. *What is the relationship between speaker and congregation?*
   The preacher/speaker only gives inspiration and a stimulus. The organist and the congregation provide the rhythm and the music, making it a kind of "improvised symphony" (l. 15).

3. *Make a list of the quotations from the Declaration of Independence (cf. Ch. VIII, Text 1) which are used as a hymn at this charismatic gathering.*
   "We hold these truths to be self-evident!" (l. 60), "That all men −" (l. 64), "Are created equal!" (l. 67), "That they are endowed by their creator!" (l. 69), "With unalienable rights!" (l. 72), "That among these are life ..." (l. 75), "Liberty!" (l. 78), "And the pursuit of happiness!" (l. 80).

4. *Why is it so ironical that Jefferson's words are turned into an ecstatic hymn?*
   He was a rationalist and an enlightened philosopher (cf. ll. 81–82), and he would no doubt have rejected this emotional outburst in the name of local politics.

5. *How would you characterize this meeting at Pleasant Hill Missionary Baptist Church? Is it a religious service or a political rally?*
   On the surface, it seems to be a religious service. It takes place in a church, the organ plays, the congregation answers as in a call-and-response prayer with "Oh, my Lord!" (l. 11), "A-men!" (l. 25), "Oh, my sweeet Lord!" (l. 28), etc. The participants go into holy fits, in which they fall to the ground, gurgle, shriek, laugh, writhe and sob. Between the lines, however, it becomes clear that it is a "political address" (ll. 15–16), in which democratic ideals are evoked and celebrated like religious beliefs, obviously for the purpose of arousing support for a local politician (cf. "to cast out devils and city bosses", l. 83). Thus, it is more a political gathering, conducted in the form of a (Southern) religious service.

6. *Pick out the words which are used to describe the ecstasy of the people.*
   "ecstatic trances" (l. 30), "They gurgled and shook" (l. 31), "They laughed, then shrieked" (l. 31), "as if they had plugged themselves into a high-voltage cable" (ll. 31–32), "writhing and sobbing" (l. 32), "they fell in heaps on the floor" (ll. 32–33).

7. *Comparing this address to "an improvised symphony" (l. 15) creates conflicting images about the atmosphere of the event. Explain. What is the overriding image?*
   This metaphor contains two elements. The idea of improvisation implies that this kind of musical interplay between preacher-politician on the one hand, and congregation and organ on the other, is unplanned, spontaneous, perhaps a bit chaotic; at the same time the comparison with a symphony implies a perfectly worked out, elaborate harmony of great complexity and variety. This impression of harmony is strengthened by the use of technical terms from music such as "syncopate" (l. 2), "riff" (l. 2), "bass"(l. 3), "vibrato" (l. 3), "chiming in" (l. 6), "rhythm on the off-beat" (l. 13), "punctuation marks" (ll. 13–14). Thus, the reader's initial impression of chaos is replaced by one of harmony.

8. *What indications are there that the author's attitude towards the "political address" (ll. 15–16) he witnesses changes?*
   Through most of the text, Raban is more of an observer than a participant in the service. Only once (cf. l. 12) in the first part of the text does he identify himself with the group. He speaks of the others at the service as "they", and he finds the speech he is hearing "strange" (l. 36). Then, in l. 54, he admits that he is "as excited as anyone". Even though he is "too inhibitedly Anglo-Saxon to join in the shouting" (ll. 54–55) at first, he would like to. And apparently he does in the end because he writes, "by the time *we* had finished with [Jefferson's words]" (ll. 58–59). Still later the identification seems even more complete: "*We* swayed, clapped, shouted" (ll. 83–84); only in retrospect, apparently, does he find the incident "ironic" (l. 81).

4 Year of the Bible – A Proclamation

Didaktische Hinweise

Das Verhältnis von Staat und Religion, dessen historische Dimension bereits in Text 2 sichtbar wurde, ist letztlich auch Thema von Text 4. Ronald Reagan umreißt in seiner Proklamation die Rolle, die die Bibel im gesellschaftlichen Leben und Denken der Amerikaner gespielt hat, und führt wesentliche Entwicklungen im sozialen und staatlichen Bereich auf den Einfluß dieser Schrift zurück: die Entstehung eines amerikanischen Nationalbewußtseins (vgl. Z. 7–9) und der amerikanischen Unabhängigkeitserklärung (vgl. Z. 14–15), die Entwicklung eines Gesundheitswesens und eines Erziehungssystems (vgl. Z. 18) und die Abschaffung der Sklaverei (vgl. Z. 18). Daß Reagans Verständnis von der engen Beziehung zwischen christlicher Religion und amerikanischem Gemeinwesen gesellschaftlich repräsentativ ist, wird durch den Verweis auf die Haltung früherer amerikanischer Präsidenten dokumentiert (vgl. Z. 19–28) und läßt sich nicht zuletzt daran ablesen, daß Reagan nicht auf alleinige Initiative und Verantwortung handelt, sondern das „Bibeljahr 1983" im Auftrag des Kongresses ausruft.

Semantic and collocational field "American values"

a sense of community, (to) forge a sense of common purpose, (to) shape the history and character of a nation, (to) lay the foundation for the spirit of nationhood ✧ the inalienable rights of the individual, the inherent worth and dignity of the individual ✧ compassion and love for one's neighbour, (to) inspire institutional/governmental expressions of benevolent outreach, (to) frame a system of law, (to) know right from wrong ✧ a deep religious belief, a shared belief, the unique contribution of the Bible, (to) recognize the influence of the Bible on sb./sth., (to) inspire sb., (to) provide sb. with strength/character/conviction/faith, (to) form the basis for an abiding belief in sth.

Talking about the text – Suggested answers

1. In the early period of the settlement of America, the Bible gave the settlers the spiritual strength to go on with their work in the face of the great hardships they had to suffer and the great dangers they were exposed to in the new and rough country (cf. ll. 4–7). Their religious beliefs gave them a "sense of common purpose" (l. 7), a sense of belonging together, which finally developed into a "spirit of nationhood" (l. 9).
2. The Bible's tenet of the "inherent worth and dignity of each individual" (l. 12) influenced the Founding Fathers' belief in the "inalienable rights of the individual" (l. 11). The Bible's "emphasis on compassion and love for our neighbor" (l. 16) inspired the government to provide assistance to the needy, to schools and hospitals for the whole population and contributed to the abolition of slavery (cf. ll. 17–18).
3. President Reagan refers to four American presidents as evidence for this "unique contribution" (l. 29). Whereas George Washington and Woodrow Wilson are mentioned without a direct quotation, Andrew Jackson is credited with the quotation that the Bible is "the rock on which our Republic rests" (ll. 21–22), and Abraham Lincoln is said to have called the Bible "the best gift God has ever given to man. ... But for it we could not know right from wrong" (ll. 27–28). These quotations are rather general remarks which cannot provide absolute historical proof of the exact origin of the ideas shaping the American Constitution or the American political system.
4. The sentences are comparatively long, involved and complicated (cf. ll. 4–7, 7–9, 29–32); high-level descriptive words are frequent (e.g. "distinctive", ll. 1–2; "fundamental and

enduring", l. 2; "inherent", l. 12; "benevolent", l. 17). There are no abbreviations, contractions or slang. The closing paragraphs (ll. 29–39) adhere strictly to the standard formalization of a presidential proclamation.

The tone of the speaker, as representative of the whole nation, suggests a serious and dignified attitude toward the subject of the proclamation, which is reflected in his usage of plural pronouns ("our greatest national leaders", l. 19; "our country's development", ll. 20–21; "our beloved America", l. 22; "as a people we may well be tested", l. 23; "we will need", l. 24). Additionally, the President gives the impression of being personally involved and committed to the topic he speaks about, since he addresses the citizens using the "I" form (cf. ll. 33, 35, 37).

5 America's Catholics: Who They Are, What They Think

Didaktische Hinweise

Text 5 stellt eine den Schülern/Schülerinnen bekannte Konfession im Kontext der amerikanischen Gesellschaft vor. Ein einleitender Text und drei statistische Übersichten werfen ein Licht auf die tiefgreifenden Veränderungen, die die amerikanischen Katholiken seit der Jahrhundertwende und in verstärktem Maße seit den sechziger Jahren erfahren haben. Diese Veränderungen betreffen zum einen die Stellung der Katholiken innerhalb des Sozialgefüges (Klasse, Status, regionale Verteilung), zum anderen die Binnenstruktur der katholischen Kirche in den USA (vgl. "The Changing Church"). Aufschlußreich sind vor allem die ethischen Überzeugungen der amerikanischen Katholiken, die aus europäischer Sicht in mancher Hinsicht erstaunlich liberal erscheinen (vgl. "The Catholic mind").

Kap. VII, Text 6c gibt eine offizielle Stellungnahme der amerikanischen Katholischen Kirche zu sozialen Fragen wieder und eignet sich als Ergänzung zum vorliegenden Text. Kap. V, Text 8 und 9 befassen sich mit den Hispanics, die etwa ein Drittel dieser Religionsgemeinschaft ausmachen. Der Liberalismus der amerikanischen Katholiken in ethischen Fragen läßt sich mit dem Konservatismus der (protestantischen) christlichen Fundamentalisten kontrastieren (vgl. Text 6).

Background information

The Roman Catholic Church in the USA: Catholicism arrived in the New World before Protestantism, being brought in the sixteenth century to Florida by the Spanish. In 1634, Maryland was founded as a colony for English Catholics to practise their religion in freedom. In 1714 the French founded New Orleans, which became a centre of French-American Catholicism. The English Protestant nature of the colonies, however, ensured that until recently Catholics were identified as a minority alien religion.

The influence of American Catholicism is a direct result of Irish, Italian and Polish immigration which dramatically increased the proportion of Catholics in the USA. Discrimination against Catholics persisted until the election of President Kennedy and the loosening of Catholic discipline following the Second Vatican Council. Today American Catholics tend to be more radical than the Vatican would like, especially in matters of morality such as birth control and abortion. In political and social matters the Catholic Church is more liberal than its Protestant counterparts, as it criticizes the government's policy on nuclear weapons, Central America and social welfare.

Abortion: Since the 1960s there has been a bitter debate in the US about whether medically-induced abortion is morally acceptable or not. From 1967 onwards legal abortion made inroads in some states, but it was only in 1973 that the Supreme Court decision in the case of *Roe vs. Wade* made abortion legal nationwide. The Roman Catholic Church, together with evangelicals and other groups, continues to oppose abortion. In 1977 the Supreme Court ruled that states are not required to spend Medicaid funds (cf. "Info-Box", SB, p. 176) on elective abortions, thus sanctioning abortion but not encouraging it. Opponents of abortion became very powerful during the Reagan years (1981–89), and the appointment of conservative judges to the Supreme Court boosted their hope that abortion might be ruled illegal again. In 1986 the Supreme Court, however, upheld the right of women to have abortions. The number of abortions has risen by 50 % since 1975: in 1985 there were 1,590,000 abortions in the USA. The highest rate of abortions is in Washington, D.C., where more pregnancies are terminated than babies are born.

Semantic and collocational field "Morality"

premarital sex, sex before marriage, birth control, contraception, (to) see nothing wrong with sth., (to) have an abortion, (to) legalize sth. (e.g. homosexual relations between consenting adults)

Talking about the text – Suggested answers

1. In 1900 an American Catholic was most likely an immigrant, or the descendant of an immigrant, from Europe, who lived in a big city and worked as an unskilled labourer. Today the "typical" American Catholic does not live in a big city and does not differ from other Americans in social standing, education or income. The exceptions to this trend are the new immigrants from Latin America who make up ca. 30 % of America's Catholic population.
2. There has been a 25 % increase in Catholic membership since 1960, however, at the same time, a 1 % drop in the shares of Catholics that make up the whole US population. There has been a substantial drop in infant baptisms, a decrease in Catholic schools of all types and fewer nuns and seminarians. Statistically, the number of converts to Catholicism has dropped sharply. In addition the Catholic birth rate is down markedly.
3. The 25 % increase in membership is due to the influx of Asian and Latin American immigrants who are primarily of Catholic faith. A 1 % drop in total shares can only mean that, despite this influx, Catholic membership is not keeping up with the general increase in population. The drop in Catholic birth rate might account for the additional decreases. Fewer babies means fewer baptisms, fewer children for the schools and fewer young people studying to become nuns and priests.
4. On the majority of issues there is hardly a difference in opinion, which indicates that American Catholics have become mainstream Americans. More importantly, however, on two major issues, i.e. homosexuality and sex before marriage, Catholics have become significantly more liberal than Protestants. These statistics are particularly surprising, since neither of these opinions have been, or are likely to become, sanctified by the Pope. On the contrary, the Catholic Church's official position is quite strongly opposed to both homosexual activity and premarital sex.

6 Nicholas Ashford: Jerry Falwell's Moral Majority

Didaktische Hinweise

Am Beispiel des in Text 6 dargestellten, in den achtziger Jahren äußerst beliebten und einflußreichen Fernsehpredigers Jerry Falwell lassen sich verschiedene gesellschaftliche Phänomene im Amerika der achtziger Jahre exemplarisch aufzeigen: die politisch konservative Einstellung der Fundamentalisten, die (versuchte) Einflußnahme religiöser Führer auf Politik und Politiker auch in weltlichen Fragen sowie der professionelle, marktorientierte Stil von Fernsehpredigern und ihren Unternehmen.

Die Verquickung religiöser Anschauungen und politischer Einstellungen, gepaart mit einem ausgesprochenen Geschäftssinn, ist schon im Puritanismus erkennbar (vgl. Text 2). Der von Falwell repräsentierte Konservatismus der Fundamentalisten kontrastiert deutlich mit dem aus Text 5 ablesbaren Liberalismus der amerikanischen Katholiken; eine vergleichende Betrachtung bietet sich daher an.

Background information

Moral Majority is the religious political organization which was headed by the Rev. Jerry Falwell until February 1988, when he stepped down as the president of the organization. He remains, however, a spiritual leader of the movement. In a wider sense, Moral Majority may be considered the whole religious constituency which makes up the New Christian Right. They are normally Evangelical Christians led by TV evangelists who proclaim fundamentalist Christian beliefs. Moral Majority was believed to have exercised great influence in the 1980 and 1984 presidential and congressional election campaigns, but significantly less in the 1988 election campaign.

Semantic and collocational field "Religion"

a born-again Christian Fundamental preacher, a hierarchy, a pastoral letter, a calling from God, (to) be born again to Christianity ✧ (to) start one's own church, (to) sign sb. on as a member, (to) train a preacher ✧ a hellfire-and-brimstone attack on sb./sth., an endless supply of biblical references, (to) spread the gospel/word, (to) denounce sb./sth., (to) be inspired by sb./sth. ✧ (to) send in a donation, (to) take a contribution from sb. ✧ a vice, an era of permissiveness, a moral perversion, moral justification, (to) question the morality of sb./sth., (to) be morally indefensible

Talking about the text – Suggested answers

1. He was "born again" to Christianity at the age of 18. At the age of 22 he started his own church and very shortly afterwards 20,000 of Lynchburg's 60,000 inhabitants were members of his church.
2. There are several reasons why one might call his religious activities an industry. Consider the number, size and nationwide range of his operations. They include the Thomas Road Baptist Church, Liberty Baptist College/Bible College, and the Gospel Hour warehouse/TV station. The operations of these different branches are also very businesslike: there are more than 2,200 employees, 80 telephones, 60 million items of mail annually. The business hours are round the clock. Moreover, the annual turnover amounts to $ 100 million. Also, Falwell's lifestyle is comparable to that of a top manager in a big corporation. He lives in a secluded estate and uses a private jet for his "business" flights to churches and schools, for a total of 400,000 miles a year (cf. ll. 40–51).

3. He uses very simple and short statements (cf. ll. 52–58) and many repetitions and anaphora: "We don't …" (ll. 53, 54), "We believe …" (l. 53), "We have …" (ll. 54, 55), "We are …" (l. 56), "Here …" (l. 57).

    He uses a contrastive technique ("We have *no beer halls*. We have *prayer rooms*", ll. 54–55; "Don't come here if you are *liberal*. We are committed to the *conservative* perspective", ll. 55–56; "This school is *not for everyone*. Here, *everyone is for Jesus*", l. 57) and tries to amplify popular prejudices of his supporters by using false contrasts, e.g. "Here you can tell boys from girls" (ll. 57–58).

    Furthermore, he uses rather drastic comparisons for sensationalism ("biological holocaust", l. 59–60, for abortion), and links the things he is against with a whole array of negative emotive concepts: abortion with "holocaust" (l. 60) and "carnage" (l. 61) or "gay organizations" and homosexuality with "moral perversion" (ll. 53–54). His own position and his values are linked with positive emotive language: "the right to be free" (ll. 23–24), "continued freedom for the western world" (ll. 24–25), "Moral Majority" (l. 28), "my calling from God" (l. 63), "a Minister of the Gospel of Grace" (l. 63–64), "Liberty Baptist College" (ll. 6–7).

    Everybody can understand this kind of language and remember what he said. He paints a rather simple yet provocative picture of right and wrong, moral and immoral, with nothing in between.

4. He is on a crusade against what he calls the vices of the era of permissiveness in the 1960s and 1970s, in particular against abortion, pornography, homosexuality and drug-taking (cf. ll. 8–10). He is very much in favour of increasing the military strength of the US and believes that nuclear deterrence is the best guarantee of freedom (cf. ll. 22–26). He is strongly anti-communist and is convinced that the Communists would defeat and take over one western country after the other. He criticizes the Democratic party and denounces their ideas as radical and dangerous (cf. ll. 35–36), whereas he supports the same ideas as the Republican Party. He is said to have mobilized the conservative religious vote in favour of Reagan (cf. ll. 30–31).

5. Since he describes all the things you are not allowed to do (such as smoking, drinking beer, staying out long at night, boys and girls living in the same dorm, thinking liberally, dressing individualistically, being gay), the term "liberty" cannot mean personal freedom and tolerance. The only liberty students seem to have is that of staying away (cf. "Don't come here if …", l. 55).

6. ***What does the writer's choice of words indicate about his attitude towards Falwell and his Moral Majority?***

    " 'Ayatollah' from Lynchburg" (l. 5) compares him to Ayatollah Khomeini and the other ayatollahs in Iran, who, in the public opinion of western countries, are considered to be religious fanatics lacking rational behaviour. "Falwell's Thomas Road Baptist Church and his Liberty Baptist College are the biggest industry" (ll. 6–7) implies that he is a businessman dealing in religion like a commercial commodity. This impression is further strengthened by the use of the term "Gospel Hour warehouse" (l. 44) for the place where the business is being conducted by his employees. " 'moral McCarthyism' " (l. 10) refers to Joseph McCarthy's witch-hunt of people who were suspected of disloyalty to the American government and of harbouring pro-communist ideas in the 1950s. This implies that Falwell would like to prosecute people who do not subscribe to the moral values of the Moral Majority. It also compares Falwell's methods with methods now generally considered to have been wrong.

7. ***The text tells you about some important aspects of religion in America. Which aspects strike you as different from what you know about religion in West Germany or your home town?***

    – –

7 Lucia Solorzano et al.: A Tough School Pays Off

Didaktische Hinweise

Text 7 ist der erste von drei Texten, die sich mit dem amerikanischen Bildungssystem befassen. Der Einstieg in das Thema kann sowohl über diesen Text als auch über die "Info-Box" (SB, S. 159 f.) erfolgen, die Informationen zu Geschichte und Gegenwart schulischer und universitärer Erziehung und Ausbildung in den USA liefert.

Eine inhaltliche Anknüpfung an das erste Thema dieses Kapitels, "Religion in America", ist möglich, wenn die Behandlung von Text 7 der von Text 6 folgt. Geht es dort unter anderem um eine Ausbildung nach konservativ-christlichen Prinzipien und für eine bereits nach solchen Prinzipien ausgewählte Studentenschaft, so beschreibt Text 7 eine staatliche High School mit überwiegend hispanischen und schwarzen Schülern und Schülerinnen, einem lange Zeit von Vandalismus und Gewalttätigkeit geprägten Klima und einem im Durchschnitt niedrigen Leistungsniveau. Thema des Textes sind die in jüngster Zeit getroffenen disziplinarischen Maßnahmen, die diesem Zustand abhelfen sollen. Damit wirft der Text nicht nur ein Licht auf den Zusammenhang zwischen sozialen und schulischen Problemen, sondern kann auch dazu anregen, über Möglichkeiten nachzudenken, Zuständen wie den hier beschriebenen dauerhaft abzuhelfen. Daß die amerikanischen Schüler/innen im vorliegenden Fall offensichtlich zustimmend auf die eingeführten Disziplinierungsmittel reagierten, kann zur eigenen Stellungnahme und zum Vergleich mit den Verhältnissen in deutschen Schulen anregen.

Vergleichend läßt sich Kap. V, Text 8 heranziehen. Dort wird deutlich, mit welchen Problemen Einwanderer konfrontiert werden, wenn sie sich im amerikanischen Schulsystem bewähren wollen, gleichzeitg aber auch, welche hohen Erwartungen und Erfolgserlebnisse damit verknüpft sein können. Auch bietet es sich an, kontrastiv dazu das englische Schulsystem zu behandeln (vgl. Kap. II, Text 3 bis 5, 10 und 11).

Background information

Public secondary school education in the USA often comes in for criticism due to poor standards of education or lack of discipline in the schools. In urban centres violence is often part of everyday life in schools. In New York City there are between 1,000 and 2,000 assaults, weapons offences and robberies every year in public schools. A survey in 1987 revealed that about 33 % of pupils had had access to a handgun, 34 % had been threatened with violence at school, and 1.5 % carried a handgun to school daily.

Semantic and collocational field "Education"

an inner-city campus, a teacher, a school meeting, a top scholar, a student-body president ✧ a climate for learning, a renewed attention to learning, individual instruction ✧ a tardy student, (to) attend class, (to) be on time, (to) run to class, (to) disrupt a class for others, (to) greet sb. as he/she arrives ✧ a disciplinary measure, (to) assign sth. to sb., (to) clean up a campus ✧ an academic problem, (to) identify a school problem, (to) present a solution to a problem ✧ (to) feel proud of one's school

Talking about the text – Suggested answers

1. Jefferson High was a troubled school with more problems than individual teachers could cope with. Many students came late to classes (cf. ll. 20–23) and therefore disturbed lessons. They painted pictures and wrote on the walls (cf. ll. 30–32). There was a lot of destructive behaviour. Students had apparently set fire to three administrative offices (cf. ll. 32–33). There was also so much gang violence that pupils were afraid to go to school (cf. ll. 48–53). Academic standards were very low.

2. Physical changes were undertaken. The burned-out areas were hidden from view (cf. ll. 40–41), buildings were repaired and redecorated to make them look attractive (cf. ll. 37–39), the sprinkler system was fixed so that the campus could look nice again with green lawn and fresh plants (cf. ll. 44–46). Strict disciplinary measures are now employed, for example the tardiness programme. The gates are locked at 8:00 a.m., and pupils who come late have to wait in a holding room until the next lesson begins. If they are late three times in a month, they have to do 20 minutes of cleaning up the campus (cf. ll. 8–17).
A remedial programme has been developed for students with low test scores. They can now get additional individual instruction, but they have to sign a contract to show their willingness to work for their academic progress (cf. ll. 71–77). An academic recognition programme has also been instituted. Students with very good marks are honoured publicly and get medals for their academic achievements, so that they can serve as positive role models to be imitated by other students (cf. ll. 55–58).

3. Progress in student discipline has been made. The number of students coming to school late has dropped by 50 % (cf. ll. 20–23). There hasn't been any gang violence for a year and a half (cf. ll. 48–49); therefore, students now feel safe at school (cf. ll. 51–52). The academic achievements of the students have improved (cf. ll. 63–65), even though they are still far from satisfactory (cf. ll. 61–62, 66–67). Most importantly, morale has been markedly elevated (cf. ll. 92–95). Students feel proud of their school (cf. ll. 46–47), and they are showing interest in their own academic improvement (cf. ll. 69–77). Teachers are more involved, as well, developing and implementing new or special programmes to meet the diverse needs of the students.

4. Both parents and the community as a whole actively support the school's efforts to provide high-quality education. More parents attend school meetings (cf. ll. 78–79). Local business provides the school with know-how and financial support. One company trained teachers in a seminar on problem-solving techniques. Another company, a dairy, gives students the opportunity to get practical experience by offering them internships. The same company also supplies the school with dairy products when the school organizes fund-raising events.

5. – –

6. *Students must sign a contract before they are given free individual instruction. Why do you think this is conducted in such a business-like manner?*
– –

7. *Which, if any, of Nakano's measures do you think are good and should be implemented in German schools, and which would you find unacceptable? Explain.*
– –

8. *Under what circumstances do you think pupils are most willing to learn and actually learn best?*
– –

9. *Pupils are continually graded and given good or bad marks for their work and their behaviour by teachers. What criteria would you use to give a teacher good or bad marks?*
– –

8 Larry McMurtry: The Conference Crown

Didaktische Hinweise

Text 8 wendet sich der wichtigen Rolle zu, die die Schule in der amerikanischen Gesellschaft, insbesondere in der Kleinstadt, spielt, und da vor allem der Sport. Aus der Perspektive eines ehemaligen Schülers und früheren lokalen Sporthelden schildert der Text den Ablauf und die Atmosphäre eines American Football-Spiels, bei dem es um einen begehrten Pokal geht. Dabei wird nicht nur der hohe Stellenwert deutlich, den der Sport im Leben der Amerikaner genießt, sondern auch die große integrative, persönlichkeitsbildende Kraft, die gerade ein Mannschafts-sport wie Football auf junge Menschen ausüben kann.

Sonny, der nicht mehr in der Mannschaft spielt, erlebt den Wettkampf als Außenstehender und erfährt dabei eine leichte Identitätskrise. Larry McMurtrys Text eignet sich daher sowohl zur Vermittlung landeskundlicher Kenntnisse als auch als Einstieg in ein Gespräch über jugendliche Sozialisations- und Ablösungs-prozesse. Der Aufgabenapparat wurde wieder im LB untergebracht.

Das Thema „Sport" wird in Text 10 wieder aufgenommen. Auf die Bedeutung der "peer group" für den einzelnen Jugendlichen, die in McMurtrys Text sichtbar ist, wird in Text 9 (vgl. Z. 13–17) erneut hingewiesen. Wohin soziale Isolation in Extrem-fällen führen kann, wird aus dem Bericht "Deadly Lyrics?" (Kap. XI, Text 12) deutlich.

Background information

Larry McMurtry (1936 –   ) was born in Wichita Falls, Texas. In the early part of his career he taught creative writing at various universities. Since 1971 he has worked solely as a novelist and free-lance writer. His works include *The Last Picture Show* (Viking Penguin, New York, 1966), from which this excerpt is taken, and *Terms of Endearment* (1984), both of which were made into successful films.

American Football is played with an egg-shaped leather ball by two teams with 11 players each. The football field is 120 yards long and 53 yards wide, with two end zones of 10 yards at either end of the field. At each goal line there is an H-shaped goal with the crossbar 10 feet high. In order to score points a team must either run with the ball over the goal line or kick the ball through the upright posts of the goal. Running or passing the ball over the goal line is called a touchdown and scores six points; an extra point can be gained after a touchdown by kicking the ball over the goal post. Kicking the ball over the goal post at any other time is called a field goal and scores three points. If the offensive team succeeds in advancing 10 yards within four plays (i.e. four downs), they keep possession of the ball and can attempt another first down. The defensive team gets the ball for an offensive of their own if they manage to prevent the other team from gaining 10 yards ground within four plays (i.e. downs). They can also gain possession of the ball by inter-cepting it or by recovering a so-called "fumble" (i.e. a dropped ball). Playing time for a match is 60 minutes, divided into four quarters.

Semantic and collocational field "Football match"

a coach, a football field, a referee, a linesman ✧ the boys on the field, (to) be out on the field, (to) play, (to) quarterback ✧ (to) stand/stride up and down on the sidelines, (to) measure a first down, (to) run the first-down chain ✧ the people in the stands, (to) play the school song, (to) be part of sth., (to) enjoy oneself, (to) congratulate sb., (to) scowl at sb., thrilling, it touches sth. in sb. ✧ a seven-point lead, (to) win the conference, (to) owe one's success to sb./sth., (to) miss a game

Talking about the text – Suggested answers

1. *Why may Sonny feel guilty about not going to the previous football matches?*
   Football enjoys great importance in the town and every male is expected to go to at least certain games. Sonny may also feel guilty because he used to play for the same high school. Furthermore, he seems to be jealous of the quarterback, Bobby Logan, who – together with Coach Popper – is the local hero.

2. *What feelings does Sonny experience at the football match?*
   At first he enjoys himself and is reminded of the days when he used to play. He almost has the feeling that he is part of it again (cf. ll. 8–9, 11–14). But during the game he watches those people who really are part of the game and realizes he is not (cf. ll. 15–16, 20). As a consequence, he feels utterly lonely. As the game progresses, this feeling of loneliness becomes worse and worse, until he finally gets the feeling that he doesn't even exist (cf. ll. 25–27, 42–45).

3. *How do Bobby Logan and Coach Popper make their presence and their involvement in the game felt?*
   Bobby Logan doesn't have to make his presence felt, because he is part of the match, he plays the decisive role, his quarterbacking is very skilful and he gets a seven point lead for Thalia (cf. ll. 29–30). Coach Popper wants to make people believe that the team's success is due to his coaching and so he tries to make his presence felt by walking up and down the sidelines and frowning upon the referees as if they were doing an awful job.

4. *What is the reason for Sonny's feeling of not being part of the game, although he runs the chain, measuring the first downs?*
   Having lost the position of being an active part of the most important activity in town (playing football), he cannot be content with a subordinate role, as in measuring downs. He has not been away from school long enough, so that he wouldn't care or could have developed sufficient self-confidence in a different role like Jerry Framingham, who goes off "with some of his truck-driving buddies to get drunk" (ll. 39–40).

5. *What factors make this football game particularly exciting for the whole town of Thalia?*
   It is an important game that could decide who will win the conference crown (cf. l. 7); many enthusiastic spectators attend (cf. ll. 32–33); the band plays the school song, emphasizing a feeling of local patriotism (cf. l. 12); the cheerleaders; the chaos after the game, everyone rushes onto the field congratulating players and coach (cf. ll. 33–38); celebrating the victory, hugging, kissing and getting drunk (cf. ll. 39–42).

6. *How does the point of view chosen in the story affect the reader's perception of events?*
   The reader learns about the event through a narrator who knows all of Sonny's thoughts but is otherwise a mere observer. This use of Sonny's viewpoint does not suggest that the reader should in any way question the importance of football for the town's social life – Sonny accepts that fact, even though he is no longer directly involved. In fact, he longs to be involved again. The reader is able to find out for him or herself, because Sonny's thoughts are presented so extensively and directly but without drawing any conclusions, that Sonny has no one but himself to blame for his state of mind. He is too busy feeling sorry for himself and jealous of others to find a place for himself in this event and be able to join in the fun. The example of Jerry Framingham shows that others in a similar position are able to enjoy themselves in a less central role.

7. ***What is the role of men and women in the world of football in the text?***
   In Thalia, men and women are both assigned strict and clear roles: "custom demanded that every male in Thalia go" (ll. 7–8). This implies that football is a man's job and that consequently men are the important spectators. The well-wishers who congratulate Coach Popper are presumably all men, important men, the farmers, the lawyers, the Quarterback Club (cf. ll. 36–38). The girls' role is to cheer, to hug and kiss, to show their admiration by clinging to the heroes (cf. ll. 33–35). The men celebrate the victory by getting drunk (cf. ll. 39–40).

8. ***What is the image of local or national sports heroes in Germany among the people you know? Take the example of some present-day sports heroes and describe what you think people admire most about these athletes.***
   – –

9. ***"Whether you win or lose is determined less by how well you play the game than by who your pharmacist is" (Dr. H. Edwards, sports sociologist at the University of California in: "Playboy", Febr. 1987, p. 68). Discuss the role of drugs and doping in professional sports today.***
   – –

9   Peter W. Cookson, Jr., Caroline Hodges Persell: Prep Schools – Tickets to the Best Colleges

Didaktische Hinweise

Während Text 7 die in vieler Hinsicht problematischen Verhältnisse an einer amerikanischen staatlichen High School schildert, befaßt sich Text 9 mit den Bedingungen an privaten Internaten, den sogenannten "prep schools". Es handelt sich dabei um die Wiedergabe eines Interviews mit den beiden Soziologen P.W. Cookson, Jr., und C.H. Persell, die über ihre Untersuchungen berichten. Insgesamt ergibt sich das Bild einer kostspieligen Eliteerziehung, die einem hohen qualitativen Anspruch genügt und gleichzeitig in hohem Maße statussichernd ist. Es wird jedoch ebenfalls darauf hingewiesen, daß diese Art von Erziehung nicht über Schwierigkeiten hinweghelfen kann, deren Ursachen im Elternhaus liegen; unter Internatsbedingungen führt dies zuweilen zu besonderen psychischen Belastungen für einzelne Schüler/innen. So bleibt durchaus offen, ob der Besuch einer "prep school" pädagogisch sinnvoll ist. Davon abgesehen tritt hier der Zusammenhang zwischen Bildungssystem und gesellschaftlicher Klassenstruktur offen zutage und fordert zur Auseinandersetzung heraus. Dabei kann der Grundsatz der Chancengleichheit dem Konzept der Eliteförderung gegenübergestellt werden. Fruchtbar ist auch ein Vergleich mit dem englischen Erziehungssystem, das mit den "public schools" und den Universitäten Oxford und Cambridge ähnliche Einrichtungen für die Ober- und obere Mittelschicht besitzt wie das amerikanische (vgl. Kap. II, Text 4 bis 9). Ihre eigenen Erfahrungen und Beobachtungen können die Schüler/innen bei einem Vergleich mit dem Schulsystem in der Bundesrepublik heranziehen. Über weitere Verknüpfungsmöglichkeiten mit anderen Texten, insbesondere zum Thema „Klassengesellschaft", informiert das „Didaktische Inhaltsverzeichnis" (LB, S. xxi).

Background information

Education in the United States has never been merely confined to academic learning, but has concentrated on the development of the individual, so that each student may be able to take up his or her place in American society. After independence, education was seen as the key to preserving democracy, since a literate, well-educated electorate could insist on their rights more successfully than an uneducated electorate. Education was also seen as the great equalizer, since if everyone was given a good education, then equal opportunities would exist for all.

However, it was not until the second half of the nineteenth century that the public high school came into being. High schools have been responsible for moulding generations of adolescents into American citizens, and a high school diploma is considered an important credential in the search for career opportunities in the US.

"the best colleges" (l. 60): often referred to as the Ivy League, a group of eight long-established eastern colleges with a high academic and social prestige. The best-known are Harvard, Yale and Princeton.

Semantic and collocational field "Prep school"

a prep-school student, a select school, a boarding school, a beautiful lawn/chapel, (to) look like something out of the last century, (to) room with sb. ✧ (to) do well academically, (to) develop one's academic skills, (to) give one's all, (to) compete ✧ student culture, (to) develop service ideals, (to) become a substitute parent for sb., (to) be moral, (to) learn the real rules of life ✧ (to) be placed under considerable stress, (to) expect sb. to do sth. ✧ an unfair advantage, (to) have connections, (to) develop networks, (to) get into the right college, (to) discuss sb. (e.g. an individual student) ✧ an intuitive grasp of how to present oneself, (to) verbalize well, (to) be tuned in to the cultural world, self-assured ✧ (to) go through an experience, (to) grow up fast, (to) see the dark side of life, (to) go through the attempted suicide of a friend, (to) make sb. cynical

Talking about the text – Suggested answers

1. The children most likely to get into an elite prep school are those from upper-class or upper-middle-class families who represent a particular style, which is further cultivated by the top prep schools (cf. ll. 72–75). Self-confidence and the ability to express oneself very well and to talk with ease about the kind of culture these schools feel a part of are required. Personal attractiveness is an additional advantage, because appearance is also important (cf. ll. 75–80).
2. The expectations of the schools differ somewhat from those of the parents, at least on the surface. Apart from expecting the students to be good scholars and to have good marks, the schools want them to have impeccable morals and to be useful members of the community, that is to be helpful and co-operative (cf. ll. 8–10). The parents' expectations are focused on their children's future success: getting into the right college (cf. ll. 11–12), marrying the right person (cf. l. 12) and getting the right job (cf. ll. 12–13).
3. The students are exposed to enormous stress (cf. ll. 6–7) because they are supposed to live up to high expectations (cf. ll. 8–10). As a consequence, they often try to escape their problems by drinking, taking drugs or even attempting suicide (cf. ll. 30–31). Many students come from materially rich, but broken homes and suffer from the divorce of their parents (cf. ll. 25–27). Students often take the place of parents for each other and give emotional support to one another in times of psychological crises (cf. ll. 28–30).
4. The prep schools' educational goals are twofold. On a practical level, they want to provide an excellent education (cf. ll. 36–38) to get their students accepted by elite universities (cf. ll. 44–48). On an ideological level, they want to instil a collective upper-class mentality into the students and make them "soldiers of their class" (ll. 90–91).
5. Student culture is the biggest influence on their lives (cf. ll. 13–15). Since the students live closely together in the dormitories, they develop an attitude of mutual assistance. They

can rely on each other in any circumstances, also in case of violating the official high morals of the school, e.g. drug abuse, alcoholism etc. They carry this attitude into their later career lives (cf. ll. 96–101), in which they can rely on each other's help as soldiers in a battle are supposed to. Also, these schools consciously instil in their students an awareness of their class and its interests (cf. ll. 115–119).

6. First, the selection of students is based on qualities acquired by belonging to a particular privileged class (cf. ll. 72–75). Secondly, their admission to colleges, which is a prerequisite for top positions, is facilitated by the school's connections with the admissions officers of prestigious private colleges (cf. ll. 38–46). Thirdly, their career success is further facilitated by life-long networks of connections which give them access to positions of power in certain fields (cf. ll. 96–112).

7. *What is the interviewees' attitude towards prep schools?*
    They admit to the excellent academic education but consider it unfair to students who are just as good, but do not get into top colleges so easily (cf. ll. 62–66).

8. *Analyze the technique of the person conducting the interview. Are his or her questions more neutral, or more suggestive?*
    Some of the interviewer's questions are fairly suggestive. While the first two questions are quite neutral, the third (cf. ll. 34–35) contains a clear presupposition, i.e. that prep schools do, in fact, help get their students into better colleges. The next three questions (cf. ll. 57–58, 67–68, 92–95) are also slightly suggestive. In their sum, it might be said that these questions lead the interviewees in a particular direction: prep schools are exclusive, elitist and part of the establishment. On the other hand, it is quite possible that the interviewer was well-prepared and knew in advance of the interview what opinions Cookson and Persell would expound. Therefore, he or she may merely have been helping the two experts get to the point more quickly.

9. *Do you think that the advantages of prep schools are worth the sacrifices the children, and perhaps the parents, too, have to make? Discuss.*
    – –

10. *Do you think that having to pay a high price for a prep school education, and the opportunities given to those who have this education, are consistent with democratic ideals? Explain your view.*
    – –

10 Paul Fussell: Class and Sports

Didaktische Hinweise

Paul Fussell behandelt zwei Themen, die bereits unter anderem Blickwinkel zur Sprache kamen: die Rolle des Sports in den USA (vgl. Text 8) und die Sozialstruktur der amerikanischen Gesellschaft (vgl. Text 7, 8; Kap. VII, Text 1 bis 6, 9a und 9b sowie die "Info-Box", SB, S. 175 f.). Fussell verknüpft die beiden Themen, indem er das Interesse an bestimmten Sportarten auf klassenbedingte Faktoren zurückführt. Dabei bleibt keine der angesprochenen Gesellschaftsschichten von Fussells Ironie verschont.

Der Text eignet sich zum einen dazu, den Schülern/Schülerinnen ein Spektrum teilweise spezifisch amerikanischer Sportarten vorzuführen, zum anderen vermittelt er eine Vorstellung von der sozialen Schichtung der USA. Schließlich lassen sich die von Fussell angesprochenen Aspekte des Sports (Sport und Klassenzugehörigkeit, Sport und Werbung, Breitensport oder Zuschauersport) ohne weiteres auf die Verhältnisse in Großbritannien (vgl. Kap. II, Text 3, 5, 6) sowie auf die Bundesrepublik übertragen (vgl. unten, Aufg. 6).

Background information

Paul Fussell (1924 –   ) [ˈfʌsl], a specialist in cultural history and literary criticism, is professor of English literature at the University of Pennsylvania. He has published many books on 18th century and modern British culture, and also literary and cultural criticism in *Harper's* and *The New Republic*. His book *Class: A Guide Through the American Status System* (1983), from which this excerpt is taken, is a sardonic look at social standing. He has received several awards for his books.

"prole" (l. 3): a term to designate someone belonging to the lower classes. The word "proletariat" gained currency due to Marxist philosophy and the Russian Revolution. As a slightly derogatory word, "prole" first appeared in the 1920s and was used by George Orwell in *Nineteen Eighty-four* to describe working-class people.
   Whereas sociologists usually distinguish five classes (Upper, Upper-middle, Middle, Lower-middle, Lower), Fussell comes up with nine classes in the book this excerpt was taken from: Top out-of-sight, Upper, Upper-middle, Middle, Higher proletarian, Mid-proletarian, Low-proletarian, Destitute, Bottom out-of-sight; this reveals that the Americans are as class-conscious as their British counterparts.

Semantic and collocational field "Sports and class"

a pro game, a yacht, tennis, golf, baseball, football, ice-hockey, boxing, stock-car racing, Roller Derby, World Series, Super Bowl, the America's Cup race ✧ (to) watch a sport live/on TV, (to) study every move ✧ participation/interest in sports, obsession with a sport, (to) be popular with sb., sb. cannot get too much of sth., an event attracts sb. ✧ a winning team, (to) win, (to) be number one, (to) identify with a winner, (to) involve oneself with a team ✧ (to) be good at sth. (e.g. sports), (to) strip down to play ✧ the class meaning of sports fanship and spectatorhood, a classic prole sport, a low prole, a destitute, an entirely wasted audience for commercials, (to) maintain upper status, (to) declass an upper-middle-class person, (to) raise the social status of sth. (e.g. a sport) by euphemism/genteelism, (to) be popular with proles

Talking about the text – Suggested answers

1. First, a "prole" wants to be able to drink and smoke while exercising his sport (cf. l. 6). Secondly, he or she appreciates the opportunity to play for a company team and get a uniform shirt with his or her name embroidered on it (cf. ll. 6–8), which increases his or her sense of being somebody important. Thirdly, proles do not like sports which require them to change clothes because they do not want people to see that they are fat (cf. ll. 8–10), presumably from sitting in front of the TV "with plenty of canned Miller's" (l. 15).
2. Sports programmes are not broadcast simply for the enjoyment of the fans, but also for the purpose of selling products advertised during those programmes. If the spectators of a particular sport do not turn out to be potential consumers of the goods advertised, the programme is simply dropped (cf. ll. 27–29).
3. They have a need to identify with winners, because in their daily lives they usually are losers (cf. ll. 30–34). In addition, it gives them the opportunity to play the role of learned experts who can conclude from their superior knowledge who is going to win or lose (cf. ll. 38–41). In this way they imitate what they see as the behaviour of the decision-making and opinion-making classes (cf. ll. 48–51), which raises their own sense of self-respect.

4. The middle-classes and proles see the upper classes as the "superior classes" (ll. 40–41) because of their "wise secret knowledge" (l. 37) and their "weighty utterance and informed opinion" (l. 41). That is why they choose to imitate them. The author, however, sees the upper orders as pedantic and dogmatic bores, who only pretend to be scholars (cf. ll. 36–38).

5. The terms used for working-class people do not refer to the positive aspect of work, but rather to their low position in a success-oriented society: "prole" (l. 3), "low-prole" (ll. 25–26), "destitute", "wasted audience" and "'Low-Reach Undesirables'" (ll. 26–28), "losers" (l. 31), "people who don't win at all in their regular lives" (ll. 33–34), "plain man" (l. 44). The author sees their activities mainly as an imitation of the upper classes (cf. ll. 40–41), which he considers an aping (cf. l. 50). Even in sports he doesn't give them credit for their knowledge, but describes the "prole" as a man who "can affect to know" (ll. 46–47).

6. *The writer names sports ranking high and low in the US. Compare them with your own list of sports which you think have the highest prestige in West Germany.*
    – –

7. *What attitude towards taking up a sport is conveyed in this text? How does it compare with your own?*
    – –

Chapter VII: Social Security and Civil Rights

Thematischer Schwerpunkt dieses Kapitels sind zwei interdependente Problembereiche: die Welt der Arbeit und die damit verknüpfte soziale Absicherung sowie die gesellschaftliche Situation von Minderheiten. Querbezüge zu anderen Kapiteln, insbesondere zu Kap. V und VIII, sind erkennbar, auf Kombinationsmöglichkeiten wird an den entsprechenden Stellen hingewiesen.

Während Text 1 Arbeit aus der Sicht des Fließbandarbeiters thematisiert, geht es in dem fiktionalen Text 2 um die Situation der „Wanderarbeiter" – beides Phänomene von landeskundlicher Relevanz. Die in Text 2 anklingende Loyalität der Arbeiter untereinander rückt in Text 3, der Fragen der gewerkschaftlichen Organisation berufstätiger Frauen aufgreift, in den Mittelpunkt. Die Mehrfachbelastungen der Frau als Arbeitnehmerin, Hausfrau, Ehefrau und Mutter spricht Betty Friedan in ihrer Rede an High School-Absolventinnen (Text 4) an. Text 5 handelt von der psychisch belastenden Situation der Arbeitslosen in Amerika, auch sie eine Minderheit in einer von puritanischen Wertvorstellungen geprägten leistungsorientierten Gesellschaft. Die diesem Text folgende "Info-Box" (SB, S. 175 f.) vermittelt Informationen über vom Staat gewährte soziale Leistungen. Daß Amerikas Kampf gegen die Armut nicht den gewünschten Effekt erzielt hat, verdeutlichen die in Text 6 zusammengefaßten Äußerungen aus unterschiedlichen Lagern. Die letzte Textgruppe (Text 7 bis 9b) behandelt Fragen der Bürgerrechtsbewegung und der heutigen Situation der schwarzen Minderheit. Integriert wurde hier die zweite "Info-Box" (SB, S. 182 f.) dieses Kapitels, die die wichtigsten Stationen im Kampf der schwarzen Amerikaner um politische und soziale Gleichberechtigung zusammenfaßt und auf ähnliche, durch die Erfolge der Bürgerrechtsbewegung ermutigte Gruppierungen hinweist.

1 Studs Terkel: A Ford Assembly Line Worker

Didaktische Hinweise

Text 1 ist ein Exzerpt aus einer Sammlung von Interviews, die Studs Terkel durchführte und erstmals 1972 unter dem Titel *Working: People Talk About What They Do All Day and How They Feel About What They Do* (New York, Pantheon Books) veröffentlichte. Der Text, ein gutes Beispiel für die in Amerika in einer langen Tradition stehende Textkategorie *oral history*, gibt die unredigierten Aussagen eines Fließbandarbeiters wieder und lenkt damit die Aufmerksamkeit auf ein amerikakundlich bedeutsames Phänomen: die Einführung des Fließbands durch Henry Ford und die dadurch ermöglichte billige Massenproduktion, die zwar auf mechanisierten und monotonen Arbeitsabläufen basiert, aber auch breiteren Schichten zu einem zumindest bescheidenen Wohlstand verhalf.

Es liegt nahe, die hier angesprochene Problematik bis in die Gegenwart zu verfolgen, das heißt, den Ersatz des Fließbands durch den Computer und die damit im Zusammenhang stehenden Auswirkungen auf die Arbeitsbedingungen zu diskutieren (vgl. unten, Aufg. 6, und Kap. III, Text 2, 6). Besteht Interesse an einer weiteren Beschäftigung mit Terkels Interviews, kann das Themenheft *American*

Dreams: Lost and Found. By Studs Terkel. Edited and annotated by G. Ulmer and D. Vater (Frankfurt, Diesterweg 1987) herangezogen werden. Auch themenspezifische Songs, über die die Schüler/innen erfahrungsgemäß gut informiert sind, lassen sich hier anschließen, etwa von Bruce Springsteen, Ian Anderson oder Mark Knopfler.

Background information

Studs Terkel (1912–   ) was born in New York City. After graduating from the University of Chicago he worked as a disc jockey, a radio commentator, actor and TV emcee. He travelled throughout America for his on-the-spot interviews with all kinds of ordinary people for his radio programme on WFMT in Chicago. His books, such as *Hard Times* (1970), *Working* (1972), *American Dreams: Lost and Found* (1980) and *The Great Divide* (1989), established his reputation as an oral historian.

Semantic and collocational field "Assembly line work"

an automobile, a welding gun, a weld, a button for high voltage, (to) push a button, (to) manoeuvre a gun ✧ (to) work a body construction, (to) clamp/fuse the metal together, (to) put sth. (e.g. a roof/a door/a frame) on, (to) be able to put things together, (to) use one's hands, (to) keep the line moving, sth. goes to another line ✧ repetition, (to) be nothing more than a machine ✧ (to) give attention to sth. (e.g. a machine), (to) have respect for sth. (e.g. a machine), (to) break down, (to) fix sth. ✧ (to) feel pride in a job, (to) be proud of one's work ✧ a noise, pressure, (to) risk being fired, (to) take sb.'s place ✧ (to) work side by side with sb., (to) reduce the chances of friction with sb., (to) let one's problems build up, (to) go out of one's mind, (to) flip, (to) strike out at sb./sth., (to) be at sb./sb.'s throat ✧ (to) dream, (to) make good money

Talking about the text – Suggested answers

1. The working conditions are relatively strenuous. For one thing, the work Stallings does is very monotonous and repetitive, e.g. he has to do more than 12,000 welding spots per shift (cf. ll. 10–12). In addition, he cannot determine the pace of his work himself, but is bound to the rhythm of the assembly line with no time to relax or even go to the toilet without first getting permission from his foreman (cf. ll. 32–35). Apart from the noise, it is also uncomfortable to stand on a small platform all day long (cf. ll. 8–9). Therefore, it's not surprising that Stallings subjectively experiences the assembly line as endless and hostile. He compares it to a serpent "all body, no tail", which "can do things to you" (l. 26). Thus the factory floor becomes a dangerous jungle, where men "have lived and died ..., never seen the end of that line" (ll. 24–25). Moreover, he feels less valued than the machines, because they are taken care of immediately when they break down, whereas ill workers are "just pushed over to the other side" (l. 51) to make room for the next worker to take over.

2. There are hardly any social relations among workers. For one thing, there is always an atmosphere of tension because of the strain of the work. Moreover, there are language barriers (cf. ll. 36–37) and racial barriers (cf. ll. 40–41). In addition, the management discourages relations of any kind, so that way no working time is lost by fighting or fraternizing (cf. ll. 43–44).

3. As a line worker, he looks upon the foremen as "them", that is representatives of the management, people who value machines more than workers. He feels "the pressure, the intimidation" (l. 32) and resents their power to "make you hold it" (ll. 33–34) when they do not allow him to go to the toilet. He also feels his pride in producing quality products is jeopardized when he is considered a troublemaker for calling "a foreman's attention to a

mistake, a bad piece of equipment" (ll. 58–59). In other words, he finds the foremen's treatment of him and the other workers demeaning.

4. First, he develops a kind of escapism into a dream world, thinking of the happiness of the past and the things he loves most (cf. ll. 18–20). Also, he thinks of the good pay he gets and reminds himself that he likes working with his hands. He gets along with his co-workers (cf. ll. 36–39) enough to stay out of trouble (cf. ll. 41–43) and, intentionally, doesn't socialize too much for the same reason. And finally, since he is forced not to be proud of his work, he directs his pride in accomplishment to his stamp collection (cf. ll. 58–62).

5. The language of the text is informal spoken American English. Stallings uses contracted forms in almost every possible instance. He also uses a number of informal and slang expressions, e.g. "guy" (ll. 17, 23, 36, etc.), "uptight" (l. 17), "kid" (ll. 19, 63, 64), "be at sb." (l. 28), "flip" (l. 45), "throw it off" (l. 61), as well as casual pronunciations, e.g. "fella" (l. 38) and "gonna" (l. 44). There are also several instances of nonstandard grammar, e.g."There is hundreds" (ll. 2–3), "You got to" (l. 15), "You got some guys" (l. 17), "me and my brothers did" (ll. 19–20), "It don't", "there's men" (l. 24), "Him and I talk" (l. 38), "he ain't", "I ain't (l. 39), "real good money" (l. 54). The use of imperatives, e.g. "Figure it out" (l. 11), "Look at the price" (l. 49) and many short or incomplete sentences also indicate informal spoken style. A certain jumping from one subject to another is a further indication of oral communication. All these characteristics add up to give the reader the feeling that he or she is actually present at the interview, a desired effect in this kind of recorded oral history.

6. *In recent years, computers and robots have taken over many monotonous routines done in factories. Discuss the advantages and disadvantages of this development.*

    – –

7. *What steps might be taken to make jobs such as the one described in the text more humane? Discuss.*

    – –

● 8. *Interview a native speaker of English living in your area about his or her job. Transcribe (and, if necessary, edit) the interview and distribute copies to the class. Discuss the interview and compare it with the text about Phil Stallings.*

    – –

2 Raymond Barrio: The Miscalculation

Didaktische Hinweise

Wurde in den persönlichen, sprachlich nicht durchgeformten Aussagen des siebenundzwanzigjährigen Schweißers (Text 1) die Welt des Fließbandarbeiters sichtbar, so entsteht im fiktional gestalteten Text 2 das Bild einer anderen Wirklichkeit – das harte Leben des für den Westen und Südwesten der USA so typischen mexikanischen Wanderarbeiters. Die soziale Ausbeutung dieser Schicht ist vielfach als Relikt aus der Zeit des Frühkapitalismus kritisiert worden. Der hier gewählte Auszug aus dem Roman zeigt aber auch erste Ansätze eines gemeinschaftlichen Widerstands der Ausgebeuteten. Dies spiegelt insofern Realität, als seit den siebziger Jahren die gewerkschaftliche Organisation der Landarbeiter in Kalifornien gegen den gewaltsamen Protest der Großgrundbesitzer beachtliche Fortschritte erzielt hat (vgl. "Background information", unten).

Raymond Barrios Roman gilt als „Untergrund-Klassiker". Er steht am Beginn einer Entwicklung, im Verlaufe derer die "minority literature" immer stärker in das Bewußtsein der literarischen Öffentlichkeit getreten ist. Da in diesem Exzerpt die Auseinandersetzung zwischen Ausgebeuteten und Ausbeutern aus der Sicht des Antagonisten erlebt wird, besitzt der Text einen hohen Motivationswert, der für den Unterricht genutzt werden kann. Die sprachliche, gestalterische und gedankliche Durchformung des Textes lassen ihn darüber hinaus besonders geeignet erscheinen für die strukturelle und stilistische Analyse (vgl. unten, Aufg. 6 bis 10).

Besteht Interesse an einer vertieften Behandlung der angesprochenen Thematik, läßt sich hier das Interview mit Roberto Acuna anschließen, das Studs Terkel in seine Sammlung aufgenommen hat (vgl. Text 1 und LB, S. 141 f.). Ausgehend von Text 2 kann durch die Einbeziehung von Text 8 und 9 aus Kap. V auch eine Unterrichtssequenz zur Chicano-Problematik entwickelt werden.

Background information

Raymond Barrio (1921–   ) was born in West Orange, N.J. As well as being a writer, he is also an artist. He had great difficulty finding a publisher for his first novel *The Plum Plum Pickers* (1969), from which this excerpt is taken, so he started his own printing press in his garden. In 1984, a second edition was published by Bilingual Press/Editorial Bilingüe, Tempe, Ariz.

Migrant labor is the term used in the USA for workers who move from place to place to find work; they are usually engaged in seasonal agricultural work. They are to be found mainly in the West and the Southwest of the US, where they pick fruit, usually unprotected by trade unions. Without fixed homes, they often live in sub-standard conditions. The status and living/working conditions of the migrant workers in California have improved in recent years, due particularly to Cesare Estrada Chavez, a revolutionary Mexican-American labour leader, who, in 1970, organized California's Chicano migrant workers into the United Union of Farmworkers. When the union was started, there were violent clashes with farmers and the Teamsters, the largest US labour union. – For information on the number of legal and illegal Chicano immigrants cf. pp. 113 f. of this book.

Semantic and collocational field "Exploitation"

a robber, a thieving brute, (to) suffer deprivation ✧ a windfall for sb., a loss of two dollars out of sb.'s pay, (to) take money from sb., (to) cheat sb., bread out of a child's mouth ✧ exhaustion, tiredness, (to) drain one's mind ✧ (to) wash one's hands of sth., (to) fulfil one's end of a bargain, not (to) care how sb. lives, it is no concern of sb.'s ✧ a spirit of will, (to) show defiance, (to) earn respect from sb., (to) count for sth., (to) experience a sense of honour and pride, (to) salvage one's money

Talking about the text – Suggested answers

1. They pick fruit all day in the hot sun (cf. ll. 1–2). The work is hard (cf. l. 32), repetitive and mechanical (cf. l. 68), exhausting (cf. ll. 4–6, 31), perhaps even painful (cf. l. 4). It is comparable to slave work (cf. l. 59).
2. Roberto Morales is a Mexican contratista with whom the American plantation owners make a contract to pick fruit for a fixed price (cf. ll. 19–20). The contratista then hires the pickers and pays them a fixed price per bucket of picked fruit (cf. ll. 28–29). Presumably

the pay is very low and, in addition, the contratista tries to cheat the pickers at the end of the day by taking two cents per bucket off the promised pay (cf. ll. 28–29, 35). The contratista has power over these people, and the workers are acutely aware of it (cf. ll. 57–58). So, the actual exploitation of the ordinary Mexican labourers is done by a fellow Mexican and not by the Americans, who only made an advantageous contract and therefore do not have to have a bad conscience (cf. ll. 15–19).

3. He is "a fellow Mexican" (l. 11) who wears "torn old clothing" and has a "crude, ignorant manner" (ll. 11–12). Sometimes he appears to be "gentlemanly, friendly, polite" (ll. 9–10). In reality he is a "robber" (l. 9), a greedy, "vicious, thieving brute" (l. 10), a "clever criminal" (l. 12) and "the shrewdest, smartest, richest cannibal" (ll. 14–15) who exploits his own people (cf. ll. 10, 16, 28–29, 34–36). He is calm, self-confident and convinced of his own strength and his own superior position (cf. ll. 43–44), which he quickly and angrily demonstrates when he is contradicted (cf. l. 47). He gives way only when in a situation that could get out of hand, making it clear, however, that he is giving in "this time" (ll. 54–55) and will likely seek revenge later (cf. ll. 57–58).

4. For one thing, it is a matter of principle, since Morales had promised to take nothing from the pickers (cf. l. 37). Secondly, Manuel needs the money he worked so hard for, because he has to feed a family (cf. ll. 61–62). Furthermore, his sense of honour and pride (cf. ll. 66–69) requires him to challenge Morales, even though he will later have to pay for his defiance (cf. ll. 57–58). As a result, Manuel earns respect from his fellow workers (cf. l. 59), who, surprisingly, support him (cf. ll. 51–53).

5. The reader sees the story mainly from Manuel's perspective, through whose mind the events are reflected, e.g. "with Lupe sitting beside him" (l. 3); "The day's work at last ended. Ended!" (ll. 6–7); " 'You promised to take nothing!' Manuel heard himself saying" (l. 37). Consequently, the reader identifies with Manuel. Since the conflict is so unevenly balanced (cf. ll. 34, 44), the reader is more likely to sympathize with the underdog, who succeeds (cf. ll. 56–57), at least for the moment.

6. In addition to exposing the system of exploitation (cf. Question 2), the characterization of Morales (cf. Question 3) and the point-of-view technique (cf. Question 5), the author uses a combination of depreciatory and descriptive terms to describe the mistreated workers, e.g. "migratory scum" (l. 23), "the tired, exhausted pickers" (l. 31), "a huge ring of red-ringed eyes" (l. 41), "exhausted animals" (l. 42). He also evokes a David and Goliath situation in which Morales can be seen as Goliath: "everyone realizing that he had the upper hand" (l. 34), "It was so unequal. ... He had the whole advantage" (ll. 43–44) and Manuel can be seen as David: "with his last remaining energy, Manuel lifted his foot" (ll. 44–45), "he had never won anything before" (l. 57).

7. ***In what way does the situation described in this text present a case in favour of trade unions?***
    It is the typical situation of the exploited workers, who, as individuals, cannot win against the exploiter. Alone, Manuel could not have won against Morales; the support by all the other workers was necessary to force Morales to back off. Thus, the story serves as an archetypal example of the advantage, as well as the necessity, of the unification of workers in order to counter-balance the power of the employer.

8. ***How does the narrator perceive the role of the plantation owners when he says that "they were honest, those gueros ... and cheated no one" (ll. 21–22)? Discuss.***
    On the surface he does not seem to hold the plantation owners responsible for the exploitation ("How could anyone know ...?", l. 16). He uses appreciatory adjectives and terms to describe them ("clean blond bloodless dirtless hands", ll. 18–19) and their activities ("They could sleep at night. They fulfilled their end of the bargain", ll. 21–22). Their seemingly played-down fault ("their only crime", l. 22) is that "they just didn't care" (l. 23). But every excuse the narrator himself puts forward, seemingly to their defense ("Their religion said it was no concern of theirs. Their wives said ... Their aldermen said

..."‚ ll. 24–25), is just another ironically worded accusation that exposes the whole white society as one that just does not care. So the narrator exposes the discrepancy between business ethics and real moral standards. On the surface they are not to be blamed, because they fulfil their business contract. But in reality they have to bear the whole blame because they don't care about the consequences of their business activities on the actual lives of the people involved.

9. *What stylistic devices does the narrator use?*

On the one hand he uses short, often elliptical sentences. On the other hand, he employs fairly sophisticated stylistic devices, e.g.

repetition/anaphora: "Despite ..." (ll. 11–12); "They ..." (l. 21); "Their ..." (ll. 22–25);

adjective strings: "gentlemanly, friendly, polite, grinning, vicious, thieving" (ll. 9–10); "shrewdest, smartest, richest" (l. 14); "clean blond bloodless dirtless" (l. 18); "slow ... stupid, accidental, dangerous" (l. 64);

alliteration: "real robber" (l. 9); "kind of clever criminal" (l. 12); "blond bloodless" (l. 18); "ring of red-ringed eyes" (l. 41); "calm, confident" (l. 43); "salvaged his money savagely" (l. 58);

play on words: "their only *crime*"/"their only *soul grime*" (ll. 22–23) ["soul" being homophonous with "sole"].

10. *In ll. 17 – 19 it says that "the anglo growers ... washed their clean blond bloodless dirtless hands of the whole matter." What effect does the author achieve with this somewhat unusual wording?*

The author plays with the (biblical) expression "to wash one's hands of sth.", which is, of course, not to be taken literally. When he writes that the hands to be washed are already "clean" and "dirtless", he points to the intended irony of the statement: the author clearly feels that the growers have, figuratively speaking, dirtied their hand in the whole affair. The fact that the first and last of the four adjectives are completely synonymous draws the words together, makes them function as a unit, an effect that is enhanced by the missing commas. "Blond" and "bloodless" here come to appear nearly synonymous, the absence of blood explaining the lack of colour. But "bloodless" has a further, figurative meaning. It refers to people who lack normal human feelings, i.e. the "blond" people, the "gueros" (l. 15), the "anglo growers" (l. 17).

3 Carey W. English: Women and Organized Labor

Didaktische Hinweise

Text 3 spricht den wichtigen Problembereich „Frauen und Gewerkschaften" an und greift damit bereits Aspekte des zweiten Hauptthemas dieses Kapitels auf. Obwohl der Anteil der Frauen an der Arbeitnehmerschaft in den USA heute laut English bereits mehr als 50 Prozent beträgt, haben Frauen erst in jüngster Zeit begonnen, sich in größerem Umfang gewerkschaftlich zu organisieren. Die amerikanischen Gewerkschaften erwiesen sich bis vor kurzem als recht frauenfeindlich (vgl. "Background information", unten) und haben erst in neuerer Zeit erkannt, daß engagierte Frauen ein nicht zu unterschätzendes gesellschaftliches Potential darstellen. Da das Equal Rights Amendment, das den Frauen in allen Bereichen verfassungsmäßige Gleichberechtigung garantieren sollte, 1982 bei der endgültigen Ratifizierung durch die Bundesstaaten scheiterte, versuchen viele Frauen über die Gewerkschaften, zumindest Gleichberechtigung am Arbeitsplatz zu erkämpfen.

Es liegt nahe, vergleichend die Situation in Großbritannien heranzuziehen. Kap. II, Text 8 und 9 sowie Kap. III, Text 5 beschäftigen sich mit der Rolle der Frau im Bildungswesen und im Berufsleben, Kap. III, Text 9a, 9b und 10 thematisieren die

Gewerkschaften. Der Text 3 zugeordnete Cartoon (SB, S. 169) zielt auf die Rollenkonflikte der berufstätigen Frau und leitet damit zu Text 4 über.

Background information

Labor Unions in the USA: With the introduction of the factory system and mass production techniques between the 1830s and 1870s, which made industry reliant on cheap labour, factory workers began to organize to protect their interests. The Knights of Labor, founded in 1869, was the first national union to combine many small local unions into one large national group. At the height of its power – it had 700,000 members in 1886 – it fought for reforms such as equal pay for men and women and the abolition of child labour. It lost prestige and power when it was blamed for the bloody riot of the Haymarket Affair in Chicago in 1886, during which a bomb was thrown at the police. In the ensuing rioting four workers and seven policemen were killed. Due to internal differences, mismanagement and disputes with other unions it ceased to be a major force in the American labor movement and was officially dissolved in 1917.

The American Federation of Labor (AFL), founded in 1886, was a federation of craft unions, i.e. unions whose members all practised the same trade and were all skilled workers. Under the legendary leadership of Samuel Gompers the AFL pursued "bread-and-butter unionism", that is better wages and working conditions. A blemish on the AFL is that, apart from the United Mine Workers, no AFL union admitted blacks or women.

The Congress of Industrial Organizations (CIO), founded in 1935, was a federation of industrial unions whose members all worked in the same industry and included both skilled and unskilled workers. It aimed at organizing the workers in such mass-production industries as the automobile, steel, oil, rubber and textile industries. It developed the "sit-down strike", which was an important and novel measure, because it prevented the employers from bringing in strikebreakers, who could be easily recruited from the masses of recent immigrants.

The two large federations remained rivals until 1955, when they merged into one gigantic federation, the AFL-CIO, to which, in the early 1980s, more than 100 different unions with altogether 17 million members (ca. 16 % of the American labour force) were affiliated. Another 4.5 million workers belong to four independent unions: the International Brotherhood of Teamsters, the United Mine Workers, the United Steel Workers, and the International Brotherhood of Electrical Workers.

Semantic and collocational field "Women and unionism"

a labor union, a work force, a departmental steward, an employee ✧ (to) have a union contract, (to) be unionized, (to) come into contact with organized labour, (to) expand membership, (to) organize a drive in a predominantly female industry, (to) stay union-free ✧ back pay, a wage increase, an issue that generates concern and interest, (to) show concern over sth., (to) improve sb.'s pay/working conditions ✧ pay equity, employment discrimination, (to) take up a cause of special interest to women

Talking about the text – Suggested answers

1. They are generally trying to expand membership (cf. ll. 20–21), and since women make up over half of the labour force (cf. ll. 22–23) and seem to be "ripe for membership" (l. 49), they are the ideal target group. In addition, "women are turning out to be among the most … dynamic leaders … in organizing campaigns" (ll. 58–61). This indicates that women who

join the union are often instrumental in getting others to join, which makes the union's job of increasing membership much easier.

2. They have special "organizing drives in predominantly female industries" (ll. 25–26). They take up causes of special interest for women, such as pay equity, which is the number one issue women are concerned about (cf. ll. 27–30).

3. They won a sex discrimination case against Washington State, whose pay system was declared discriminatory by a federal judge (cf. ll. 37–44). As a consequence, other states are considering changes in their (discriminatory) pay systems (cf. ll. 45–47).

4. They recognize the ramifications of this change and are worried about its possible effect on their corporations (cf. ll. 64–69). They are taking steps to "minimize their vulnerability" (l. 79).

5. The author quotes insiders and people concerned, who can speak with authority and supply trustworthy information, e.g. Kathy Kerr, departmental steward (cf. ll. 12–13); Richard Bensinger, regional organizing director of a union (cf. ll. 61–63). The credibility of these people is further supported by a quotation from a company lawyer (Attorney Martin Payson, cf. ll. 69–72) who, as an opponent of unions, confirms the need for unionization of female employees.

6. – –

7. **What issues surrounding women and employment are of greatest concern in the Federal Republic of Germany? Discuss.**
– –

4 Betty Friedan: The 100 Percent Perfect Superwoman

Didaktische Hinweise

Betty Friedan, prominente Vorkämpferin für die Gleichberechtigung der Frau, wendete sich in ihrer 1986 gehaltenen Rede an Absolventinnen einer High School, an eine Generation also, denen Gleichberechtigung weitgehend als eine Selbstverständlichkeit erscheint. Sie thematisiert die Mehrfachbelastung der Frau durch Beruf, Ehe, Haushalt und Kindererziehung, warnt vor zu hochgespannten Erwartungen, geht auf die Anfänge der Frauenbewegung ein, nennt gegenwärtige und künftige Probleme und spricht von der Notwendigkeit, die überholte Frontstellung der Geschlechter zugunsten eines partnerschaftlichen Miteinanders aufzugeben. Inhalt und Form dieses Textes sind besonders geeignet, die Schüler/innen direkt anzusprechen, sie zur Stellungnahme und zu Vergleichen mit ihrer eignenen Situation herauszufordern. Auffallend ist die inhaltliche Übereinstimmung Betty Friedans (vgl. Z. 30–35) mit Aussagen von Katherine Whitehorn (Kap. III, Text 5, Z. 43 ff.) über die prägende Rolle, die die Erziehung der Mädchen bei ihrem späteren Verhalten im Berufsleben spielt. Auch hier bieten sich fruchtbare Diskussionsansätze. Unter dem Aspekt der Textanalyse ist dieser Text besonders geeignet, Argumentationsstrategien und rhetorische Techniken zu demonstrieren und ihre Funktionen zu untersuchen (vgl. Aufg. 6).

Background information

Betty Friedan (1921–   ) is one of America's leading feminists. Her book *The Feminine Mystique* (1963) turned the nation's attention to the problems facing women in modern America. She was the founding president of the National Organization for Women (NOW) and helped organize the National Women's Political Caucus. *It*

Changed My Life (1976) concerns her participation in the women's movement, and *The Second Stage* (1981) outlines an agenda for a future human equality.

"equal opportunity in every field of society "(l. 15): for information on the Women's Movement for Equal Rights cf. "Info-Box", SB, p. 183.

Semantic and collocational field "Women and career"

(to) have control over one's life, (to) grow up confident in one's ability to do what one wants, (to) make choices/decisions about marriage/children, (to) take oneself seriously, (to) have it all ❖ one's race for success, (to) compete for career success, (to) be entitled to equal opportunity in every field of society ❖ a world that is structured in terms of men's lives, a male-defined corporate career, (to) play by the rules laid down for/by men ❖ the guilt/conflicts of the double burden of work and home, maternity leave, (to) take time off to have a baby, (to) interrupt one's professional life, (to) share equal responsibility for parenting ❖ job security, (to) be protected by law ❖ (to) strive for the social changes needed, (to) empower one another, (to) change one's life

Talking about the text – Suggested answers

1. They grow up believing that they have the same opportunities men have, i.e. that they can choose jobs which formerly were considered male occupations (cf. ll. 3–5, 13–15). At the same time, they believe they can also fulfil the traditional role and aspiration of women, i.e. to have a family with a (nice, wealthy) husband and children (cf. ll. 6–7). They believe that they have control over their lives and the choices they make regarding their career, marriage and children (cf. ll. 9–17).

2. The corporate world is structured for married men whose wives "take care of the details of daily life" (ll. 25–26). In order to be successful at their jobs, women have to follow rules that were made for men, by men, and are, therefore, unsuited to them. Women have to overcome the handicap of their still traditional upbringing, which makes them a little passive and overconscientious (cf. ll. 30–33). All these disadvantages can only be compensated by working harder and more hours than men (cf. ll. 34–35).
    If a woman decides to interrupt her professional career to have a baby, she is unlikely to get maternity leave and job security (cf. ll. 39–46). If she does decide to have a baby and return to work, she will be faced with the problem of who will take care of the baby, since there are very few child-care facilities (cf. ll. 55–60). Moreover, the double burden of work and home may cause feelings of guilt and conflicts within the family (cf. ll. 80–81).

3. Nowadays women have much greater job opportunities than they used to (cf. ll. 3–5). Moreover, the women's movement has produced husbands who share responsibilities at home by helping with the children (cf. ll. 62–66).

4. Living in suburbs, alone with the children during working hours, they were frustrated housewives, who developed a guilt complex because they wanted more from life at a time when they were supposed to be content with their families, their homes and their appliances. They also quite often developed an inferiority complex because they tended to think that they were abnormal if they wanted more (cf. ll. 84–94).

5. On the one hand, men are perceived negatively when they are operating within the corporate world, presumably taking advantage of their traditional position of power and privilege (cf. ll. 26–30). On the other hand, Friedan recognizes that the women's movement has produced a new kind of man who shares the responsibility for parenting (cf. ll. 62–65). Men are seen as partners necessary in the process of changing society (cf. ll. 133–138).

6. Friedan uses contracted forms throughout the text, which is characteristic of spoken, informal language. She addresses her readers (audience) directly - note the frequent use of "you" - and even imitates dialogue with the audience (cf. "I can hear you say", ll. 2–3,

and the rhetorical questions, e.g. ll. 21–22, 56, 61–62). The exclamation "Well, that's great" (l. 9) is also more characteristic of spoken than of written language. The personal touches appeal to the audience, thus increasing the persuasive effect of the text.

7.   – –

● 8. *Gather information on a famous woman you admire, and report in class about her life and achievements.*
   [Some famous British and American women the teacher may want to suggest for reports: Jane Addams (1860–1935), American social activist; Susan B. Anthony (1820–1906), American suffragist; Elizabeth Cochrane (pen name Nellie Bly, 1867–1922), American investigative journalist; Amelia Earhart (1898–1937?), American aviator; Emmeline Pankhurst (1857–1928), English suffragist.]

● 9. *Analyze the image of women shown and promoted by at least five different magazines. Report your findings to the class.*
   [Students should give careful thought to the kinds of magazines they choose to analyze: all women's and girls' magazines, all men's magazines, general-interest magazines or a mixture? Care should also be taken to find a wide range of portrayals within the chosen category.]

● 10. *Collect pop or rock songs that deal with the role of women in a relationship or in society in general, then present and analyze one in class.*
   – –

5 Frank Trippett: The Anguish of the Jobless

Didaktische Hinweise

Während sich die Texte 1 bis 4 mit unterschiedlichen Aspekten des Themas „Arbeit" beschäftigen, wendet sich Text 5 dem Problem der Arbeitslosigkeit und ihren wirtschaftlichen, vor allem aber psychischen Auswirkungen zu. Zwar geschieht dies hier auf dem Hintergrund einer Gesellschaft, die seit ihren Anfängen von den Wertvorstellungen einer protestantisch-puritanischen Arbeitsethik geprägt ist (vgl. Kap. VI, Text 2, und "Info-Box", SB, S. 143), dennoch wird über den konkreten landeskundlichen Bezug hinausgehend ein Grundkonflikt menschlichen Zusammenlebens – die Kluft zwischen denen, die Arbeit haben, und denen, die Arbeit suchen – angesprochen, der zur persönlichen Stellungnahme herausfordert. Damit bietet der Text die Möglichkeit, vergleichend auf die Verhältnisse in Großbritannien (Kap. III, Text 2, 3, 4) und in der Bundesrepublik (vgl. unten, Aufg. 7 bis 9) einzugehen.

   Über staatliche soziale Leistungen im Falle von Arbeitslosigkeit gibt die "Info-Box" (SB, S. 175 f.) Auskunft. Unterschiedliche Meinungen über den Erfolg solcher finanzieller Hilfen präsentiert Text 6.

Background information

"The new unemployment rate" (l. 1): In 1987, the average unemployment rate was 6.2 % – the rate being 5.4 % for white men and 5.2 % for white women, as compared to 11.5 % for non-white men and 11.7 % for non-white women (based on *Information Please. Almanac, Atlas & Yearbook*. Houghton Mifflin, Boston, 1989, p. 67).

Semantic and collocational field "Unemployment"

the unemployment rate, joblessness, worklessness, an out-of-work person, a victim of the system ✧ a firing, a (government) layoff, a company closure, a plant shutdown, the loss of a job, (to) lose one's job, (to) lose the position one held ✧ unemployment benefit, financial assistance, a staggering cost ✧ an unlucky citizen in need of assistance, the struggle to pay the rent, (to) make (financial) ends meet ✧ the search for new work, (to) seize the opportunity to switch careers ✧ a sense of powerlessness, (to) be cut off from personal and social power, (to) be condemned to uselessness ✧ a confusion of emotions, the psychological cost of joblessness, a feeling of rejection/ worthlessness, self-administered condemnation, (to) take a (cruel) psychic bruising, (to) suffer a sharp loss of self-esteem/a diminished sense of identity/a sense of estrangement, (to) take an uncharitable view of one's ordeal, (to) take away sb.'s self-confidence, (to) destroy sb., (to) blame oneself

Talking about the text – Suggested answers

1. Unemployment is extensive, if considered in terms of the number of individuals – 9.5 million (cf. ll. 6–8). This figure translates into roughly $ 19 billion of potential wealth, in federal revenues, lost (cf. ll. 10–12), not to mention $ 6 billion paid out by the government to assist the jobless (cf. ll. 12–14).

2. The first reaction of a person losing his or her job is one of disbelief. When the reality of the event has dawned upon him or her, there is a shock which is followed by a phase of numbness. This phase gives way to one of rage, characterized by outbursts of destructive behaviour, e.g. "wife beating, child abuse, neglect of friends, drunkenness" (ll. 99–101).

3. The jobless tend to blame themselves for their ordeal (cf. ll. 124–125). As a result, their self-confidence is shattered (cf. ll. 113–114) and they feel useless (cf. l. 65) and worthless (cf. ll. 97–98). They "suffer a sharp loss of self-esteem" (l. 36), lose their "sense of identity" (l. 37) and become unclear and uncertain about what they want to achieve in life (cf. ll. 37–38). They develop a feeling of being rejected (cf. ll. 80–81) by society and of being alienated from friends (cf. ll. 38–39). Thus they feel "cut off from personal and social power" (ll. 118–119) and finally feel destroyed (cf. l. 114).

4. American society has never been sympathetic toward joblessness (cf. ll. 134–137). Usefulness is honoured (cf. l. 66), and the basic view of work being sacred and worklessness being a sin still prevails (cf. ll. 143–145).

5. On the one hand, society pays vast sums of unemployment benefits. On the other hand, the jobless person is often "treated like an alien culprit in need of interrogation" (ll. 71–72).

6. He seems to have a sympathetic view of the unemployed, referring to them as "unlucky citizen[s] in need of assistance" (ll. 72–73). He also reminds the reader that "most of today's idleness is involuntary" (ll. 142–143), and he, if with expression of regret, even points out the value of a certain amount of unemployment (cf. ll. 149–161).

7. ***What attitudes towards the unemployed are common in your part of Germany? Discuss.***
   – –

8. ***Write a fictional text in the form of several diary entries about losing a job and the emotional changes that follow.***
   – –

● 9. ***Interview someone who is currently unemployed. Find out how this person feels, what he or she thinks of unemployed people, and how he or she views service and treatment at the unemployment office. Report your findings to the class without disclosing the name of your interview partner. Discuss the findings of different people's intentions and compare them with what is said in the text.***
   – –

6 Some Voices in the American Social Welfare Debate

Didaktische Hinweise

Die hier zusammengestellten Exzerpte aus einem Zeitschriftenartikel (Text 6a), einer Buchkritik (Text 6b) und einem Hirtenbrief der katholischen Bischöfe (Text 6c) repräsentieren – vor dem Hintergrund der in der zweiten Hälfte der achtziger Jahre stattfindenden öffentlichen Debatte über das staatliche Wohlfahrtssystem Amerikas – divergierende Meinungen. Der zusammenfassend referierende Bericht von L.D. Maloney über die von dem amerikanischen Soziologen Charles Murray in seinem Buch *Losing Ground: American Social Policy 1950–1980* (1984) vertretenen Thesen gibt wohl die Meinung der konservativen Mehrheit wieder. L.C. Thurow weist in seiner Kritik an Murrays Buch (Text 6b) auf Schwachstellen in der Argumentation des Soziologen hin. In ihrem 1986 veröffentlichten Hirtenbrief *Economic Justice for All: Catholic Social Teaching and the U.S. Economy* (Text 6c) widerlegen die Vertreter der katholischen Kirche Murrays Behauptungen, ohne ihn freilich namentlich zu nennen, mit einer Gegenstatistik, verurteilen aber vor allem die unbarmherzige Haltung der amerikanischen Gesellschaft gegenüber den Armen. Letztlich zielen alle drei Texte auf die grundsätzliche Frage, wie ein westlicher Industriestaat am Ende des 20. Jahrhunderts mit seinen gesellschaftlich benachteiligten Mitbürgern umgeht.

Um zu gewährleisten, daß die Schüler/innen sachlich angemessen zu den Problemen Stellung nehmen können, sollte die "Info-Box" (SB, S. 175 f.) in die Textbesprechung einbezogen werden. Auch die in der "Background information" (vgl. unten) genannten Zahlen können in das Unterrichtsgespräch integriert werden. Weitere Angaben über das Phänomen der „neuen Armut" in den USA finden sich im LB, S. 189.

Background information

Lester C. Thurow (1938–   ) is a professor of economics and management at the Massachussetts Institute of Technology in Cambridge, Mass. Among other books, he has published *Generating Inequality* (1975), The *Zero-Sum Society* (1980) and *Dangerous Currents* (1983).

Households receiving Aid For Dependent Children (AFDC) in 1986:

Race of recipient		*Number of children in the family*	
Black:	40.7 %	One:	43.4 %
White:	39.7 %	Two:	30.8 %
Hispanic:	14.5 %	Three:	16.0 %
Asian	2.3 %	Four or more:	9.8 %
Other:	2.7 %		

Age of youngest child		*Time on AFDC*	
Under 3:	38.4 %	Under 7 months:	17.2 %
3 to 5:	22.7 %	7 to 12 months:	12.7 %
6 to 11:	24.3 %	One to two years:	17.3 %
Over 11:	14.5 %	Two to five years:	26.8 %
		Over five years:	25.9 %

Mother's age

21 or younger:	15.8 %
22 to 29:	41.3 %
30 to 39:	30.3 %
40 or older:	12.7 %

Mother's education

Under grade 12:	47.4 %
High school graduate:	42.9 %
Some college education:	8.5 %
College graduate:	1.2 %

Fathers of the children	*1986*	*1973*
Not married to mother:	52.6 %	31.5 %
Divorced or separated:	31.7 %	46.5 %
Unemployed or disabled:	9.0 %	14.3 %
Deceased:	1.7 %	5 %
Other or unknown:	5.1 %	2.7 %

Semantic and collocational field "Welfare"

a crusade to wipe out poverty, a social welfare system, a welfare programme, a programme for the poor/designed to help sb., an affirmative-action programme, an AFDC recipient, a handout, an entitlement, (to) receive AFDC, (to) obtain benefits ✧ a huge outpouring of aid, an increasing amount of government aid, (to) provide more for the poor, (to) cost the government billions of dollars, (to) scrap a welfare programme ✧ (to) be worse off, (to) become deeply mired in poverty, (to) destroy individual initiative, (to) undermine family life, (to) be/stay on welfare, (to) move on and off welfare, (to) build a (poverty) trap, dependent on the dole ✧ (to) raise one's allowance, (to) escape work, (to) be poor by choice/through laziness ✧ a desire to work, (to) escape (from) poverty by hard work

Talking about the text – Suggested answers

1. They believe the money has been wasted because the programmes have not really helped the poor, but have contributed to their staying poor and even getting poorer (cf. ll. 8–13). As the title of Murray's book implies, the poor are "losing ground" (l. 18), or the government is losing ground in its war on poverty. According to the critics, government aid has increased the number of poor (cf. ll. 24–25) and made them dependent on benefits by destroying people's individual initiative (cf. ll. 21–23). Some apparently go so far as to blame welfare programmes for ruining families (cf. l. 22) and causing an increase in illegitimate births (cf. ll. 57–58).

2. Thurow ridicules Murray's basic argument on an issue as complex as welfare by comparing it with the simple logic of Aesop's fable. To Thurow, Murray's welfare recipients are Aesop's fiddling, happy-go-lucky grasshoppers, who are supposed to be jeopardizing the whole system by asking for food from the hard-working ants. Just as it is unproved that ants would stop working if the grasshoppers were fed in the winter by those with the means to help them, so it is unproved that workers would prefer welfare to earning their living.

3. Misconception: Most are racial minorities (cf. ll. 77–79). People stay on welfare for years (cf. ll. 81–82). Welfare recipients do not work (cf. l. 82). Poor people do not want to work (cf. l. 83). Poor women have more children to get more benefits (cf. ll. 93–95).

   Facts: Two-thirds are white (cf. ll. 79–80). Less than 1 % stay on welfare continuously for 10 years (cf. ll. 84–87). Nearly half of all families receiving AFDC have a working member (cf. ll. 99–101). Research shows that poor people share the work ethic with everybody else (cf. ll. 102–105). 70 % of AFDC families have only one or two children. Little money is to be gained by having more (cf. ll. 96–99).

4. They criticize what they call "a punitive attitude toward the poor" (ll. 111–112). Apparently, many people believe that the poor themselves are to blame for their poverty, and that all that is needed is hard work for somebody to escape from poverty (cf. ll. 114–115). They are especially strong in their criticism of people calling aid to the poor "handouts" (l. 125),

which, as such, is given only grudgingly, while subsidies to well-off individuals and corporations are referred to as "entitlements" (l. 123) and are taken for granted.

5. – –
6. *Organize a debate in class. Topic: All welfare programmes should be abolished.* – –

7. *Do you believe that religious leaders should speak out on social issues the way the US Catholic bishops did, or should they confine their statements to religious matters? Discuss.* – –

7 Alice Walker: Freedom March

Didaktische Hinweise

Dieses Exzerpt aus Alice Walkers Roman *Meridian* (1976) bietet die Möglichkeit, vier für die Behandlung der amerikanischen Bürgerrechtsbewegung wichtige Aspekte herauszuarbeiten: die Lebensbedingungen der Schwarzen in der amerikanischen Gesellschaft vor dem Beginn des Civil Rights Movement; den friedlichen Charakter der Protestbewegung; die ungerechtfertigte und unangemessen harte Reaktion weißer Behörden; schließlich die bedeutende Rolle der Kirche im Kampf der schwarzen Amerikaner um ihre Gleichberechtigung.

Die gewählte Erzählperspektive, die die Unvermitteltheit des staatlichen Zugriffs und das völlige Unverständnis der Demonstranten besonders deutlich macht (vgl. unten, Aufg. 5), kann den Jugendlichen einen Eindruck davon vermitteln, was es bedeutete, noch in den sechziger Jahren ein schwarzer Bürger/eine schwarze Bürgerin der Vereinigten Staaten zu sein. Gegen diesen Hintergrund tritt in Text 8 und 9b dann umso deutlicher zutage, welche Fortschritte im Verlauf von zwei Jahrzehnten erzielt wurden, auch wenn noch immer Fälle von Diskriminierung zu finden sind (vgl. auch Kap. V, Text 7). Den historischen Verlauf der Bürgerrechtsbewegung (einschließlich eines Rückblicks auf die Geschichte der Sklaverei in Amerika) zeichnet die "Info-Box" (SB, S. 182 f.) nach.

Eine Unterrichtssequenz zum Thema „Minoritäten in den USA" wird nicht nur die Situation der schwarzen Amerikaner/innen (Text 7 bis 9b), sondern auch die der zweitgrößten Minderheitengruppe, der Hispanics (vgl. Kap. V, Text 8, 9 und 11), berücksichtigen. Eine Vertiefung der Diskussion durch die Einbeziehung von Texten, die zu den menschlichen Grundrechten Stellung nehmen (vgl. Kap. XII, Text 9, 12), ist ohne weiteres möglich.

Background information

Alice Walker (1944–   ) was born in Eatonton, Ga. She is regarded as one of America's most gifted black writers, having published a number of novels, including *Meridian* (Harcourt Brace Jovanovich, New York, 1976), *The Color Purple* (1982), for which she won a Pulitzer Prize, and *The Temple of My Familiar* (1989). Several collections of her poetry and short stories, as well as a biography of the poet Langston Hughes, have appeared.

Semantic and collocational field "Demonstration"

a demonstration, a freedom march/song, a demonstrator, a civil rights worker, an attempt to have sb. released, (to) be in protest against sb./sth., (to) demonstrate against sth., (to) testify ✧ a State trooper, a police car, a jail, segregated (hospital) facilities, (to) be arrested ✧ a bludgeon, tear gas, (to) surround sb., (to) turn on sb., (to) knock sb. to the ground, (to) be trampled by sb., (to) punch sb., (to) kick sb. in the back, (to) grab sb. by the hair, (to) beat sb., (to) finish sb. ✧ (to) scream, (to) burst into tears, (to) tremble, (to) twitch with dread

Talking about the text – Suggested answers

1. *What do we learn from the text about blacks' living conditions before the changes brought about by the civil rights movement?*

   A number of facilities were segregated according to race, including the jail (cf. ll. 6–7), the hospital (cf. l. 13) and the buses, where blacks had to sit in the back (cf. l. 61). Apparently, all public toilets in the town are reserved for whites (cf. ll. 63–64). Conditions in the black section of these facilities were poor: reports of conditions in the black jail were so bad that they "caused Meridian's body to twitch with dread" (l. 7). Many black people were illiterate (cf. ll. 55–56) [and were, therefore, kept from voting].

2. *What are the aims of the civil rights workers, and what do they do to achieve them?*

   They have three aims: to desegregate the hospital and other facilities (cf. ll. 12–13, 56), to get their fellow demonstrators out of jail (cf. ll. 13–14) and to make blacks more politically aware. The first two goals are to be achieved by peaceful demonstrations, the third by political education in the form of "canvassing, talking at rallies" (ll. 43–44) and teaching uneducated blacks to read and write (cf. ll. 55–56).

3. *What is the attitude of the black community towards the civil rights movement?*

   The majority support the movement – at least morally – and encourage the civil rights workers (cf. ll. 54–55). Some, however, are less than sympathetic. Mrs Hill, for instance, has apparently been brainwashed into believing that the existing order is God's will (cf. ll. 59–60). She refuses to see the disadvantages of segregation and even rationalizes them into being advantages (cf. ll. 61–62).

4. *What can you conclude from information given in the text about the role churches play in the civil rights movement?*

   Churches provide, first of all, a meeting place for the civil rights activists. They also provide leadership – a Reverend is "in charge" (l. 5) – and organization. Most important, however, is the legitimacy they give to the movement: a prayer (cf. l. 5) gives participants the notion that God is on their side.

5. *What effect does the author achieve by concentrating on Meridian in this excerpt?*

   Concentrating on Meridian makes the story more personal, credible and therefore effective than a general overview would have been. The reader experiences events with her: the feeling of dread from reports on conditions in the local jail (cf. l. 7), her observations about those who had been arrested before her and her sudden realization that she would be next (cf. ll. 22–26), the pain inflicted upon her inside the jail (cf. ll. 32–33), but especially her development from a rather naive marcher who was unable to comprehend the tactics she herself was participating in (cf. ll. 14–16) to a fully-fledged member of the movement (cf. ll. 55–57, 66).

6. *Describe the atmosphere created by the author's choice of words.*

   The atmosphere is definitely one of violence and cruelty, but the tone remains peculiarly unemotional. Even before Meridian experiences violence herself, she hears about (cf. l. 7) and sees the effects of violence (cf. ll. 23–25). The words used to relate Meridian's own experience of beatings at the hands of the sheriff and his deputies are very sober, direct, lacking in vividness. Even the panic that ensues is described with a minimum of words: "she was trampled by people running back and forth over her" (ll. 28–29).

8 Taylor Branch: The Tenth Federal Holiday

Didaktische Hinweise

Dieser Text spannt den zeitlichen Bogen von den Verhältnissen, wie sie vor Beginn der Bürgerrechtsbewegung in Amerika herrschten, zu den tiefgreifenden gesell–schaftlichen Veränderungen, die es 1987 ermöglichten, einen zu seinen Lebzeiten von Teilen der weißen Mehrheit geschmähten Mann wie Martin Luther King zwanzig Jahre nach seinem gewaltsamen Tod mit einem Nationalfeiertag zu ehren. Aus Taylor Branchs Darstellung werden nicht nur die Leistungen und das Charisma Kings deutlich, sondern auch der von ihm bewirkte Wandel in der gesellschaftlichen Situation der schwarzen Amerikaner/innen.

Es liegt nahe, die im Text nur in zwei kurzen Ausschnitten zitierte Rede "I Have a Dream" vollständig in den Unterricht einzubeziehen (u.a. verfügbar in: Staats-institut für Schulpädagogik und Bildungsforschung München [Hrsg.]: *Religion in America.* [Handreichungen zur Amerikakunde im Leistungskurs Englisch am Gymna–sium, Bd. 2] Donauwörth, Verlag Auer 1985, S. 100 f.). Die Rolle des schwarzen Predigers ist Thema der sehr lesenswerten Kurzgeschichte von Lerone Bennett, Jr.: "The Convert" (in: Martin Mirer [ed.]: *Modern Black Stories.* Woodbury, N.Y., Baron's Educational Series, 1971).

Literaturhinweise: H. Sittkoff: *The Struggle for Black Equality 1954–1980.* New York, Hill & Wang 1981. David J. Garrow: *Bearing the Cross: Martin Luther King, Jr, and the Southern Christian Leadership Conference.* New York, Morrow 1987. Adam Fairclough: *To Redeem the Soul of America: The Southern Christian Leadership Conference and Martin Luther King, Jr.* Athens, Ga., University of Georgia Press 1987. Eine ausführliche Rezension beider Bücher schrieb George M. Frederickson: "The Stirring of Black America". In: *The Times Literary Supplement,* July 17, 1987, pp. 759 f.

Background information

Taylor Branch (1947–   ) grew up in Atlanta, Ga. He attended the University of Chapel Hill, N.C., and was a staff member of *Harper's, The Washington Monthly* and *Esquire.* In 1988 he published *Parting the Waters: America in the King Years, 1954–1963* (Simon & Schuster, New York), which was the result of six years of research. A second volume of this critically acclaimed biography is due to appear in the early 1990s.

Martin Luther King, Jr. (1929–1968) was born in Atlanta, Ga. He studied theology and received his PhD from Boston University in 1955. He became a Baptist minister and leader of the Civil Rights Movement from the mid-1950s until his death by assassination. Following the principles of Gandhi (cf. Ch. I, Text 2), he advocated a policy of non-violence to oppose the segregation laws, and in 1964 was awarded the Nobel Peace Prize. He is best remembered for leading the March on Washington (1963), during which he made his famous speech "I Have a Dream."

"our tenth federal holiday": (ll. 32–33) There are no official holidays in the USA, only days on which federal organizations are closed, although in practice many offices, etc. also shut down on these days. The ten federal holidays are New Year's Day (Jan.1); King Day (the third Monday of January); Washington's Birthday (the third Monday of February); Memorial Day (the last Monday in May, honouring the dead of all wars); Independence Day (July 4, commemorating the signing of the Declaration of Independence in 1776); Labor Day (the first Monday of September, since 1894); Columbus Day (the second Monday of October, commemorating the discovery of America by Columbus); Veteran's Day (November 11, honouring American service personnel, past and present, introduced after World War I as Armistice Day); Thanksgiving (the fourth Thursday of November); Christmas Day (December 25).

Talking about the text – Suggested answers

1. King appealed in his speech to the strong sense of patriotism shared by most Americans. He cited words from a song he could be sure everyone in his audience knew. He spoke to all Americans, "black men and white men, Jews and Gentiles, Catholics and Protestants" (ll. 19–21), from all parts of the US (cf. ll. 9–14). By emphasizing the oneness of his fellow Americans and not the differences, he implied that, as long as blacks were not free, everybody would suffer; when blacks were finally free, everyone could feel their relief and cry, " 'Thank God Almighty I'm free at last!' " (ll. 23–24). The use of anaphora, e.g. "from …" (ll. 8–13), "free at last" (ll. 22–24) and parallel structures with "and" (ll. 19–21) add to the forcefulness of the rhetoric.
2. Before this new holiday, all the people honoured by the US government had been politicians or military men. King is also the first black to receive such recognition, the first person with a doctorate, the first preacher, the first to have been at odds with the US government and the first who had never even tried to get a public office (cf. ll. 56–60).
3. The South has been "liberated" (l. 71) and is on the rise. Blacks now hold elected offices, work in the professions and are represented in TV shows and college sports. They are watched – and to a large extent respected – not only by the black community, but by all Americans, or in King's own words, by "all of God's children" (l. 19).
4. King's message is universal, applying to all people (cf. ll. 19–21) and to all countries, esp. to South Africa and the Middle East (cf. ll. 76–78). Recent incidents of racial hatred (cf. ll. 78–79) show that there is still a need for his words in the US. But the more important changes are in the hearts and minds of people, allowing them "to recommit ourselves to the proposition that all men are created equal" (ll. 103–105) and nourishing the "spirit of reconciliation" (l. 105–106).
5. Bethune, it would appear, has gone through profound changes. He comes from a Southern state in which there was great opposition to the Civil Rights Movement (cf. "travail", l. 93). In addition, he was once with the FBI, an organization that long considered King an enemy.
6. *Are there any national heroes in your country you think should be honoured with a holiday? If so, argue their case.*
   – –
● 7. *Write a profile of a famous black American, living or dead, and present the information to the class.*
   [Possible source: the black magazine "Ebony", available at international newsstands in the railway stations and airports of most major cities in Germany, and at the Amerika Häuser.]

9a A Permanent Black Underclass?

Didaktische Hinweise

Text 9a und 9b (Graphik) gehören inhaltlich eng zusammen (vgl. auch Aufg. 1 zu Text 9b). Sie zeigen, wie sich die wirtschaftliche und gesellschaftliche Stellung der schwarzen Amerikaner/innen in den vergangenen zwei Jahrzehnten entwickelt hat. Auffallend ist das Auseinanderfallen der schwarzen Bevölkerung in zwei Gruppen: Während ein schwarzer „Mittelstand", was Einkommen, Schulbildung, Besitz und öffentliches Ansehen anlangt, erhebliche Fortschritte gemacht hat (vgl. Text 9b), droht einem anderen Teil Verelendung. Text 9a und 9b beschränken sich auf die Wiedergabe der Fakten, die Gründe für eine solche Entwicklung werden kontrovers diskutiert und hängen von der jeweiligen politischen Überzeugung ab. Während die einen sie im "vacuum of values" sehen, das nur durch eine veränderte Einstellung der Betroffenen selbst beseitigt werden könne, machen vor allem ältere Vertreter des Civil Rights Movement den noch immer latenten Rassismus der amerikanischen Gesellschaft für die Zustände verantwortlich (M.B. Zuckermann: "The Black Underclass". In: *US News & World Report*, April 14, 1986, p. 78). Auch die in Text 5 und 6c erwähnte weitverbreitete Meinung über die „selbstverschuldete Armut" wird als Erklärung herangezogen.

Die Interdependenz der beiden Themenkomplexe „soziale Absicherung" und „Minoritätenproblematik" wird an Text 9a und 9b besonders deutlich. Beide sind über den spezifisch landeskundlichen Bereich hinaus von allgemeiner Bedeutung und werfen damit Fragen auf, mit denen auch deutsche Schüler/innen direkt konfrontiert werden können.

Background information

For information on unemployment rates cf. p. 150, for information on poverty levels cf. p. 189 of this book.

Semantic and collocational field "Inner-city poverty"

an inner-city neighbourhood, a ghetto, urban poverty, a black underclass, a swelling population of have-nots, (to) be down ✧ an income below the poverty line, dependence on government support, a high rate of joblessness/crime/drug abuse, (to) live in poverty ✧ a broken life, a sense of hopelessness, a spirit of defeatism, economic/spiritual impoverishment, (to) be left behind

Talking about the text – Suggested answers

1. Most of these people live in inner-city neighbourhoods, where there are high rates of crime, drug abuse and joblessness. Large numbers come from fatherless households. They are both perpetrators and victims of crime much more often than whites. Many are, as a result of their situation, subject to a strong "sense of hopelessness ... – a spirit of defeatism" (ll. 45–46).
2. The prospects are bleak, especially since it is hard for people who have grown up in poverty to believe that they will ever know a better life. As Jesse Jackson puts it, "the odds are overwhelming" (l. 37), so many "surrender spiritually" (l. 36). Eventually the underclass may explode (cf. ll. 50–51), but until then it seems likely that "today's inner-city children will become a forever-lost generation of adults" (ll. 53–54).

3. According to the text, the government is considering reforms in the welfare system. It is not reported what the nature of these reforms might be, only that the goal is to encourage self-help and to provide conditions that would lead to a higher standard of living, jobs and two-parent families (cf. ll. 19–20).
4. – –

9b Changes over 20 Years

Didaktische Hinweise

Vgl. die Hinweise zu Text 9a, LB, S. 158.

Talking about the text – Suggested answers

1. Texts 9a and 9b do not contradict each other. Text 9a, though its writers present a very negative view of the situation of black Americans, admits that "the civil-rights movement has brought better life to large numbers of blacks" (ll. 12–14). Text 9b simply emphasizes the improvements, while Text 9a deals only with those not affected by these improvements.
2. – –
3. Besides the fact that such graphs liven up the pages of the magazine printing them, they are very effective ways of communicating statistical information. The visual presentation creates a more vivid and lasting impression on the reader than a dry explanation of the statistics.
4. A median income is the value that divides exactly one half the *number* of incomes from the other half. Taking the 1982 median income of $ 25,359 as an example, the figure tells us only that one half of black "families" – whatever that may mean – earned more than that amount, while one half earned less. The figure does not tell us how much more or how much less those people earned. [An extreme example might help to illustrate the concept: If 10 people earned $ 25,360, one person earned $ 25,359 and 10 people earned only $ 5,000, then the median income of these 21 people would be $ 25,359].

    An average income counts each individual income equally, emphasizing the *value* as opposed to the number of incomes counted. [In the extreme example above, the average income of the 21 people counted would be $ 15,665.] Both median and average incomes tend to obscure individual cases.

Chapter VIII: Constitutional History and Political Reality

Kapitel VIII beschäftigt sich mit Aspekten der politischen Geschichte und mit der politischen Realität der Vereinigten Staaten von Amerika. Dabei spielt die Frage der Menschenrechte eine besonders große Rolle. Insofern dienen die Texte nicht nur der Faktenvermittlung, sondern erfüllen auch eine erzieherische Aufgabe. Verfassungsrechtliche Fragen werden berührt, wo es um historische und aktuelle Aspekte der Staats- und Regierungsform geht, werden aber auch im Zusammenhang mit den Rechten und der stets zu verteidigenden Identität des Einzelnen angesprochen. Eine Reihe von Texten thematisiert schließlich das Verhältnis der USA zu Europa sowie zu anderen Teilen der Welt und trägt damit dazu bei, die oft nicht genügend reflektierten Einstellungen der Schüler/innen zu den Vereinigten Staaten auf der Basis größerer Sachkenntnis zu revidieren.

Kapitel VIII beginnt mit einem Auszug aus der "Declaration of Independence", einem grundlegenden, für die westliche Welt und ihre politischen Strukturen höchst einflußreichen Dokument. In der amerikanischen "Bill of Rights" (Text 2) wurden die Persönlichkeitsrechte festgeschrieben. Ohne Kenntnis dieses Dokuments ist die verfassungsgeschichtliche Entwicklung der USA kaum nachvollziehbar. Während Text 3 den Blick auf den historischen Verlauf der Menschenrechtsdiskussion und ihre jeweilige Umsetzung in Verfassungstexte lenkt, geht Text 4, ein Auszug aus R. Bradburys *Fahrenheit 451*, von einer fiktiven drastischen Einschränkung der Menschenrechte und der Aufhebung der Gewaltenteilung in einer durchaus vorstellbaren Zukunft aus. Die Texte 5, 6 und 7 befassen sich mit den beiden großen politischen Parteien bzw. mit den drei Gewalten, die in einem für die amerikanische Verfassung charakteristischen System von "checks and balances" miteinander verknüpft sind (vgl. dazu auch "Info-Box", SB, S. 190 f.). Text 8 problematisiert den bisher im historischen Kontext diskutierten Freiheitsbegriff aus heutiger Perspektive, verknüpft die Vergangenheit mit der Gegenwart und leitet damit zum weltweiten politischen und wirtschaftlichen Engagement der USA über, das Gegenstand der beiden letzten Texte ist. Sie bieten die Möglichkeit, die in diesem und den Kapiteln V bis VII angesprochenen Teilthemen systematisierend zusammenzufassen, in größere Zusammenhänge einzuordnen und so zu einer auf Sachkenntnissen beruhenden Einstellung zu den Vereinigten Staaten zu gelangen.

1 Excerpt from the Declaration of Independence (1776)

Didaktische Hinweise

Die amerikanische Unabhängigkeitserklärung gehört zu den verfassungsrechtlichen Dokumenten, die weit über die Grenzen des Landes hinaus bekannt sind; möglicherweise kennen Schüler/innen den Wortlaut, zumindest in Auszügen, aus dem Geschichtsunterricht. Aufgenommen wurde daher ein Ausschnitt, der die Schlüsselsätze dieses Dokuments enthält. Mit den hier wiedergegebenen Passagen erreichten die bis dahin philosophisch postulierten Menschenrechte Verfassungsrang und fanden Eingang in die praktische Politik. Im ersten Abschnitt verweisen die Verfasser auf die historische Situation, die aus ihrer Sicht zur Unabhängigkeitserklärung geführt hat und sie rechtfertigt; gleichzeitig heben sie sie durch die moralische Begründung aus ihrer historischen Bedingtheit heraus und verleihen ihr eine über den Tagesanlaß hinausgehende Bedeutung.

Die amerikanische Unabhängigkeitserklärung bzw. das Thema „Menschenrechte" werden auch in den Texten 2 bis 4, 7 bis 10 sowie in den Kapiteln IV, V, VII und XII angesprochen. Über Verknüpfungsmöglichkeiten gibt das „Didaktische Inhaltsverzeichnis" (LB, S. xxiv ff.) Auskunft. Soll der Einstieg in die Menschenrechtsproblematik über einen stärker grundsätzlich orientierten Text erfolgen, kann auch mit Maurice Cranstons Erörterungen (Text 3) begonnen werden.

Background information

For more than 10 years before the Declaration of Independence, tension had been growing between Britain and her American colonies. The British expected the colonists to share in the costs of administering and defending the colonies, and so imposed taxes on various items to raise money. However, these taxes were strongly opposed by the colonists and were eventually repealed. Only one tax remained: the Tea Tax. The "Boston Tea Party" of 1773, in which colonists boarded British ships in Boston Harbor and dumped their cargoes of tea into the water, was the colonists' response. Parliament countered with a number of laws to punish Massachusetts. These laws came to be known as the Intolerable Acts and helped to unite the colonies against the mother country.

In 1774 the First Continental Congress, made up of delegates from all the colonies except Georgia, met in Philadelphia. The delegates decided to boycott British goods to force Britain to change her policies. When the Second Continental Congress met a year later, British policy had not changed and there had already been some fighting between colonists and British troops. Congress decided to form an army and a navy and to issue money to finance the war effort. A final appeal was sent to King George III to change his attitude towards the colonies.

The independence movement grew rapidly, and on June 7, 1776, a resolution was introduced in Congress to declare America independent. On June 10, Congress decided to appoint a committee to draft a declaration of independence to use in case the resolution passed. The committee was made up of five members, three of whom would become very important in America's early history: Thomas Jefferson (cf. "Info-Box", SB, p. 190), who drafted the text in a two-week period, John Adams (1735–1826; second president of the US, 1797–1801) and Benjamin Franklin (1706–1790; American statesman, scientist and author). The committee's draft was debated and amended in Congress. On July 2, the resolution to declare America independent was passed; the final draft of the Declaration of Independence was approved by Congress two days later.

July 4 is considered to be the birthday of the US and is America's most important non-religious holiday. The original parchment copy of the Declaration, which carries the signatures of 56 members of the Continental Congress, is on display in the National Archives Building in Washington, D.C.

"Life, Liberty and the pursuit of Happiness" (ll. 7–8): This concept goes back to Michel-Guillaume Jean de Crèvecœur and his ideas of "the American"(cf. Ch. V, Text 2), which developed from philosophical perspectives of the Enlightenment. The term "pursuit of happiness" is just as elusive and hard to define as it is inspiring and motivating; it was therefore able to grow into the myth of the American

Dream and become a dominant force in American life and thought, where it is still present today. In the latter part of the 19th century the American Dream grew to be understood more materialistically as a relentless pursuit of success, a right to the acquisition of wealth, which would produce a high degree of self-esteem and a respected position in society. Although many Americans have realized that there is a gap between the ideals and reality, the myth nevertheless persists.

Talking about the text – Suggested answers

1. *How did the authors of the Declaration of Independence describe the relationship between government and the governed?*
   They stated that governments are established in order to secure the rights of individuals. They added that the source of a government's legitimacy is the consent of the people who are governed. If the people are not satisfied with the way a government is doing this job, they have the right to change or even abolish the government.

2. *In an American encyclopedia or other source, find the complete text of the Declaration of Independence. Summarize its contents for the class.*
   – –

2 The Bill of Rights (1791)

Didaktische Hinweise

Als eine schriftliche Garantie für die individuellen Rechte der Bürger ist die amerikanische "Bill of Rights" ein Dokument von größter Folgewirkung bis hinein in die Gegenwart. So spielt z.B. in einer Zeit, in der die Massenmedien zunehmend die Kontrollfunktion der Parlamente übernehmen und Fehlverhalten der Regierungen aufdecken (vgl. auch LB, S. 216), das First Amendment eine herausragende Rolle. Die aus den ersten 10 (von mittlerweile 26) Zusatzartikeln bestehende "Bill of Rights" zeigt, daß die amerikanische Verfassung kein starres, unveränderliches Dokument, sondern die flexible Kodierung einer stets anpassungsfähigen Staatsform ist. Unter diesem Gesichtspunkt ergibt sich ein enger Bezug zu Text 7, in dem der Einfluß des Supreme Court auf das politische Leben der USA dargestellt wird. Es empfiehlt sich, bei der Arbeit an diesem Text die "Info-Box" (SB, S. 190 f.) und das Themenheft *The US Bill of Rights in Action.* (Ed. by Ruth Williams. Berlin, Cornelsen Verlag 1990. SB Best.-Nr. 52168, LH 52176) heranzuziehen.

Background information

The Bill of Rights: Following independence, there was an important debate in America concerning the political nature of the newly-founded nation. Out of 13 independent and distinct colonies, a new nation was formed with a centralized government to coordinate national and foreign policy. The suspicion of authority and the reluctance of states to forego their privileges can be seen in the division of opinion concerning the Constitution. In 1787 state delegates drew up the Constitution, but only 39 of the 55 delegates signed it. Those who opposed it did so for two main reasons: the fear of a centralized government destroying the rights of individual states, and the belief that the Constitution did not safeguard the freedom of the individual citizen. In Rhode Island the opposition to a strong federal government was so intense that it was not until 1790 that the state ratified the Constitution.

George Mason, the author of the Declaration of Rights of Virginia, was one of the delegates at the Constitutional Convention who refused to sign the Constitution. He stressed the importance of a document protecting the civil liberties and rights of the individual. He was opposed by the majority of the delegates, who believed that the federal government would not be given the power necessary to impose restrictions on individual freedom and that the constitutions of the states would be sufficient to protect civil rights. So the final draft of the Constitution which was sent to the 13 states for ratification did not include a Bill of Rights.

However, in state ratification conventions – particularly in Virginia – arguments between Federalists (those who accepted the idea of a strong federal government) and Anti-Federalists (those who wanted the states to have more power than the central government) often centred around the question whether or not to add a Bill of Rights. The Federalists managed to win over the advocates of a Bill of Rights by promising to support their demands. Massachusetts made the addition of 10 amendments protecting individual liberty a condition of its ratification, and other states followed suit. When the First Congress convened in 1789, the feeling in favour of adopting the amendments was such that Congress set about drafting them. In 1791 they were officially added to the Constitution, after most of the states had ratified them, and they were given the name Bill of Rights (cf. "Info-Box", SB, p. 190 f.)

Semantic and collocational field "The law"

common law, the due process of law, (to) make a law, (to) prohibit sth., prescribed by law ✧ a criminal prosecution, an indictment, an accusation, (to) issue a warrant, (to) search sb./sth., (to) seize sb./sth., (to) require bail, (to) inflict punishment, the accused ✧ a (law) suit, a public trial, a trial by jury, an impartial jury, a grand jury, a witness, counsel for the/one's defense, an oath, an affirmation

Talking about the text – Suggested answers

1. The first group, consisting of Amendments 1–4, protects the rights and liberties of individuals from interference from the federal government. The second group, Amendments 5–8, describes the legal rights of individuals accused of a crime or involved in any kind of legal controversy. Amendments 9 and 10 state that rights not expressly given to the federal government are to be retained either by the states or the people.
2. The original reasons colonists had for leaving Europe, among them religious intolerance and censorship, help to explain the First Amendment. Also, the colonists had repeatedly – and unsuccessfully – petitioned George III asking him to stop Parliament passing laws concerning the colonies. The Second Amendment can be explained with the War of Independence itself. America's Founding Fathers had found it necessary to turn to armed rebellion to free themselves from a government they considered intolerable. They wanted to keep this possibility open for the future.
3. All the amendments apply to all [white] people, and so reflect the idea that "all men are created equal" (Text 1, 1. 6). The essentials of life are guaranteed indirectly in various amendments, directly, though, in the Fifth Amendment, where it says that nobody will be "deprived of life ... without due process of law" (ll. 40–42), and in the Eighth Amendment, which prohibits "cruel and unusual punishments" (ll. 68–69). Liberty, in some sense, is protected by the first seven amendments and by the Eighth. [Here the student may be expected to enumerate and elaborate.] As far as "the pursuit of Happiness" (Text 1, 1. 8) is concerned, one might state that all the amendments together give individual citizens the security they need to even consider any attempts at finding happiness.
4. – –

3 Maurice Cranston: Human Rights

Didaktische Hinweise

Maurice Cranstons Ausführungen können als theoretische Grundlage für die Auseinandersetzung mit Fragen der Menschenrechte und ihrer Verwirklichung bzw. Suspendierung dienen und daher auch als Basistext für eine entsprechende Unterrichtssequenz fungieren, also der Behandlung von Text 1 und 2 dieses Kapitels vorgeschaltet werden. Weitere Bezüge lassen sich zu den Texten 4, 7 bis 9, aber auch zu Kap. IV, Text 1a und 1b, herstellen. Über andere Verknüpfungsmöglichkeiten gibt das „Didaktische Inhaltsverzeichnis" (LB, S. xxiv) Auskunft.

Background information

Human rights: It was not until after World War II, with all its accompanying atrocities, that active concern for human rights on an international level began to make itself felt. The preamble to the Charter of the United Nations (1945) (cf. Ch. XII, Text 9) declares its faith "in fundamental human rights, in the dignity and worth of the human person" (ll. 4–5). Although a vague statement, it does mean that all countries that are signatories to the Charter do, in theory, accept the concept of human rights.

In 1948 the General Assembly adopted the Universal Declaration of Human Rights, which upon ratification by governments would become legally binding upon them. Despite this and various other international charters and declarations, the violation of human rights continues in the majority of countries in the world.

The first time that it seemed some concrete commitments to human rights in the Soviet bloc might be achieved was in 1969, when the Soviet Union asked for a European Security Conference to deal with security, economic cooperation, human rights and institutional matters. In 1975 35 countries signed the Helsinki Declaration, which sought to promote rights in the signatory countries, but which produced few results. A follow-up conference early in 1989 in Vienna revealed willingness on the part of the Soviet Union to allow its citizens greater freedom.

"The Age of Reason" (l. 17): another term for the Enlightenment, a cultural and philosophical movement that aimed to replace orthodox beliefs, which were based on religious and political authority, with beliefs that were a result of rational thinking and scientific inquiry and that would stand up to the critical examination of the individual. The movement began with the unparalleled scientific inquiry into the natural world and the universe that took place in 16th century Europe. During the 17th and 18th centuries moral and religious beliefs as well as social structures were questioned; as scientific knowledge increased, seemingly basic truths were criticized and established assumptions were challenged. Philosophers of the time attacked dogmatic religion and demanded individual liberty and equality. The movement culminated in the French Revolution in 1789. Some of the most notable thinkers were Bacon, Hobbes, Hume and Locke in Britain, Voltaire, Rousseau and Montesquieu in France and Lessing and Kant in Germany.

Semantic and collocational field "Human rights"

human rights, the rights of man, an inherent/a natural right, a right to life/liberty/property/a fair and public trial by jury, (to) be endowed with an inalienable right, (to) be free/

independent ✧ a natural law, (to) be created equal ✧ the enjoyment of life/liberty, the pursuit of happiness, (to) pursue/obtain happiness ✧ a fair and public trial by jury ✧ (to) adopt/enact a bill of rights ✧ (to) deprive/divest sb. of sth.

Talking about the text – Suggested answers

1. The only new idea in the Virgina bill of rights is the concept of "pursuing and obtaining happiness". John Locke had, a century earlier, already spoken of man's right to life, liberty and property. Other thoughts expressed in the Virgina document show the influence of the English Bill of Rights of 1689. That the idea of a right to happiness could be added to the list was only made possible by a change in social thought away from puritanical morals.

2. Natural law presents man with certain facts, including his own weakness and vulnerability. Natural rights were thought to be derived solely from the nature of man (cf. "there is something about man's nature", ll. 66 ff.), and not as a result of philosophizing or a law-making process. Vulnerability has forced man into social structures which, in turn, demand rules of behaviour – and rights. Such rights are universal, inherent and inalienable. No government could possibly take them away, and no one could ever give them up – not even of his or her own free will.

3. *There are many international agreements to protect human rights, notably the Charter of the United Nations (1945; cf. Ch. XII, Text 9), the Universal Declaration of Human Rights (1948) and the European Commission on Human Rights (1971). Efforts to establish international committees to enforce these agreements have been mostly failures. Can you think of reasons why this might be the case? Discuss.*
   – –

4. *What dangers to human rights can you discover in the world today? Write a brief essay detailing these dangers.*
   – –

4 Ray Bradbury: The Happiness Boys

Didaktische Hinweise

Dieses Exzerpt aus Ray Bradburys *Fahrenheit 451* (1953) wurde gewählt, weil bereits in den beiden ersten Sätzen ein Leitmotiv dieses Kapitels, jetzt in sein Gegenteil pervertiert, angeschlagen wird: "We must all be alike. Not everyone born free and equal, as the Constitution says, but everyone *made* equal. … then all are happy" (ll. 1–2). Das Thema „Bücherverbrennung" als Mittel zur Zerstörung tradierter geistiger Werte, kritischer Distanz und damit jeglicher Individualität ist – nicht nur angesichts deutscher Geschichte – für Schüler/innen von großer Aktualität, und so kann erwartet werden, daß sie sich engagiert an der Diskussion der vom Text aufgeworfenen Fragen beteiligen werden. Bezüge zu Ereignissen der Gegenwart sind mühelos herzustellen.

Bradburys Anti-Utopie eignet sich ausgezeichnet als Klassenlektüre. Eine ungekürzte Taschenbuchausgabe mit dazugehörigem Study Guide und Lehrerheft ist verfügbar (hrsg. von D. Vater. Berlin, Cornelsen Verlag 1985. SB Best.-Nr. 20339, Study Guide 20347, LH 20355). Der Roman entwickelte sich aus Bradburys Kurzgeschichte "The Pedestrian", die in der Sammlung *Read and Respond*. Ed. by J. Ashton and G. Bolt (Berlin, Cornelsen Verlag 1984. SB Best.-Nr. 1806, Cassette 1814) enthalten ist. Bei einer intensiveren Beschäftigung mit dem Roman kann als

Vorbereitung darauf die Kurzgeschichte von den Schülern/Schülerinnen zu Hause gelesen werden. Die Verfilmung von *Fahrenheit 451* unter der Regie von François Truffaut (1966) wurde ein Welterfolg. – Weitere Exzerpte aus bekannten Utopien finden sich in *Utopian Literature*. Hrsg. von G. Thiele. (Frankfurt, Cornelsen Verlag Hirschgraben. SB Best.-Nr. 662190, LH 662150 [Unterrichtsmodelle für die Sekundarstufe II]; *Science Fiction USA: Eight Stories*. Hrsg. von H. Heuermann und W. Schubert. (Berlin, Cornelsen Verlag. SB Best.-Nr. 7650, LH 7669); *Heading for Tomorrow. Fact and Fiction*. Hrsg. von A. Steinbrecher und G. Weiß. (Berlin, Cornelsen Verlag. SB Best.-Nr. 10023, LB 10031 [CVK Modell English]). Angaben zur Sekundärliteratur finden sich im LB, S. 62.

Background information

Ray Bradbury (1920–   ) was born in Waukegan, Illinois, but as a teenager moved with his family to Los Angeles, Calif., where he still lives. He is best known as a science fiction writer, but has also been successful in other literary fields, including poetry and drama. He published his first science fiction story in 1941, but it was *The Martian Chronicles* (1950) that made him famous. His best-selling anti-utopian novel *Fahrenheit 451* (1953) was well-received by the critics and established his reputation as a social critic in an age of technology. He is a prodigious writer, having published over 500 stories, novels, poems, essays, etc. Among his works are *The Illustrated Man* (1951), *The Golden Apples of the Sun* (1953) and *Long After Midnight* (1976), which are collections of short stories, *Something Wicked This Way Comes* (1962), a novel, and *When Elephants Last in the Dooryard Bloomed* (1973), a collection of poems.

Fahrenheit 451 is today considered a modern classic of anti-utopian fiction, and, like Huxley's *Brave New World*, Orwell's *1984* and Burgess's *A Clockwork Orange* and *1985*, it raises the question of an individual's position in a technologically perfect and ideologically totalitarian world. However, in contrast to the others, Bradbury does not elaborate on the philosophy of the future state but rather concentrates on certain present-day trends which he pushes to their extremes. In *Fahrenheit 451* the pursuit of happiness is the distinctive feature of society and equality is the precondition to achieve this aim. Books, the last signs of individuality and cultural non-conformity, of critical thought and contemplation, must consequently be destroyed. Firemen are responsible for burning books (paper starts to burn at 451° Fahrenheit, hence the title of the book).

One of the firemen, Guy Montag, is the protagonist of the novel. He meets a young girl, Clarisse, whose probing questions and non-conformist attitude to life make him reevaluate his role in society. His anxiety and dissatisfaction are increased when he sees an old woman die rather than part with her books. He starts to read books, and gradually turns against society, which caters only for mass pleasure.

When it is discovered he has books in his house, he kills his boss and escapes from the city. In a wood he meets a group of people who have made it their job to preserve the great works of literature in their heads for the day when society will be ready for books again.

"We have our fingers in the dike" (l. 75): This is an allusion to the story of the young Dutch boy who, on noticing a leak in a dike, stuck his finger in the hole and

waited for help. He thus averted an inundation which would have destroyed much of the country. The story first appeared in a collection called *Hans Brinker; or, The Silver Skates,* written by an American, Mary Mapes Dodge (1831–1905).

Talking about the text – Suggested answers

1. The state is meant to ensure the happiness of its citizens. It does so by relieving them of the necessity to think. It prevents people from reading or hearing about controversies and takes all decisions of importance for them. Instead, people are filled with useless, "noncombustible [!] data" (ll. 58–59) to keep their minds busy. They are kept on the move, titillated at all times.

2. As official censors, the firemen are a decision-making body in that they determine what may and may not be said or even thought. In other words, they have at least a certain legislative function. As judges and executors, they also unite the judicial and executive functions in their persons. All governmental powers are held by one group, with no one left to check these powers. The firemen are, in a way, absolute dictators.

3. Clarisse had become a problem, an embarrassment, for the state. In a system that is based on conformity and is afraid of conflicting thought, she had slipped through the net. She asked critical questions, always wanting to know *why* things were done, not *how.* Her questions might have set others thinking – "she was a time bomb" (l. 45). And, according to the standard of the society described in "Fahrenheit 451", as a thinking person she was unhappy. Someone, probably the firemen, put her out of her misery – she is "better off dead" (ll. 48–49).

4. Being born equal means that everyone starts out in life with equal opportunities. How he or she makes use of those opportunities supposedly depends on him or her alone, i.e. on that person's talent and aspirations. Being made equal seems to imply that everyone, regardless of his or her talents and aspirations, is pressed into a single mould. [The discussion of the advantages and disadvantages of each will probably revolve around the students' concepts of tolerance towards the individual and of productivity for society.]

5. *To what extent does this excerpt seem typical of (anti-)utopian literature?*
   Utopian, or anti-utopian, literature by definition portrays a society based on certain ideas and ideals. These phenomena are generally observable in the real world, but they are taken to extremes in the ideal society. In the case of this excerpt from Bradbury's novel, two ideas that are developed to their apparently logical conclusions are especially obvious. One is the concept of the "pursuit of happiness", which can already be found in its extreme form amongst the contented, apathetic, free-living, happy-go-lucky elements of all modern western societies. The other is the idea of equality, which forms the theoretical basis of democratic society.
   Another element common to many anti-utopian novels is the benevolent, apparently quite reasonable representative of the society being portrayed [e.g. O'Brien in Orwell's "1984", the Controller Mustapha Mond in Huxley's "Brave New World", Dr. Branom in Burgess's "A Clockwork Orange", or here, Beatty]. In the form of a lecture this person typically explains the principles the society is based on to some rebel [e.g. Winston in "1984", the Savage John in "Brave New World", Alex in "A Clockwork Orange", Bev in "1985", or here, Montag].

6. *What does Beatty's use of language in the last paragraph tell you about him?*
   His speech is that of an educated person, as words such as "clarify" (l. 72), "melancholy" and "drear philosophy" (l. 76) show. In this short passage he also uses a literary allusion, if only to a children's story: "We have our fingers in the dike" (l. 75). Based on this story and its image of water, he sustains a clear metaphor: "small *tide*" (l. 74), "*torrent* of melancholy" (l. 76). One might even get the impression that Beatty is a well-read individual in this book-burning society.

5 Political Parties

Didaktische Hinweise

Gerade weil die Bedeutung der politischen Parteien in den USA – auch aus historischen Gründen – ungleich geringer ist als in Europa, erscheint es notwendig, sie im Rahmen dieses Kapitels zu thematisieren, um den Schülern/Schülerinnen ein möglichst umfassendes Bild der politischen Wirklichkeit zu vermitteln. So wird auch die Bedeutung anderer Institutionen, etwa des Präsidentenamts oder des Supreme Court, die in den beiden folgenden Texten behandelt werden, deutlicher. Schließlich stellt der Text notwendiges Hintergrundwissen für das Verständnis amerikanischer Wahlkämpfe bereit und bietet außerdem die Möglichkeit, das amerikanische Parteiensystem nicht nur mit dem Parteienspektrum in der Bundesrepublik (vgl. SB, Aufg. 3), sondern auch mit dem in Großbritannien zu vergleichen (vgl. Kap. IV, Text 4).

Background information

Political parties: The emergence of political parties in the US occurred not long after independence, when the issue of whether the federal government or the individual states should have more power became hotly debated. Those favouring a strong federal government were called Federalists and were led by Alexander Hamilton; the Anti-Federalists, led by Thomas Jefferson, supported the rights of the individual states. The Federalists tended to be the party of the North and were more conservative, while the Anti-Federalists were the party of the South and were more liberal.

Under Presidents Jefferson and Madison, the Anti-Federalists (or Democratic Republicans as they became known) pursued such highly successful and popular policies, e.g. the Louisiana Purchase of 1803 and the War with England of 1812–1815, that by 1820 the Federalists had ceased to exist, due to lack of support.

After 1824 a split in the Democratic Republican Party resulted in the formation of two parties: the National Republican Party, under John Quincy Adams, and the Democratic Republican or Jefferson Republican Party, under Andrew Jackson, which in 1828 renamed itself the Democratic Party. In 1832 the National Republicans changed their name to Whigs; they fell into decline after 1854 when many of their eminent politicians and supporters joined the newly-formed Republican Party.

The Republican Party was formed in 1854 as an alliance of Whigs and northern Democrats; it was a liberal party with a pro-union, anti-slavery attitude. Its first president was Abraham Lincoln. Since 1869 the president has always been a candidate of one of the two big parties, the Democrats or the Republicans.

Until the 1930s, the Democrats were considered more conservative than the Republicans, but since the New Deal, introduced by Democratic President F.D. Roosevelt, they have been associated with social welfare for the poor and civil rights. Despite originally being pro-slavery, the Democrats now receive the overwhelming majority of black votes. The Republicans, often called the Grand Old Party, tend to be more conservative; they oppose state control, high taxes and social benefits for the poor. Compared to European parties, there are few major political differences between the two main American parties. They are both non-ideological, centrist parties.

Semantic and collocational field "Government and politics"

the federal/a state government, an elected official, (to) take over/run a government ✧ a(n) government/social/economic programme, (to) establish a programme, (to) be opposed to a programme, (to) vote on/create a law ✧ a taxpayer, (to) raise taxes ✧ a major political party, a liberal/conservative party, a party leader, loyalty to a party, (to) band together, (to) form a party, (to) belong to a party ✧ (to) participate in an election, (to) attract supporters, (to) achieve a national goal, (to) represent sb.'s views/interests, (to) embrace a wide range of political viewpoints

Talking about the text – Suggested answers

1. Political parties were considered a danger because their members might prefer to represent party interests rather than those of the people as a whole. Parties might produce a conflict of interests.
2. Competition between different ideologies is essential to the democratic spirit, and such competition is most easily realized through party structures. The necessity of mobilizing large numbers of voters in order to be elected, and the need to find like-thinking individuals to run the government once one is elected, make party organizations essential.
3. The Democrats place more emphasis on the social role of government. It is they who have introduced most of the social welfare programmes that exist in the USA today. The Republicans, on the other hand, tend to stress the importance of individual initiative and believe that big government stands in the way of free enterprise. The official Democratic line is in some respects close to the Social Democratic Party of Germany (SPD), while the Republicans probably have more in common with the Free Democratic Party (FDP) or the Christian Democratic/Social Union (CDU/CSU). The major difference between American und European parties, however, is that the former barely differ. Party loyalty also tends to be much greater in Europe, whereas "cross-voting", i.e. voting across party lines, is common in the US.
4. *In your opinion, should elected officials be bound by the platforms of their particular parties, by the will of the people they represent, or by their consciences? Discuss.*
    – –

6 John Steinbeck: Americans and Their President

Didaktische Hinweise

Dieses Exzerpt aus John Steinbecks kritischer Bestandsaufnahme *America and the Americans* (New York, Viking Penguin 1966) beschreibt – nicht ohne Pathos – die ambivalente Haltung der Amerikaner zu ihrem Präsidenten und die hohen moralischen Anforderungen, die – ein Erbe der "Founding Fathers" – an den Inhaber des "most powerful office in the world" (Z. 31) gestellt werden. In einer Zeit, in der der amerikanische Präsident als Staatsoberhaupt einer der beiden Supermächte weltweiten Einfluß ausübt, aber auch weltweiter Kritik ausgesetzt ist (vgl. auch Text 10), ist die Kenntnis dieser Beziehungen besonders wichtig, damit Klischeevorstellungen und Vorurteilen entgegengewirkt werden kann. Das Themenheft *The White House, Washington, D.C.* von K. Carlson-Kreibohm (Berlin, Cornelsen Verlag 1988. Best.-Nr. 3388) bietet eine Fülle von Informationen, die vertiefend genutzt werden können.

Background information

John Steinbeck (1902–1968) was born in Salinas, Calif. After leaving school he spent six years at Stanford University, Calif., and then turned to writing. He became one of the best-known American novelists and received the Nobel Prize for Literature in 1962. Steinbeck preferred to describe the "have-nots", the homeless and socially deprived and, at the same time, he critically but sympathetically analyzed American society. Among his most famous works are *Tortilla Flat* (1935), *Of Mice and Men* (prose and drama version 1937), *The Grapes of Wrath* (1939, made into a successful film), for which Steinbeck received the Pulitzer Prize, *Cannery Row* (1945), *East of Eden* (1952, whose film version made James Dean famous) and his last novel *The Winter of Our Discontent* (1961). Besides numerous short stories Steinbeck also wrote film scripts and travel books, among them *A Russian Journal* (1948) and *Travels with Charley* (1962), a selection from which is available in an annotated edition (John Steinbeck: *In Search of America,* Ed. by H. Weyand. Berlin, Cornelsen Verlag. Best.-Nr. 5569).

The Presidency: The president is elected for a four-year term and may serve no more than two terms in office. (President F.D. Roosevelt was an exception; he was elected president four times. The 22nd Amendment limiting the president to a two-term office was only ratified in 1951.) In order to stand for president, one must be a native-born American, at least 35 years of age and have lived in the United States for at least 14 years.

The presidential candidates are chosen at the national convention of the party. Then, in the presidential election, the electorate cast their vote for electors and not for the president. Each state has as many electors as it has senators and representatives together. The electors cast their vote for the president in their respective state capitals, and Congress then counts the votes and officially declares the winner of the election. It is possible for a president to be elected by a minority of the electorate. Presidents Lincoln (39.9 % of the popular vote in 1860), Kennedy (49.7 % in 1960) and Nixon (43.4 % in 1968) were all minority presidents.

"assassination" (l. 21): Four American presidents (Abraham Lincoln, James A. Garfield, William McKinley and John F. Kennedy) have been assassinated, and unsuccessful attempts have been made on five presidents this century.

Semantic and collocational field "Public opinion"

(to) respect sb./sth., (to) admire sb./sth., (to) praise sb./sth., (to) have a love for sb./sth., (to) stand together ✧ the gift of the people, (to) give sb. responsibility/work/pressure ✧ the suspicion of overuse/misuse of power, (to) inspect sb.'s every move, (to) subject sb. to constant scrutiny, (to) fear/suspect power ✧ a torrent of accusation and abuse, a derisive press, a sullen electorate, (to) blame sb. for sth., (to) denounce sb. for sth., (to) abuse sb., (to) raise a storm of protest, (to) give sb. trouble ✧ (to) wear sb. out, (to) destroy sb./sth. ✧ to find oneself hamstrung/straitjacketed/helpless

Talking about the text – Suggested answers

1.   Besides the other two branches of government, Steinbeck cites the federal bureaucracy, the military, the press and the voting public as factors that limit executive power. The president   must also deal with smaller governmental units, capital and labour, the churches as well as other organizations, all of which can make life difficult for him.

2. If the president is to exercise his powers, he must be very knowledgeable of all three branches of government. He must be open for discussion, but he must also be able to persuade others sensitively to his way of thinking. His behaviour must be up to the country's high moral standards for his office, and he must never act in such a way that anyone suspects he is misusing or abusing the powers of his office.

3. Steinbeck has structured his text in two closely related ways that make his points easy to follow. As a whole, the text takes on a listing order. The writer goes through all the points he wants to get across, one by one. Because each of these items involves a contradiction, Steinbeck proceeds contrastively. Some typical contrastive expressions are: "Of course we ..., but at the same time we ..." (ll. 2–3), "in spite of" (l. 7), "It is said that ... . What is not said ... is that ..." (ll. 31–32).

4. By using the first-person plural through most of the text, Steinbeck shows that he identifies with his fellow Americans in their contradictory attitudes towards the president. He, too, feels a close, almost personal relationship to the him.

● 5. a) *Compare the duties of the American president to those of the British prime minister or the West German chancellor.*
   – –

   b) *Compare the American presidential system to the British or German parliamentary system.*
   – –

7 Dick Pawelek: The Highest Judicial Power in the Land

Didaktische Hinweise

Die Bedeutung des Supreme Court für verfassungsrechtliche Entwicklungen in den Vereinigten Staaten ist kaum zu überschätzen. Paweleks Hinweis auf Entscheidungen des Supreme Court zur Rassentrennung bzw. zur Gleichstellung der Schwarzen (Z. 81 ff.) läßt sich anhand von Texten aus Kapitel VII (etwa Text 7 bis 9b und "Info-Box", SB, S. 182 f.) weiterverfolgen und vertiefen bzw. rekapituliert dort vermittelte Informationen. Aber auch ein Blick auf Großbritannien ist in diesem Zusammenhang aufschlußreich. Zwar gibt es dort aufgrund des Fehlens einer geschriebenen Verfassung keine dem amerikanischen Supreme Court vergleichbare Institution, aber auch eine ungeschriebene Verfassung wie die britische besitzt ihre Schutzmechanismen (vgl. Kap. IV, Text 3).

Background information

The Justices of the Supreme Court are appointed for life by the president in office when a Court position becomes vacant (by death, resignation or – theoretically – impeachment). Like other major presidential appointments, these are subject to approval by the Senate. The first black to serve on the nation's highest court was Thurgood Marshall (1908 –   ). He was appointed in 1967 by President Johnson. The first woman on the Court was Sandra Day O'Connor (1930 –   ), who was appointed by President Reagan in 1981.

"Marbury vs. Madison" (l. 49): After John Adams lost the 1800 presidential election to Thomas Jefferson – the first time in modern history that an opposition candidate peacefully replaced a nation's leader – he created a number of posts for his political friends so that they could retain the power, privileges and responsibilities they

had grown accustomed to. These "last-minute" appointments were confirmed by the Senate on Adams's last day in office. Among those nominations was that of William Marbury to a position as justice of the peace.

Although Marbury's appointment had passed all the legal hurdles, the letter of commission had not yet been delivered when the Jefferson administration took office. This served James Madison, Jefferson's Secretary of State, as an excuse for refusing Marbury the commission. Marbury appealed to the Supreme Court for help. When the Court ruled that Marbury was entitled to his commission, it said, in effect, that Madison's refusal was not in accordance with the law.

With this ruling the Marshall court claimed the Supreme Court's right of judicial review, i.e. the power to examine acts of another branch of government and to declare them illegal or even unconstitutional. The decision became the platform on which the Supreme Court developed into the third branch of the US government.

"Plessy vs. Ferguson" (ll. 81–82): Although the 13th Amendment abolished slavery, racial prejudice continued in the South. So-called "Jim Crow laws" (ll. 85–86) were passed in southern states to keep blacks separate from whites. A group of black leaders formed a Citizen's Committee to test the constitutional validity of the Separate Car Law in Louisiana. Homer Plessy, who was one-eighth black and lived in Louisiana, acted for the Citizen's Committee. He bought a train ticket in Louisiana and took a seat in a compartment reserved for whites. When he refused to move he was arrested. Plessy and his lawyer claimed that the Louisiana law denied him "equal protection of the law" as set down in the 14th Amendment and that it violated the 13th Amendment.

The Supreme Court ruled 8 to 1 against Plessy and in effect reinforced state-controlled segregation. Southern states required blacks to use separate toilets, means of transport, waiting rooms, hospitals, schools, churches, cemeteries, etc., and segregation became a fact of life. Segregation was to dominate social, political and judicial life in the South for the next 50 years. The doctrine "separate but equal" turned out to be "separate but unequal".

"Jim Crow laws" (ll. 85–86): Originally "Jim Crow" was the name of a 19th century slave's song. The American entertainer Thomas D. Rice (died 1860) used the name for a character in one of his acts, after which it came to be applied – derogatorily – to any black person. Today the term applies only to policies of discrimination against, but especially segregation of, blacks. It is used only in AE and is considered relatively informal.

"Brown vs. Board of Education, Topeka, KS" (l. 91): It was only in 1954 that the Plessy judgment was overruled. In the early 1950s parents of black children asked lower courts to remove laws requiring segregated schools and to provide really equal education for their children. Five separate cases from South Carolina, Virginia, Delaware, Kansas and Washington, D.C., were taken together and heard by the Supreme Court as *Brown vs. Board of Education of Topeka, Kansas.* The case got its name from Mr and Mrs Brown, who sued the school board of Topeka for not permitting their 7-year-old daughter to attend the school nearest their home, which was for whites only.

The Supreme Court unanimously struck down the "separate but equal" doctrine and declared it an unconstitutional violation of the 14th Amendment. The Court argued that segregation gave children a feeling of inferiority and that segregated education could never be equal even if it provided equal facilities. By this decision state-supported segregated education was made illegal.

Although there was enormous resistance to school integration, the decision was also instrumental in promoting the civil rights movement that followed (cf. "Info-Box", SB, pp. 182 f.).

Semantic and collocational field "The law "

a law, a provision of the law ✧ the judicial branch of government, the Supreme Court, judicial power, a court decision, (to) make a ruling on a law, (to) exercise a power ✧ (to) set up a safeguard ✧ (to) reverse a decision, (to) knock out a law, (to) overturn an act of Congress, (to) rule sth. unconstitutional, (to) violate the Constitution

Talking about the text – Suggested answers

1. The Court keeps watch over the other two branches of government and decides whether their actions are in accordance with the US Constitution. It also reviews decisions made by lower courts and strikes them down if necessary. Another major responsibility is guarding individual rights guaranteed by the Constitution.This sometimes involves knocking down police actions or business practices that do not conform to the Constitution. In some cases the Supreme Court may even review previous Supreme Court decisions and update them.

2. The power of judicial review is not given to the Supreme Court by the Constitution. It was Chief Justice John Marshall and his court who, in the early part of the 19th century, believed this power had been intended by the writers of the Constitution and claimed it for themselves.

3. The *Plessy vs. Ferguson* decision, announced in 1896, laid the foundation for discrimination against blacks through segregation. It was a major setback in that it either limited or virtually negated the progress that had been made since the Civil War. There was once again a legal basis for a racist society. It took the Court over 50 years to reverse the *Plessy vs. Ferguson* decision in the case *Brown vs. Board of Education*. The effects of this 1954 case were just as dramatic as the earlier decision it struck down and is considered one of the milestones of the civil rights movement and a major step towards truly "equal justice under law".

4. – –

5. *The 22nd Amendment to the Constitution, which was ratified in 1951, prohibits anyone from being elected president more than twice. What effect does this two-term rule have on the Supreme Court?*
   The 22nd Amendment declared that no one can be president for more than eight years. Since Supreme Court Justices serve for life, it is unlikely that any one president will have the chance to appoint more than a few Justices; this means that the president is unable to gain more influence over the Court than would be in the spirit of the Constitution.

6. *In an almanac or other up-to-date reference book, find out who the current members of the US Supreme Court are. Give a brief report on all the Justices, including the information when they were appointed, by whom, and what political tendencies they generally represent.*
   – –

8 James Reston: Liberty Unlimited?

Didaktische Hinweise

Diesem Text kommt innerhalb dieses Kapitels eine Schlüsselfunktion zu. Die Diskussion des Freiheitsbegriffs gibt den Schülern/Schülerinnen die Möglichkeit, die anhand der vorangehenden Texte (auch der Kap. V bis VII) gewonnenen Kenntnisse und Einsichten aus einer neuen Perspektive zu sehen. Gleichzeitig kann diese Diskussion die Auseinandersetzung mit den Grundsätzen der amerikanischen Außenpolitik (Text 9) vorbereiten. Vor allem aber werden die Jugendlichen durch die Erörterung des Spannungsverhältnisses zwischen der Freiheit des Einzelnen und den Zwängen der Gesellschaft in ihrer Rolle als Heranwachsende direkt angesprochen.

Background information

James Reston (1909–   ) was born in Scotland, but as a young man emigrated to the USA, where he attended the University of Illinois. After working as a journalist for various newspapers, he joined the *New York Times* and became the Washington correspondent.

"sweet land of liberty" (l. 64): This is the second line of the poem "America" (1831) by Samuel Francis Smith (1808–1905). The poem is often referred to by its first line "My country, 'tis of thee".

"The Organization of American States" (ll. 72–73): abbreviated OAS, an organization founded in Bogota in 1948. Its aim is to achieve mutual understanding, cooperation and solidarity between the nations of the Americas. It holds to the principles of non-interference in each other's affairs and mediation between countries in the case of conflict. Each country guarantees protection of the member states in case of an attack from a foreign power. The history behind the OAS can be traced back to the Monroe Doctrine of 1823, in which President Monroe stressed the independence of the New World from the Old World at a time when Spain's colonies were declaring independence.

There are 27 members of the OAS; they include most of the North, Central and South American nations and the Caribbean Islands. Canada and Guyana are not members; neither is Cuba, which was suspended in 1962 when it accepted nuclear missiles from the Soviet Union. Cuba has, however, since been given observer status (for Nicaragua cf. also pp. 177 f. of this book). There is an annual general assembly of the foreign secretaries of the member states; a permanent council of ambassadors has also been set up.

"The World Court" (ll. 74–75): The International Court of Justice was set up by the United Nations as its supreme legal body to administer justice under international law. It sits at The Hague in the Netherlands. For information concerning its judgment against the USA cf. p. 178 of this book.

"bombers against Libya" (l. 78): In December 1985 there were Palestinian terrorist attacks on Rome and Vienna airports. It was alleged that Moammar Gadhafi, Libya's revolutionary leader, supported the terrorists with arms and money. Tension increased when the Libyans attacked American planes operating off the coast of

Libya. In 1986, following a terrorist attack on a West Berlin disco frequented by American service personnel, President Reagan retaliated and sent bombers against Libya; 39 people, mostly civilians, were killed and hundreds more were injured. Amongst its allies, only Britain supported the USA, allowing the bombers to take off from British bases; France and Spain refused to allow the American bombers to use their air space.

Semantic and collocational field "Liberty"

liberty, personal liberty, a democracy, an open discussion, a free election ✧ establishment of justice under law, (to) pass judgment on sb./sth. ✧ license to do sth., (to) be/feel at liberty to do sth., (to) put one's interests ahead of the general good ✧ terror, a dictatorship, an oppressed people, (to) use violent means to achieve sth., (to) violate a commitment, (to) break the law, (to) be deprived of sth.

Talking about the text – Suggested answers

1. At the beginning of the century, Western democracies with their open discussions and free elections were expected to lead the world on the path of human progress. But today these ideals are challenged, doubted and violated, not least in the Americas.
2. Reston gives several examples of people taking liberties in political life, including terrorists feeling free to use violence to further their causes, or the dictators of the Soviet bloc or the racist leaders of South Africa demanding liberty for the few to destroy the liberty of the masses. He also cites President Reagan's feeling at liberty to topple the Nicaraguan government or to bomb Libya without regard for the authority of treaties, international law and the World Court. From American civil life he uses examples of people feeling at liberty to break the law, to push drugs, to leave their families and to put personal satisfaction ahead of the common good. In all these cases, someone is taking advantage of freedoms without considering the responsibilities he or she has towards others.
3. The writer makes his opinion quite clear throughout the text. We might even say he editorializes. He openly regrets the fact that Western ideals are no longer universally accepted when he says that that is "all the more reason ... to renew efforts to defend what is left of a common civilization" (ll. 26–30). He pleads for a paring of "liberty" with some other value that would keep it in check. To support his belief he quotes Lippmann and then goes on to present evidence which, he claims, "is all around us" (l. 52).
   He makes no attempt to conceal his harsh judgment of Soviet bloc nations or of South Africa, and his criticism of Reagan is perfectly clear. When he points out abuses of personal liberty, he assures the reader that his arguments are "not mere moralizing" (l. 89). He later uses the symbol of the Statue of Liberty and the emotion-packed images of "the hungry and oppressed people of the world" (ll. 104–105) to defend immigration, while at the same time employing the metaphor of "a river without banks" (ll. 116–117) to argue in favour of sensible limitations to immigration.
   Reston has skilfully prepared the reader for this final, apparently balanced viewpoint on immigration by taking the middle ground throughout the text.
4. ***Take any one of the "value pairs" mentioned in the text, e.g. "liberty and authority" (ll. 37–38) or "liberty and morality" (l. 92) and write a text of no more than 500 words explaining how the two terms are in conflict and how they might be reconciled.***
   – –

9   G. Calvin Mackenzie: Realpolitik

Didaktische Hinweise

Dieser und der folgende Text befassen sich mit der Rolle der Vereinigten Staaten als einer Weltmacht und mit dem Verhältnis der USA zu Europa. Damit werden Probleme angesprochen, deren Aktualität durch die Tagespolitik ständig deutlich wird. Zugleich handelt es sich um Themen, die bei den Schülern/Schülerinnen häufig kritische Reaktionen hervorrufen. Text 9 und 10 bieten daher die gute Gelegenheit, möglicherweise stark affektiv besetzte Amerikabilder im Klassengespräch zu artikulieren, zu analysieren und so zu versachlichen.

Background information

G. Calvin Mackenzie holds a Ph.D. in government from Harvard University. His government experience is based on his time with the US Army in Vietnam, where he worked as Senior Research Analyst for the Commission on Administrative Review of the US House of Representatives, and as a consultant to congressional committees and executive agencies. He has also done research work on such topics as the American political system and the presidential appointment process. Mackenzie is a professor of government at Colby College in Waterville, Maine. He is on the board of several journals and academic organizations. His publications include *The Politics of Presidential Appointments* (Free Press, New York, 1980), *The House at Work* (University of Texas Press, Austin, 1981) and *Government and Public Policy in America* (Random House, New York, 1986), from which this excerpt is taken.

"Iran" (l. 35): America's relations with Iran have always been determined by Iran's vicinity to the Soviet Union and by the importance of oil. Prior to the Islamic Revolution of 1979, America had supported the Shah, Reza Pahlavi, despite the brutality with which his secret police, SAVAK, suppressed opposition to the Shah's rule. The USA's support for the Shah resulted in anti-American protests in Teheran after the revolution and the storming of the American embassy, following which the embassy staff were held as hostages for over a year.

"Philippines" (l. 35): The USA supported Ferdinand Marcos, the president of the Philippines, from 1965 until his downfall in 1986, mainly because of his anti-communist stance, in an area of the world where communism was gaining ground. The American government distanced itself from Marcos in the last years of his rule, but due to the need for American military bases in the country rarely put pressure on him. The United States welcomed the election of the new president, Corazon Aquino, in 1986, after Marcos fled to the US, and maintains good relations with the present government.

"South Korea" (l. 35): South Korea's position as a bastion against communist North Korea has ensured that the US has been a loyal ally since the Korean War (1950–1953). As with the Philippines, the US policy has been to maintain friendly relations with whichever government is in power; until 1988 there were no proper democratic elections and the country was ruled by military strongmen.

Semantic and collocational field "Foreign policy"

foreign policy, international relations, international influence, world affairs ✧ a policy of *detente*, realpolitik, national security policy, human rights policy, an objective of American policy ✧ hostility, brazen anticommunist rhetoric, opposition to communism, conflict, cooperation, containment policy, (to) contain Soviet influence/Soviet expansion/the spread of communism, (to) drive a wedge in the rift between (two countries), (to) turn one's back on sb./sth. ✧ a friendly posture toward sb./sth., a search for allies, a foreign alliance, (to) seek allies, (to) ally (oneself) with sb./sth., (to) befriend sb./sth. (e.g. a country) ✧ support for sb./sth. (e.g. a dictator), (to) support sb./sth. (e.g. a foreign regime) with sth. else ✧ (to) reopen relations with a country, (to) recast Soviet-American relations, (to) increase foreign trade

Talking about the text - Suggested answers

1. Realpolitik is based on a highly pragmatic view of the world. It entails a belief that conflict rather than cooperation is the norm in international relations, and that power is a more reliable source of international influence and of national security than are idealism and moralism.
2. The overall *strategy* of American national security policy has not changed. Its objective is still the containment of communism, but the means, or *tactics*, by which this aim is pursued are different. Reopening political and diplomatic relations with the People's Republic of China, for example, was an attempt to drive a wedge between China and the Soviet Union. The effort to increase foreign trade with the USSR was an attempt to relax US-Soviet tensions in the hope that Soviet aggression, and therefore Soviet expansion, might be reduced.
3. – –
4. – –
5. [E.g. budgetary concerns; difficulty in obtaining accurate, unbiased information about events in other countries; problems in predicting political strategies and reactions of other – even allied – nations and their leaders; frequent necessity of acting quickly; pressure from one's own people to act; need for secrecy prevents open discussion with everyone who might have advice on the matter.]

⚏ 10 Paul Belien: Europe, Europe, Europe - Yurrop, Yurrop, Yurrop

Didaktische Hinweise

Dieser Auszug aus Paul Beliens Kommentar ist thematisch eng mit Text 9 verbunden: Beide Texte befassen sich mit der Rolle Amerikas als einer Weltmacht. In ihrer dezidiert „amerikanischen" Sichtweise des Verhältnisses zwischen Amerika und Europa sind Beliens Ausführungen geeignet, Widerspruch zu provozieren. Hiervon ausgehend können die Schüler/innen zu einer Auseinandersetzung mit ihrer eigenen Position gelangen, die schließlich zu einer sachlichen Betrachtung der ganz und gar nicht einfachen Problematik und zu einer ausgewogenen Beurteilung führen sollte. Abgesehen von dieser wichtigen Funktion bietet dieser Text jedoch auch Gelegenheit, die bei der Behandlung der Texte dieses Kapitels (und eventuell auch der drei vorausgehenden) gewonnenen Einzelkenntnisse in größerem Zusammenhang zu sehen und so Beliens Behauptungen zu relativieren.

Background information

"Nicaragua" (l. 60): one of the largest countries in the Central American isthmus, with a population of approximately 3,500,000 (1987).

US involvement in Nicaragua began in 1909 when a naval force was dispatched to intervene in the country after the execution of two American citizens. From 1912 until 1933 US marines were stationed in the land. In 1934 General Tacho Somoza took control of Nicaragua and ruled as a dictator. He murdered General Sandino, a guerilla leader who had fought a war against the US Marines. In 1979, the Sandinista guerilla movement (named after Sandino) finally ousted President Anastasio Somoza, Tacho's son, and took power.

In 1981 the US government accused Nicaragua, which had become a close ally of Cuba, of supplying arms to El Salvadorian guerillas. Nicaragua denied the charges. However, President Reagan considered Nicaragua to be a destabilizing factor in "America's backyard" and started to give aid to Contra guerillas fighting the Sandinista government. In 1984 the Americans mined Nicaraguan ports, despite the World Court's ruling against the action as a violation of international law (cf. Text 8). President Reagan refused to accept the results of the Nicaraguan general election of 1984 which returned the Sandinistas to power, and in the following year imposed a trade ban on the country, which, however, failed to remove the government. The controversy and civil war continue with no real end in sight.

"Poland" (l. 63): Since 1945 Poland has been a satellite of the Soviet Union, and as such has known very little political freedom in its recent history. The terrible economic situation of the country resulted in a number of strikes. In 1980, led by the Gdansk shipyard worker Lech Walesa, the workers formed themselves into a free trade union called Solidarity and gained considerable concessions from the government. The government signed a binding agreement which allowed the formation of free trade unions. However, continuing strikes and economic chaos resulted in Prime Minister Jaruzelski, obviously under Soviet pressure, reneging on the agreement and imposing martial law. Thousands of pro-Solidarity activists were arrested, among them Lech Walesa. Martial law was lifted in 1982, and amnesties resulted in the release of most of the political opponents, but the struggle for more political and economic freedom went on. Eventually, an agreement between the government and opposition representatives was signed early in 1989, arranging for the union's legalization and substantial constitutional and economic changes.

"Grenada" (l. 65): a Caribbean island with about 100,000 inhabitants (1987). A British colony, it was granted independence in 1974. Its first prime minister was Eric Gairy, a Conservative, who was overthrown in 1979 by Maurice Bishop, an admirer of President Castro of Cuba. In 1983 Bishop was overthrown and murdered by left-wing officers, whereupon the USA, at the request of other Caribbean islands, invaded the island. The official reason for the invasion was to safeguard the lives of Americans on the island and to restore democracy.

"Afghanistan" (l. 67): a central Asian state bordered by the Soviet Union, China, Iran and Pakistan, with a population of about 14,000,000 (1987). In the 19th century Afghanistan became a battleground between the British and Russian Empires, but the country's terrain made Afghanistan unconquerable. In 1978 Taraki, a Marxist, seized power and sought to establish a pro-Soviet state, but he was overthrown by Prime Minister Amin in the following year. Amin was a doctrinaire communist, who had thousands of opponents executed. Shortly afterwards the Soviet Union organized a coup and invaded the country, despite worldwide protests. The Muslim tribal

leaders (Mujahedin) formed a rebel organization which managed to harass the Soviet forces quite successfully. The inconclusive nature of the war prompted the Soviets to withdraw their troops. The last Soviet soldiers left Afghanistan in February 1989, but fighting continued between government and rebel forces.

Semantic and collocational field "International relations"

the complexity of the present world difficulties, moral equivalence, a political system, a pluralist democracy, a communist totalitarian regime, a parliamentary democracy ✧ a superpower, the North Atlantic Treaty Organization, the Warsaw Pact, American/Soviet domination, (to) maintain the domination of sb./sth. (e.g. a country) ✧ sb.'s politics toward sb. else, (to) distance oneself from sb./sth., (to) have sympathy for sb./sth., (to) stand for sth., (to) represent sth., (to) be an enemy of sb./sth., (to) be peaceful/aggressive ✧ America's backyard, an intervention in sth. (e.g. a country), an invasion of sth. (e.g. a country)

Talking about the text - Suggested answers

1. Belien's attitude towards Europeans is quite negative. He characterizes them as being frustrated and irrational, ignorant yet arrogant. He also believes West Europeans to be without economic ambition as a result of their governments' welfare state policies.

2. La Fontaine's fable sets the tone for the text and serves as a basis for an extended comparison. Fables have the advantage of being very simple, representing types rather than individuals, with a clear and usually explicitly stated moral. In the quoted fable, the frog is obviously silly, her obsession with size eventually leading to her destruction. The moral of the story is that everybody should know their place. Belien would have us believe that "contemporary Western European politics toward the U.S." (ll. 17–18) is as simple as the story of the frog. He uses the fable to prove his point that Western Europe is being silly and should learn to be satisfied with its size and, by implication, its role as a junior partner to the United States.

3. According to Belien, Western Europeans see only certain superficial characteristics when they equate America with the Soviet Union. First and foremost, they see that both countries are much bigger than they are. They note that both are involved in military activities in other countries, and that the USSR and the USA seemingly intimidate their smaller neighbours. They believe that the two superpowers use their military alliances to dominate "their" parts of Europe (cf. l. 79). The mistake lies in Europeans' not recognizing the underlying differences between the USSR and the USA, namely that America stands for the same things they believe in, i.e. "parliamentary democracy and freedom of expression" (ll. 93–94). They ignore the fact that the Soviet Union is "a communist totalitarian regime" (ll. 90–91).

4. "Moral equivalence" means that two persons, actions or things have the same ethical value. In the examples Belien uses to characterize European attitudes, it would mean that there is absolutely no ethical difference between the behaviour of the two superpowers, that one is just as bad as the other.

5. In his first example (ll. 59–63), Belien describes Nicaragua, America's neighbour, as "little", while Poland, as a neighbour of the Soviet Union, is in a "poor" position. The implication, of course, is that there is no reason to feel sorry for Nicaragua. Being little is simply a fact. Poland, on the other hand, is in a pitiable position.

   In the second example (ll. 64–67), the writer refers to US military activity in another country as an "intervention", to Soviet military activity in another country as an "invasion". This choice of words makes American actions seem basically harmless, like nothing but a little interference, a corrective measure, while Soviet actions are portrayed as merely hostile.

   In the third example (ll. 68–72) Belien uses quotation marks to point to what the writer considers an essential difference between the US and the Soviet Union. By putting the words "American domination" in inverted commas, Belien implies that American behaviour towards Western Europe is merely perceived as domination. "Soviet domination", though, does not rate quotation marks, as Belien believes that the Soviets do, in fact, dominate Eastern Europe.

In his fourth example (ll. 73–79), the writer simply states that there are "fundamental differences" between NATO and the Warsaw Pact. He does not, however, state what these differences are.

6. *The writer sees a significant difference between Western Europe and the USA in attitudes towards economic freedom. Describe this difference and explain whether or not you agree with him.*

– –

Chapter IX: Town and Country

Kapitel IX leitet den dritten Teil des Lesebuchs ein, der sich mit länderübergreifenden Fragen befaßt. In Text 1 tritt der bekannte britische Architekt Michael Manser unter Hinweis auf Beispiele, die vorwiegend aus der englischen Architekturgeschichte stammen, vehement für die grundsätzliche Freiheit des Architekten von einengenden Normierungen und Regulierungen ein. Das Teilthema „Städtebau" rückt durch den fiktionalen Text 2 in den Mittelpunkt. Hier geht es um die allgemeine Kritik am Bau von Hochhäusern während der von Wohnungsnot geprägten Nachkriegsjahre. Die darauf folgende "Info-Box"(SB, S. 219) faßt Grundsätzliches zum Thema „Umwelt" rück- und vorblickend zusammen. Die Texte 3 bis 6 lenken den Blick auf amerikakundliche Teilaspekte, etwa den verschwenderischen Umgang mit Grund und Boden, die Verkehrsentwicklung und das Leben in einer Großstadt. Durch das Gedicht der Amerikanerin Joyce Carol Oates (Text 3), das schlaglichtartig bestimmte Erscheinungsformen des amerikanischen Lebensstils beleuchtet, werden emotionale Bereiche miteinbezogen. In Text 4 berichtet W.J. Weatherby mit Frische und Witz über seine persönlichen Erfahrungen als Wohnungssuchender in New York City. Ähnlich temperamentvoll beschreibt New Yorks prominenter Bürgermeister Edward I. Koch in Text 5 Probleme des Zusammenlebens und -wohnens verschiedener Rassen und Klassen in seiner Stadt. Aspekte der Großstadtkriminalität werden in dem Exzerpt aus Saul Bellows Roman *Mr. Sammler's Planet* angesprochen (Text 6). Um die konkrete, mit starken Kontrasten arbeitende Kritik an den „Wohnsilos" mancher britischer Großstädte geht es Stephen Gardiner in Text 7, in dem auch die Rolle der Straße als eines Elements menschlichen Zusammenlebens betont wird. Wie Jugendliche gelegentlich in Abrißgebieten aufwachsen, läßt der fiktionale Text 8 von Barry Hines miterleben. Die Stadtsanierung wird am Beispiel Glasgows in Text 9 thematisiert, einer *reportage* mit ausgeprägt historisch-landeskundlichem Bezug zu Schottland. Die beiden das Kapitel IX abschließenden Texte befassen sich mit den Teilthemen „Naturzerstörung" und „Naturschutz". Roger McGoughs Gedicht (Text 10) und das Interview mit dem amerikanischen Wissenschaftler Lester R. Brown (Text 11) greifen explizit über die Zielsprachenländer Großbritannien und die Vereinigten Staaten hinaus, ergänzen sich in ihren Aussagen und runden die Behandlung der Gesamtproblematik ab.

1 Michael Manser: The Nonsense of Conformity

Didaktische Hinweise

In diesem argumentativen und landeskundlich sehr bezugsreichen Text tritt der bekannte und erfolgreiche britische Architekt Michael Manser (vgl. "Background information", unten) sehr engagiert für weitgehende Freiheiten bei architektonischen Planungs- und Gestaltungsmöglichkeiten ein. Auf seine Ansichten wird man nicht nur anläßlich der Besprechung des Photos im SB, S. 217, sondern auch bei der Arbeit mit den weiteren Texten dieses Kapitels, insbesondere den Texten 2, 7, 8 und 9, immer wieder zurückkommen und sie auf der Basis der dort dargestellten Sachverhalte und Meinungen kritisch diskutieren.

Background information

Michael Manser (1929–   ) has been the president of the Royal Institute of British Architects since 1983. Besides having his own private architectural practice, he also works as an architectural journalist. This article was published in *The Observer* in 1981 as part of an on-going debate concerning modern architecture. In 1984 the debate was brought to the attention of the general public when Prince Charles launched an attack on certain aspects of modern architecture. Since then Manser has sought to justify the position of architects.

Semantic and collocational field "Architecture and design"

architecture, a style, a scale, a colour, a material, a builder ✧ a new/modern/ huge/small building, a timber/three-storey/tile-roofed building, a cathedral, a church spire, an urban area, a(n) historic/ancient town, a village ✧ a Jacobean court, a classical library, a Georgian imitation ✧ good design, a street elevation, (to) be inserted into older fabric, (to) savage the existing skyline, (to) be sharp against sth., (to) be in keeping with sth., (to) be built all of a piece ✧ cavalier unconcern, conformity, diversity, (to) bother about sth. ✧ the timelessness of great buildings, an insincere quality, by today's conservation standards, (to) be of one's own time, appealing ✧ a hardworking local authority official, a pressure group, (to) prevent construction

Talking about the text – Suggested answers

1. He wants to voice his criticism of the current British planning authorities as well as architects (cf. ll. 1–10). He is concerned about and rejects the predominant approach to town planning and building, which, according to him, leaves too little freedom for creative architects to realize their concepts (cf. ll. 11–13, 77–78). Planners and bureaucrats are conformists, likely to give in to pressure groups and block different modern approaches (cf. ll. 64–67, 72–78).
2. Modern buildings do not have to be "in keeping" (l. 6) with their surroundings. "Diversity" (l. 19), not "conformity" (ll. 26–27), makes the appeal of towns. "Replicas" (l. 31) of past styles are to be rejected. What counts in the esteem of future generations is innovation and creativity. "Good design" (l. 10) is nothing absolute, what is criticized today may be praised tomorrow. Architects must be ready to stand up and fight for their ideas.
3. By giving numerous examples from the history of western architecture, which are all about outstanding achievements still attractive today. At the time, the architects of these works did not conform to existing styles and designs, but were willing and able to realize their revolutionary projects unhampered by strict regulations or controls and in spite of contemporary criticism.
4. By perplexing the reader, they help to underline the writer's basic contention that only innovation and modernness in architectural design make for lasting values and assure recognition by future generations.
5. *How does the structure of this comment help the writer to achieve his aim?*
   He wants to win the reader's consent by structuring his argumentation in a particular dialectical order: He first summarizes the predominant approach to planning and building in Britain, which he opposes (cf. ll. 1–10), then rejects it on historical grounds and briefly states his belief in architectural diversity (cf. ll. 11–21). After conceding that there are justifiable exceptions, he reaffirms his view (cf. ll. 22–35), which he verifies by means of various examples (cf. ll. 36–72). He concludes by seeing the reasons for these architectural achievements in the absence of the restrictive and bureaucratic approach prevalent today (cf. ll. 72–79). Thus he gives proof of the correctness of his view and links up the end with the beginning, bringing his argumentation to a convincing conclusion.

6. *How strongly does this architect seem to be involved in his topic? Consider his way of arguing and his choice of words.*

   He is deeply committed, even polemic in places, and does not allow for nuances of opinion. He totally rejects the current bureaucratic practice of building in Britain while emphatically supporting his own perspective. He argues in absolute terms such as "totally unjustified" (l. 1), "All of this is nonsense. No previous generation" (ll. 11–12), "any" (ll. 13, 14), "no justification" (ll. 30–31), "All replicas" (l. 32), "only" (l. 33), "absolute" (l. 48), "all these buildings" (ll. 60–61), "no bureaucracy" (l. 73), "No amorphous pressure groups" (l. 74). In addition to a number of intensifying adverbs (e.g. ll. 1, 18, 23, 28, 40, 42, 64), he mainly works with emotive words with either positive or negative connotations, e.g. "nonsense" (l. 11), "comical" (l. 18), "insincere" (ll. 32–33), "slapped" (l. 39), "brutal" (l. 42), "magnificent" (l. 46), "vandal" (l. 48), "savaged" (l. 48), "monstrous" (l. 51), "pile" (l. 51), "shattered" (l. 56), "loved and revered" (ll. 61–62), "sentiment and nostalgia" (ll. 63–64), "bitter" (l. 70), "amorphous" (l. 74), "peaceful" (l. 77), "heritage" (l. 79). All this shows his subjective, even sensational, treatment of a controversial topic.

7. *Who would you side with, Manser or the current British planning authorities he is concerned with? Discuss, giving reasons.*

   – –

8. *In your view, what basic rules should an architect follow when designing a private house or a block of flats?*

   – –

2 Brian Clark: Architectural Hindsight

Didaktische Hinweise

Landeskundlicher Bezug dieses Textes ist der Bau der "New Towns" in Großbritannien nach dem Zweiten Weltkrieg (vgl. "Background information", unten). In diesem Exzerpt aus dem ersten Akt von Brian Clarks Drama *Can You Hear Me at the Back?* (1979) reflektiert der Architekt und Stadtplaner Philip Turner selbstkritisch über die Projekte, die er vor etwa 15 Jahren plante und verwirklichte. Die Bewohner der nach seinen Ideen gebauten Hochhäuser leiden unter den Lebensbedingungen, für die er verantwortlich ist, einige von ihnen sind jetzt Patienten seiner Frau Sarah, einer Ärztin. Bereits in diesem Text lassen sich Bezüge herstellen zu Mansers Vorstellungen von Architektur und Stadtplanung, aber auch zu den nicht-fiktionalen Texten 7 und 9. Verknüpfungsmöglichkeiten bestehen ferner zu Kap. I, Text 11, und Kap. III, Text 2 und 4, in denen die Aufmerksamkeit auf die soziale Komponente einer unterlassenen Stadtsanierung gelenkt wird.

Brian Clarks Drama *Can You Hear Me at the Back?* ist in einer von A.-R. Glaap herausgegebenen und annotierten Schulausgabe verfügbar (Frankfurt, Diesterweg). Ebenso wie Clarks Drama *Whose Life Is It Anyway?* (Hrsg. von A.-R. Glaap. Frankfurt, Cornelsen Verlag Hirschgraben 1981. TAGS, Textausgabe Best.-Nr. 665906, LH 666015) eignet es sich gut als Klassenlektüre.

Background information

Brian Clark (1932–   ) was educated in Bristol and then studied at the Central School of Speech and Drama and at Nottingham University. He worked as a teacher in various schools and also taught drama at Hull University. He has written a large number of television plays and some full-length dramas for the theatre, among them *Whose Life Is It Anyway?* (1972, rewritten in 1978) and *Can You Hear Me at the Back?* (1979), from which this excerpt is taken.

The New Towns Act of 1946 formed the basis for the creation of 32 "new towns" in Britain. The objectives of the "new town" policy were to disperse population and industry from congested cities to the surrounding areas and, at the same time, to stimulate the regional economy in other areas. Eleven new towns, amongst them Harlow, Milton Keynes and Crawley, are within 80 miles of London, and are intended to relieve the population pressure on the capital. The total population of the new towns is about two million, and should rise by another half million.

Practically all the features that comprise a town have been taken care of: there are schools, shops, health centres, libraries, police stations, churches, youth clubs and other recreational facilities, so that many of the new towns have become regional centres for shopping and office accommodation.

The development of the new towns programme, which was nearing completion in the late 1980s, has proved a successful achievement of successive British governments. Nevertheless, new towns have been the target of a certain amount of criticism. Farmers and conservationists bemoan the loss of good farmland, depressed industrial areas envy the privileges of the new towns, but, above all, they are attacked for lacking atmosphere and the feeling of neighbourliness.

However, the whole programme of new towns has been slowed down due to the reduction in public expenditure, the unexpected fall in population growth and the adoption of new policies, such as inner-city revitalization and the formation of enterprise zones. (Based on T. Byrne, C.F. Padfield: *Social Services.* Heinemann, London, 1985, pp. 238, 240–241; *Britain 1989. An Official Handbook.* Her Majesty's Stationery Office, London, 1989, p. 191).

Talking about the text – Suggested answers

1. *What seems to be the general situation of Philip's professional life in this excerpt?*
   He looks back on his career of designing and building a New Town years ago. He is frustrated and beset by self-doubts because his good intentions have come to nothing, as he fears.

2. *What were this architect's original ideals and what has become of them in his judgment?*
   He did not want to adapt himself to common tastes and imitate historical styles to make his money from private customers (cf. ll. 25–26) but intended to work in the interests of society, to be creative and realize modern forms of architecture (cf. ll. 26–27, 31–32). He was convinced that in a "'visually exciting environment'" (l. 35) with "high-rise development" (l. 32) and accommodation for large numbers of residents people could live "free and happy lives" (l. 27). These ideals have been proved wrong by reality. The life of the citizens in the buildings designed by him is characterized by boredom, loneliness, vandalism and lack of communication (cf. ll. 33–36).

3. *What reasons for this development are suggested in the text?*
   Originally, i.e. after the wartime slump in building, large numbers of people needed accommodation (cf. l. 8), and architects went to work with renewed energy and a spirit of community after the war was won (cf. ll. 21–24). What made itself felt were the false prognoses of growing wealth and sufficient energy supply (cf. ll. 10–11), the ecstasy of the young, inexperienced architect (cf. ll. 5–7, 26–28) and the arrogance of the profession (cf. ll. 11–14).

4. *How would you sum up Philip's view of the future?*
   He is worried, pessimistic and despondent because he realizes that the effects of his professional decisions are not only long-lasting but also affect large numbers of people (cf. ll. 12–13). Moreover, he wonders whether architects have learned anything from the situation, and he is not sure whether even well-intended projects of the present time will not be proved false in the future (cf. ll. 38–39).

5. *How is his state of mind reflected in this dialogue?*
   Philip is highly upset, very emotional and under an urge to talk and voice his concerns and self-doubts. This becomes obvious from the dominant role he plays in the dialogue and in his speech, which is characterized by emotive language (e.g. ll. 5–7, 11–12, 22, 26–27, 33–34, 35, 39), requests (cf. ll. 9, 30, 31), exclamations (cf. ll. 9, 23, 30), emphasis (italics in ll. 10, 28, 33), rhetorical questions (cf. ll. 3, 38–39) and the exaggerations in his judgments.

6. *What seems to be Margery's function in this excerpt?*
   She makes brief comments and objections in an attempt to bring Philip down to earth and to justify his actions to some extent. As her remarks, however, have the opposite effect, she goads him into responding with further accusations and self-doubts.

7. *Why may the two speakers have chosen the illustrations in ll. 2–3 and 16–17?*
   Each of them refers to the professional experience of the other – Philip chooses his example from Margery's job as a dress designer, and Margery takes one of her illustrations from the sphere of architecture and the other from the general knowledge of what cancer is. In this way they hope to make themselves better understood and to win the other's consent more easily.

8. *Philip remembers a time when, according to him, " 'Welfare' was a term of praise, of pride, not a term of abuse" (ll. 24–25). In the light of your knowledge from Ch. III, Texts 2, 3 and 4, explain this statement.*
   – –

9. *Later in this drama, the main character criticizes the town he helped to build as "Lego Land". What does this metaphor imply?*
   – –

10. *In her response to Philip's final rhetorical questions (ll. 38–39), Margery draws the provocative conclusion, not printed in this excerpt, that from now on he will design "cosy little converted windmills for Sunday Supplement people". Would this be a meaningful alternative? Discuss.*
    – –

3 Joyce Carol Oates: Dreaming America

Didaktische Hinweise

Während die beiden ersten Texte dieses Kapitels am Beispiel Großbritanniens die Gestaltung unserer urbanen Umwelt durch Architekten und Städteplaner thematisieren, reagiert Joyce Carol Oates in ihrem Gedicht auf die Veränderung und Zerstörung der amerikanischen Natur- und Agrarlandschaft als Folgeerscheinung der modernen Zivilisation. Gerade in den USA trug die Entwicklung des Automobils zur Be- und Zersiedlung des Landes, zur Prägung des Landschafts- und Städtebilds sowie zur Herausbildung eines spezifischen Lebensstils bei. Das möglicherweise als abrupt empfundene Ende des Gedichts mag zum Anlaß genommen werden, über Haltung und Intention der Autorin zu spekulieren.

Inhaltlich bestehen enge Bezüge zu Roger McGoughs Gedicht "The Lake" (Text 10, vgl. auch LB, S. 197), der sich mit dem Problem der Umweltzerstörung ganz allgemein auseinandersetzt. Denkbar ist jedoch auch die Einbeziehung des Gedichts "New Way, Old Way" von Dave Martin Nez (Kap. V, Text 6), der als Native American seine Version des "American Dream" in Worte kleidet, wobei insbesondere Z. 34 des Oates-Gedichts als Anknüpfungspunkt dienen könnte.

Background information

Joyce Carol Oates (1938–   ) was born in Lockport, New York, of an Irish-Catholic working-class family. She studied English and philosophy, then taught English at the University of Windsor in Ontario, Canada, and at Princeton. She is best known for her fiction, especially her short stories, but she has also published collections of poems. She has received many literary awards. Among her works are *By the North Gate* (1963), *The Wheel of Love* (1970), *Dreaming America and Other Poems* (1973), *The Fabulous Beasts* (1975), *Crossing the Border* (1976), *The Assignation* (1988). Her essays and critical writings are collected in *The Edge of Impossibility* (1971), *New Heaven, New Earth* (1974) and *Contraries* (1981).

Talking about the text – Suggested answers

1. The construction of more and more highways, wider and more closely connected (cf. ll. 1, 8–13), the destruction of nature, farmland and farms (cf. ll. 2–7, 13–17, 25, 34), the creation and expansion of service facilities and areas for motorized travellers such as restaurants, filling stations and shopping malls (cf. ll. 18–19, 27–28), the spoiling of the scenery by obtrusive advertisements (cf. ll. 18–23, 26), the detraction from the natural rhythm of day and night (cf. ll. 24, 26–30, 35–36).
2. There are, on the one hand, the teenagers, who are not aware of the changes but have accepted this environment as part of their life-style. They are falling prey to this world characterized by illusions, glamour and consumption (cf. ll. 29–30, 33, 35–36). On the other hand, there are the grown-ups, who hardly have the time to realize the changes and regret them (cf. ll. 31–32, 37).
3. The speaker regrets the transformation of America by its highly technological civilization and longs for the times when the country was less determined or controlled by man. The last line seems to suggest that she/he may be resolved to become active and appeal to people's awareness of the losses and values worth preserving, perhaps even restoring.
4. The American Dream is alive, but it has become an illusion of speed, glamour and consumption. The poet's dream seems to be a nostalgic remembrance of America in a more natural state. The title is ambiguous, as the reader does not know whether this is the writer dreaming up her own America or whether this is America adhering to false dreams.
5. *How is the speaker's view of America's changing environment reflected in structural units?*
   There are two major parts to this poem, each consisting of three stanzas. Those in the first part deal with important stages in the transformation of the countryside by the spread of motor traffic and are bound together by the use of the past tense, a number of passive voices and the parallelisms and anaphora of the first lines and l. 14. Those in the second part contrast the natural state of the past with the conditions and life-style of the present, which is reflected in the connection of past and present tenses. They are also unified by parallelisms and anaphora, in this case "where", not "when".
6. *What may be the reasons for the car becoming so dominant in American society?*
   – –
7. *Cars and highways have been essential elements in American art and entertainment. Discuss an example from cinema or television, literature or music.*
   – –

4 W. J. Weatherby: Apartment-Hunting in New York City

Didaktische Hinweise

Nach der eher grundsätzlichen Diskussion von Fragen der Stadtplanung und -architektur zu Beginn dieses Kapitels (Text 1 und 2) und der dichterischen Auseinandersetzung mit einer amerikaspezifischen Variante der Umweltproblematik (Text 3) wenden sich dieser und die beiden folgenden Texte konkreten Einzelproblemen des Wohnens und Lebens in einer modernen amerikanischen Großstadt, hier New York City, zu. Zieht man im Rahmen dieser Unterrichtssequenz zusätzlich Text 3 aus Kap. V zur Betrachtung heran, so entsteht ein Porträt dieser für viele Schüler/innen noch immer interessantesten amerikanischen Metropole. Neben der Thematisierung von Einzelaspekten, etwa der Wohnungsknappheit, den Mietpreisen, der Entfernung zwischen Wohnung und Arbeitsplatz, der Verkehrsdichte und Kriminalität, verdeutlicht dieser sehr persönliche Bericht auch die rassische und ethnische Vielfalt New Yorks – und Amerikas –, die bereits einer der zentralen Aspekte des Kap. V war und im folgenden Text in ihrer spezifischen Problematik nochmals im Mittelpunkt stehen soll. Eine weitere Vertiefung läßt sich erreichen durch die Einbeziehung des Themenhefts *American City in Crisis. Landeskundliche Materialsammlung.* Didaktisch bearbeitet von Raphael Wunsch, Nicoline Kokxhoorn, Helga Pfetsch. Berlin, Cornelsen Verlag 1978 (CVK Modell Englisch, SB Best.-Nr. 9947, LH 9955).

Background information

New York City originally consisted only of Manhattan Island, but in 1898 it joined with the boroughs of Brooklyn (formerly Kings), Queens, the Bronx and Staten Island (formerly Richmond) to form Greater New York. Each borough has a president, and above them is the mayor of New York City. With a population of 7,263,000 (1986 estimate), New York ranks as the largest US city and is the financial, commercial and business centre of the United States.

New York has managed throughout the years to retain its character as a singularly liberal, exciting and cosmopolitan city with a feeling that it is nearly a nation in itself. Despite having had a high percentage of foreign-born, it has always resisted any exclusive ethnic identification. However, the city has been highly segregated along racial lines. The Black population, forming approximately one quarter of the city's population, is concentrated in Harlem, in northeastern Manhattan, which is more of a ghetto than any other minority neighbourhood, Brooklyn and certain areas of the Bronx. About a fifth of the population is Hispanic, and is concentrated in upper Manhattan. There are also considerable communities of European origin, such as German, Greek, Hungarian, Irish, Italian, Polish and Russian. With about two million Jews in addition, no other city can boast such a wide representation of various cultures, races and ethnic entities as New York City.

Semantic and collocational field "City housing"

an apartment, a condo(minium), a one-room studio ✧ (a) management, a manager, an estate agent, a superintendent, a tenant ✧ a real estate boom, a buyer's/seller's market ✧ a safe area, segregated housing, (to) live behind multi-locks and barred windows ✧ a rent, a fee, gas and electricity included, (to) go for ($ 1,000) a month, (to) be a bargain, (to) afford sth. ✧ a first-comer, (to) search for sth., (to) follow up an ad, (to) be close to giving up, (to) move/settle in

Talking about the text – Suggested answers

1. *What are housing conditions like in New York City, according to the text?*
   Roomy apartments are hard to come by. The prices for property and rents are very high. There seems to be discrimination of certain resident groups against outsiders. Streets and houses are often unsafe, views are obstructed and the air is polluted.

2. *How does life in Yonkers differ from that in Manhattan, in the writer's view?*
   There is a lower population density; there are consequently more apartments available, often in more pleasant surroundings (cf. ll. 53–58, 70–74); the rents and the real-estate agents' fees are lower; there is less crime, traffic, noise and pollution. On the other hand, those who have business in Manhattan or take part in its cultural life must rely on public or private transport over long distances. The group rivalries between residents still exist (cf. ll. 30–40, 61–69, 74–78) but can, in the writer's experience, be overcome more easily (cf. ll. 79–84).

3. *Considering what Weatherby observes about the population in and near New York City, would you say it is more appropriate to describe this area as a "melting pot" or as a "salad bowl" (cf. Ch. V, "Info-Box", pp. 121 f.)?*
   It is more appropriate to speak of a "salad bowl" because different races and ethnic groups are distinguishable and tend to concentrate in proper neighbourhoods (cf. ll. 25–27, 30–40, 51, 59–69, 75–78).

4. *Why may this form of text exercise a greater appeal than a sociological study on the housing situation in New York City?*
   Because the writer uses the first-person point of view and narrates his own experiences in a kind of story rather than an abstract exposition. He reduces the distance between himself and his readers by employing a large number of elements of informal style. In addition to this, he strikes a humorous or ironical tone (e.g. ll. 21–23, 27–29, 32–34, 38–41, 47–49, 51–53, 57–58, 92), which, at times, even becomes sarcastic (e.g. ll. 16–20, 45).

5. *How does the writer adapt himself to the fact that the text is published in "The Guardian" and most of his readers can be expected to be English, fairly educated and liberal-minded?*
   His reference to Manchester (cf. l. 27) and his critical treatment of the Irish (cf. ll. 34–41) may appeal to English readers, the pejorative comparison with the "old English class system" (l. 78) complies with their liberal-mindedness, and the literary allusions to Cheever (l. 72) and Huxley (l. 75) can only be appreciated by people with some such background.

6. *Why is Manhattan the only place a typical New Yorker believes he or she could live in (cf. ll. 21–23)?*
   – –

5 Edward I. Koch: Racial Integration in Housing

Didaktische Hinweise

In den Ballungszentren der Großstädte leben Menschen auf besonders engem Raum zusammen. Die daraus entstehenden Schwierigkeiten vergrößern sich noch, wenn Bevölkerungsgruppen mit unterschiedlichem rassischem, ethnischem oder sozialem Hintergrund aufeinandertreffen. Vielfach konzentrieren sich bestimmte Gruppierungen in einzelnen Stadtteilen, Versuche, sie zu integrieren, scheitern häufig. Solche Verhältnisse, früher vor allem für amerikanische Großstädte typisch, werden heute in fast allen Metropolen sichtbar und sind vielen Schülern/ Schülerinnen auch aus persönlicher Erfahrung bekannt.

Bereits in Kap. V, Text 3, wurde New Yorks Bevölkerungsproblematik, dort aus historischer Sicht und mit dem Blick auf jüdische Immigranten, thematisiert. Sie wird mit diesem Auszug aus Edward I. Kochs *Politics*. (New York, Simon & Schuster 1986) wieder aufgegriffen. Die Meinung des New Yorker Bürgermeisters wird für die Schüler/innen von besonderem Interesse sein, da sie hier sehr deutlich und in einer lebhaften, fast an eine Rede erinnernden Form geäußert wird.

Background information

Ed(ward) I. Koch [kɒtʃ ☆ kɑːtʃ] (1924–   ) was born in the Bronx, New York City, of Polish-Jewish parents. He studied law at New York University and practised as a lawyer. He later entered politics, serving on the New York City Council from 1967 to 1968. He was a Democratic member of Congress for New York State from 1969 to 1978, when he was elected mayor of New York City, a post which he has held since then. He is a colourful and controversial figure, who is always prepared to say what is on his mind.

For further information on New York City cf. p. 187 of this book.

"poverty level" (l. 17): In the USA a family of four is judged as living below the poverty level if the total family income is less than $ 11,203 per year (1989 figure). Until January 1989 only the taxable income was taken into account when determining whether or not a family lived below the poverty level. Now, however, the definition of income has been broadened to include benefits from Social Security, e.g. Medicare and Medicaid, rent subsidies and food stamps (cf. also "Info-Box", SB, pp. 175 f.). This has meant an overnight drop in the number of people living below the poverty level from 32.4 million (i.e. ca. 13.6 % of the population) to 27.6 million Americans (i.e. ca. 11.6 % of the population).

Approximately 31 % of all blacks, 27 % of all Hispanics and 11 % of all whites lived below the poverty level (according to the 1986 figures). Certain areas of the US are worse affected than others – the states around the Mississippi delta (Mississippi, Arkansas, Alabama and Louisiana) have the highest poverty rates, and in New York City poverty is concentrated in the areas of Manhattan, Brooklyn and the Bronx where blacks and Hispanics form the majority of the population.

Semantic and collocational field "Class and race in housing"

a neighbourhood, a housing project, a futile programme, a slum, a property owner ✧ low/middle income, the wealthy, people of different economic strata, a lifestyle, economically deprived, (to) live on welfare, (to) live at the poverty line ✧ a class/race problem, racial integration, (to) prohibit racial discrimination in housing, (to) enforce a law, to stop/prevent sb. from moving into an area, (to) violate sth.

Talking about the text – Suggested answers

1.The middle class is said to be unwilling to live together with lower-income people because they see their own values threatened and fear the frustration, anger and violence of their poorer neighbours. Indignities seem to happen at times, some of them "racially motivated" (l. 10). The better-off are inclined to move out. Thus the area is left to turn into a slum that is socially and economically homogeneous.

2. It puts up housing projects in middle-class neighbourhoods and lets them out to low-income and welfare families. It is hoped that all can live together and that the poorer will adapt to the lifestyle of their middle-class neighbours.

3. He emphatically recognizes everybody's right to move wherever they want to as long as they can afford it, but criticizes the government's measures to enforce this right by mixing families with different economic backgrounds. He is convinced that such integration does not work because, in his opinion, class is a "determinant of social attitudes" (l. 38) and therefore the poor do not make the middle-class lifestyle and value system their own. He shows his understanding for middle-class people who try to preserve their style of living by moving.

4. It may strike the reader that Koch mainly uses the first-person point of view, often in connection with phrases expressing opinion and preference, e.g. "believe" (ll. 1, 30), "like" (l. 10), "in my judgement" (ll. 14, 20), "think" (ll. 20, 27), "my position" (l. 29). Similarly he employs a large number of attitudinal adverbs or their equivalents, e.g. "There's no question" (l. 3), "quite correctly" (l. 5), "there's something wrong" (l. 14), "is just wrong" (l. 19), "rightly" (l. 20), "They are wrong" (l. 38), and emphasizes statements by means of emphatic constructions (ll. 1, 19–20, 33) and intensifying adverbs, e.g. "particularly" (ll. 21–22), "really" (l. 30), "very" (l. 31), "always" (l. 33), "exactly" (l. 34). Moral obligation is expressed in the auxiliaries "should" (ll. 1, 8) and "ought not to" (l. 32). In some cases the writer also interrupts himself to qualify his own terms or phrases (cf. ll. 5, 10–11, 12–13, 17, 20–21, 21–22, 25, 37). All this shows a high degree of personal involvement combined with a lively temperament, striking outspokenness and frank subjectivity.

5. *In what respects may lifestyles and values differ between economic classes? Discuss.*

– –

6. *What arguments may those "who are obsessed with race, on the right and the left" (l. 37), put forward? Discuss them.*

– –

7. *Are there similar housing policies of mixing neighbourhoods in your own home town? If so, report on how successful they are.*

– –

6 Saul Bellow: I Want to Report a Crime

Didaktische Hinweise

Dieser fiktionale Text, ein Auszug aus Saul Bellows Roman *Mr. Sammler's Planet* (1969), gewinnt seine Spannung aus dem Konflikt zwischen Erwartung und Enttäuschung eines europäisch erzogenen Immigranten in einem von Gleich-gültigkeit, Resignation und Gewalt geprägten New York. Amerikanische Großstädte sind wegen ihrer hohen Kriminalitätsrate berüchtigt. Nachdem dieser Aspekt der Großstadtproblematik bereits in den beiden vorausgehenden Sachtexten ange-sprochen wurde, rückt er hier, am Einzelschicksal exemplarisch verdeutlicht, in den Mittelpunkt. Obwohl seit dem Erscheinen des Romans mehr als zwanzig Jahre vergangen sind, hat Bellows sarkastische Kritik an den bestehenden Verhältnissen noch nichts von ihrer Aktualität verloren. Sie beruht auf Erfahrung einer Realität, die den Schülern/ Schülerinnen wahrscheinlich nicht fremd ist und die sie daher nachvollziehen können.

Background information

Saul Bellow (1915–   ) was born in Canada, the son of Russian-Jewish immigrants. He grew up in Chicago, studied sociology and literature and then taught at various universities. He is one of America's best known writers of fiction and was awarded the Nobel Prize for Literature in 1976. His most successful novels are *The Adventures of Augie March* (1953), *Seize the Day* (1956), *Henderson the Rain King* (1959), *Herzog* (1964), *Mr. Sammler's Planet* (1969) and *Humboldt's Gift* (1975).

Mr. Sammler's Planet (1969) deals with an immigrant Polish Jew and the everyday problems he has to confront in New York's Upper West Side. The novel's strength lies in the contrast between Sammler, an educated, lonely man who worked as a journalist in London in the 1920s and 30s, then survived a German concentration camp in World War II, and the attitudes of the society of which he has become a part.

Semantic and collocational field "Crime"

the police, an officer, a detective, a criminal, a pickpocket, an interrogation, (to) rob sb. ✧ (to) report a crime, (to) point sb. out ✧ (to) arrest sb., (to) catch sb., (to) cover sth.

Talking about the text – Suggested answers

1. *What does this episode suggest about crime and security in Manhattan?*
   Petty crime such as pickpocketing and telephone vandalism seem to be too common to be prosecuted seriously. Entrances to apartment buildings are guarded – in theory at least – by doormen and television surveillance. The police are understaffed and are too busy protecting more important people or investigating major offences.
2. *How does American reality as experienced by Artur Sammler compare with his previous image of this country?*
   Whereas he had firmly believed that America was universally recognized as a model nation, he must now realize that ethical standards seem to be rather low. Apart from the fact that delinquency is a more or less accepted part of daily life, the police are lethargic and indifferent, and the doorman at his building (cf. l. 3) neglects his duties.
3. *How does the protagonist react to conditions as he finds them in America?*
   Although he does not attempt to stop the pickpocket on the spot, he takes pains to describe the man to the police and thus be helpful in making an investigation possible. When he realizes the indifference and resignation of the authorities, his confidence in America and his admiration for the country are shattered (cf. ll. 48–51).
4. *For what reasons may the author have chosen to use dialogue here?*
   Apart from the fact that this form of scenic presentation makes for variety and brings about a dramatic effect, its main function is to characterize both speakers implicitly by their communicative behaviour. The policeman's lack of interest and his resignation are reflected in his short utterances and the monotonous repetition of "O.K.", his carelessness and impoliteness show in his addressing Sammler by his Christian name, even misusing it, and his refusal to answer the caller's last question. The protagonist's determination to help can be seen in his coming to the point directly, his insistence and the precision of the description he gives. His politeness and education find expression in the use of complete sentences and more formal forms of address.
5. *Discuss possible reasons for the high crime rate in all major cities.*
   – –

6. *What would you think of neighbourhoods organizing themselves into active groups to safeguard life and property?*
   – –

7 Stephen Gardiner: The Biggest Blunder of All

Didaktische Hinweise

Nachdem in den Texten 4, 5 und 6 die Problematik städtischer Umwelt unter ameri-
kakundlichem Aspekt behandelt wurde, vermitteln die Texte 7, 8 und 9 Einblicke in
entsprechende Phänomene in Großbritannien. Der vorliegende Text ist ein Auszug aus
einem Artikel, der im Rahmen einer Serie in der Sonntagszeitung *The Observer*
erschien. In ihr äußerten sich – teilweise recht kontrovers – namhafte britische
Architekten zu verschiedenen Aspekten der Städteplanung (vgl. LB, S. 182).
Stephen Gardiner reflektiert hier über Fehlentwicklungen im britischen sozialen
Wohnungsbau der vergangenen Jahre. Die Zerstörung gewachsener Stadtviertel im
Rahmen von Neubaumaßnahmen, die vorwiegend profitorientierte, übereilte
Errichtung billiger "Wohnsilos" und -anlagen für möglichst viele Menschen sowie
die unzureichende Berücksichtigung der Kommunikationsbedürfnisse der Bewohner
durch die mangelnde Einbeziehung traditioneller Begegnungsräume, etwa von
Straßen und Plätzen, führten in seinen Augen zu einem Verlust an Lebensqualität, zu
Vereinsamung, Aggression, Vandalismus und Kriminalität. Querverbindungen,
insbesondere zu dem Auszug aus Brian Clarks Drama *Can You Hear Me at the Back?*
(vgl. Text 2), aber auch zu den amerikakundlichen Texten 5 und 6 lasssen sich
mühelos herstellen. Die Einbeziehung des Cartoons, SB, S. 227, in die Besprechung
des Textes, auch als Einstieg, bietet sich an.

Background information

The redevelopment of overcrowded and derelict urban areas often started with slum
clearances, but this policy more or less came to an end in the first half of the 1980s.
The existence of basic utilities, local employment and easy access to city centres
suggested that these areas should be retained, rather than destroyed.

   For many years high-rise flats seemed to be a solution to housing problems and
they did help to improve housing conditions considerably. High-rises, however,
were not acceptable to many of their residents in the long run, especially to families
with children and the elderly. After running up high maintenance costs and being
plagued by serious structural defects, many high-rises were demolished. Local
authorities, with the government's encouragement, now tend either to sell council
houses and flats favourably to the private sector or at least to refurbish them.
Where it is necessary to preserve high population density, planning now insists on
low-rise blocks of up to four storeys, usually grouped closely together (based on the
1989 edition of *Britain. An Official Handbook.* Her Majesty's Stationery Office,
London, 1989, p. 196–202).

Semantic and collocational field "City planning"

an architect, architecture, a town planner, a manufacturer ✧ a (local authority) housing
estate, a tower block, a terrace, a square, a street ✧ a neighourhood link, neighbourhood
design, an ideal community form, a housing programme, a rebuilding operation, the shape
and proportion of sth., to adjust a balance, (to) design a facade ✧ privacy, surroundings, a
secluded space, (to) have a view ✧ height, a material, a factory-made building part, prefab-
ricated ✧ demolition, (to) devastate sth., (to) uproot a community, (to) obliterate street
patterns, (to) demolish a neighbourhood, (to) leak, (to) crack, (to) fall apart, a wall drips with
condensation, a maintenance bill rockets

Talking about the text – Suggested answers

1. Town planning was too much concerned with the erection of housing estates and tower blocks, thereby destroying old communities, traditional street patterns and historic architecture (cf. ll. 5–8, 20–28, 85–87). Construction relied increasingly on the assembly of pre-fabricated parts, which was time-saving, but resulted in low standards of quality (cf. ll. 55–72). This led to high maintenance costs and a generally bad state of repair; in some cases, it even became necessary to demolish these buildings. Lack of social communication and poor quality of life resulted in frustration, violence and vandalism among the residents and even caused them to abandon their dwellings (cf. ll. 28–40).

2. There were the local governments, which competed to provide more and more accommodation all the time and were ready to subsidize such projects heavily (cf. ll. 16–19, 55–59, 66–69). There were the planners, who recklessly disregarded past organic growth, and the architects (cf. ll. 26–28, 120–125), who willingly carried out what was expected of them instead of considering the people's genuine needs and devoting themselves to original designing and aesthetic values. Last but not least, there were the manufacturers, who put profits above the quality of their products (cf. ll. 28–35).

3. Planners and architects should take their time and concentrate on aesthetic qualities, which are the results of attention to proportions, materials, the design of details and harmony with existing streets, buildings and natural surroundings (cf. ll. 49–54, 84–91). They should also take into consideration human values, such as the need for security, intimacy, comfort and relaxation, but also opportunities to meet and communicate easily with one other (cf. ll. 91–120).

4. He may have wanted to assess the past mistakes and their causes in retrospect, draw conclusions for present and future building projects, and warn against the high material costs and the human unhappiness that such blunders entail (cf. ll. 41–54, 119-125). By publishing the article in "The Observer" he can expect to reach a large, engaged, educated readership with a certain influence on decision-making.

5. He tries to impress his warnings on his readers by sharp contrasts, underlining the negative aspects of the past and opposing them to the positive features of his own suggestions. He achieves this effect by making blunt judgments and using words with strong emotive qualities, e.g.
   negative: "blunders" (l. 3), "worst" (l. 4), "appalling" (l. 6), "horrible" (l. 6), "biggest" (l. 8), "uprooted" (l. 21), "obliterated" (l. 22), "devastated" (l. 24), "horrific" (l. 30) ;
   positive: "superb" (l. 23), "useful" (l. 88), "importance" (l. 89), "continuity" (l. 91), "harmonious" (l. 96), "ideal" (l. 101), "balance" (l. 108),"perfectly" (l. 109), "retreat" (l. 114).

6. [Manser would probably accept his demands for careful design and solid building and his criticism of the planning authorities' power. He might pay less attention to grown structures.]

7. *Considering the living conditions of the population at large in the 18th and 19th centuries, in what respects could a critic dismiss some of Gardiner's statements on the past as half-true and nostalgic?*
   [Streets used to be unpaved and unlit, narrow and noisy. Kerbstones and street "furniture" like bollards or seats were long unknown. The interiors of houses were often narrow, ill-ventilated and unhygienic. Until well into the 19th century cities were unpoliced and in the worst parts of industrial towns there were often only cellars and slums for the mixed labour force.]

8. *What may have made life in tower blocks appear a necessity, even an ideal, to some architectural schools?*
   – –

9. *Would you say that blunders like those criticized in the text have occurred in your home town? If so, what is being done about them?*
   – –

8   Barry Hines: The Playground

Didaktische Hinweise

Dieser Auszug aus Barry Hines' Roman *Looks and Smiles* (zum Inhalt und zur Verwendung als Klassenlektüre vgl. LB, S. 53) vertieft als fiktionaler Text die von Stephen Gardiner in Text 7 beklagten Entwicklungen im sozialen Wohnungsbau Großbritanniens, hier vor dem Hintergrund des wirtschaftlichen Niedergangs traditioneller Industriezweige in den Midlands, der damit verbundenen öffentlichen Kapitalknappheit und einer hohen Arbeitslosenquote. Den Jugendlichen, die in der hier beschriebenen Arbeitersiedlung leben, fehlen sinnvolle, altersgemäße Freizeiträume, sie schaffen sie sich mit viel Phantasie und unter nicht ganz ungefährlichen Bedingungen selbst (vgl. unten, Aufg. 1 bis 3). Der mit ihnen sympathisierende, leicht amüsierte Erzähler beobachtet sie, wie sie sich auf diese tristen Verhältnisse auf ihre Weise einstellen.

Um den spontanen Zugang zum Text zu gewährleisten, wurde der Aufgabenapparat wiederum im LB untergebracht.

Background information

Barry Hines: cf. p. 53 of this book.

Semantic and collocational field "Wasteland"

a piece of wasteland, a dirt track, devastation, damage, a pile of bricks and rubble, a crater, a(n) derelict/empty house, (to) board sth. up ✧ a digger, a bulldozer, (to) knock sth. down, (to) demolish sth., (to) clear a site ✧ a mound of (compressed) earth, a lump of soil, (to) use sth. (e.g. land) as a playground

Semantic and collocational field "Motorbiking"

a (motor) bike, a motor-cycle, a handgrip, petrol, (to) adjust the brakes ✧ (to) kick-start sth. (e.g. a motorbike), (to) rev the engine, (to) roar louder, (to) accelerate, (to) slow down, (to) ride up on a motorcycle, (to) ride off ✧ a course, a finishing flag, (to) flag sb. down, (to) complete a lap ✧ (to) absorb the impact of landing, (to) skid, (to) spin, (to) slide away from underneath sb.

Talking about the text – Suggested answers

1. *How well, in your opinion, do leisure facilities for young people seem to have been taken into consideration by the planners and builders?*
   They seem to have been neglected, if not altogether disregarded. If they were planned, they have not been realized. It is up to the children to find themselves a place where they can play and have a good romp. In this case it is just a half-cleared demolition site.
2. *What sort of a playground is described here?*
   The playground is an open lot of land with a few deserted houses and covered with debris. Its rough surface is strewn with all sorts of disused or demolished objects that were once part of the building structures or belonged to the contents of the houses. All this suggests an unhygienic and dangerous refuse pit rather than a proper and safe area to play in.
3. *What use do the young people make of the particular qualities of this setting?*
   They are quite creative and transform the seemingly useless objects and the uneven, loose surface into functional components of their games. Thus the craters, mounds and other obstacles become parts of a cross-country race-track. The boards of the front and back doors are turned into a tunnel to make the course more exciting. The torn tights and

the broken umbrella serve as the flag of a race-track official. The discarded settee furnishes an imaginary open-air children's room.

4. *How do the children's and grown-ups' attitudes towards law and authorities appear to be reflected in the text?*
   The children have stolen the bike and their behaviour when the police arrive hints at the fact that they have got into conflicts with the law before. Though not liked by some people, they are protected against the authorities by the solidarity of parents and neighbours, who tolerate delinquency.

5. *How much does the narrator know about the setting and the characters?*
   Although he is mainly an observer of the playground and the actions there, he knows more than what might be expected from just watching the scene. He repeatedly proves omniscient, e.g. when relating the planners' intentions and their reasons for stopping work (cf. ll. 3–5), the misuse of some materials (cf. ll. 13–14), the previous experience and the present thoughts of the police (cf. ll. 64–67).

6. *What seems to be the story-teller's relationship to the youngsters?*
   The elements of comedy, even absurdity, suggest that the narrator regards the children and their surroundings with a good deal of humour and amusement as well as understanding and sympathy (cf. ll. 11–16, 27–28, 33–36, 51, 59–62).

7. *What, in your opinion, should planners and architects provide for children and adolescents when designing a neighbourhood? Add your own experiences.*
   – –

9 L. Garrison, M. Cronin: Scrubbing the Grime from the Sandstone

Didaktische Hinweise

Dieser Auszug aus einem Artikel, der 1986 in der amerikanischen Wochenzeitschrift *Time* erschien, ist als positives Gegenstück zu den Texten 2 und 7 zu sehen und zeigt am Beispiel der schottischen Stadt Glasgow, wie man aus den von Brian Clark und Stephen Gardiner beklagten Fehlern zu lernen beginnt und Stadtsanierung sinnvoll verwirklichen kann. Da die beiden Journalisten in erster Linie für nicht-britische – insbesondere amerikanische – Leser/innen schreiben, können sie nur ein bestimmtes Maß an Vorwissen voraussetzen und müssen daher möglichst umfassend berichten. Diese landeskundlichen Informationen kommen den Bedürfnissen der Schüler/innen entgegen, die so gleichzeitig ein anschauliches Bild von der Entwicklung einer bedeutenden britischen Stadt erhalten. Die in Kap. III, Text 2 beschriebenen Veränderungen in der britischen Wirtschaftsstruktur werden hier an einem konkreten Beispiel noch einmal demonstriert, so daß sich durchaus Verknüpfungs-möglichkeiten mit dem Hewitt-Text ergeben (vgl. LB, S. 55).

Background information

For information on inner-city housing in Britain cf. p. 192 of this book.

Semantic and collocational field "Urban decay and rejuvenation"

an urban centre/area, an industrial city, a ghost town, a city doomed to decay, a city's grim past, a bleak decade, a steady decline ◇ a housing estate, an apartment house, a dwelling, a substandard home, a teeming slum, an abandoned/derelict tenement, a shuttered store-front ◇ an exhibition centre, a café theatre, a warehouse, a mall, an art gallery, an office building ◇ a hub of shipbuilding and heavy industry, a shipyard, an absence of heavy industry, (the) service/tourist industry, a growth industry, a manufacturing job ✧ private/public investment, private funding ✧ rejuvenation, renovation, a transformation, a face-lift, a city's revival, a steam blaster, (to) restore sth., (to) refashion sth., (to) transform sth., (to) convert sth. into sth. else, (to) scrub away the soot, (to) scrub the grime from sth. ✧ a developer, a planner, a property development, a project, a residential tower, (to) relocate/resettle sb. (e.g. a resident)

Talking about the text – Suggested answers

1. The city was a thriving centre of shipbuilding and heavy engineering and thus one of the most important and populous cities in Britain from the 19th century up to the middle of the 20th century (cf. ll. 6–11). With the deterioration of Britain's traditional industries (cf. Ch. III, Text 2) Glasgow rapidly declined (cf. ll. 11–18). Since the 1960s there has been a development towards a whole range of service industries such as banking, insurance, advertising and catering, and even the arts were supported by a great deal of private and public investment. This has amounted to a transformation and revival of Glasgow's economic life (cf. ll. 37–51, 63–65, 69–72, 86–91).

2. Originally Glasgow was a predominantly industrial town, with factories, shipyards and warehouses. Its population of workers lived in lower-class neighbourhoods, which deteriorated into slums with the city's economic decline. The structural transformation and financial revival have brought about changes in Glasgow's appearance. Older buildings have been pulled down, restored or converted, façades have been cleaned, a large number of new projects have been carried out such as hotels, banks, insurance and office buildings, shops and galleries. The slums have been cleared and the residents have been offered new dwellings.

3. They cleared the slums in inner urban areas and relocated their residents in modern housing estates with high-rise buildings on the edge of Glasgow. This meant a complete disintegration of the old neighbourhoods, perhaps with a loss of homeliness, which tower blocks simply could not offer, and the necessity to adapt to life on the outskirts of the city. The social situation of the people did not change (cf. ll. 69–77, 95–96).

4. They stopped wholesale demolition and relocation. As far as possible they preserved the old neighbourhoods, restored, renovated, modernized and cleaned buildings, added thousands of new homes in the inner areas and made sure that all public amenities were available in these residential districts. All this contributed to making the city of Glasgow more livable again (cf. ll. 77–85, 100–104).

5. Their intentions seem to be to inform their readers about a successful attempt at bringing a decaying city back to life again and to present Glasgow as an "object lesson" (l. 63) to other cities in a similar situation. The writers try to make their information precise and objective by giving quite a lot of figures, dates and quotations from experts. They make their case more concrete, appealing and vivid by repeatedly comparing past and present conditions (cf. ll. 1–18, 28–31, 52–60, 66–68, 81–84) and by personifying Glasgow to a certain extent, using expressions like "face-lift" (l. 27), "long-dormant" (l. 49), "breathe" (l. 50), "alive" (ll. 53, 103), "hardworking, hard-drinking" (l. 56), "teeming" (l. 58), "fighting back" (l. 64), "rejuvenation" (l. 69) and "savior" (l. 86).

6. *What would Michael Manser (cf. Ch. IX, Text 1) probably think of the new ideas and activities of town planners in Glasgow?*
   [He might be suspicious of public and private funding as an expression of vested interests of pressure groups; he might distrust preservation, restoration and renovation as an obstacle to disparity and diversity; he might denounce the Scottish Development Agency as bureaucratic machinery.]

7. *In   your opinion, what should planners consider to make slum clearance economically and aesthetically acceptable to residents?*
   – –

10 Roger McGough: The Lake

Didaktische Hinweise

Die Gefahren einer Zerstörung der natürlichen Umwelt durch den Menschen sind ein weltweites Problem und werden deshalb – mit unterschiedlicher Ausführlichkeit und aus verschiedenartigen Blickwinkeln – in der Schule in mehreren Fächern erörtert. Es kann daher erwartet werden, daß die Schüler/innen bereits Vorkenntnisse besitzen, auf die bei der Arbeit mit den beiden letzten Texten dieses Kapitels (Text 10 und 11) zurückgegriffen werden kann. Eine thematische Erweiterung an dieser oder späterer Stelle durch die Einbeziehung des Gedichts von Joyce Carol Oates (Text 3) und/oder der Texte 7 und 8 aus Kap. XII ist ohne weiteres möglich.

Roger McGough gehört wie Brian Patten und Adrian Henri zu den "Liverpool Poets", deren Gedichte bei den Schülern/Schülerinnen in der Regel auf großes Interesse stoßen. Sein Gedicht mit dem Titel "The Lake", der Naturlyrik vermuten läßt, spricht nicht nur durch seine verblüffenden und teilweise rätselhaften Aussagen die Neugier und Phantasie an, sondern fordert durch die Nichtgesagtes andeutenden Punkte geradezu dazu heraus, die absichtlich gesetzten Leerstellen mit Bedeutung zu füllen und so am Produktionsprozeß aktiv teilzunehmen. Die Textcassette *Selected Texts on Cassette* (Best.-Nr. 54861) enthält die Aufnahme einer Lesung des Gedichts durch den Autor. Sein Vortrag verstärkt noch den Eindruck des Bedrohlichen, die Aufnahme sollte daher nach Möglichkeit in die Arbeit mit diesem Text integriert werden.

Background information

Roger McGough [məˈgɒf] (1937–   ) was born in Liverpool and studied at the University of Hull. He worked as a teacher for three years and played in various pop groups before becoming famous as one of the "Liverpool Poets" around the time of the Beatles. He has published several collections of poetry, among them *Holiday on Death Row* (Jonathan Cape, London, 1979), from which the text was taken.

Talking about the text – Suggested answers

1. The lake has served as a kind of refuse pit for a long time. It has been filled with debris, waste matter, rubbish and carcasses. The pollutants have destroyed the water quality, thus killing off all animal and plant life.
2. They shut their eyes to the biological collapse of the lake and ignore their responsibility for this development (cf. ll. 2–3). Instead of trying to reverse the process, they seem to resign and withdraw into their limited perverted world devoid of all nature (cf. ll. 26–32).
3. On the one hand, there are lakes which have been so heavily polluted that they are biologically dead. On the other hand, it is incredible, even absurd that pigs should thrive under such conditions and threaten human life in the end. This clearly symbolizes an inversion of the natural order. Here the water does not give life but is portentous of death. With regard to people, the poet portrays the children's world as barren though still imaginable, the grown-ups, however, as anglers in living-rooms, which is paradoxical, and in fact utterly unbelievable. All these activities in the homes are related to water but reflect a perversion of the original relationship.
4. The realistic and the paradoxical elements of the description address the readers' intellect. The unsavoury details and some connotations, e.g. people's conventional dislike for pigs and their gluttony, for plastics and stale bread, appeal to their emotions and

imagination. Thus the author is able to impress his readers, fill them with disgust, shock them, frighten them with this vision of a nightmare and make them wonder about his message.

5. They give the poem a structure in three fairly large parts, i.e. first the lake seen from the outside, devoid of plant and animal life, then from below as a refuse pit and breeding-ground for pigs, and finally human habitation as threatened by these animals. This betrays a certain gradation towards a climax. The marks of ellipsis indicate that something is left out, which the readers are challenged to fill in from their own imagination. They feel compelled to become active, reflect, continue the poet's suggestions and draw their own conclusions. The final ellipsis, in this way, creates a kind of open ending.

6. *What does the author do to give his poem general validity?*
   He uses the timeless present-tense group and generalizing plurals, and leaves the setting undefined as to geographical location.

7. *In the light of your analytical attempts so far, what would you understand as the ultimate message the poet intends to convey?*
   He may want to convey the message that men should take better care of nature because the destruction of their natural surroundings will engulf them, too, in the end. Everybody should face up to their responsibilities, not ignore reality and its dangers and not withdraw into a world of escapist illusions.

11 Lester R. Brown, Mary Hager: Tread Lightly on the Earth

Didaktische Hinweise

Der letzte Text dieses Kapitels lenkt abschließend die Aufmerksamkeit auf die globale Dimension der Umweltgefährdung und ihre wichtigsten Ursachen und Implikationen und bietet damit die Möglichkeit, die in diesem Kapitel angesprochenen Teilaspekte integrierend zusammenzufassen, zu vertiefen und gegebenenfalls zu ergänzen, etwa durch den Bericht über die Tschernobyl-Katastrophe (Kap. XII, Text 8). Nach dem Dichter (Text 10) kommt nun der Experte zu Wort, der sich an seine Zeitgenossen wendet und sie auf der Basis umfangreicher wissenschaftlicher Untersuchungen knapp und sachlich informieren und eindringlich ermahnen will. Die international verständliche Lexik der Wissenschaftssprache macht diesen Text sprachlich leicht zugänglich, und die Form des Interviews verleiht Browns Appell seine besondere Unmittelbarkeit.

Background information

Lester R. Brown (1934–   ) was born in Bridgeton, N. J.. He obtained degrees from Rutgers University, N. J., the University of Maryland and Harvard. From 1959 until 1969 he worked at the Department of Agriculture. He has served on many boards and committees dealing with economic and agricultural development, and since 1974 he has been president of Worldwatch Insitute, Washington, D.C.. Among the many books he has published are *Man, Land and Food* (1963), *Seeds of Change* (1970), *By Bread Alone* (1974) and *Population Policies for a New Economic Era* (1983). Since 1983 he has been co-editor of Worldwatch's annual publication *State of the World. A Worldwatch Institute Report on Progress Toward a Sustainable Society.*

Semantic and collocational field "Environmental problems"

the state of the world's environment, a global/local environmental problem, a profound global challenge, a race against time ✧ a(n) political/environmental/ economic issue, environmental politics, energy/population policy, overpopulation, population growth, an effective political response, public awareness, (to) create a new kind of global environmental politics, (to) affect the entire world, (to) head in the right direction ✧ (the) biosphere, the rising level of carbon dioxide and other greenhouse gases, the climate change, a/the warming of the earth, (to) alter the earth's climate ✧ forest cover, acidification, the effect of acid rain on forests, acid-rain forest die-off, (to) show signs of damage/disease ✧ the use of fossil fuels, fossil-fuel use, (to) contribute to deforestation ✧ the depletion of the ozone layer, a hole in the (ozone) shield, ozone depletion, (to) be exposed to ultraviolet radiation, an increase in skin cancer, a weakening of (the) immune system, (to) affect the ozone shield ✧ biological diversity, a reduction in crop yields, overgrazing, top soil, wholesale land degradation, (to) accelerate soil erosion

Talking about the text – Suggested answers

1. Brown points to "the effects of acid rain on forests" (l. 16); "the depletion of the ozone layer" (ll. 21–22) by the industrial and private overuse of chlorofluorocarbons; an eventual "climate change" (l. 127–128) as a result, for example, of the "warming of the earth" (l. 49–50); "deforestation" (l. 119); "land degradation" (l. 123) and a "loss of biological diversity" (l. 121) in plant and animal life. The main cause of these problematical developments is seen in the rapid population increase. This means more people need ever more food, living-space and energy, and demand more basic necessities as well as luxury goods. In other words, they occupy more land, use up more fossil fuels and other resources, and influence, or even pollute, their environment by industrial production.
2. They are taking place more rapidly than predicted and have not only local but also global dimensions, with those who cause them not necessarily being the ones most affected. They are often interrelated, although the cause-and-effect relationship has not always been clearly recognized. Finally, they produce long-term effects, which may be hard to reverse.
3. More research into causes and effects, uninhibited and worldwide information, greater private, public and international awareness, the recognition of mutual moral responsibilities and a readiness to act accordingly, i.e. to subordinate private interests and national economic profits to the common good.
4. Up to now scientists have been content to make predictions based on necessarily limited knowledge and have often been proved wrong as to the speed and magnitude of effects. They should learn from this and not limit themselves to research and information; they should also become politically active to strengthen their immediate influence.
5. They may have wanted to startle their readers by a direct request to act responsibly towards their environment. This request becomes more insistent still when repeated in the final sentence and when the readers realize that the headline is a quotation from Brown, which he here introduces with the sentence "I would urge" (l. 128) and contrasts with the dreadful final alternative.
6. *Why may Hager have decided to inform her readers on Lester R. Brown's opinion in the form of an interview instead of, for example, a report?*
   The journalist practically does not mediate between the interviewee and the readers but presents Brown's statements directly, without comments or relevant alterations. This makes for greater objectivity and leaves the responsibility for the form and contents of what he says with the scientist. Brown expresses himself quite eloquently. Perhaps Hager felt that the interview format would be more effective than an article. Such a presentation also brings about the effect of a dialogue, in which the readers may feel like silent listeners.

7. *Although in this form of the text the interviewee is practically the exclusive source of information, certain possibilities and functions rest with the interviewer. What use does the journalist make of them?*
   She briefly introduces Brown's work up to now (cf. ll. 1–3) and directs the conversation to certain distinct aspects of the topic. First she has him report on some results (cf. ll. 3–36), then calls for his evaluation and interpretation of previous analyses (cf. ll. 37–98) and their implications for the future (cf. ll. 99–111). Finally, she makes him summarize and highlight the most important results for the readers to keep in mind and gives him a chance to voice his personal opinion on priorities (cf. ll. 112–129). In two cases (cf. ll. 63, 74) we can see that the oral interview has been slightly edited, perhaps more alterations have been carried out, e.g. in order to adapt the original to the conventional one-page interview of "Newsweek" and to some level of written English.

8. *Choose one of the main environmental issues referred to in this text and report on it in somewhat greater detail to the class.*
   – –

9. *What powers should international organizations such as the United Nations or the European Parliament have, in your opinion, to deal effectively with environmental problems?*
   – –

10. *Groups such as "Greenpeace" and "Robin Wood" try to prevent environmental damage in their own ways. What do you think of their activities and tactics?*
    – –

11. *There are other global dangers threatening human life which have not been mentioned by Brown. Which ones can you think of and which of them can be connected with environmental problems? Discuss.*
    – –

Chapter X: Language and the Media

Das zweite der vier Kapitel mit länderübergreifenden Themen stellt das Englische als Weltsprache in den Mittelpunkt: seine globale Bedeutung als *lingua franca* (bzw. "world English", "world language", "global English" oder "universal language") in Politik, Wissenschaft, Wirtschaft und in der Unterhaltungsbranche (Text 1); die wichtigsten Varianten des Englischen (Text 2 und 3); Sprache als Mittel der Manipulation, etwa in den Bezeichnungen für Nicht-Weiße und Frauen (Text 4 und 5); und schließlich Sprache als Kommunikationsmedium in Zeitung, Rundfunk und Fernsehen (Text 6 bis 11). Eine erste "Info-Box" (SB, S. 244 f.) orientiert über Sprache in ihrer Bedeutung als menschliches Verständigungsmittel allgemein, während eine zweite "Info-Box" (SB, S. 250 f.) die spezielle Rolle des Englischen in den Medien Großbritanniens und der USA – einschließlich ihrer historischen Entwicklung – beleuchtet.

Von Kapitel X aus können vielfältige Verbindungslinien zu den übrigen Kapiteln des Buches gezogen werden: etwa zum Thema "Commonwealth" (Kap. I), insbesondere im Zusammenhang mit Susanna McBees Bemerkungen über Englisch als Weltsprache (Text 1) oder Alem Mezgebes Gedanken zum Zusammenhang zwischen Sprache und Rassismus (Text 4). Eine andere Verbindung läßt sich herstellen zum Thema „Erziehung" und „Klasse" (Kap. II) im Anschluß an die Ausführungen zu "Standard English" (Text 3). Christopher Priests Überlegungen zum Unterschied zwischen Amerikanischem Englisch und Britischem Englisch (Text 2) lassen sich darüber hinaus mit Texten aus den amerikakundlichen Kapiteln V bis VIII koppeln. Und aus der grundsätzlichen Forderung, gegen einen sich in der Sprache manifestierenden Sexismus anzugehen (Text 5), lassen sich Querverbindungen ziehen zum Thema "Oxbridge" (Kap. II, Text 8 und 9) oder zu Beaties Ringen um sprachlichen Ausdruck (Kap. II, Text 1). Der zweite große Themenbereich dieses Kapitels, „Medien", bietet Verknüpfungsmöglichkeiten mit zentralen landeskundlichen Aspekten, etwa der geschriebenen Verfassung Amerikas (insbesondere Kap. VIII, Text 2, 4, 8 und "Info-Box", SB, S. 190 f.) oder der ungeschriebenen Großbritanniens (Kap. IV, Text 1 bis 4 und "Info-Boxes", SB, S. 88 ff., S. 94 f.).

Da der hier skizzierte thematische Rahmen des Kapitels über nicht-fiktionale Texte erschlossen wird, sollten fiktionale Texte der übrigen Kapitel immer wieder hinzugezogen und in Erinnerung gerufen werden, um eingeführte Differenzierungen zur englischen Sprache mit konkreten Beispielen zu füllen. Ein vertiefender Kurs „Sprachbetrachtung" wird auch die Arbeit mit Themenheften einschließen, etwa B. Sülzer: *Language. Ein Kurs zur Sprachbetrachtung*. Berlin, Cornelsen Verlag 1978 (CVK Modell Englisch, SB Best.-Nr. 14118, LH 14126); I. Zimmermann: *The English Language and Linguistics*. Düsseldorf: Cornelsen Verlag Schwann 1982 (Courses in English, Arbeitsbuch Best.-Nr. 547049, LH 547820).

1 Susanna McBee: English, the Language of Prestige

Didaktische Hinweise

Susanna McBees Beitrag wurde als Einleitung für dieses Kapitel gewählt, weil er in knapper und anschaulicher Zusammenfassung grundlegend über die historischen wie gegenwärtigen Gründe für Englisch als Weltsprache orientiert. Bedeutsam ist dabei, daß die Verfasserin nicht nur den Siegeszug des Englischen gegenüber konkurrierenden ehemaligen Kolonialsprachen wie Spanisch, Portugiesisch oder Französisch herausstellt, sondern auch auf das Problem des "cultural imperialism" (Z. 49) aufmerksam macht, mit dem ehemalige Kolonialstaaten nach der Übernahme des Englischen als Amtssprache zu kämpfen haben (vgl. auch "This is a battle for people's minds", Z. 60–61).

Neben der thematischen Verknüpfung insbesondere mit Kapitel I (vgl. oben) lassen sich auch Texte aus diesem Kapitel direkt anschließen, etwa Text 4 und 5, in denen die Zusammenhänge zwischen Sprache und Denken im Detail aufgezeigt werden.

Background information

"obscure Germanic tribes who invaded England" (ll. 1–3): According to ancient British sources, the conquest of Celtic Britain, which had previously been ruled by Rome, was initiated by the Jutes who came from the northern peninsula of contemporary Denmark as early as 428 A.D. They were followed by the Angles and Saxons from the coastal lowland regions of northern Germany. Some of the geographical regions of Southern England derive their names from the Anglo-Saxons who settled in these areas, e.g. Essex (< East Saxons), Sussex (< South Saxons), Wessex (< West Saxons) and East Anglia. By the eighth century, the word "Angle" was being used to describe all the Germanic peoples who lived in England, and "England" as a geographical term had become universal by 1000 A.D.

"A Patchwork Quilt" (l. 63): This is a metaphor that has often been used to refer to the ethnic and racial make-up of the United States, since, while forming part of the greater whole, the various races and national groupings still manage to retain some of their distinctness (cf. Ch. V, Text 3, and "Info-Box", SB, pp. 121 f.).

Semantic and collocational field "The English language"

the English language, a (rude) tongue, a dialect, a jargon, (to) speak English, (to) talk in/communicate in/ swear in English, (to) use English as one's first language, (to) claim some knowledge of English, (to) write sth. (e.g. a manual) in simple English, (to) publish sth. in English/in an English-language journal ✧ a native language, a(n) official/semiofficial tongue, (to) conduct sth. (e.g. government business) in English ✧ a demand for English-language broadcasts/texts/material, 6 years of required English, (to) learn English, (to) enroll in a language school, (to) provide an in-service course, (to) choose sth. (e.g. a language) over sth. else (e.g. another language), (to) master irregular verbs/strange idioms/irrational spellings ✧ the (official) language of aviation/shipping, a language of prestige/practical success, a medium of exchange in science/technology/commerce/tourism/diplomacy/pop culture, a medium for 80 % of information stored in computers, a key to jobs ✧ a weapon of cultural imperialism, a battle for people's minds, (to) ban/restrict sth. ✧ a language spreads/ circles/encompasses the globe/is augmented by/infused with words of another language ✧ (to) make a propaganda point, (to) alert sb. to sth., (to) cut a deal with sb.

Talking about the text – Suggested answers

1. The writer gives three reasons why English spread around the globe (cf. ll. 36–44): 1) its initial spread with the growth and expansion of the British Empire; 2) its support "by U.S. economic and political power" (ll. 39–41) after World War II; and 3) its lead as the medium for storing information, resulting from "the knowledge explosion" (l. 41).

2. People everywhere in the world "struggle daily" (ll. 112–113) to learn English, since it has become the only international "medium of exchange in science, technology, commerce, tourism, diplomacy and pop culture" (ll. 24–27). As lingua franca, the English language is the key to "prestige" and "practical success" (ll. 115–116).

3. The demand for English has grown in direct proportion to the internationalization of certain areas of life in every country. Pilots, scientists, entrepreneurs, propagandists and pop singers all use or need a language for communicating with an international community of participants.

4. The writer uses concrete examples to illustrate first what is meant by describing English as the language of aviation or science, technology, commerce, etc. Simultaneously, her personalized illustrations (with stereotyped concepts of the area in which a country excels, e.g. "German physicists", l. 9) enable her to convey a more particular idea of why one can speak of English "dominating the planet as *the* medium of exchange" (ll. 24–25). References to Argentina, Turkey, Germany, Japan, Scandinavia, Bangkok, the Soviet Union, the Mideast or Hong Kong all evoke the picture of particular countries and geographical areas "around the world" (l. 32). By thus combining the particular with the general in her presentation, the writer is clearly attempting to hold the readers' interest and at the same time to ensure that they grasp her information about the English language.

5. She chooses two formal strategies to hold the readers' interest and make for easy reading and understanding: she starts a new printed paragraph for each of her examples and sentences; and she chooses structural parallelism for the opening clause in each of her five sentences, at the same time clearly pointing to this structure through the anaphoric repetition of the clause-initial "When". The writer thus creates a list of detailed information about the English language as lingua franca before condensing the details in one summary sentence ("dominating the planet ...", ll. 24–27).

6. [Use of English in former colonies emphasizes their colonial background and perpetuates the British way of thinking, even after independence. Use of English political, judicial or economic terms surpresses native ways of handling a country's affairs and leads to the destruction of native cultural traditions in government, trade, law and language, since these are considered inferior or inadequate. Thus an alien cultural identity is assumed.]

7. *How could you explain the fact that English is still an "official" language in a country such as India?*
On the Indian subcontinent, hundreds of different languages and dialects are spoken. When India became independent in 1947, English was the only medium by which the intranational language barriers could be transcended. English is therefore needed as the official language of the government. Though associated with the former colonial rulers, it is retained for purely pragmatic reasons.

8. *What view of American English is expressed when the writer refers to it as "English with a twist - American jargon" (ll. 37–38)?*
Though the writer's choice of the word "jargon" to refer to American English may be understood in its technical sense (the technical language of a group of specialists), its dominant connotations are negative. American English is presented as merely a lesser dialect of English. Susanna McBee's choice of this slightly derogatory reference may be explained as her ironical introduction of an attitude towards American English that is sometimes found among purists biased in favour of British English.

🎧 2 Christopher Priest: American English and British English

Didaktische Hinweise

Während Susanna McBee generalisierend von „Englisch" als einer Weltsprache spricht, soll Text 2 die Schüler/innen mit der wichtigen Tatsache vertraut machen, daß mit dem Begriff „Englisch" viele Arten von Englisch gemeint sind. Sie sind als eigenständige "dialects" (vgl. Z. 1–3) zu begreifen, die – wie das Amerikanische – zwar ihren Ursprung im Mutterland England haben, aber vor allem auf Grund ihrer räumlichen und historischen Distanz nicht mehr als weniger akzeptable Varianten des Britischen Englisch zu betrachten sind (vgl. S. McBees leicht geringschätzige Formulierung "English with a twist – American jargon", Text 1, Z. 37–38).

Die Thematisierung des Amerikanischen Englisch – aus der inzwischen umfassenderen Gruppe von "New Englishes", etwa "Indian English, Philippine English, Singapore English and African Englishes of nations such as Nigeria and Ghana" (John Platt, Heidi Weber, Ho Mian Lian: *The New Englishes*. London, Routledge and Kegan Paul 1984, S. 3) – bietet sich nicht nur auf Grund seiner historischen Stellung an, sondern auch wegen seiner Bedeutung für die noch immer wachsende Verbreitung und Festigung des Englischen als Weltsprache.

Der informelle und unterhaltende Ton Christopher Priests kann einen eigenständigen Leseanreiz geben, der im Unterricht auch ohne eine differenziertere Analyse genutzt werden kann. Aufgabenstellungen wurden daher in das LB aufgenommen. Um den Schülern/Schülerinnen eine Vorstellung von dem im Vergleich zum Britischen Englisch anders gearteten Klang des Amerikanischen zu vermitteln, kann auf entsprechende Texte der Textcassette *Selected Texts on Cassette* (Best.-Nr. 54861) zurückgegriffen werden (etwa zu Kap. V bis VIII).

Background information

"emptying trash ... automobile" (ll. 33–36): AE trash = BE rubbish; AE can = BE dustbin; AE sidewalk = BE pavement; AE hood = BE bonnet; AE automobile = BE car

"a bumper is a fender" (l. 84): In fact, the word "bumper" (Stoßstange) is used in both AE and BE. The AE word "fender" (Kotflügel) is given as "wing" in BE.

"Americans wear their vests outside" (l. 93): The AE equivalent for BE "vest" is "undershirt".

Semantic and collocational field "Varieties of English"

a dialect, cultural assumptions, rhythm, cadence, intonation, clause structure ✧ the intrusion of Britishisms, (to) mouth American slang, (to) be read in American/British English ✧ interdialect translation, a modification from sth. (e.g. a dialect) to sth. else (e.g. another dialect), (to) be palatable to a reader, (to) make sth. comprehensible to sb. ✧ a spelling variant, a difference between American and British usage, (to) be untranslatable, (to) appear in a language (profoundly) different from sth. else/quite distinct from sth. else/(uncannily) like one's own

Talking about the text – Suggested answers

1. *What view of the "two dialects" (l. 2) is Christopher Priest trying to correct?*
   The common view that American English and British English are only marginally different (in particular, in spelling and vocabulary) is, according to Priest, wrong. "The real differences have very little to do with vocabulary" (ll. 118–119).

2. *Why does the writer consider it important that other people should come round to his view?*
   Publishers have always felt tempted to adapt texts by British authors for the American market and vice versa. Though publishers had to put an end to the work of "copy editors" in recent years because of rising typesetting costs (cf. ll. 10–16), the new possibilities of computers threaten a return to the former practice of "inter-dialect translation" (ll. 52–53). People should realize, the writer maintains, that though "inter-dialect programs can be written to professional standards for use by publishers" (ll. 75–77), such translations would produce texts "profoundly different" (l. 21) from the original.

3. *In this connection, what importance does the writer attach to his own experience with a manuscript "translated" into American English (cf. ll. 23–39)?*
   Priest uses his own experience with "a story set emphatically in England" (ll. 31–32) to illustrate his argument that inter-dialect translations from British English into American English result in texts in which one area of word choice ("true-Brit characters, moving through a story set … in England") contradicts the suggestions of another ("true-Brit characters" now "mouthing American slang" and using everyday American words such as "trash", "cans", "sidewalks", "hoods" and "automobiles", cf. ll. 31–36). Even at this relatively simple level of word equivalents, Priest is saying, deeply unpalatable distortions are likely to result.

4. *How do the writer's examples in ll. 88–102 differ from the earlier ones?*
   Priest's later examples illustrate a further difficulty connected with British and American English vocabulary. British and American speakers often seem to use the same words, but the meanings they associate with them may differ profoundly. While the slang word "fag", for instance, may refer to a cigarette for a British English speaker, a speaker of American English tends to understand it as a reference to a homosexual. [For the other examples cf. the "Annotations".]

5. *The writer closes his argument with the assertion that "the real differences have very little to do with vocabulary" (ll. 118–119). How would you explain the fact that he only names these "real differences" (ll. 119–122), but does not illustrate them?*
   Priest's calling these the "hidden intangibles" (l. 120) indicates that elements of writing such as the rhythm, style, cadence or intonation of sentences and texts are extremely difficult, if not impossible, to describe, so that the reader could actually produce an authentic American or British English equivalent on the basis of such a description and illustration. What Priest does point to by merely naming these "real differences" (l. 118) is that, put simply, an American English sentence has, apart from minor differences of word pronunciation, a totally different flow and sound than its British English counterpart.

6. *In this context, how would you explain the writer's choice of language when he speaks of "boffins" (ll. 50 and 123)?*
   The writer uses the informal term "boffins" in a slightly derogatory way. In one instance he even calls them "square-eyed", implying that they take their inventions so seriously and spend so much time with them that they have begun to resemble the square screens of their computers. Priest puts scientists and technicians into a category and suggests that all members of the group are ignorant of what language is really about, i.e. "rhythm and style and cadence, the intonation, clause structure, cultural assumptions" (ll. 120–122). To the "boffins", all these things are just "meaningless ideas" (l. 123). The writer further blurs the distinction between the machine and its creators when he refers to the "computer

mind" (l. 58). Here it is not clear whether he is referring to the part of a computer that processes data, or if he means a human mind possessed by the notion of computers. Thus the writer stylistically loads his text against those who view language and languages too simplistically, be they "boffins" or "copy editors".

7. *How does Priest's view of American English compare with Susanna McBee's, who speaks of "English with a twist – American jargon" (cf. Ch. X, Text 1, ll. 37–38)?*
While McBee gives expression to a view that considers American English the less refined variety of English, Priest acknowledges each as a dialect in its own right. Lest Americans feel discriminated against by the example of his "true-Brit characters [...] *mouthing* American slang" (ll. 31–33), he at once adds a sentence for good balance: "I am certain there must be many American authors who have had *equivalent experiences,* for whom the intrusion of Britishisms has had the same unnerving effect" (ll. 41–45).

8. *Historically, how might one explain many people's view that American English is merely "English with a twist"?*
Historically, American English derives from the kind of English spoken by British settlers in North America since the beginning of the seventeenth century. Susanna McBee refers to it as the "transoceanic leap" that British English took with the settlement of Virginia in 1607 (cf. Ch. X, Text 1, ll. 78–81). However, just as geographical boundaries in, for instance, Britain resulted in the development of different dialects, so the geographical distance of English speakers from England resulted in a distinct development of an American English "dialect", with all the changes in pronunciation, vocabulary and sentence formation that growing independence from the former mother country and new influences tended to bring about in the course of time.

3 Peter Trudgill, Jean Hannah: Standard English

Didaktische Hinweise

Nach Christopher Priests differenzierender Betrachtung des Amerikanischen und Britischen Englisch (Text 2) wird mit diesem Exzerpt aus Peter Trudgills und Jean Hannahs Publikation *International English: A Guide to Varieties of Standard English* (London, Edward Arnold 1985) der Blick auf weitere Unterschiede innerhalb Großbritanniens, vor allem auf die grundlegende Unterscheidung zwischen "Standard" und "non-Standard", gelenkt. Gleichzeitig vermitteln die Autoren einige Fachtermini für die Kommunikation über die verschiedenen Arten von Englisch. Im Rückgriff auf fiktionale Texte der anderen Kapitel dieses Buches können Schüler/innen selber die Leistung von Begriffen wie "variety", "dialect", "style" oder "accent" überprüfen. Auch eine Einbeziehung von Jilly Coopers Reflexionen über "accents" (Kap. II, Text 2) liegt nahe. Zur allgemeinen Orientierung über weitere "varieties" des Englischen (etwa "pidgin" und "creole") kann die "Info-Box" (SB, S. 244 f.) herangezogen werden.

Die Thematisierung von "Standard English" im Laufe des Oberstufenunterrichts kann darüber hinaus auch zum Nachdenken über die Aussprachenorm anregen, die dem Englischunterricht und den Unterrichtsmaterialien in der Bundesrepublik zugrundegelegt wird. Die z. Zt. noch wenig verbreitete Angabe der amerikanischen Aussprache (neben der britischen), wie sie in den Annotationen des Schülerbuchs praktiziert wird, könnte dabei mitdiskutiert werden.

Detaillierte Informationen zu den hier angesprochenen Fragen bietet Dieter Bähr: *Standard English und seine geographischen Varianten.* München, Wilhelm Fink Verlag 1974 (UTB 160).

Background information

The pronunciation model currently followed in England (and Western Europe) is that laid down in *Everyman's English Pronouncing Dictionary* (J.M. Dent & Sons, London), which was originally compiled in 1917 by Daniel Jones and revised and edited in its 14th edition by the late A.C. Gimson in 1977 and Susan Ramsaran in 1988. Gimson summarizes the history of changes in the definition of "Standard English" in his introduction: "In the first edition of this Dictionary (1917), Daniel Jones described the type of pronunciation recorded as 'that most usually heard in everyday speech in the families of Southern English persons whose menfolk have been educated at the great public boarding-schools'. Accordingly, he felt able to refer to his model as 'Public School Pronunciation' (PSP). In later editions, e.g. that of 1937, he added the remark that boys in boarding-schools tend to lose their markedly local peculiarities, whereas this is not the case for those in day-schools. He had by 1926, however, abandoned the term PSP in favour of 'received pronunciation' (RP). ... Its regional base remains valid and it continues to have wide intelligibility throughout Britain (in a way that other regional forms do not) – one of the reasons why this type of pronunciation was originally adopted by the BBC for use by its news-readers" (op.cit., p. X).

"North American English (NAmEng)" (l. 33): For further differentiation, the following observations may come in useful: "Like the English at the BBC, [American broadcasting] evolved its own all-American accent, known as 'Network Standard', the accent of television newscasters, in which the regional characteristics of Southern or Texan or Brooklyn speech would be modified in the interests of clarity, intelligibility, and neutrality" (R. McCrum, W. Cran, R. McNeill: *The Story of English*. Faber and Faber, London, 1986, p. 35). However, it is important to note the authors' rider that "unlike Britain, the Network Standard has virtually no class connotation. A strong regional accent has never been a hindrance in reaching the White House" (ibid., p. 36).

Semantic and collocational field "English in foreign language teaching"

a student of English as a Foreign or Second Language (EFL/ESL), a school, a university, grammar, vocabulary, pronunciation, an educated speaker of English, (to) receive formal instruction, (to) learn English at school, (to) study for a time in a country ✧ (to) teach/require (one variety of) English, (to) be (widely) taught to students of EFL and ESL /students learning English/foreigners ✧ (to) offer conflicting models, (to) be exposed to more than one model, (to) encounter sth. (e.g. a dialect), (to) establish a norm, (to) relax a requirement, (to) permit sb. (to) do sth., (to) be consistent

Talking about the text – Suggested answers

1. The writers deal with the following four topics: 1) definition of Standard English as opposed to non-standard dialects (cf. ll. 1–16); 2) definition of English English on the basis of the RP accent (cf. ll. 17–31); 3) definition of North American English (cf. ll. 32–38); 4) the conflict of models, i.e. between so-called NAmEng and EngEng, in European foreign language teaching (cf. ll. 39–56).
2. Standard English is 1) "normally employed in writing" (l. 2); 2) "normally spoken by 'educated' speakers" (l. 2); 3) "often refers to grammar" and 4) to "vocabulary *(dialect)*" (l. 5); 5) "includes informal as well as formal styles" (ll. 13–14); 6) does not refer to "pronunciation *(accent)*" (ll. 5–6).

3. It is predominantly the combination of Standard English grammar and vocabulary with the RP accent, i.e. the norm here called "English English", and much more commonly known as British English (cf. ll. 30–31). (Exceptions are made, though, in cases like those mentioned by the writers in ll. 45–56.)

4. Since a native-like competence in the combination of Standard English with the RP accent is considered "a prestigious accent" (l. 27) by many speakers of British English, the student might wrongly be associated with more social status than is his or her due. He or she may, for instance, be viewed as having been to a prestigious public school in England or viewed as the son or daughter of upper-middle or upper-class parents (cf. ll. 26–27).

5. The main justification is that "some norm" (l. 41) is needed that teachers and students can follow. If "conflicting models" (l. 42) were offered, confusion would arise for teachers, for the publishers of school books and for students, who are normally taught by different English language teachers in the course of their school careers. Another justification is only implied by the writers. Just as the North American model is followed "in many parts of Latin America" (ll. 37–38) and in a number of Asian countries because of their geographical proximity, so the Standard English model is predominantly followed in European countries because of the closeness and historical prestige of England.

6. – –

7. *What are the main descriptive terms the writers use to distinguish between different forms of English, and what do these terms refer to?*
The terms are: "variety" (l. 1) to refer neutrally to any kind of English that can be more clearly defined as a form belonging to the same general type; "dialect" (l. 11) to refer to non-standard regional kinds of English, with their distinct forms of "grammar and vocabulary" (l. 5); "style" to refer to "formal" and "informal" kinds of Standard English (cf. ll. 14–15); "grammar" (l. 5); "vocabulary" (l. 5); and "pronunciation" or "accent" (ll. 5–6, 24–31) to refer to the combination of regional and social aspects of the kind of English spoken (cf. ll. 24–27).

8. *Use some of these terms to characterize the kind of English spoken by Arnold Wesker's Beatie (cf. Ch. II, Text 1).*
The variety of English Beatie speaks can be characterized as a mixture of the Standard English dialect with forms of grammar (e.g. "she say", l. 33), choice of vocabulary (e.g. "Blust", l. 32) and pronunciation (e.g."ent", "bin", "hev", l. 7, 15) that are typical of a non-standard dialect. Concerning Standard English, she makes choices both from formal style (e.g. "living in mystic communion with nature", l. 52–53) and informal style (e.g. "vegies" for "vegetables", l. 26).

4 Alem Mezgebe: Language as a Tool of Racist Attitudes

Didaktische Hinweise

Dieser und Text 5 lenken den Blick auf folgenreiche Wechselbeziehungen zwischen Sprache und Ausdrucksformen einerseits und Denken und Verhalten der Sprecher andererseits. Die verfremdende Distanz, die Schüler/innen schon früh beim Erlernen einer Fremdsprache erfahren, kann in besonderer Weise die Einsicht vorbereiten helfen, daß bestimmte Ausdrucksformen eine bestimmte Weltsicht beinhalten, die so suggestiv vermittelt wird, daß die Sprecher/innen sich dieses Einflusses nur selten bewußt werden.

Alem Mezgebe zeigt am Beispiel der Konnotationen, die sich für die Farbbe-zeichnungen „schwarz" und „weiß" seit Jahrhunderten in christlicher Metaphorik herausgebildet haben, wie bis heute aus solchen Sprachprägungen rassistische Einstellungen gegenüber „Schwarzen" gespeist werden. Es ergibt sich hier die Möglich-keit, den Schülern/Schülerinnen die wichtige Unterscheidung zwischen „Denota-tion" und „Konnotation" bestimmter Wörter und Wortverbindungen im Englischen exemplarisch zu verdeutlichen (vgl. auch Aufg. 3 und 4). Damit werden trans-ferierbare fachmethodische Kenntnisse vermittelt, die auf andere Situationen, in denen die Sprache bewußt manipulativ verwandt wird, übertragen werden können, etwa bei der Verwendung von "loaded terms" in der Werbung oder Politik. Zu denken ist hier besonders an die Ersetzung von "multiracial" durch "multicultural" in dem Bestreben, Vorurteile allmählich abzubauen. Dieser Aspekt kann schließlich zur Diskussion der sprachlichen Diskriminierung von Frauen (vgl. auch Aufg. 6 zu Text 5, LB, S. 212) führen: Genügt es, die seit Jahrhunderten tradierten Ausdrucks-mittel auszutauschen, um eine „objektivere" Weltsicht zu vermitteln?

Background information

"Whites ... see things in black and white" (ll. 1–3): This view of the relationship between language and thought may be seen in connection with the so-called Sapir-Whorf hypothesis developed by the American linguist and anthropologist Edward Sapir (1884–1939) and his pupil Benjamin Lee Whorf (1897–1941). Their hypothesis states a) that the language we speak determines the way in which we think, and b) that the way in which the patterns of one language dissect the world differs from that in any other language (cf. David Crystal: "The Sapir-Whorf hypothesis". In: *The Cambridge Encyclopedia of Language.* Cambridge University Press, Cambridge, 1987, p. 15). Though it is no longer accepted in its full form, Crystal notes, "a weaker version of the Sapir-Whorf hypothesis is generally accepted. Language may not determine the way we think, but it does influence the way we perceive and remember, and it affects the ease with which we perform mental tasks" (op.cit.). For more information cf. Benjamin Lee Whorf: *Language, Thought, and Reality: Selected Writings.* Ed. by John B. Carroll. M.I.T. Press, Cambridge, Mass., 1964, p. 252; George Lakoff, Mark Johnson: *Metaphors We Live By.* University of Chicago Press, Chicago, 1980, p. 3.

Semantic and collocational field "Racism in language"

racism in the (English) language, white values, a language is littered with sth., (to) be racist, (to) be colour conscious in one's vocabulary, (to) equate black with evil, (to) associate black with sin/calamity, (to) have negative connotations, (to) use words to keep sb. in fear and subjugation, (to) see things in black and white ◇ (to) live in the shadow of sth., (to) be imbedded in the black psyche ◇ a fight against racism in language, a move to discard racist terms, (to) change a concept/the negative definition of blackness

Talking about the text – Suggested answers

1. Mezgebe's *thesis* is that whites have become and are racists through the connotations that the colour terms "black" and "white" carry in European languages. He *supports his view* with a look at how the colour terms came to be equated with good and evil in Judaeo-Christian civilization. Among other things, the Biblical equation of black with evil made possible the endorsement of the slave trade by the Roman Catholic Church. Mezgebe *concludes* from his linguistic evidence that racist prejudices can be overcome only if colour terms that denigrate the black race are discarded from European languages. The writer attaches a list of 20 terms he believes ought to be replaced.

2. The story of Ham was interpreted by "leaders of Christendom" in such a way as to fit their need for cheap labour (cf. ll. 39–45). Since the father of one of the three genealogical lines descended from Noah was cursed to be "a servant of servants ... unto his brethren" (Genesis 9:25), one section of the human race became permanently "relegated ... to a condition of servitude"(ll. 26–27). Since sinning, in Christian colour metaphor, is equated with blackness (cf. ll. 57–63), outward appearance (e.g. black skin colour) could be construed to point to specimens of the cursed servant race descended from Noah's sinful son Ham. It became possible to say (as the Spanish Dominican friar, Bartolomé de Las Casas, did) that African Negroes were the race marked for permanent punishment and servitude. This interpretation was confirmed by papal bulls (cf. ll. 53–54).

3. [Students may think of examples from literary texts they have read, e.g. Shakespeare's "Macbeth". When Macbeth first begins more definitely to contemplate murdering Duncan, he refers to these his innermost thoughts as *"black* and deep desires" (I, v, 51). Similarly, when Lady Macbeth seeks to steel herself for the evil deed, she implores the powers of darkness with "Come, thick *Night,* And pall thee in the dunnest smoke of Hell ..." (I, v, 50f.). The connotations here are that Macbeth's desires are evil, allied with, as Mezgebe puts it, "Satanic, diabolical forces" (l. 61). For Lady Macbeth, the darkness of night connotes the possibility of an evil deed, such as the murder of King Duncan.]

4. – –

5. *In his introduction, the writer concedes that people are perhaps "unwittingly" racist, since "they see things in black and white" (ll. 1–3). What general connection between language and thought are the writer's reflections based on?*
   Language forms, e.g. the words a person uses, are automatically equated with his or her thoughts. Simultaneously, the denotations and connotations of words determine a person's perception of others and the world in which he or she lives. The writer subscribes to a determinist view of language.

6. *In ll. 72–75 the writer sums up and quotes Grace Halsell as saying: "Western culture as the dominant culture ... has 'deliberately used words to keep others in fear and subjugation'." Think of areas in our own day where such "deliberately" discriminatory language is used to establish or reinforce dominance.*
   – –

7. *How would a "move to discard racist terms and concepts in European languages" (ll. 124–126) work ? For comparison, think of the move to discard a "sexist bias" (cf. Ch. X, Text 5).*
   – –

5 Casey Miller, Kate Swift: Sexist Bias in Language

Didaktische Hinweise

Mit dem Beitrag dieser beiden Autorinnen kann nicht nur der diskriminierende Einfluß von unbewußt verwendeten Ausdrucksformen auf menschliches Denken und Handeln in einem weiteren Bereich gezeigt werden (vgl. Text 4), sondern darüber hinaus auch verdeutlicht werden, wie weit der bewußte Austausch tradierter sprachlicher Inventare bereits vorangetrieben worden ist, um geschlechterspezifische Stereotypen in der englischen Sprache zu korrigieren (zur Verbindung dieser sprachreformerischen Bewegung mit der amerikanischen Frauenrechtsbewegung vgl. "Info-Box", SB, S. 183). Als konkrete Beispiele für die Problematik rollenspezifischen

Verhaltens können Kap. I, Text 9 (junge pakistanische Frauen in Großbritannien), Kap. II, Text 8 (Frauen in den Colleges von Oxbridge) und Kap. III, Text 5 (Frauen im Beruf) herangezogen werden.

Background information

Unlike Grace Halsell's view that "Western culture as the dominant culture ... has 'deliberately used words to keep others in fear and subjugation' " (cf. Text 4, ll. 72–75), Casey Miller and Kate Swift observe: "Most of the sexist offenses committed through language are not deliberate. They creep in as a result of laziness, habit, or overreliance on what the rule books say is correct, and they yield to the test of exactness. Although some solutions cannot be applied across the board, since their appropriateness varies with the circumstances, most involve nothing more than a healthy respect for fairness and precision" (*Words and Women*. Victor Gollancz, London, 1977, p. 158). The writers give a list of chief areas where language use ought to be more accurate with reference to either male or female gender (pp. 158–164), e.g.

Animals: "Many people [...] habitually refer to the rabbit, the turtle, the cockroach, and the gull as 'he'. Why, is a mystery, especially since the pronoun 'it' provides an acceptable way to avoid a 50 per cent chance of error."

Babies: "All babies are not alike, and all babies are not male, despite the impression most baby-care books give to the contrary. ... Eliminating the generic 'he' avoids the suggestion that males are more important or more typical than females."

-ess ending: "Tacking an -ess ending onto a common gender English word because the person referred to is a woman is reasonably resented by most people so identified. When it is relevant to make a special point of someone's sex, pronouns are useful and so are the adjectives 'male' and 'female'."

Forms of address: "One often conveys more respect for a woman by avoiding the conventional courtesy titles than by using them, since the distinction they make is related to a woman's marital status rather than to the person herself. ... One reason people are uneasy about using 'Ms.', an obvious solution to the 'Miss/Mrs.' dilemma, is that it is still so new it makes them self-conscious."

Order: "In pairs like male and female, men and women, husbands and wives, sons and daughters, boys and girls, Adam and Eve, males need not always come first. Occasionally reversing the order has two advantages: it counters the implication that members of the male sex rate a priority, and it helps to jog attention by avoiding the habitual."

–person compounds: " 'Salesperson' is a word that doesn't seem to throw anyone into a tizzy. ... '–person' compounds will come to seem more natural. They are especially useful when candidates for a job or elective office are being considered without regard to sex."

Semantic and collocational field "Sexism in language"

a sex-stereotyped role/character trait, the social conditioning of a reader, a sexist bias in language, sb.'s language mirrors the sexist assumptions of society, (to) show favouritism to one sex or the other, (to) perpetuate/drop sexist assumptions ✧ an example featuring a female, (to) affirm sb.'s positive qualities, (to) correct sexist biases through examples/the wording of definitions, (to) adopt nonsexist guidelines, (to) restore the gender balance, (to) ascribe to women the (active/inventive/ adventurous) traits traditionally reserved for men ✧ (to) use language to liberate/ expand thought, (to) be more accurately phrased

Talking about the text – Suggested answers

1. Two aspects were reflected: 1) girls and women are grossly under-represented as characters, which suggests that girls and women play a less prominent role in the world; 2) sex-stereotyped roles and character traits of males and females are perpetuated, suggesting that males are "active, inventive, and adventurous" (ll. 30–31), while females are passive, soft and prone to crying.

2. The reasoning behind the corrections was the desire to do justice to the demographic fact of one half of the human race being female and thus deserving equal treatment. In a society where more and more women are part of the work force (cf. ll. 65–66), it is simply wrong to allow young readers to be socially conditioned by the traditional "sex-stereotyped roles and character traits of females and males" (ll. 25–26).

3. In contrast to English, the German language uses a definite article with nouns to mark them as masculine, feminine or neuter. So "der Weise" (and, using the indefinite article, "ein Weiser") excludes women from the reference. A German dictionary maker who aims at correcting the sexist bias in the German language, would have to do more than only exchange examples or reword the definitions.

4. In German, every effort is made to mention both women and men in most situations, e.g. "Schülerinnen und Schüler" or "Schüler/innen". Sometimes the German word "man" (English "one") is replaced by invented words such as "frau" or "man/frau". In English, one tries to avoid differentiating between the sexes wherever possible by using forms such as "everyone … they" instead of the earlier "everyone … he", or by coining new words, e.g. "postal carrier" instead of "postman/postwoman", "flight attendant" instead of "steward/stewardess", etc.

● 5. *Language use is only one of several areas in which the feminist revolution has brought about profound social change. Report to the class on the short history and kinds of changes introduced since the 1960s.*
   [Cf., for instance, "Women at odds" in Edmund Fawcett and Tony Thomas: *America and the Americans*. Collins Sons & Co., London, ²1985, pp. 83–128 (Fontana Paperback); "Info-Box", SB, p. 183.]

6. *How is the discovery of a sexist bias in language use similar to the bias in language towards black people? To help you with your answer, you may like to read Ch. X, Text 4.*
   Like the sexist bias, the racist bias in language has only recently been recognized as influencing people's thought, usually without their becoming conscious of this influence. Moreover, the racist language bias, too, has long served to undermine the democratic principle of equality, "to keep others in fear and subjugation" (cf. Ch. X, Text 4, ll. 74–75).

7. *To what extent have forms of "showing favoritism to one sex or the other" (l. 28) been eliminated in your own social environment (e.g. in the classroom)? Discuss.*
   – –

6 Truth and the Press – A Discussion

Didaktische Hinweise

Mit diesem Ausschnitt aus einer Diskussion beginnt eine Gruppe von sechs Texten, die die Rolle der Medien aus anglo-amerikanischer Perspektive thematisieren. Im Mittelpunkt der Texte 6, 7 und 8 stehen grundsätzliche Fragen zur Bedeutung von Pressefreiheit und zu den Grenzen, die sich Journalisten und Journalistinnen in Eigenverantwortung auferlegen müssen (Text 6 und 7) oder die ihnen von Regierungen in bestimmten Zeiten aufgezwungen werden (Text 8). Darüber hinaus werden als weitere Aspekte in dieser Textgruppe Fragen der Nachrichtenauswahl, der möglichen Objektivität in der Nachrichtenübermittlung, der Organisation in konventionalisierten Textformen sowie des langfristigen Einflusses bestimmter Medien auf die Lebensgestaltung des heutigen Menschen angesprochen. Die "Info-Box" (SB, S. 250 ff.) orientiert über die historische Entwicklung und Bedeutung von Presse, Funk und Fernsehen in Großbritannien und den USA.

Zur Vertiefung der hier diskutierten Fragen bieten sich Texte aus anderen Kapiteln des SB an, etwa zum Thema „Zensur" Kap. VIII, Text 2, zum Thema „Beeinflussung (durch Werbung usw.)" Kap. II, Text 4; Kap. XI, Text 4; Kap. I, Text 5a und 5b, aber auch Kap. III, Text 3; Kap. VI, Text 6. Darüber hinaus können Textformen wie etwa "(interpretive) news story", "feature story", "report", "comment", "letter to the editor" usw., die für die Informationsübermittlung in Zeitungen typisch sind, mit Hilfe weiterer Texte des SB verdeutlicht werden. Eine gute Hilfe bei der Auswahl bietet das „Didaktische Inhaltsverzeichnis" (LB, S. x ff.).

In der Diskussion wird die fundamentale Frage nach der Pressefreiheit aus wechselnder Perspektive beleuchtet: als notwendige Freiheit gegenüber staatlicher Kontrolle, als Problem für den Schutz des Einzelnen vor möglicher Verleumdung und daraus entstehenden weitreichenden Konsequenzen für Privat- und Berufsleben, als Problem der Objektivität in der Nachrichtenübermittlung und als eine Freiheit, die ein vielfältiges Informationsangebot mit wechselseitiger Selbstkontrolle und öffentlicher Überprüfbarkeit ermöglicht.

Zur weiteren Präzisierung der verfassungsrechtlichen Grundlagen für eine freie Presse (bzw. deren Einschränkung durch die Verschärfung des britischen "Official Secrets Act" 1988, vgl. auch LB, S. 218) können die "Info-Boxes" zu Kap. IV (SB, S. 88 f.) und Kap. VIII (SB, S. 190 f.) sowie das Themenheft *The US Bill of Rights in Action*. Ed. by R.B. Williams. (Berlin, Cornelsen Verlag 1990. SB Best.-Nr. 52168, LH 52176) herangezogen werden.

Background information

The participants in this discussion about the role of the press in American society had been invited by *Harper's Magazine*. They were Tom Wicker, an associate editor of *The New York Times* and a syndicated columnist; Walter Karp, a frequent contributor to *Harper's* and *American Heritage*, whose books include *The Politics of War*; Herbert Schmertz, Mobil Oil Corporation's vice president for public affairs; Sidney Zion, a former reporter for *The New York Times* and the author of *Read All About It! The Collected Adventures of a Maverick Reporter*; Frances Fitzgerald, a contributor to *The New Yorker* and *The New York Review of Books*. Her books include *Fire in the Lake* and *America Revised*; Charles Rembar, an attorney specializing in First Amendment issues. He is the author of *The End of Obscenity* and *The Law of the Land*; Lewis H. Lapham as moderator of the discussion.

"prior restraints on the press by the government" (ll. 33–34): a key term in US constitutional law, meaning censorship by the government.

"I exempt from this criticism editorialists, and newspaper columnists" (ll. 50–52): News magazines such as *Time, Newsweek* and *U.S. News & World Report* have specialized in interpretative journalism: "They see their role as weekly summarizers and explainers, putting the news of the week into historical, political, or

scientific perspective, to express the meaning in the news" (Ray Eldon Hiebert, Donald F. Ungurait, Thomas W. Bohn: *Mass Media. An Introduction to Modern Communication.* Longman, London, 1982, p. 494).

Semantic and collocational field "The media"

an editorialist, a newspaper columnist, a straight-news reporter, (to) write a story, (to) interview sb., (to) report an event, (to) construct a written account in a certain way ✧ (to) employ a questionable tactic, (to) depend on an unnamed source, (to) intrude on sb.'s privacy, (to) look like an adversary/a threat to sb. ✧ a free press, the freedom of the press, the press's constitutional rights, the right to publish without prior restraint, the right to publish sth. without the threat of legal consequences, (to) protect the press from government interference, (to) allow sb. to have information ✧ a legitimate constraint on the press, (to) advocate prior restraints on the press, (to) abridge the freedom of the press, (to) prevent the press from printing whatever it chooses ✧ the surrogate of the people, a sense of obligation to the people, (to) disseminate information, (to) protect/strengthen the government of the people, (to) make sth. available to sb. ✧ objectivity in writing, evenhandedness, ethical standards in journalism, (to) be neutral, (to) observe standards of accuracy/fairness, (to) get the facts right ✧ advocacy journalism, (to) influence/report/make policy, (to) slant a (supposedly objective) story, (to) select what is important, (to) bend the facts to suit one's political agenda, (to) let one's politics dictate one's reporting, (to) come to an event with a fixed conviction, (to) advocate a particular position, (to) present sb./sth. as corrupt/self-seeking/a villain ✧ a progressive loss of trust in the press, (to) go with the flow of public opinion

Talking about the text – Suggested answers

1. *Concerning the definition of a free press, what question are the five speakers trying to answer?*
   The speakers' question is where the limits to the freedom of the press in the US ought to be drawn. The key term in their discussion that points to this problem is "constraints" (ll. 19, 23–24, 30, etc.), which is varied as "restraint" (ll. 33, 37, etc.).

2. *How do the speakers' answers differ?*
   Herbert Schmertz is the only speaker who argues for certain "constraints" on the press (i.e. by the marketplace, but not by the government, cf. ll. 31–34), whereas the other four speakers support the unrestrained freedom of the press as guaranteed by the First Amendment to the Constitution (cf. ll. 84–88). To prevent journalists from abusing their freedom, these four speakers tend to place trust in the journalists' ethical code to investigate and "get the facts right" (ll. 92–93).

3. *Why do the speakers disagree about libel laws in connection with a free press?*
   The disagreement about libel laws is again between Schmertz and the others. Schmertz wants to see individuals protected against "untrue statements" (l. 74), since both people's rights to "privacy" (l. 69) and their businesses (cf. ll. 60-62) may be harmed. Sidney Zion counters that "the libel laws now in effect" can "bankrupt a newspaper ... through pretrial discovery procedures in a libel suit" (ll. 93–96).

4. *When criticizing what he considers the press's abuse of its freedom, why does Schmertz "exempt from this criticism editorialists" (ll. 51–52)?*
   Schmertz makes a basic distinction between the objective reporting of facts ("objective stories", l. 55) and comment and opinion published in a separate section of a newspaper and written by "editorialists" and "columnists". Since editorials can be recognized by readers as the editorialist's and/or paper's opinion on separately printed news stories, they do not pose a threat to the readers' independence of thought. A slanted news story,

i.e. one in which a reporter "bend[s] the facts to suit his own political agenda" (ll. 176–177), is, in his view, an illegitimate encroachment on the politicians' territory (cf. ll. 42–51).

5. **In this connection, why do Wicker and Fitzgerald also exempt "straight-news reporters" (l. 54) from criticism?**
   Schmertz's opponents point to two important aspects: 1) all news stories are based on the reporter's selection of facts; all reporters have to make "basic choices" as to "what to include and what to leave out" (ll. 151–152); 2) "a set of conventions" (ll. 160–161), such as standards for investigating a story, of "accuracy" and of "fairness" (cf. ll. 166–172), now safeguard the reader against "deliberate distortion of the news" (ll. 147–148). This set of conventions, then, will serve as the kind of constraint that reporters have to accept when making their basic choices in writing their story.

6. **In view of the fact that under the American Constitution every newspaper is free to inform and influence the public without "prior restraints" (l. 33) by the government, why does Schmertz's fear of the politically biased reporter appear to be unjustified?**
   The complete freedom of the American press creates competition among newspapers in the marketplace, with the attendant variety of reporting and opinion-making that tends to correct one-sidedness. Readers can always get information from a variety of sources, so the truth about certain events usually does come out. Only when the press is totally controlled by the government (or by laws such as the British Official Secrets Act; cf. Ch. X, Text 8) can the news become effectively distorted. If the press is free, the politically unfair and biased reporter will always find critics amongst his fellow journalists.

7. **Before elaborating on his view, Schmertz states, "I've never advocated prior restraints on the press by the government" (ll. 32–34). Considering what the other people say, why may this sentence be said to be basic to their arguments, as well?**
   Though they disagree about detail, this sentence sums up the tenet to which all five agree. As Sidney Zion puts it, "No press in the world has ever had a better warrant than we've got under the Constitution" (ll. 84–86). Frances Fitzgerald pinpoints the question they are discussing: it is not "the issue of its [the press's] rights and freedoms under the Constitution" (ll. 118–119), but "the press's own sense of obligation" to the public (ll. 116–117). In contrast to policy in other countries (e.g. Great Britain , cf. Ch. X, Text 8), the First Amendment to the American Constitution emphasizes and guarantees what can be considered essential for a really free press: it is, in Fitzgerald's words, "that the government cannot prevent the press from printing whatever it chooses" (ll. 124–125).

8. **From the point of view of language use, which of Frances Fitzgerald's lexical and syntactic choices can be considered characteristic of the text form she uses in ll. 130–143?**
   Frances Fitzgerald uses language forms which organize her ideas in the argumentative text form of a comment. Characteristic are the lexical choices: "we discuss", "versus", "points out", "objects to", "his objection"; the syntactic choice of opposed negative and affirmative sentences, linked by a contrastive "but": "we are *no longer* talking about ... *but* about ..."; "when Schmertz points out that journalists *are not* ... his objection *must stand outside* any definition ..."; the syntactic choice of a causal clause, here one introduced by the coordinator "for": "*For,* seen as ..., the press *has* a perfect right to ..."; the syntactic choice of verb and preposition plus a gerund with a subject of its own, to include another speaker's view: "and ... *objects to their trying* to influence ... ." For her listeners, these choices serve as clear signals that the speaker is continuing to express herself in the basic text type argumentation.

7 David Anderson, Peter Benjaminson: The Classic Ethical Dilemma

Didaktische Hinweise

David Anderson und Peter Benjaminson, Reporter bei der *Detroit Free Press*, zeigen in diesem Auszug aus ihrem grundlegenden Buch *Investigative Reporting* (Indiana University Press, Bloomington, Ind., 1976), wie bedeutsam es für das gesellschaftliche Wohl ist, daß neben den "straight news report" und den interpretierenden "comment" als weitere Variante die "investigative story" tritt. Sie ist dadurch gekennzeichnet, daß sie generell verborgen gehaltene Information öffentlich macht und damit insbesondere auch jene Funktion erfüllt, die die Hüter der amerikanischen Verfassung im Sinn haben, wenn sie die Presse und ihre Freiheit als Kontrollinstanz des Volkes gegenüber den regierenden Volksvertretern schützen (vgl. Text 6 und "Background information", unten). Als herausragendes Beispiel verweisen die Autoren auf den Watergate-Skandal (vgl. Z. 33). Die Darstellung der beiden Journalisten erhellt zugleich, welche Gefahren und Fehlentwicklungen sich ergeben können, wenn Presseleute selbst das Recht für sich in Anspruch nehmen, unlautere Methoden einsetzen zu dürfen, um die Öffentlichkeit über Mißstände zu informieren.

Weitere Bereiche, in denen "investigative reporting" erfolgreich in der Aufdeckung von Mißständen war, werden in der "Info-Box" (SB, S. 252) genannt. Als Beispiel für die Beschränkung der Pressefreiheit in Großbritannien kann anschließend Text 8 behandelt werden.

Background information

Looking back at the "McCarthy years" in the US, i.e. the time from 1950 to 1954 when Senator Joseph McCarthy of Wisconsin was able to engage official America in a prolonged hunt of Communists in high government or public office, some commentators maintain that the lack of interpretive and investigative reporting by the press in those years helped McCarthy continue unchecked for so long. The press's adherence to the principle of objectivity, to "straight-news reporting", kept the public from being informed fairly and fully. Edwin R. Bayley observes in this connection: "McCarthy's tactics produced lasting changes in the media. Newspaper people realized that it was not enough simply to tell what had happened or what was said, but that they had to tell what it meant and whether or not it was true" (Edwin R. Bayley: *Joe McCarthy and the Press*. The University of Wisconsin Press, Madison, Wis., 1981, p. 219).

In a case involving *The New York Times* and *The Washington Post*, which, at the height of the Vietnam War, had acquired copies of a multivolume classified study of the government's Vietnam policy in 1971, the Supreme Court ruled in favour of press freedom. Justice Brennan stated: "In the absence of the governmental checks and balances present in other areas of our national life, the only effective restraint upon executive policy and power in the areas of national defense and international affairs may lie in an enlightened citizenry – in an informed and critical public opinion which alone can here protect the values of democratic government. For this reason, it is perhaps here that a press that is alert, aware, and free most vitally serves the basic purpose of the First Amendment. For without an informed and free press there cannot be an enlightened people" (Alpheus Thomas Mason and Donald Grier Stephenson, Jr.: *American Constitutional Law. Introductory Essays and Selected Cases*. Prentice-Hall, Englewood Cliffs, N.J., [8]1987, pp. 485–486).

Semantic and collocational field "The media"

the newsgathering profession, a hostile press, investigative reporting, a(n) accurate/thorough reportage of events, a professional journalist, an investigative reporter, bias, sensationalism, a story appears ✧ sb.'s right to information, (to) bring sth. (e.g. corruption) to public attention, (to) inform the public, (to) gather information, (to) seek confirmation of sth., (to) obtain/withhold sth. (e.g. information), information remains concealed ✧ (to) be candid in dealing with sb. under investigation, (to) confront sb. (e.g. the subject of an investigation) ✧ (to) act ethically, (to) question the ethics of a profession, (to) question sb.'s motives, (to) label sth. as dishonest/fraudulent, (to) shock sb.'s ethical sensibilities, (to) take criticism from sb., (to) receive an accolade ✧ (to) use deceptive methods, (to) resort to questionable methods, (to) err on the side of dishonesty, (to) pose as sb., (to) lie to sb., (to) find oneself afoul of the law, (to) be indicted/convicted/jailed for a story

Talking about the text – Suggested answers

1. Two aspects are characteristic: 1) It "aims at bringing corruption, hypocrisy, and lawbreaking to public attention" (l. 3); in other words, the investigative reporter tries to gather news that is difficult to find and uncover. 2) It often uses "deceptive methods" (l. 21) to get at the news and thus violates the profession's usual ethical code.
2. The investigative reporter works under two obligations which often cancel each other out. It is his job to report corruption, but in getting at the source of corruption he must become dishonest himself. In terms of Greek drama, the investigative reporter is in a tragic situation: "he's damned" if he uses the deceptive methods needed for his job, "and damned" if he fails to uncover corruption and thus protect the public (cf. ll. 15–16).
3. According to the writers, the responsible journalist thinks in terms of a hierarchy of values. To him, the public's right to be informed and protected comes first, the corrupt individual's right to expect "complete candor" (l. 21) comes second. The "theory" (l. 19) is that a "reporter should never resort to questionable methods if the information can be obtained in any other way" (ll. 23–25).
4. They must respect certain limits to protect "the subjects of newspaper investigations" (l. 36) as well as "the friends and families of people they expose" (ll. 34–35). Further, they must be prepared to live with "tremendous criticism" (l. 34). And they often have to face prosecution for the "illegalities involved in many investigations" (ll. 42–43).
5. [Students could start by reading Günther Wallraff's book "Ganz unten" (Kiepenheuer & Witsch, Köln, 1985). The journalist tells of how he changed into a Turkish immigrant labourer to expose attitudes and malpractice in the West German labour market.]
6. – –
7. *In the context of their reflections, what reason do you think the writers had for referring to "the burden of glamor which Watergate has given the profession" (l. 33)?*
   Watergate may be considered the greatest success story of investigative reporting. Two reporters from "The Washington Post" succeeded in bringing down a president (Richard Nixon) on the charge that he had authorized an unlawful break-in. This immense success of two investigative reporters puts others under pressure to be just as good. As a result, some pay less attention to the ethics of the profession.
8. *What additional light does the concluding sentence (ll. 46–48) throw on the role of the press in a democracy?*
   Public offices such as those of the public prosecutor are reached only via elections at the local, state and federal levels. A prosecutor seeking re-election needs backing from the electorate every few years. Reporters, on the other hand, can reach the electorate every day, a fact that makes them extremely powerful. They are in control of the major means of argument and persuasion and could influence people to vote either for or against a particular candidate.

8 Alastair Hetherington: Media Censorship in Times of Crisis?

Didaktische Hinweise

Alastair Hetheringtons Beitrag verdeutlicht exemplarisch, daß keine der in den Texten 6 und 7 genannten Formen der journalistischen Informationsübermittlung oder Kommentierung noch eine Chance hat, den Bürger zu erreichen, wenn die Rahmenbedingungen durch verschärfte staatliche Pressezensur verändert werden. In den Vereinigten Staaten setzt die Verfassung mit dem First Amendment sowie die Kontrolle von Exekutive und Kongreß durch die Entscheidungen des Supreme Court einen Rahmen, der die Zensur der Presse auch in Notzeiten verhindern kann (vgl. LB, S. 216). In Großbritannien dagegen fehlt, bedingt durch seine "Unwritten Constitution" (vgl. "Info-Box", SB, S. 88 ff.), ein solches Korrektiv, so daß eine Regierung, die über eine starke Mehrheit im Parlament verfügt, jederzeit Grundfreiheiten einschränken kann (vgl. Hetheringtons Hinweis, Z. 33–34). Eine solche Situation entstand im Laufe des Jahres 1988, als die konservative Regierung unter Margaret Thatcher in einem "Government White Paper" eine Verschärfung des *Official Secrets Act* von 1911 verkündete (vgl. "Background information", unten).

Als Beispiel für eine Berichterstattung, die nicht dem Anspruch von "calm and unemotional reports" (Z. 19) entspricht, können die Schlagzeilen der Titelseite aus *The Sun* vom 4. Mai 1982 (SB, S. 258) herangezogen werden. Auch bietet sich ein Vergleich mit Kap. XII, Text 6, einem Bericht über den Abwurf der ersten Atombombe, an. Zur Vertiefung der angesprochenen Problematik eignet sich ferner der Artikel "Few Britons Raise an Outcry on Curbs for Press and Trial" aus *International Herald Tribune* (3.11.1988), der von E. Werlich interpretiert wurde *(Sammlung Lensing 2*, Jahrg. 18, 4. Lfg., No. 359. Dortmund, Lambert Lensing 1989).

Background information

In an editorial on freedom of the press and expression in Britain, *The Observer* (4.12.1988) wrote: "A Government elected by a minority of British voters is preparing to enact, by means of its Commons majority and a House of Lords that represents nobody, a new law which is – or should be in any civilised democracy – unconstitutional. Under this proposed law, Ministers will personally be empowered to authorise agents of their secret police to break into the homes and tap the telephones of – say – their political opponents at election time. Any Crown servant who revealed that he had been ordered to do that, even to his Member of Parliament, could be jailed. There would be no defence available against such a charge, for the Government has decreed that the new Official Secrets Act will contain no mention of 'the public interest'. ... Even if an official were brave enough to defy this law and speak out, anyone who published or broadcast his disclosures would also face jail. They, too, would have no legal defence. No one – whistle-blower, parliamentarian or editor – would be allowed to plead to a jury that he had exposed wrongdoing in the public interest, even where it could be manifestly shown to be true. Such a law can only find its way on to the British statute book because we have no written constitution".

"Listening to the BBC's World Service, he had a fair idea of how much from his messages was being used" (ll. 3–4): Voice reports, such as those by Brian Hanrahan for the BBC and Michael Nicholson for ITN, were the only material that journalists

could get out immediately from the war scene in the Falklands. All other news, including pictures and film, was effectively delayed and censored by the Ministry of Defence. To overcome the total lack of film and photographs, newspapers used drawn pictures to illustrate their articles.

Semantic and collocational field "Media censorship"

a censor, a trickle of information, censorship of messages from (a place), (to) impose censorship, (to) prevent useful reporting, (not to) permit a television camera, (to) mislead the press/public ✧ (to) accept censorship in war, (to) suspend one's normal practice of inquiry, (to) temper one's reporting to sth. ✧ (to) achieve limited coverage, (to) be at odds with sb. ✧ an open information policy

Talking about the text – Suggested answers

1. Hanrahan mentions two phases. The first was when he thought he would have to use "fairly stark terms" (l. 7) to spell out "that there were men here who might get killed" (ll. 9–10). The second was when he realized that it was enough to give "the descriptions" (l. 18), to report "in a very flat way what [he] saw and heard and not get too tied up" (ll. 16–17) into evaluating the descriptions.

2. He reacted to the threat of government censorship through "the naval authorities" (l. 10), who made reporters feel that they preferred them to be "a bit less bloody in some of [their] choice of words" (ll. 11–12).

3. Some journalists, being at a loss for information, faked their reports, giving "'eye-witness' accounts … of events that never took place" (l. 25). Another consequence was that officials were made to hand on information to journalists that "deliberately misled the press and public" (l. 26).

4. He indicates that these accounts were labelled as such at the time, but were actually the opposite of what the word suggests, namely stories that had been made up by the journalists, fictional war reports.

5. *Considering the questions that Hetherington asks in connection with the role and responsibilities of war correspondents (cf. ll. 28–31), what basic rights of journalists in a democracy do they touch upon? (For additional information on these principles, you may also consult Ch. X, Texts 6 and 7).*
    The questions all touch upon the freedom of the press. The first question indicates that in times of "war or near-war" (ll. 28–29) the British government, "with the backing of Parliament" (ll. 33–34), imposes censorship, i.e. suppresses the truth. The second question refers to journalists' style of reporting and the standards of accuracy their profession expects them to obey. Under censorship, they are expected to adapt their style to the changing demands of patriotism and government propaganda. Finally, the third question, too, is directly linked with journalists' freedom and ethical standards. Under censorship, they are expected to accept being gagged, i.e. to act against their obligation to serve the people and reveal corruption.

6. *What would you consider as more important in times of crisis or even war – the government's right to impose censorship to keep the enemy in the dark, or the public's right to be informed fully and accurately? Discuss.*
    – –

7. *How does Hetherington's reference to US information policy at the time of the Vietnam War (cf. ll. 46–47) aim to modify British readers' expected support of their own government in war?*
    In contrast to Britain, US information policy during the Vietnam War was quite open, i.e. in agreement with the press's constitutional right to freedom. This allowed the press to mobilize the American public against continuing the war once its "human cost" had

become "unacceptable" (ll. 57–58). In other words, the press acted in the wider public's interest, against a government that had lost sight of the people's rights and interests.

8. *In view of Britain's newly revised and strengthened Official Secrets Act, how may the intention behind Hetherington's two concluding paragraphs be understood?*

   He makes a veiled plea for more openness in Britain, for revising the Official Secrets Act and following the democratic example set by the United States.

9 Jules Feiffer: What Is News?

Didaktische Hinweise

Dieser Cartoon, nach der Diskussion der grundsätzlichen Fragen in den Texten 6, 7 und 8 hier als *comic relief* fungierend, kann auch ohne die dem LB beigegebenen Aufgaben besprochen werden. Werden die unten formulierten Aufgaben in das Interpretationsgespräch integriert, kann die visuelle Vorgabe auch dazu genutzt werden, oberstufengemäße Formen der bewußt strukturierenden Bildbeschreibung zu üben, insbesondere die Erarbeitung des transferierbaren Textformwortschatzes für Anfang, Mitte und Schluß in Bildbeschreibungen (vgl. hierzu E. Werlich: *Student's Guide to Text Production*. Berlin, Cornelsen 1988, S. 14–19 und S. 83–84).

   Zu dem von Feiffer thematisierten Problem eines Überangebots von Informationen in den Medien könnte ein weiterer Cartoon ("No news today", SB, S. 252) herangezogen werden, der die Schein-Objektivität der Nachrichtenmedien ins Absurde steigert. Darüber hinaus bietet sich ein Vergleich zwischen Feiffers Figur und der offiziellen Sicht in dem Exzerpt aus Ray Bradburys *Fahrenheit 451* (Ch. VIII, Text 4) an. Im Zusammenhang mit dem behandelten Thema relevante Cartoons von Jules Feiffer finden sich in E. Werlich: *Comics & Cartoons. Translating visual elements into language*. Dortmund, Lambert Lensing 1980, S. 37–40.

Background information

Jules Feiffer (1929–   ) was born in New York City. After studying at art school, he became a professional cartoonist. His first cartoons were published in *The Village Voice*, for which he received a Pulitzer Prize in 1986. The British Sunday newspaper *The Observer* and the magazine *Playboy* began publishing his cartoons in the late 50s. His cartoons usually involve a character's monologue which satirically exposes his or her insecurities.

Talking about the text – Suggested answers

1. *Explain the relationship between the first and the last picture as opposed to the other pictures.*

   Picture 1 presents the character in a state of indecision about the newspaper in his hand: he can still choose not to read it and remain ignorant about the latest news. In fact, he seems to feel that not knowing what the papers say may even be good for him. After he has spent time putting himself in the know about the "latest" news in pictures 2 to 5, his feelings as expressed in the first two pictures are confirmed in picture 6. At the end he has reached his decision about the paper and cast it aside. Reading the paper has made him feel sick. The development is from indecision to decision.

2. **What sort of textual organization can be found in this sequence?**
   The cartoon shows the order of a plotted story. The character's situation develops in time (temporal ordering); his reactions to what he reads increase in intensity (climactic ordering); his encounter with so much bad news and the sensational reports produce in him a clear result, i.e. sickness and disgust (cause-and-effect ordering).

3. **Judging from the information the cartoon character is given and the way he reacts to it, what message do you get from Feiffer's cartoon?**
   [There are three basic angles the cartoon can be viewed from: 1) World events – What sort of life is possible in a world full of bad news and sensational events? 2) The press – To what extent is the press at fault for its choice of news and its way of reporting it? 3) The reader – What sort of reader is shown here? What are his expectations? Do his reactions to the newspaper he is reading seem appropriate? How logical is his conclusion in the final picture?]

4. **How may one explain the meaning of the changing background to the character in pictures 2 to 5?**
   While the background is blank in picture 1, there gradually rises a darkness behind the character as he goes on taking in more and more bad news, until he is finally completely framed by darkness in picture 5. So the increasingly darkening background can be understood as symbolizing what the newspaper depicts as the true state of the world: it is a world full of evils homing in on its human inhabitants. Put differently, through the newspaper the reader has adopted an increasingly darker view of the world in which he lives.

5. **At first sight, the final news item does not seem to belong in the same category as the other items. Why may "the latest sexual breakthrough" come here as the climax of disappointment?**
   If the latest news about sex is considered worth publishing, then the public's interests appear to have reached such a low level that the distinction from the instincts of the animal world is difficult to keep up. Papers raising sex to this level of newsworthiness aim at their readers' gut reactions. Picture 6 shows the cartoon character as an adversely affected reader, one who is still sensitive to what ought to concern rational beings.

10 Rushworth M. Kidder: Television and the News

Didaktische Hinweise

Obwohl die in Text 6 bis 9 angesprochenen zentralen Aspekte wie Pressefreiheit und Nachrichtenauswahl auch für das Fernsehen gelten, wird dieses Medium noch einmal gesondert und mit dem Blick auf seine eigenen Strukturen und Wirkungen thematisiert. Die das Kapitel X beschließenden Texte 10 und 11 tun dies, indem Text 10 vor allem Aufschluß gibt über die für "television news", typischen Bedingungen (auch im Hinblick auf sein "visual lexicon", Z. 72), während Text 11 sich stärker auf die Wirkungen konzentriert, die extensiver Fernsehkonsum nach sich zieht. Als thematische Erweiterung bietet sich der Beitrag über die Fernseh-Evangelisten in den Vereinigten Staaten an (Kap. VI, Text 6), ein Phänomen, das inzwischen auch in der Bundesrepublik zu beobachten ist.

Background information

In the United States, there are approximately 1,600 TV stations. There are three main TV networks: the American Broadcasting Company (ABC), the Columbia

Broadcasting System (CBS) and the National Broadcasting Company (NBC); many local stations are affiliated to these three. All television networks are private, but the Public Broadcasting Service (PBS) was set up in 1977 to dispense federal and private funds for the production of educational and cultural programmes. 98 % of American homes have a TV set, 50 % of them also receive cable television. The average American watches approximately 30 hours of television a week.

Semantic and collocational field "Television"

television, a television newsman/crew, a co-anchor of a news show, a viewer, (to) take a shot of sth., (to) see sb./sth. on screen, (to) get one's view of sth. through the news, news comes through television ✧ the strength of television news, a feeling of immediacy, the subtle effect of television news, a "visual lexicon", (to) use visual images, (to) combine timeliness with visual excitement, (to) mould the nation into a community of viewers, (to) magnify sth. for sb., (to) build a sense of trust, (to) appeal to sb. ✧ (to) inculcate sth. (e.g. an idea), television news ranks above sth. else ✧ oversimplification, trivialization, sensationalism, (to) surrender attention to sb./sth., (to) reduce the news to X minutes, (to) compress a story to fit a time frame, (to) produce a kind of headline service, (to) reinforce sb.'s previous conclusions

Talking about the text – Suggested answers

1. Firstly, television has gradually replaced the other media, newspapers and radio, as the main source of "news" for the public (cf. ll. 16–18). Secondly, in the US, television reduces all news items to pictures (cf. ll. 66–83) and, because of the constraints of time, to little more than headlines. In the conventional two-minute run for a "piece on the news" there is no time for putting things in "context" (cf. ll. 94–96).

2. West German TV news presentation is not (yet) cut up into pieces by "commercials" (l. 86). American television stations depend on the money raised by running advertisements. The major West German TV stations are state run.

3. It is this medium's dependence on a narrow "visual lexicon" (l. 72). This induces the TV journalist to simplify complex ideas and situations, or just to leave out what cannot be represented by means of visual images (cf. ll. 66–83).

4. [In the political field, up-to-date information makes it possible for people to react in an up-to-date way; regional differences, misunderstandings or envies can be modified; differences in the use of language for new ideas and situations tend to be harmonized, so that people can make themselves understood anywhere in the nation.]

5. It is above all the use of symbol and metaphor: an object from a familiar visual area is made to stand for another, more abstract, area since it shows certain similarities with it. If one part is made to stand for the whole, this is related to the verbal strategy of synecdoche, e.g. "dead bodies" for "war" (cf. ll. 77–78).

6. *In the wider context of human communication, what long-term effects may people's dominant exposure to visual news presentation have?*
   In communication, people still depend on language. However, if they receive news about the changing world around them predominantly through picture sequences, with only the barest verbal contextualization, their language competence tends to atrophy. They will increasingly lack the words and structures to cope with what they have seen, or to organize the information received for long-term memory and their own communication. Kidder mentions another closely related effect resulting from people's concentration on pictures: "television news segments are frequently misinterpreted in such a way as to reinforce the viewers' previous conclusion" (ll. 98–101). On this basis, "well-considered decisions" (l. 106) are hardly to be expected from the citizen.

7. *How do you think viewers could reduce the negative effects of TV exposure?*
   – –

11 Milton Shulman: Like Pandora's Box

Didaktische Hinweise

Milton Shulmans Beitrag lenkt den Blick auf langfristige Wirkungen, die intensiver Fernsehkonsum in der Gesellschaft nach sich zieht. Dabei bemüht sich der Autor, Vorzüge und Nachteile des relativ jungen Mediums abwägend einander gegenüber-zustellen. Für die Behandlung im Unterricht empfiehlt es sich, nicht nur – unter Einschluß des Fernsehens in der Bundesrepublik – in der Beurteilung der Aussagen des Autors nach Ländern zu differenzieren, sondern auch Raum zu geben für weitere länderspezifische Besonderheiten (vgl. unten, Aufg. 6, 7 und 8).

Background information

At present there are four television channels in the United Kingdom: BBC 1, BBC 2, ITV and Channel 4. The BBC (British Broadcasting Corporation) is responsible for programmes on BBC 1 and 2; BBC 1 broadcasts programmes of general interest, e.g. light entertainment, current affairs, sport, etc., while BBC 2 broadcasts minority interest programmes which are usually considered highbrow, e.g. documentaries, dramas, etc. The IBA (Independent Broadcasting Authority), soon to become the ITC (Independent Television Commission), controls ITV and owns Channel 4. The IBA supervises but does not produce television programmes; 15 television programme companies hold contracts to provide programmes for the 14 independent television regions. Channel 4, set up in 1982, caters for tastes which are not provided for by ITV and is intended to broadcast more experimental programmes. More recently cable and satellite television have been introduced into Britain.

Households with television must buy an annual licence costing £ 18 for a black and white TV or £ 58 for a colour TV. The licence fee, together with the sales of its programmes, finance the costs of the BBC. The IBA's finances derive mostly from advertising.

In Britain about 95 % of the population watch television, the average viewing time per person being about 25 hours a week.

Semantic and collocational field "Television"

a TV set, a TV commercial, (to) see a programme, (to) be a light viewer, (to) view X hours a day/a lot of TV, (to) adjust one's habits to the TV schedules, leisure time is dominated by the small screen ✧ the power of the TV image, exposure on the box, (to) change the shape and pattern of life, (to) become a spectator society ✧ (to) provide pleasure to sb., (to) broaden sb.'s horizons, (to) bring the cultural heritage of the past to the present, (to) keep society in touch with sth., (to) uncover sth. (e.g. injustice) ✧ the addictive nature of TV, encouragement of violence, (to) have a(n) (baleful) impact on sb./sth., (to) become addicted to viewing, (to) demand a higher standard of life

Talking about the text – Suggested answers

1. He strongly criticizes the use "we" (l. 11, etc.) make of television. People "are on the verge of becoming addicted to viewing" (ll. 12–13).
2. Shulman shifts the point of view from the first-person plural "our" and "we" (cf. ll. 4–36) to an impersonal third-person "a new report shows" (l. 38) and "it has been proved" (ll. 40–41). The intended effect may be first to capture the reader's interest in a development that he or she has, perhaps unwittingly, become a victim of. However, in order to perhaps

persuade the reader to the writer's view of the dangers connected with TV addiction, he needs more than subjectively persuasive language. Shulman's switch to the point of view of an objective "report" (l. 38), based on scientific research, introduces the kind of factual evidence that is needed in more formal argumentation. For the reader, this shift introduces an independent, intersubjectively acceptable viewpoint.

3. The sentence has a "right-branching" structure, i.e. starts from a main clause, inverted for emphasis, that is then extended by a long series of nominal groups to the right, five in all, each connected with the previous one through anaphoric "its". If viewed in connection with what the main clause speaks of and announces, i.e. something that must be balanced against the "positive benefits" (l. 54) of TV, then this expressive right-branching sentence structure conveys the impression of a setting loose or release of a host of evils from "the box" (l. 58), one coming on top of the other, almost with no end in sight. [Significantly, the last group of the right-branching serialization is not announced by "and", as is normal in monosyndetic serialization]. The sentence thus serves as a prelude to the simile of "Like Pandora's Box" that the subsequent sentence introduces as a climactic synthesis (cf. ll. 62–64).

4. Television, too, is informally referred to as "the box" (l. 58). By likening it to Pandora's Box, the writer most memorably suggests that, though "hope still remains inside waiting to be released" (ll. 63–64), television was sent into the world first of all to let loose a host of evils among people.

5. [The quoted sentences are likely to be rejected by those who, because of quite different habits, feel that the writer's all-embracing "we" is highly presumptuous. To explain the writer's risk-taking with this kind of reader, students may come to the conclusion that he disregards the non-addictive viewers because these constitute a definite minority today.]

6. *Draw up a list of the negative aspects of TV that the writer mentions. Which would you accept as true, probably true for some, or definitely not true?*

   – –

7. *Against the background of your own experience (and/or investigation), what view do you take of the writer's claim that we "have become a spectator society" (ll. 11–12)?*

   – –

8. *If you wanted data on TV viewing habits, you would have to conduct a survey. To get representative results through interviewing others, what characteristics of your interviewees would you have to consider?*
   [Important factors: age, occupation, size of family, kind of home, hobbies, etc.]

Chapter XI: Literature and the Arts

Dieses Kapitel wurde nicht als ein in sich geschlossenes Angebot für einen bestimmten literarischen Kurs konzipiert, sondern bietet vielmehr Material für Kurse mit unterschiedlicher Thematik. Sein Schwerpunkt liegt bei Fragen der Rezeption von Literatur, Musik und Kunst. Als Rezipienten sind die Schüler/innen in doppelter Weise betroffen: unmittelbar durch die Aussagen der fiktionalen Texte, mittelbar durch die Auseinandersetzung mit den Inhalten der Sachtexte. Dabei kann anregende Spannung aus der Konfrontation von eigener und vermittelter Rezeption erwachsen.

Je nach den konkreten Fragestellungen können sich Verbindungen mit Themen anderer Kapitel ergeben (vgl. dazu „Didaktisches Inhaltsverzeichnis", LB, S. xxx f.). Umgekehrt können Texte aus anderen Kapiteln zum Ausgangspunkt der hier entwickelten Fragestellungen werden. Die augenfälligsten Möglichkeiten zur Sequenzbildung innerhalb dieses Kapitels ergeben sich aus der Tatsache, daß drei der vorliegenden Texte (Text 2, 3 und 4) unter ganz unterschiedlichem Blickwinkel dem Thema "Poetry" gewidmet sind und vier weitere sich implizit (Text 5) oder explizit (Text 6, 7 und 8) auf Shakespeare beziehen. Damit wird zum einen die Möglichkeit geboten, sich ausführlicher mit einer im fremdsprachlichen Literaturunterricht zuweilen vernachlässigten Gattung zu befassen, zum anderen wird der Bedeutung Shakespeares Rechnung getragen. Möglichkeiten der Vertiefung der hier angesprochenen Fragen durch selbst gewählte fiktionale und nicht-fiktionale Texte sind selbstverständlich gegeben, über sie wird wohl gemäß der Unterrichtssituation entschieden. Als Einstieg in die Thematik kann die Auseinandersetzung mit den Aussagen der absichtlich essayistisch gehaltenen "Info-Box" (SB, S. 272) dienen.

1 T. L. Wymer et al.: Why Didn't He Come Right Out and Say It?

Didaktische Hinweise

Im Rahmen dieses Kapitels kann Text 1 als programmatisch angesehen werden. Hier wird Literatur als etwas zu jeder menschlichen Gemeinschaft Gehörendes verstanden, dessen Wesen und Wirkungsmöglichkeit darin bestehen, Erfahrung als gelebt und erlebbar zu vermitteln. Der Text ist vielfältig kombinierbar, auch mit fiktionalen Texten eigener Wahl. Innerhalb dieses Kapitels liegt eine Überprüfung der hier aufgestellten Thesen an Ted Hughes' "The Thought-Fox" (Text 2) oder ein Vergleich mit Robert Penn Warrens Aussagen über den Akt des Schreibens (Text 3) nahe, aus anderen Kapiteln könnten Texte etwa unter gattungsspezifischem Aspekt herangezogen werden.

Es liegt nahe, Text 1 zu Beginn eines ersten, vorwiegend literarischen Texten gewidmeten Semesters/Kurses zu behandeln. Die im Text gestellte Frage nach den Gründen für eine systematische Beschäftigung mit Literatur (Z. 28 ff.) kann den Einstieg bilden, als Basis lassen sich bereits bekannte literarische Werke heranziehen (vgl. unten, Aufg. 6). Ebenso denkbar ist die Arbeit an diesem Text jedoch auch zu einem späteren Zeitpunkt innerhalb eines Kurses oder einer Sequenz, wenn es darum geht, das eigene Vorgehen zu reflektieren und zu begründen. Und schließlich läßt sich der Text am Ende eines Literaturkurses/-semesters einsetzen, da er die Möglichkeit zu Rückschau und Bilanz eröffnet (vgl. unten, Aufg. 7).

Semantic and collocational field "Literature"

a literary artist, storytelling, the medium of a story, a rich tradition of stories ◇ a reading habit, a literary response, the effect of literature, a shock of recognition, (to) respond to sth., (to) partake in sth. ◇ (to) portray a character, (to) imagine an event, (to) imply a sense of order ◇ entertainment, a source of fulfillment and joy, (to) enjoy sth. for its own sake, (to) take delight in sth., (to) appeal to sb., (to) capture/hold sb.'s attention ◇ (to) be created for educational purposes, (to) teach sb. sth., (to) inform/instruct sb., (to) illustrate a fact/a model, (to) illuminate, (to) explore the deepest mysteries of existence, (to) make meaning manifest, (to) question the basis of sb.'s behaviour/morals

Talking about the text – Suggested answers

1. (1) Story telling as a universal phenomenon; (2) three kinds of purposes and effects of literature; (3) the good (ideal) story; (4) reasons for studying literature; (5) literature as the presentation of experience as lived.
2. Their main intention is to motivate (their) students for the study of literature. Their justification is that, once readers have learned how to respond properly to language as the medium of literature and to the ways in which meaning is presented in literature, reading will become more rewarding in itself and enrich the readers' experience of life.
3. They start with positive aspects, i.e. everybody's knowledge and enjoyment of literature. By using the pronoun "we", they blur the distinction between themselves and the readers/students. This may make the latter feel more inclined to follow their argument when they actually suggest taking a course in literature. At this point (cf. ll. 28–29), and at other decisive points in their argumentation as well (cf. ll. 48–49; l. 52), they cunningly take the readers'/students' possible objections into account and provide answers to likely questions. In their subsequent remarks on language, the medium of literature, and on the mode of presenting meaning in literature, emphasis is put on the characteristics of literature and the rewards the readers/students can expect, rather than on the details of learning. In the end, the writers seemingly identify with their less keen students, when they begin the last but one sentence with "unfortunately" (l. 63), instead of with "of course" or, at least, with some neutral expression.
4. Fiction, in contrast to philosophy, does not confront the readers with abstract statements but with "experience as lived" (l. 55). It affects the readers immediately because it involves them as complete persons instead of challenging select (mental) capacities only.
5. According to the text, fiction presents "experience as lived" (l. 55). The readers respond to this imagined experience on the basis of their own actual experience (cf. ll. 61–63). Together with the connotative rather than denotative use of language in fiction (cf. ll. 33–39), this allows for certain variations in the interpretation of a particular fictional work.
6. *Choose one of the stories you have read in class (including Sekundarstufe I), and discuss how it might best be described with regard to the three purposes of literature mentioned in the text.*
   – –

● 7. *Against the background of what the text has to say about literature, name one fictional work (i.e. novel, story, poem, play) that you have read and understood better after studying it in some detail. Discuss your different choices in class, compile a "Recommended Reading List" and pass it on to your juniors at school and to their teachers so that it may help them to choose their texts.*
   – –

2 Ted Hughes: The Thought-Fox

Didaktische Hinweise

Die Texte 2 bis 4 zum Themenbereich "Poetry" wurden so gewählt, daß sie als eine in sich abgeschlossene Textsequenz behandelt werden können, darüber hinaus aber auch in anderen Kombinationen einsetzbar sind. Neben Rezeptionsfragen werden hier auch Fragen der Inspiration und des dichterischen Schaffensprozesses erörtert.

Folgt man der im SB gewählten Reihenfolge der Texte, so werden die Schüler/innen in Text 2 ohne textgebundene Hinführung mit der Thematik direkt konfrontiert. Sie sollen die Möglichkeit erhalten, die beiden Ebenen der Tier-Chiffre unmittelbar zu erfassen, was bei einer Text 2 vorausgehenden Beschäftigung mit den Ausführungen von Robert Penn Warren (Text 3) infolge der damit in eine bestimmte Richtung gelenkten Erwartungshaltung entfallen würde. Sollten bei einem solchen Vorgehen Schwierigkeiten voausgesehen werden, kann Text 3 auch vor dem Gedicht von Ted Hughes behandelt werden. – Unabhängig von der gewählten Reihenfolge bietet Text 4 die Möglichkeit zur erneuten Überprüfung und Zusammenfassung des bereits Erkannten (vgl. Aufg. 9 und 10 zu Text 4, LB, S. 233).

Besteht vertieftes Interesse an Fragen nach dem Zustandekommen und dem Wesen eines Gedichts, kann die Textsequenz entsprechend erweitert werden (vgl. unten, Aufg. 8 und 9). Unter dem Aspekt der Wirkung kann auch der Bogen geschlagen werden zu Text 12 dieses Kapitels (vgl. LB, S. 244). Losgelöst von der im SB gewählten Reihenfolge ließe sich "The Thought-Fox" einbeziehen in Sequenzen zum Werk des Dichters, zur englischen Nachkriegslyrik und zu Tiergedichten verschiedener Autoren und Epochen.

Auf jeden Fall empfiehlt es sich, für die Arbeit an diesem Text die Textcassette (*Selected Texts on Cassette*, Berlin, Cornelsen Verlag 1989. Best.-Nr. 54861) heranzuziehen, die eine von Ted Hughes gesprochene Aufnahme des Gedichts enthält.

Literaturhinweise: Keith Sagar: *Ted Hughes*. Harlow, Longman for the British Council 1972 (Writers and Their Work, No. 227); Ders.: *The Art of Ted Hughes*. Cambridge, Cambridge University Press 1975; Terry Gifford, Neil Roberts: *Ted Hughes: A Critical Study*. London, Faber and Faber 1981; Leonard M. Scigaj: *The Poetry of Ted Hughes: Form and Imagination*. Iowa City, Iowa, University of Iowa Press 1986.

Background information

Ted Hughes [hjuːz] (1930 –   ) was born in West Yorkshire. He went to Cambridge, where he studied anthropology and archaeology. In 1956 he married the poet Sylvia Plath. His first volume of poetry, *The Hawk in the Rain* (1957), in which "The Thought Fox" appeared, was well-received by the critics. His work reveals a wide variety of subject matter and form. Besides his poetry, he has produced an experimental play, *Orghast* (1971), written mainly in an invented language, and plays for children. In 1984 he was appointed Poet Laureate, a title which dates back to the seventeenth century (among Hughes's famous predecessors were John Dryden and William Wordsworth). The poet laureate is appointed for life and receives a small salary as an officer of the Royal Household.

For the American version of "Poet Laureate" cf. pp. 229 f. of this book.

In a BBC programme for schools, "Listening and Writing" – later published as Ted Hughes: *Poetry in the Making: An Anthology of Poems and Programmes from "Listening and Writing"*. Faber and Faber, London, 1970 – Ted Hughes equates capturing animals with writing poems. For him, poems, like animals, have their own – independent – life. In order to illustrate his views, he uses "The Thought-Fox" as an example: "This poem does not have anything you could easily call a meaning. It is about a fox, obviously enough, but a fox that is both a fox and not a fox. What sort of a fox is it that can step right into my head where presumably it still sits ... smiling to itself when the dogs bark? It is both a fox and a spirit. It is a real fox; as I read the poem I see it move, I see it setting its prints, I see its shadow going over the irregular surface of the snow. The words show me all this, bringing it nearer and nearer. It is very real to me. The words have made a body for it and given it somewhere to walk. ... In some ways my fox is better than an ordinary fox. It will live forever, it will never suffer from hunger or hounds. I have it with me wherever I go. And I made it. And all through imagining it clearly enough and finding the living words" (op. cit., pp. 20–21).

Talking about the text – Suggested answers

1. He is apparently up at midnight, alone in a room, wanting to write something (cf. l. 4) . It is dark outside, but as he thinks of the forest, he is no longer the only one alive. There is "something else" (l. 2). What he imagines he sees coming towards him, from somewhere nearer than the invisible stars but even "deeper within darkness" (l. 7), turns out to be a fox, whose "sharp hot stink" (l. 21) he smells at the moment when it "enters the dark hole of the head" (l. 22). His surroundings, inside the room and outside, have not changed by the end of the poem, with the exception of the page in front of him, which is no longer "blank" (l. 4) but "printed" (l. 24).

2. The poem conveys the speaker's experience of conceiving a poem. It could be considered to be either a straightforward or a symbolic rendering of the creative process. On the surface level, it seems to be about a fox, or, more precisely, about how a fox-poem comes into being. On a symbolic level, the fox might stand for inspiration (originating, most likely, in the speaker's personal experience of nature), and thus it would be a poem about inspiration. In both cases, explanatory emphasis is on the initial, inspirational phase of the creative process, with no definite information on what (technical) stages have to be completed before the final version of the poem is achieved – unless we take the final line to suggest that the fox-poem has been created at one go.

3. Once again the question may be dealt with on two different levels. Choosing an undomesticated animal for a poem about the process of creation seems to be fitting for a poet who has often taken his subject matter from nature and the world of animals in particular [cf. "Background information", above, on Hughes's own interpretation of this poem]. Considering the fox's proverbial quality of cunning (in addition to agility, swiftness and the like), this animal seems to be particularly well-chosen as a symbol of inspiration.

4. Among the words chosen, the nouns and verbs are precise; the adjectives and adverbs are not ornamental but functional. Thus the choice of words contributes to the impression of realness, vividness and immediacy in the presentation of the fox and its surroundings.

5. The movement is reflected through the sentence starting in l. 11 and continuing to l. 22. The haltingness of the fox's progress and its changes of speed are reflected in the rhythm; in the variable length of the lines (signalling perhaps a zigzag pattern, a change of direction, although the sentence goes on); in the unusual word order, e.g. ll. 14–16; and in the visual gaps between stanzas 3 and 4, 4 and 5 (connected by means of enjambe-

ment), which might be taken to symbolize the "clearings" (l. 17) that the fox decides to cross.

6. The term "thought-fox" seems to indicate that the fox in the poem, though realistically described, is no depiction of any particular fox actually being, or having been, observed. In the poem, imagining the forest seems to make the fox appear, its vividness, most likely, based on the former experience of observing foxes in general. At the same time the term "thought-fox" could also serve as a clue for the possible interpretation of the fox as a symbol of inspiration (cf. question 2).

7. *The word "print" is used twice (cf. l. 13 and l. 24). In the context of this poem, why is this a particularly well-chosen word?*
The noun "prints" in l. 13 refers exclusively to the marks that the fox leaves in the snow. The verb "print", as it is used in l. 24, refers to what the fox has left with the speaker, and has a double meaning: 1. The speaker has had an inspiration of what to write ("printed" referring in this case to the traces of the fox, i.e. inspiration, from which to start). 2. A fox-poem (possibly dealing with inspiration) has come into being ("printed" in the sense of "ready for publication").

8. *How has the process of creation been dealt with by other poets that you know?*
– –

9. *In the USA, students are frequently offered courses in creative writing at school. Although such courses are rarely found in German schools, quite a number of German students try and write poems at some (decisive) point in their development. If you are among them, discuss what your initial stimulus was, and how you proceeded.*
– –

3 Robert Penn Warren: A Poem You Can Feel to Your Toes

Didaktische Hinweise

Robert Penn Warrens Ausführungen nehmen in ihrem ersten Teil (bis Z. 38) Ted Hughes' poetische Reflektion des eigenen Schaffensprozesses (Text 2) wieder auf und ergänzen sie um Überlegungen zur angemessenen Rezeption. Seine Vorstellung von "poetry" als "vital experience" (Z. 36) – und zwar sowohl für den Dichter als auch für den Rezipienten – weist zurück auf Wymers Definition von Literatur als "presentation of experience as lived" (Text 1, Z. 54–55). Abgesehen von den bereits erwähnten Ergänzungsmöglichkeiten (vgl. LB, S. 225 f.) bietet es sich hier an, Warrens Äußerungen an seinen eigenen Gedichten zu messen. Sie finden sich u.a. in R. Ellmann (Ed.): *The New Oxford Book of American Verse*. New York, Oxford University Press 1976.

Background information

Robert Penn Warren (1905–   ) was born in Kentucky. He studied at Vanderbilt University, the University of California, Yale University and finally at Oxford University (as a Rhodes scholar). He has held many academic posts, among them professor of drama at Yale University. He has published numerous novels and collections of poetry, and has won three Pulitzer prizes – in 1947 the fiction prize for *All The King's Men*, in 1958 the poetry prize for *Promises: Poems, 1954 – 1956* and in 1979 the poetry prize for *Now and Then*. He was the first poet laureate of the

United States (1986–1987), a post which is held for one year. The title came into being in 1986 and includes the honour of the consultantship in poetry to the Library of Congress, Washington, D.C.

"And wretches hang that jurymen may dine" (ll. 28–29): a line from Alexander Pope's "The Rape of the Lock", Canto III, l. 22.

Semantic and collocational field "Poetry"

poetry, an idea for a poem, a rhyme, a symbol, an image, signs on paper ✧ the meaning of a line, a statement of some kind, (to) understand poetry ✧ a vital experience, (to) be fragmentary autobiography, (to) trace an idea back to a fragment of memory, (to) exist in sb.'s head, (to) make sense out of an event, (to) provoke sb. into sth. ✧ the feel of a poem, (to) become aware of the basic physicality of sth., (to) feel a poem to one's toes ✧ (to) read a poem to oneself, (to) memorize sth. (e.g. a poem), (to) recite sth. (e.g. a poem)

Talking about the text – Suggested answers

1. Warren emphasizes personal experience as the most frequent source of ideas for his poems (cf. ll. 5–7). He does not give any definite information, though, as to the actual process of selecting past experience and transforming it into a poem. At least the initial phase of the creative process seems to take place without the author's active participation (cf. ll. 7–13).
2. Robert Penn Warren transfers the basic idea of the symbol as a poetic device, an element of imagery in which a concrete object is simultaneously suggestive of an abstract idea, to the poem as a whole. In his opinion, the poem is a symbol because its meaning encompasses more than the author himself is aware of, and more than the reader is directly informed about. This inherent symbolic (i.e. suggestive) quality distinguishes the poem from the mere statement.
3. What Warren suggests as help is closely connected with his basic idea of poetry as a "vital experience" (l. 38). The experience has to be responded to in an appropriate, i.e. comparable, way. Reading a poem properly to yourself provides the (sense) experience of hearing, tasting, feeling, seeing (i.e. visualizing) and thus, according to Warren, understanding it (cf. ll. 39–48). Memorizing it facilitates the process, and actually reciting it may possibly be seen as perpetuating the experience.
4. The author, of course, has the idea for the poem, which originates mostly in his own experience of life (cf. ll. 5–7); but, according to Robert Penn Warren, the meaning of the poem, once it is finished, is neither limited to what the author consciously intended (cf. ll. 14–16), nor can it be grasped objectively and definitely by any one individual reader (cf. ll. 14–17). It might even be argued that the reader in fact actively, though unconsciously, contributes to the meaning of the poem when trying to experience its physicality (cf. esp. ll. 34–35, 39–48). Thus, the meaning of a poem is not fixed once and for all; instead, it may be realized in possibly infinite shades, depending on who experiences it. Author, poem and recipient together are instrumental in establishing a meaning which is neither fully objective nor merely subjective.
5. The overall impression the reader gains of Penn Warren is that of a dedicated artist and educator. The original conversation is reduced to Warren's own contributions (presumably answers to the interviewer's questions, as can be derived from the very first sentence), and the immediate effect of Warren's words is not impaired by any summarizing on the interviewer's part. The informality of the conversation still shows in such characteristics as the frequent use of short forms, informal expressions (cf. ll. 21 and 35) and the general tendency to use fairly uncomplicated sentence structures. It is in ll. 37–38, though, that Warren's fervent commitment to poetry and his desire to communicate it is most vividly reflected.

6. *According to your own experience, what has proved to be most helpful for your personal understanding of poems?*
– –
7. *To what extent can learning about poetry teach you "how to live" (cf. ll. 61–66)?*
– –

4 S. I. Hayakawa: Poetry and Advertising

Didaktische Hinweise

Text 4, der dritte und letzte Text zum Thema "Poetry", scheint zunächst thematisch von den in Text 2 und 3 angeschnittenen Fragen deutlich abzuweichen. Über den ungewöhnlichen Vergleich von Dichtung mit Werbung gelingt es S. I. Hayakawa jedoch, zur Reflektion darüber anzuregen, worin die Wesensunterschiede zwischen den beiden Bereichen bestehen, obwohl technisch vergleichbare Strategien nicht in Abrede gestellt werden können.

Text 4 läßt sich jedoch auch in eine Sequenz zum Thema „Werbung und Propaganda" einfügen, für die etwa Kap. II, Text 4 (Anzeige), Kap. I, Text 5a und 5b und Kap. III, Text 3 (Informations- und Werbeschriften) herangezogen werden können.

Background information

Samuel Ichiye Hayakawa (1906-   ) was born in Vancouver, Canada, of Japanese parents. After graduating from the University of Manitoba, Winnipeg, he settled in the United States. He has been successful in both the academic world and the world of politics. From 1955 to 1973 he worked at San Francisco State College. He was a Republican senator for California from 1977 to 1983 and a leading figure behind a California initiative seeking a constitutional amendment making English the official language of the USA. Among his publications are *Language in Action* (1941), *Our Language and Our World* (1959), *Symbol, Status and Personality* (1962) and *Language in Thought and Action* (1972), from which this excerpt is taken.

Semantic and collocational field "Poetry and advertising"

poetry, a poem, a poet's eye, the loftiest of verbal arts ✧ advertising, a copywriter, an object for sale, the handmaiden of commerce, the poeticizing of consumer goods, a play on words, (to) be a part of everyday life, (to) act upon sth., (to) laugh over sth. ✧ (to) exploit ambiguities, (to) appeal to sb.'s vanity/fear/snobbery/false pride, (to) carry connotations of half-truth/deception/outright fraud ✧ (to) appreciate sth., (to) enjoy sth., (to) think about sth., (to) study sth., (to) be beyond sb.'s comprehension ✧ the denotative content, a connotative value, (to) symbolize sth., (to) invest sth. with meaning/significance, (to) become symbolic of sth. beyond itself, (to) give meaning to everyday experience

Talking about the text – Suggested answers

1. The impatient reader might well be convinced that a high degree of similarity between poetry and advertising is being advocated in this text. The initial reference to the unusual combination in the title (cf. l. 1) is apparently followed by the enumeration of the contrasts between the two elements (cf. l. 7). The larger part, however, seems to be devoted to their similarities in general (cf. l. 13) and to one important aspect among them

in particular (cf. ll. 30, 43, 46), the last line forming the climax with the two elements amalgamated in the phrase "poeticizing consumer goods" (l. 52).

2. The notion of advertising is expressed in straightforward statements of the simple type of "advertising is" (ll. 2–3; 8–9; 12). There is only one exception, where the writer refers to the connotations of the name of advertising and modifies the statement (cf. ll. 3–6) by adding an evaluating comment. In contrast, all his statements on poetry – even though two of them are basically of the same type as those on advertising (cf. ll. 1 and 9) – are modified either by an addition ("universally conceded to be", ll. 1–2; "in the general apprehension", ll. 9–10) or by a restriction ("The best poetry *seems* to be...", l. 7). Although the two additions seem to make the statements more valid at first sight (*"universally"*, *"general* apprehension"), they do not act as intensifiers in this context (cf. esp. the influence of "seems" in the second statement). It might be argued that the writer is less certain about what poetry really is, or how to define it, and therefore hides behind so-called general views.

3. Reference to the symbolic quality covers the larger and most prominent final part of the text. The symbol is usually considered to be among the most encompassing and complex of poetic devices. The examples mentioned in ll. 42–51 may be taken to reflect some of the complexity of the poetic symbol (including positive and negative aspects of the experience of life). Symbolic qualities in advertising, on the other hand, will never cover the full range of human experience because they must be desirable (cf. the four examples in ll. 49–51). They are chosen to attract specific groups of buyers and thus to increase the sales figures of the object concerned (cf. l. 3). Therefore they are much more easily seen through and explained (cf. the examples in ll. 48–51). The "objects of experience" are "symbolic of something beyond themselves" (ll. 34–36) only in the crudest sense. Thus, the application of the idea of "symbol" to advertising is neither altogether refutable nor fully conclusive.

4. The term "poeticizing" is closely related to "poetic", "poet", "poetry". In view of the examples quoted in paragraph 3 (cf. ll. 13–29) and the ideas about the applicability of the idea of symbol to advertising (cf. answer to task 3), there seems to be some justification for accepting "poeticizing" as a description of the process by which so-called "poetic" devices are incorporated into advertising. Because of their reduction to mere technique in advertising, their use results only in superficial similarities between poetry and advertising. The difference is, in fact, implied in the restrictive modification added to one of the sentences expressing similarity ("although on a much more *primitive* level", ll. 24–25).

5. Although "poeticizing" (as shown in the answer to task 4) can be interpreted as a technical process that results only in superficial (i.e. apparent) similarities between poetry and advertising, the term seems to be misleading because it unduly blurs the copywriter's basic task, for which the technical process is but a means, i.e. for making people memorize the names of goods (and their desirable "symbolic" qualities) so that they will recognize them or even ask for them in the shops and buy them (cf. ll. 3 and 47, and also tasks 3 and 6).
   [Some students might argue, though, that focusing on the technical side of the copywriter's task, without referring to the underlying intention, does not render the definition inadequate, but only incomplete.]

6. In the arrangement of his ideas Hayakawa employs three different kinds of ordering principles, which he interrelates in an extremely sophisticated way. Contrastive order is most obviously used within paragraphs 1 and 2, but it is also used to distinguish between section 1 (paragraphs 1 and 2) and section 2 (paragraphs 3 to 6) and in the illustrative part of paragraph 5. Listing order is suggested in paragraph 3 and is most prominent in paragraph 6. Climactic order is employed from paragraph 3 onwards.
   The first impression gained by the reader is most likely that of logicality and complexity in the relation of contrasts (roughly corresponding to contrastive order) and similarities

(partly represented by listing order) between poetry and advertising. But the arrangement of ideas does not fully reflect the underlying meaning of the text. Although an impatient reader might get the impression that poetry and advertising are being presented as more or less the same thing (cf. task 1), more careful study has shown that the similarities between the two are merely technical and superficial.

The contrast expounded in the first paragraph can be seen as fundamental. By comparison, the seeming climax ("poeticizing of consumer goods", l. 52) is an argumentative or structural fallacy. Advertising, in contrast to poetry, "is but the handmaiden of commerce" (l. 3). The "poeticizing of consumer goods" is but the surface structure of a deeper paradox (poems vs. consumer goods / experience vs. consumption) and the fundamental incompatibility of poetry and advertising. What the writer basically achieves through his complex arrangement is a deeper insight into poetry *and* advertising.

● 7. *Collect typical examples of advertising that make use of poetic devices such as rhyme, rhythm, symbol, ambiguity, etc., and analyse the function(s) of these devices.*

   – –

● 8. *Form small groups and make up your own advertising copy to "poeticize consumer goods".*

   – –

9. *Take a poem of your own choice, and show the way in which the poet "strive[s] to make the objects of experience symbolic of something beyond themselves" (ll. 34–36).*

   – –

10. *Sum up in a few sentences the central ideas behind each of the three texts on poetry (Ch. XI, Texts 2, 3 and 4). Discuss which of these views you found new/interesting/baffling, etc. Discuss whether the concepts/notions/definitions exclude one another.*

   – –

5 Hiram Haydn: The Elizabethans and Modern Man

Didaktische Hinweise

Hiram Haydn vertritt hier eine Literaturauffassung, die das dichterische Werk in seinem zeitlich-geistigen Gesamtzusammenhang sieht. Text 5 kann daher zum einen den Blick für Beziehungen zwischen historisch weit auseinanderliegenden Epochen schärfen und Verständnis für zeitlich Entlegenes fördern. Als Charakterisierung des Lebensgefühls des Elisabethanischen Zeitalters und damit der Shakespeare-Zeit kann er zum anderen aber auch in enger Verbindung mit der Behandlung eines Shakespeare-Dramas gelesen werden. Diese doppelte Funktion begründet seine Anfangsstellung innerhalb der Shakespeare-Sequenz (vgl. dazu auch LB, S. 235).

Weitere Informationen über die Shakespeare-Zeit finden sich in *Shakespeare and his Times*. Hrsg. von G. Thiele. Frankfurt, Cornelsen Verlag Hirschgraben 1982 (Unterrichtsmodelle für die Sekundarstufe II, Textsammlung Best.-Nr. 662206, Unterrichtsmodell 662257).

Background information

Hiram Haydn (1907–1973) was a New York publisher and editor of the learned quarterly *The American Scholar* (1944–1973). He wrote several novels, among them *By Nature Free* (1943), *Manhattan Furlough* (1945), *The Hands of Esau* (1962), as well as *Words and Faces* (1974), a memoir about publishing and authorship.

Talking about the text – Suggested answers

1. According to Haydn, the Elizabethan Age is a period which saw a radical change in the explanation of the universe (and mankind's place in it). The change from the geocentric view, i.e. the belief that the earth was the centre of the universe, to the heliocentric view, i. e. that the sun was the centre of our planetary system, affected people in a way they could not cope with easily. The process of adjusting to the new idea and its consequences was slow, so that the two world views existed side by side in the Elizabethan Age, finding their outlet in contradictions in everyday life as well as in literature.

2. Haydn's intentions can be seen as twofold. On the one hand, he does not want literature to be looked at as a separate phenomenon but as an expression of its time as a whole, regardless even of national boundaries. On the other hand, he intends to look at periods in the past (here the Elizabethan Age) not only from a historical point of view. Past and present, he claims, show surprising parallels. They are interrelated. Considering the past can help us to understand and to cope with the present.

3. After two paragraphs referring exclusively to the Elizabethan period, the third paragraph begins like a conclusion drawn from the preceding paragraphs, or like an explanation; but instead of "the Elizabethans" we find "we" at the beginning of the second sentence (cf. l. 12), and the rest of the paragraph down to l. 19 contains a description of the writer's own time (cf. "we" in ll. 14, 15, 17, 18; "our, ourselves" in ll. 14, 16, 18; "us" in l. 16). Only in the last paragraph does he return to the Elizabethans, who, in his own words, "experienced a similar dilemma" (l. 20; cf. also the very similar expressions in ll. 18–19 and ll. 23–24). The very last sentence encourages readers to use this parallel creatively when trying to cope with their own time. The unexpected deviation from chronology in l. 12 causes the readers to become aware of the parallel before it is actually named by the writer. The arrangement reflects the writer's view of the interrelation of periods which are historically separated by centuries.

4. Both periods (the Elizabethan Age and the writer's own time, i.e. the time immediately after World War II) are seen as times when the changes in people's thinking made necessary by scientific discoveries are too radical to come about immediately. The result in both cases is a time of deep unrest, during which traditional values and convictions are constantly queried.

5. Towards the end of the 20th century readjustment is necessary in view of the dangers of further scientific progress (cf. Chernobyl, genetic engineering, etc.). There are changes taking place in many people's attitudes towards the hitherto seemingly unlimited possibilities of technological progress and exploitation of natural resources, and towards the resulting pollution or destruction of the environment (and mankind).

6. *Is the phrase "chaos in God's cabinet" (l. 26) a suitable keyword for describing your own time? Discuss.*
   – –

7. *Discuss the writer's statement "The whole structure ... to survive" (ll. 14–16) with reference to your own time.*
   – –

6 Charles Lamb: Painful Reality on the Stage

Didaktische Hinweise

Die Lektüre eines Shakespeare-Dramas in Verbindung mit seiner Präsentation über Videorecorder und/oder einem gemeinsamen Theaterbesuch bietet ohne Zweifel einen besonders günstigen, wenn auch nicht den einzigen Rahmen, in dem dieser Text gelesen werden kann. Die hier zum Ausdruck kommende Vorliebe Charles Lambs für die Lektüre von Shakespeares Werken gegenüber ihrer Aufführung kann zum Anlaß genommen werden, einen auch von heutigen Schülern/Schülerinnen erfahrbaren Unterschied in den Reaktionen auf Shakespeare-Text und Shakespeare-Aufführung zu diskutieren und zu begründen (vgl. unten, Aufg. 5). Wegen seiner grundsätzlichen Thematik kann dieser Text auch im Zusammenmhang mit der Behandlung anderer als der explizit genannten Stücke *Macbeth*, *Richard III* und *Othello* im Unterricht besprochen werden.

Einen kommentierten Überblick über für die Schule geeignete Shakespeare-Ausgaben, visuelle Medien und Sekundärliteratur bietet N. Timm: "Shakespeare in der Sekundarstufe II". In: *Neusprachliche Mitteilungen*, 4, 1988, S. 253 ff. Kritik, Anregungen und bibliographische Hinweise enthält auch R. Ahrens (Hrsg.): *William Shakespeare. Didaktisches Handbuch*. 3 Bände. München, Wilhelm Fink Verlag 1982 (UTB 1111-1113). Eine einführende oder vertiefende Auswahl wird präsentiert in *Shakespeare's Tragedies. Essential Passages*. Hrsg. von R. Gocke. Frankfurt, Cornelsen Verlag Hirschgraben 1986 (Unterrichtsmodelle für die Sekundarstufe II. Textsammlung Best.-Nr. 662303, Unterrichtsmodell 662354); *Highlights of Shakespearean Comedy*. Hrsg. von R. Gocke. Frankfurt, Cornelsen Verlag Hirschgraben 1988 (Unterrichtsmodelle für die Sekundarstufe II. Textsammlung Best.-Nr. 662400, Unterrichtsmodell 662451).

Background information

Charles Lamb (1775–1834) was born in London and educated at Christ's Hospital. For most of his life he worked for the East India Company. A strain of insanity in his mother's family manifested itself in Charles in 1795 and had a devastating effect on his sister Mary, who, in a fit of madness, killed their mother. Thereafter Charles acted as her guardian. Together they wrote *Tales from Shakespeare* (1807), which was designed to introduce children to Shakespeare's work. Charles Lamb is best known as an essayist and a critic, but he also wrote poetry and drama.

"Shakspeare" (l. 1): one of several ways of spelling Shakespeare's name which were widespread until the 20th century.

Semantic and collocational field "Tragedy"

a criminal character, ambition, an impulse, (to) murder sb., (to) commit a crime, (to) leap over a moral fence ✧ a semblance of reality, an object of meditation, a state of sublime emotion, painful anxiety about sth., a natural longing to prevent sth., an uneasiness

Talking about the text – Suggested answers

1. Reading Shakespeare's plays stimulates our psychological interest in his criminal characters, regardless of the reprehensible deeds they commit. Seeing Shakespeare's plays performed involves us directly because the deeds/crimes seem to become real and

of immediate relevance. Seeing his plays performed thus excludes the aesthetic pleasure that his verbal art brings about when we read his plays.

2. – –

3. Lamb seems to prefer the aesthetic pleasure of the reading experience, although he highly appreciates Mr K.'s performance. Only in connection with the reading experience does he use such phrases and words like "state of sublime emotion" (l. 7), "we are elevated" (ll. 7–8), "images of night and horror" (l. 8), "solemn prelude" (l. 10), "the delight which the words in the book convey" (l. 25–26; note that this delight is "destroyed" when seeing the play), "the sublime images", "the poetry alone" (ll. 31–32). Apart from using the above-mentioned phrases, he expressly refers to "that vantage ground of abstraction which reading possesses over seeing" (ll. 14–15).

4. – –

5. *If you have had the experience of both reading and seeing a play by Shake-speare, was your reaction to seeing it on the stage (or on TV) different from your reaction when reading the play? Give details.*
   – –

7 Willy Russell: It's Fun, Tragedy, Isn't It?

Didaktische Hinweise

Im Rahmen dieses Kapitels kommt Text 7 eine besondere Bedeutung insofern zu, als Fragen der Literaturrezeption, hier auf Shakespeares *Macbeth* bezogen, in einem fiktionalen Text thematisiert werden. Dieses Exzerpt kann daher die *Macbeth*-Lektüre vorbereiten oder aber ergänzen.

Text 7 unterscheidet sich von Text 6 nicht nur hinsichtlich der Textsorte, sondern auch im Hinblick auf die hier geäußerten Ansichten über die größtmögliche Wirkung Shakespeares. Während Charles Lamb seine Betroffenheit durch die Lektüre eines Shakespeare-Dramas betont, geht im vorliegenden Exzerpt die Wirkung des Dramas auf Rita zunächst einmal von seiner Aufführung aus (vgl. auch die auf der Textcassette enthaltene Aufnahme). Dieser Kontrast kann für die Besprechung der in diesem Kapitel im Mittelpunkt stehenden rezeptionsästhetischen Fragen genutzt werden. Um sie nicht zu präjudizieren und den Zugang zum Text offenzuhalten, wurde der Aufgabenapparat wiederum im LB untergebracht.

Die in Text 7 angesprochenen Fragen erlauben es, ihn auch im Zusammenhang mit dem Themenkomplex „Erziehung" zu behandeln und Texte aus Kap. II (etwa Text 1, 3, 5, 10 und 11) anzuschließen. Ebenso kann der Russell-Auszug seinen Platz in einer Unterrichtssequenz zum englischen Drama der Nachkriegszeit finden. Und schließlich bietet es sich an, das Stück als Ganzes zu lesen (Willy Russel: *Educating Rita.* Ed. and annotated by A.-R. Glaap. *Comment and Study Aids.* By A.-R. Glaap. Frankfurt, Diesterweg 1984). Vorschläge zur Einbettung in den Unterricht, auch im Zusammenhang mit der Shakespeare-Lektüre und speziell mit dem im SB enthaltenen Exzerpt, finden sich bei A.-R. Glaap: „'Educating Rita': Literatur für jedermann. Zur Interpretation einer Komödie von Willy Russell." In: *Der fremdsprachliche Unterricht* 62, 1982, S. 108 ff.

Background information

Willy Russell (1947–   ) was born near Liverpool. He left school without any formal qualifications and worked as a ladies' hairdresser from 1963 to 1969, during which time he started to write songs, sketches and poetry. After taking his school examinations in his early twenties, he pursued his studies further and worked as a teacher for a few years. Since the early 1970s he has written continuously, especially for television and the stage, his most famous play being *Educating Rita* (1981), also made into a film.

Educating Rita is the story of a Liverpudlian hairdresser who decides to take a course at the Open University in order to educate herself. The play can be seen as another adaptation of the classical legend of Pygmalion. According to Greek mythology, Pygmalion was the King of Cyprus who fell in love with a statue of the goddess Aphrodite he had made. The goddess then endowed the statue with life. *Pygmalion* (1913) by Shaw, adapted as the musical *My Fair Lady* (1956), is also based on the myth.

The Open University is a non-residential university that offers part-time degree courses to anyone who wants to take part; no formal academic qualifications are required, but the standards of the University's degrees are equal to those of other universities. Students follow the courses through correspondence, television and radio broadcasts and summer schools. In 1988 some 150,000 students were following Open University courses.

Semantic and collocational field "Tragedy"

tragedy, tragic event, preordained ✧ a flaw in one's character, (to) be flawed by one's ambition ✧ (to) bring sth. on, (to) dictate sb.'s end, (to) take the inevitable steps towards one's own doom, (to) tread the path to doom, (to) go blindly on, (to) ignore a warning, (to) be warned

Talking about the text – Suggested answers

1. *What do we learn about Shakespeare's "Macbeth" through Rita and Frank's conversation?*

   Through Rita we do not get any coherent information on either plot or characters (cf. her fragmentary hints in ll. 33–34). Instead, we learn about her impression of the play (cf. ll. 19–20, 30–31, 37) and the effect the play and the character of Macbeth had on her (cf. ll. 20, 30, 34–35, 39). Her tentative use of the term "tragedy" (l. 39) cannot be seen as a logical conclusion drawn from the information she has just given. From Frank's explanation of the difference between "tragic" in everyday usage and "tragedy" in dramatic terms (cf. ll. 47 ff.) we learn that "Macbeth" is a tragedy of character in the Aristotelian sense.

2. *How would you characterize the way Rita and Frank inform each other (and the readers)?*

   Rita's way of telling Frank about her experience of "Macbeth" is highly emotional and subjective. With the exception of the term "tragedy" (and she is not quite sure whether this is the right word, cf. l. 39), her words could refer to anything that has greatly impressed her. Frank, on the other hand, uses the appropriate terms from objective literary criticism.

3. ***Characterize Rita from what you learn about her in this scene.***
   Rita is uneducated but eager and able to learn, good-humoured, spontaneous and
   genuine, though emotional and subjective, in her verbal reactions. She is sometimes
   hampered in her impulsiveness by a vague knowledge of what one is or is not supposed
   to do in certain circumstances, e.g. in the theatre (cf. ll. 37, 70).

4. ***How does Frank adapt his speech to his student?***
   Frank's anxiousness to adapt his speech to his student is particularly obvious in the
   second part of the scene (cf. ll. 47–85). It shows in his choice of a contrastive example to
   "Macbeth" (cf. ll. 60–61) as well as in his specific image for (character) tragedy (cf. ll. 79–
   80). Together with his repeated use of verbs like "look" (ll. 53, 64), "see" (ll. 57, 79, 81),
   "understand" (l. 77), of questions (cf. ll. 54, 57, 81) or question tags (cf. ll. 66–67, 73, 77) and
   his reference to Rita's own words, they show his personal involvement as a teacher who
   wants his student (without this sort of formal education) to understand, and thus – apart
   from using the terminology of literary criticism when absolutely necessary – tries to avoid
   explanations which are still too abstract for Rita's mind.

5. ***How would you explain Rita's seemingly paradoxical statement in the final
   sentence: "It's fun, tragedy, isn't it?"***
   The objectively inappropriate use of the term "fun" in connection with "tragedy" is
   subjectively quite appropriate. On the one hand, it connotes her fascination with the play
   itself, and, on the other hand, it refers to her experience of learning, which she thoroughly
   enjoys. The contradiction stems from her inability to use critical jargon.

6. ***Considering your own knowledge of Shakespeare's play, is Frank's explanation
   of Macbeth's character and actions correct? Quote from the text and any other
   additional material to support your view.***
   – –

8 Yet Another Version of Shakespeare

Didaktische Hinweise

Mit der Aufnahme von Text 8 wurde bewußt ein ungewöhnlicher Zugang zu
Shakespeares Dramen gewählt. Ein Auszug aus *Macbeth* in Form eines Comic wird
mit Sicherheit Diskussionen auslösen, etwa über die Rolle, die Illustrationen in
einer Shakespeare-Ausgabe spielen (vgl. unten, Aufg. 7). Eine Grundsatzdebatte
über Ziele und Grenzen einer Modernisierung klassischer Werke – sei es hinsichtlich
der Inszenierung oder der Übertragung auf andere Medien (vgl. Z. 1–10) – läßt sich
anschließen. Text 8 kann aber auch am Ende einer Shakespeare-Sequenz behandelt
werden, etwa im Anschluß an Text 6 und als Kontrast zu Lambs Aussagen (vgl. unten,
Aufg. 6). Er leitet ferner zum Thema „Literaturbegegnung durch moderne Medien"
über, das Gegenstand der beiden folgenden Texte ist.

Semantic and collocational field "The performing arts"

a director, (to) stage a play, (to) produce a play in countless forms, (to) open a season with a
play ✧ a theatrical tradition, a musical version, a full-scale ballet, a television presentation ✧
(to) take another form, (to) bring sb. (e.g. Shakespeare) to life for a generation

Talking about the text – Suggested answers

1. *In what ways may the comic book version influence young readers' initial attitudes?*
   Young readers will most certainly recognize a well-known form and, depending on their attitude towards comics in general, will probably look forward to dealing with the book, and its pictures in particular, because they will not envisage any difficulties.

2. *What strikes you about the drawings and their intended effects?*
   – –

3. *Although the text is unshortened, it has somehow been changed. In what way?*
   Because of the arrangement in the balloons, verse is no longer printed in the traditional manner, a fact which is most obvious in the first speech bubble in the bottom frame.

4. *Why might the publishers of the cartoon edition of "Macbeth" feel relatively certain that the work will be a success?*
   The rather surprising combination of the traditional and the relatively new make the "Macbeth" comic an apparently safe bet. Shakespeare is required reading for virtually every student in the English-speaking world and for many foreign learners of English, so any Shakespeare edition promises to be at least mildly successful. One can assume that the comic is a form enjoyed by most of the above-mentioned students, and that those students voluntarily purchase at least the occasional comic. An edition of Shakespeare in comic form thus combines work and pleasure, obligation and inclination, in such a way that the financial success of the project seems likely.

5. *What advantages do you see in a cartoon edition of Shakespeare? Would you personally prefer such an edition or a traditional rendering?*
   – –

6. *How would Charles Lamb (cf. Ch. XI, Text 6) most likely have reacted to this Shakespeare comic?*
   According to Lamb, performance prevents us from concentrating on Shakespeare's verbal art; aesthetic pleasure and psychological interest in the persons are replaced by our moral involvement. The pictures as such do not offer a valuable experience in the way a performance, much less pure reading, can. Therefore Lamb would probably have seen them as a mere nuisance, i.e. a distraction from the text.

7. *Compare and contrast the effect of the pictures in the cartoon edition and in other illustrated versions of Shakespeare's plays, e.g. the "Oxford School Shakespeare".*
   – –

9 William Scobie, Nick Goodway: Books on Tape

Didaktische Hinweise

Während Text 1 bis 8 entweder selbst Beispiele fiktionaler Gestaltung sind oder sich im wesentlichen auf solche Texte beziehen – wobei Hayakawas vergleichende Ausführungen (Text 4) eine gewisse Sonderstellung einnehmen –, wird in Text 9 (und später Text 11) durch die Einführung des Oberbegriffs "book" die Unterscheidung zwischen "fiction" und "non-fiction" aufgehoben. Hier und in den drei folgenden Texten steht die Rolle der modernen Medien in ihrer den Umgang mit dem gedruckten Wort fördernden Funktion zur Diskussion. Eine weitere thematische Gemeinsamkeit besteht darin, daß sie nicht nur Einblicke in kulturelle Belange der Zielsprachenländer gewähren, sondern in besonderem Maße auch zum Vergleich mit der Situation im eigenen Land anregen.

Text 9 wirft unter anderem die Frage auf, inwieweit Adaptionen schwieriger Originaltexte zulässig sind. Deutlicher als in Text 8 wird hier auf den kommerziellen Aspekt hingewiesen. Damit wird die Aufmerksamkeit der Schüler/innen auf einen Bereich gelenkt, in dem wirtschaftliche und – zumindest partiell – literarische Interessen aufeinander treffen und nicht in jedem Fall in Einklang zu bringen sind. In die Überlegungen, welche Auswirkungen der zunehmende Ersatz des Buches durch visuelle und akustische Medien nach sich ziehen kann (vgl. auch SB, Aufg. 4), läßt sich Isaac Asimovs Science-Fiction Story "The Fun They Had" (in: *Science Fiction*. Stories chosen by J. Gibson, annotated by F.-K. Opitz. Best.-Nr. 66316; *Fact and Fantasy. Six Science Fiction Stories*. Ed. by H.G. Stenzel. Best.-Nr. 16940; beide Frankfurt, Cornelsen Verlag Hirschgraben) einbeziehen.

Background information

Predictions concerning the sales figures of audio books seem to have been realistic: sales in the USA reached more than $ 250 million in 1986. An expected 50 % to 100 % growth in the next five years will probably even surpass the predicted "annual sales of $ 500 million by the end of the decade" (ll. 55–56). Up to 1986, about 12,000 titles, covering the whole subject range of an average library (with special emphasis on fiction and self-help books), have been recorded in the United States. They were either read by their respective authors or by professional readers; some of the recordings include various background noises, music, etc. (cf. S. Kanfer: "Heard Any Good Books Lately?" In: *Time,* July 21, 1986, p. 53 f.).

Audio publishing is not restricted to Britain and the USA. In Germany, the number of publishing houses interested in "books on tape" has increased steadily. Lately, publishing houses such as S. Fischer, Rowohlt, Suhrkamp and Goldmann have announced their intention to enter the audio market.

Semantic and collocational field "Audio books"

audio publishing, a double cassette pack, a tape deck, a headset, (to) bring out one's own "audio books" line, complete on tape ✧ (to) come over the car's stereo cassette player, (to) listen to a bestseller/a book on tape, (to) be engrossed in sth. ✧ (to) change sb.'s reading habits, (to) be introduced to sth. (e.g. great literature), (to) be given access to sth. (e.g. information) ✧ drastic condensation/editing/adapting, (to) provide the essence of a book

Talking about the text – Suggested answers

1. Listeners who do something else while they are listening cannot fully concentrate on what they are listening to, as is most obvious from the first example mentioned in the text. The phrase "a driver is engrossed in a book" (ll. 3–4) cannot possibly imply that the driver forgets everything else because the book takes up all his or her attention. The impact of the book may therefore be less intense, or even superficial, depending, in this particular case, on the traffic, not necessarily on the book.
2. The writers' choice of examples in the first section of the text (paragraphs 1 and 2) shows their intention to appeal to male and female readers of different professions and literary interests. The middle part (covering paragraphs 3 to 8) is relevant to both American and British readers, and it provides information for a specialist interest in facts and figures. The last section (paragraphs 9 and 10) challenges all those readers who tend to get morally involved in such a discussion, regardless of their other personal data.

3. Sound provides an experience different from that of reading. It may be seen as a distraction from, or as a distortion or intensification of, the "original" (reading) experience.

4. [E.g. the loss of variety in the shape and the binding of books, the only difference preserved being the number of cassettes; the writers' adjustment to the rules of audio publishing in order to get their work published at all; a rise in book prices due to the dwindling numbers of books actually published in book form; a reduction in the range of readers' interests (books on tape only); a gradual loss of literacy.]

5. The reference is to "Kentucky Fried Chicken", the name of a chain of shops specializing in take-away fried chicken: ready-made, handy pieces of approximately the same size and little difference in flavour. As "the fast food of the publishing industry", "Kentucky Fried Literature" is also ready-made (by the publishing industry) and cut to size (lasting less than an hour). As with Kentucky Fried Chicken, you save time with Kentucky Fried Literature, but you have to do without the unmistakable individuality of what you listen to.

6. *With reference to the information given in the text, what advantages and/or disadvantages do you, personally, see in the possibility of "listening to books on tape" (ll. 27–28)?*
   – –

7. *The text gives two different views on adapted versions of books (cf. ll. 75–90). What is your opinion, against the background of your own experience of reading adaptations?*
   – –

10   A. P. Sanoff: What It Takes to Make a Good Book a Good Movie

Didaktische Hinweise

Möglichkeiten der sinnvollen Einbeziehung von Film und Video in den fremdsprachlichen Literaturunterricht werden seit längerem in der Fachliteratur intensiv diskutiert (vgl. etwa das Themenheft "Filme". In: _Anglistik und Englischunterricht_, H. 36, 1988; E. Platz-Waury: "American Short Stories On Film. Ein Projekt zur Neuorientierung des Literaturunterrichts an Schule und Hochschule." In: J. Paech (Hrsg.): _Methodenprobleme der Analyse verfilmter Literatur_. Münster, Nodus Publikationen 1988). Ohne zu stark ins Detail zu gehen, bietet Text 10 die Gelegenheit, die Schüler/innen an der Diskussion des Themas „Verfilmung literarischer Werke" aktiv zu beteiligen. Im Zentrum stehen Fragen, die sich auf die (notwendigen) Veränderungen der literarischen Vorlage durch das Medium Film beziehen. Daher liegt es nahe, den Text im Zusammenhang mit der Film- oder Video-Vorführung eines gemeinsam erarbeiteten literarischen Werkes zu behandeln (vgl. unten, Aufg. 7). Der Text kann aber auch als Einstieg in eine (eventuell als Projektarbeit konzipierte) umfänglichere Untersuchung verfilmter Literatur benutzt werden. Der Einsatz von Video-Cassetten erlaubt in beiden Fällen vielfältige unterschiedliche methodische Zugriffe. Auch liegt es nahe, die Grundsatzdiskussion über die Berechtigung (und die Grenzen) der Bearbeitung literarischer Texte (vgl. LB, S. 238) unter den im Text genannten Aspekten weiterzuführen.

Kritisches Material zu verfilmter englischsprachiger Literatur, einschließlich der notwendigen englischen Fachtermini, enthalten die beiden Bände P.G. Buchloh, J.P. Becker, R.J. Schröder (Hrsg.): _Filmphilologie_ und _Literatur und Film_. (Kiel,

Kieler Verlag Wissenschaft + Bildung 1982 und 1985 [Kieler Beiträge zur Erweiterung der Englischen Philologie, Bd. 1 und 4]. Ein Verzeichnis der Fachtermini bietet ferner J. Monaco: *How to Read a Film* (New York, Oxford University Press 1977). Video-Cassetten für den Einsatz im Unterricht leihen die Landesbildstellen, das British Council, die Amerika-Häuser und das Institut für Film und Bild in Wissenschaft und Unterricht (FWU, Bavaria-Film-Platz 3, 8022 Grünwald) aus.

Für die Untersuchung einer Film-Version im Zusammenhang mit dem Thema „Shakespeare", insbesondere *Macbeth* (vgl. auch Text 6 bis 8), bietet sich Roman Polanskis *Macbeth*-Verfilmung an. Kritische Stellungnahmen dazu finden sich u.a. in R. Borgmeier: " 'Ein Filmdrehbuch von William Shakespeare?' Polanskis Macbeth und die Probleme der Shakespeare-Verfilmung." In: H. Grabes (Hrsg.): *Literatur in Film und Fernsehen.* Kronberg/Ts., Scriptor 1980, S. 81 ff. (Auslieferung Bielefeld, CVK Cornelsen Verlagskontor); G. Schröder: "Polanskis Macbeth im Englischunterricht". In: P.G. Buchloh, J.P. Becker, R.J. Schröder (Hrsg.): *Literatur und Film* (vgl. oben, S. 113 ff.).Weiteres Material zum Thema „Shakespeare-Verfilmungen" findet sich in R. Ahrens (Hrsg.): *William Shakespeare. Didaktisches Handbuch.* München, Wilhelm Fink Verlag 1982, Bd. 2, S. 729 ff., Bd. 3, S. 987 ff. und S. 1044 ff. [UTB 1112, 1113].

Semantic and collocational field "Film adaptations"

a movie based on a novel, (to) make a film version of a play, (to) bring sth. (e.g. a novel) to the screen, (to) transfer a play to film, (to) turn words on a page into images on a screen, (to) become a movie, (to) be the product of a film maker's love affair with a piece of literature ◊ (to) adapt a novel/book for film, (to) wrest a screenplay from a novel, (to) reconcile the differing demands of film and print ◊ a knack for screenwriting, (to) come up with a script, (to) script a book, (to) write/do the screenplay, (to) know what to leave out, (to) have obligations to the material ◊ (to) be faithful to the spirit/letter of the book, (to) keep the dramatic dialogue/coherence/framing, (to) remain intact, (to) translate well ◊ (to) get the Hollywood treatment, (to) add lines/a character to a movie, (to) expand the role of sb./sth., (to) change the locale ◊ (to) rely on literature for raw material ◊ (to) own the film rights to a novel

Talking about the text – Suggested answers

1. Many of the reasons mentioned in the text point in one direction: Books are exploited for financial reasons. With a book as raw material it is easier to find financial backers for a film (cf. ll. 96–103). A film based on a novel will be favoured by the middle class (cf. ll. 26–27). Generally, it may be expected to attract a large audience (not of teenagers, though, according to the writer; cf. ll. 29–31), more numerous, in fact, than the readers of the book itself would be (cf. ll. 33–36; 214–216). The ultimate goal is a success comparable to that of "Gone with the Wind" (cf. ll. 217–219).

2. One of the major problems in connection with a screenplay based on a novel has to be solved before the actual work can start: Who may be considered to be a suitable scriptwriter (cf. ll. 51 ff.; 104 ff.)? Once that person has been found, he or she will be confronted with problems concerning quantity and quality. With, usually, about a hundred minutes allowed for a film and one page of script being equivalent to one minute of film, most novels have to be shortened drastically. The question of what to cut is not easily solved (cf. ll. 63 ff.). Language, and especially "lyrical language" (l. 5), can pose a further problem relating to quality. Other problems of quality concern the possible changes of topic, plot, characters and ending (cf. ll. 6–14, 131–134, 141–143, 144–165, 196–199, 204–206). All these features have to be adjusted to what is considered to be appropriate for the new medium.

3. The writer himself touches upon the questions of cast (cf. ll. 82–87, 159–165, 169–171) and setting (cf. ll. 176–181). He does not mention any "technical" details, such as camera work, colour, background music and the like. All these things determine, after all, how the tone and atmosphere of the book will "translate" into a film.

4. What viewers can expect of a film is a manifold, though primarily visual (and auditive), experience. While it lasts there is little room for them to use their imagination. Images realized on the screen guide them more strictly than words alone normally do. It might be argued that, in general, the medium film does not demand much creativity of the audience while they are actually exposed to it, whereas readers must continually create their own images from the printed word.

5. The writer makes extensive use of namedropping. Although the text is mainly about five films which are based on novels or a short story respectively, he mentions more than thirty names of persons and thirteen titles of books and films. He is very careful, though, to balance the numbers referring to persons involved in film making on the one hand, and to authors and books on the other, and thus to hold the attention of both readers and film fans.

6. *If "a film is not made for lovers of a book" (ll. 142–143), why do you suppose many of them go and see the film version nonetheless?*
    – –

7. *Discuss the main differences between a book that you know and its film version, and show what effect these differences have.*
    – –

8. *From your own experience, support or challenge the contention that "schlock fiction makes the best movies and great literature does not" (ll. 206–208).*
    – –

11 Gordon A. Sabine: Books Are like Vitamins

Didaktische Hinweise

Auf die Gemeinsamkeiten der Texte 9 und 11 wurde bereits hingewiesen (vgl. LB, S. 239). Ergänzend sei angemerkt, daß im Zusammenhang mit beiden Texten ein Vergleich mit den jeweiligen (nationalen) Bestseller-Listen interessant sein kann.

Während Text 9 den wirtschaftlichen Aspekt stärker betont, konzentriert sich Text 11, gestützt auf eine amerikanische Studie, auf die von solchen Aspekten freie Buchwahl. Bei dem untersuchten Leseverhalten bleibt allerdings weitgehend offen, in welchen Fällen es sich um eine bewußte Wahl handelte und in welchen Fällen die Befragten durch Zufall auf das in der Rückschau als wichtig bezeichnete Buch stießen. Hiervon ausgehend kann die Diskussion in der Klasse durchaus zu der nicht mehr landeskundlich gebundenen grundsätzlichen Frage führen, warum wir überhaupt lesen.

Semantic and collocational field "The role of books"

(to) be interested in a (tremendous) range of books, (to) read a book at a stress point, (to) be important at different periods in sb.'s life ✧ an enlarging and expanding activity, (to) make a difference in sb.'s life, (to) make sb. feel good, (to) have great impact, (to) be instrumental in sb.'s career choice, (to) make sb. decide on sth.

Talking about the text – Suggested answers

1. The books mentioned in the answers of particular persons and in Sabine's statistics can be categorized as follows: The Bible (a category in itself, heading religious and theological literature); handbooks (self-help books, dictionaries and other reference books); autobiographical literature (of various leanings); science fiction (politically orientated); escapist or popular literature (romances). In short, the books which are frequently read all belong to "literature" in a broad sense, including fiction and non-fiction.

2. As for escapist or popular literature, the motive is explicitly stated as the desire to feel good (cf. ll. 28–31). The Bible meets people's spiritual needs. Handbooks can be consulted for information. Autobiographies may be read out of historical or topical interest, but also, just like the particular kind of science fiction mentioned, in search of answers to topical questions.

3. – –

4. He specifically refers to books for adults that are considered to be unfit reading material for young people.

5. – –

6. The original conversation has become a monologue by means of leaving out the interviewer's contributions. For the convenience of the reader the editor has introduced sub-headings to indicate individual topics. These may, in fact, be related to some of the original questions from the interview. The editor may have decided on the present form because it is easier to read than a standard interview and puts more emphasis on what Sabine says and on his actual findings.

- 7. *Find out more about censoring books and plays:*
     a) *For what reason were books censored in Germany between 1933 and 1945?*
     b) *Is there any possibility of censoring books in Germany today?*
     c) *For what reasons were plays censored in Britain until 1968?*
     [For information on censoring plays in Britain, cf. Appendix I to "The Oxford Companion to English Literature". 5th edition, edited by Margaret Drabble. Oxford University Press, Oxford, 1985, pp. 1105–1112.]

- 8. a) *Devise a questionnaire similar to the one Sabine may have used in his study.*
     b) *Use the questionnaire you have drafted to conduct interviews with visitors to your local library. Compare the results of your survey (distinguish between different age-groups) with those that Sabine describes.*

     – –

12 Deadly Lyrics?

Didaktische Hinweise

Auch dieser Text beschäftigt sich mit dem, was ein Kunstwerk (im weitesten Sinne) bewirken kann, und führt damit die in den vorausgegangenen Texten angesprochene Thematik fort. Der 1986 in der Tageszeitung *Milwaukee Journal* erschienene Bericht bezieht sich auf ein Ereignis, das tatsächlich stattgefunden hat. Anhand dieses Textes lassen sich mögliche Abhängigkeiten thematisieren und problematisieren, wobei jedoch mit Behutsamkeit verfahren werden sollte. Dem Fragezeichen in der Überschrift entsprechend läßt sich der Text eher als Hinweis auf eine nicht zu unterschätzende Einflußmöglichkeit denn als Nachweis einer tatsächlich erfolgten fatalen Einflußnahme verstehen.

Semantic and collocational field "Suing"

an attorney, a law, a suit, a court paper, a lawsuit, (to) amend/file a lawsuit, (to) be named in a lawsuit, (to) prohibit sth., (to) claim sth., (to) teach sb. a lesson, (to) seek unspecified monetary damages, a suit relies on a law

Talking about the text – Suggested answers

1. – –
2. The writer has been very careful not to give his personal view on a pending case. Neither his words nor his arrangement of information allow any conclusions as to his opinion. He carefully avoids summarizing phrases that might be open to interpretation. Instead, he relies on direct and indirect quotation, appropriately introduced by the non-committal verb "say" (e.g. ll. 5, 33, 36, 42, etc., plus "tell", l. 60, and "call", l. 69), unless the correct rendering of the suit demands more specific terms such as "name" (ll. 7, 34) and "claim" (ll. 9, 13).
3. – –
4. Among the parents' overt motives may be their intention to find the culprit and get at least financial compensation for their loss, and, at the same time, to prevent any future cases of this kind. It is not unlikely, though, that by pointing out someone else's guilt they may also hope to alleviate their own pangs of conscience when they ask themselves whether they failed their son at some point in his development.
5. – –
6. [Students will most probably differentiate between legal and moral responsibility. The words of Attorney Thomas Anderson (cf. ll. 33–45) show that he holds the record company responsible. As for the parents, attention has to be drawn to the fact that they apparently did not react to their son's unusual behaviour, and, what might be of legal relevance, the father did not keep his pistol safely locked away from his son.]
7. *In the case of John McCollum it is by no means clear whether – and, if so, to what extent – the text of the rock song pushed him into committing suicide. Do you know of any works of art or events that have actually influenced people in a fatal way? Give reasons for your answer.*
    [The best-known example may be Goethe's *Die Leiden des jungen Werther*. A rash of suicides, which often occurs after the death of a famous person, particularly if that person committed suicide, is known in psychology as the "Werther effect".]

13 Arthur Koestler: Who Can Tell the Difference?

Didaktische Hinweise

Mit Text 13 wird, dieses Kapitel abschließend, ein weiterer Teilaspekt des Themas „Kunstrezeption" angesprochen und damit der Problemkreis abgerundet. Arthur Koestler geht es um die grundsätzliche Frage menschlichen Verhaltens gegenüber dem Original bzw. der Reproduktion. Berichte über die in jüngster Zeit aufgedeckten Fälschungen großer Werke der Malerei und die damit im Zusammenhang stehende Frage nach dem materiellen Wert eines Kunstwerks können zur Vertiefung der angesprochenen Thematik herangezogen werden. Der Einstieg in die Textbehandlung über den Cartoon (SB, S. 289) bietet sich an.

Background information

Arthur Koestler (1905–1983) was born in Budapest, Hungary. In 1940, after studying at the University of Vienna and travelling through much of Europe, he settled in England. His writings reveal a wide range of interests, including politics (he was at one time a Communist), science and parapsychology. He committed suicide, together with his wife, having frequently expressed his belief in the right to euthanasia. Among his publications are *Darkness at Noon* (1940), *The Trail of the Dinosaur and Other Essays* (1955) and *The Act of Creation* (1964).

Semantic and collocational field "Original and reproduction"

a line drawing, (to) bear a serial number ✧ an aesthetic equivalence between an original and a reproduction, a second-rate original, as first-rate reproduction, the aesthetic effect of a copy/an original, (to) be indistinguishable from the original, (to) look like a lithograph, (to) take sth. to be a reproduction, (to) turn out to be an original, (to) be guided by aesthetic considerations ✧ a contempt for reproduction, poor quality ✧ modern printing techniques, an age of stereotyped mass production

Talking about the text – Suggested answers

1. Manuscripts of books are usually only of interest to collectors, biographers and editors; for the general public the essence of literature, i.e. the words, is not affected by its being printed and published in either a leather-bound hard-cover edition or a cheap paperback edition. Music, for most people, comes to life when it is performed. Records offer the opportunity of listening to different interpretations. The music itself does not fundamentally change when it is reproduced, although the surroundings may change the experience of listening to it.
    With the exception of – perhaps – the line drawing, an original painting is, in the true sense of the word, substantially different from its reproduction. Even the best reproduction cannot reproduce perfectly the original quality of the colours and the stroke of the brush on paper, cardboard or canvas.
2. From what the text tells us, Brenda does not appreciate the quality of the drawing as long as she believes it to be a reproduction (cf. l. 7). Her praise of the drawing as a whole and of some of its details, once she has learned that it is an original, sounds insincere (cf. ll. 9–11). It seems to be nothing but the money paid for the original that makes the difference for her.
3. – –
4. – –
5. *What functions may excellent reproductions of masterpieces have?*
    They can introduce people (regardless of their financial status) to great art, and, without being fully equivalent to the originals, develop and keep up people's awareness of what has been achieved. With regard to the original works, they can either prepare us for them, or they can remind us of them.
6. *What would be your answer to the writer's last sentence but one (cf. ll. 33–35)?*
    – –
7. *What would be your reasons for choosing a particular picture for your room?*
    – –
8. *Visits to art museums may have confronted you with the originals of works of art you had been introduced to in your schoolbooks. Try and verbalize your reaction to one particular original.*
    – –

Chapter XII: War and Peace

Das letzte Kapitel lenkt den Blick zunächst auf wissenschaftlich-technische Entwicklungen, die neben der Bewunderung für die Forscherleistung und den zivilisatorischen Fortschritt zunehmend den Ruf nach Kontrolle, Sicherheitsrichtlinien und nationaler wie internationaler Gesetzgebung ausgelöst haben. Es beginnt mit einer Textgruppe, die Einblicke in die Möglichkeiten und Gefahren der Gentechnologie eröffnet, die mit ihrem Griff in den Zellkern den Urbaustein irdischen Lebens zu analysieren und zu manipulieren begonnen hat (Text 1 und 2). Ihr folgt eine Textgruppe über jenen anderen technischen Durchbruch, den die Nukleartechnologie mit ihrem Griff in den Atomkern, den Urbaustein der Natur, nur wenige Jahrzehnte zuvor erzielte (Text 3, 6, 7 und 8). Ähnlich wie die Zündung der ersten Atombombe im Jahre 1945 als Einstieg in das atomare Zeitalter begriffen wurde, gilt die Entdeckung der Trägersubstanz des Erbguts (DNS) im Jahre 1951 durch J.D. Watson und F.H. Crick als Eintritt in das biotechnische Zeitalter.

Die Texte veranschaulichen darüber hinaus exemplarisch, wie die Probleme, die sich auf Grund technologischer Entwicklungen weltweit ergeben haben, eindringlicher als je zuvor in der Menschheitsgeschichte auf ambivalente Antriebskräfte im Menschen selbst zurückweisen. Gefragt wird heute nachdrücklicher als früher nach der Verantwortung des Wissenschaftlers, nach seiner Einstellung zu drängenden ethischen Fragen (vgl. S. Papcke: „Wissenschaft und Ethik – ein Dilemma". In: A.-A. Guha und S. Papcke [Hrsg.]: *Entfesselte Forschung: Die Folgen einer Wissenschaft ohne Ethik.* Frankfurt, Fischer 1988, S. 23).

Abgerundet und zugleich auf eine allgemeinere Ebene gehoben werden diese beiden Themenkomplexe durch Texte, die sich den grundsätzlichen Fragen des menschlichen Miteinander in einer kleiner gewordenen Welt zuwenden (Text 4, 5, 9 bis 12). Viele der in den vorausgehenden Kapiteln angesprochenen Einzelaspekte können hier wieder aufgegriffen und in einen größeren Zusammenhang integriert werden.

1 Aldous Huxley: Bokanovsky's Process

Didaktische Hinweise

Dieser Auszug aus Huxleys utopischem Roman bietet einen motivierenden Einstieg in das Thema „Gentechnologie". Die fiktionale Antizipation gezielter Manipulationen der Erbsubstanz (vgl. insbesondere das Verfahren der „Bokanovskyfizierung") kann den Schülern/ Schülerinnen erste Vorstellungen von den gentechnischen Möglichkeiten vermitteln. Hierzu zählt, daß heute mittels DNS-Rekombination *(DNA recombination),* auch als Verschweißen von Genen *(cloning)* bekannt geworden, neue Organismen produziert werden können. Huxleys Biotechniker arbeiten für den Fortbestand eines entindividualisierten, emotionsfreien und daher aggressionslosen Weltstaats. Aus dieser Perspektive bieten sich Vergleiche mit R. Bradburys Projektionen einer „glücklichen Welt" (Kap. VIII, Text 4) an. Auch eine Fortführung der Diskussion anhand der Texte 9 bis 12 ist möglich, in denen andere Wege zur Erreichung dieses Ziels gewiesen werden.

Brave New World (1932), von vielen Lehrplänen zur Lektüre empfohlen, ist in zahlreichen Paperback-Ausgaben erhältlich. Huxleys kontrovers diskutierte "novel of ideas" hat unterschiedliche Interpretationen erfahren, von denen hier zwei genannt seien: A.R. Wells: "Aldous Huxley: Brave New World". In: J.V. Hagopian und M. Dolch: *Insight II. Analyses of Modern British Literature.* (Frankfurt, Cornelsen Verlag Hirschgraben ⁵1979, S. 175 ff. Best.-Nr. 127106); C. Bode: *Aldous Huxley: 'Brave New World'.* (München, W. Fink 1985 [UTB 1312]), mit kommentierter Bibliographie. Weitere Literaturhinweise zur Gattung „Utopie" finden sich im LB, S. 62.

Background information

Aldous Huxley (1894–1963) was born in Surrey, England. He was educated at Eton and Oxford. He then started to write verse and short stories, but made his name as a satirical novelist. His first novel, *Crome Yellow*, appeared in 1921. From the 1920s onwards, he lived successively in Italy, France, where he wrote *Brave New World* (1932), and the USA, where he settled in 1937. In 1958 Huxley brought out *Brave New World Revisited*, a collection of essays, in which he reexamined the prophecies he had made in his 1932 novel.

Brave New World: Set in the 26th century, Huxley's novel (whose title is an ironical allusion to a line from Shakespeare's *The Tempest* V,i,183) intends to demonstrate how social stability, world peace and personal happiness could be brought about through the systematic use of, among other means, bio-engineering. This seemingly ideal utopian state is made to rest on the nearly perfect control that the government exercises through the genetic standardization of human beings. In *Brave New World Revisited*, Huxley characterizes the products of the Bokanovsky Process: "The creatures finally decanted were almost subhuman; but they were capable of performing unskilled work and, when properly conditioned ..., could be counted on to give no trouble to their superiors" (Harper & Row, New York, 1958, p. 15).

Genetic research has in the last couple of decades turned into a profitable multi-million-dollar industry, with the number of bio-engineering firms in the United States increasing rapidly every year. In the 1970s such firms were rare, but by 1985 the number had risen to about 350 (cf. J. Wille: „Wissenschaft im Gen-Rausch". In: A.-A. Guha und S. Papcke: *Entfesselte Forschung: Die Folgen einer Wissenschaft ohne Ethik.* Fischer, Frankfurt, 1988, pp. 122 f.). It is estimated that the universities of Stanford and of California at San Francisco will earn $ 1 billion from only two of the patents they hold in gene-technology. For information concerning the patenting of animals, cf. p. 250 of this book.

Semantic and collocational field "Genetic engineering"

the fertilizing process, a fertilized ovum, a supply of ova, a ripened egg, the technique for preserving the excised ovary alive, (to) undergo a process, an egg remains unfertilized ◇ an incubator, a receptacle, optimum temperature, racks upon racks of test-tubes, the warmed slide of a microscope, (to) be immersed in sth., (to) be kept in a liquor, (to) keep sth. at blood heat ◇ (to) proliferate, (to) bud, (to) divide, (to) grow into a perfectly formed embryo, (to) be inspected for abnormalities, (to) check the normal growth rate ◇ (to) sterilize, (to) draw off liquor from a test-tube

Talking about the text – Suggested answers

1. They are introduced to "the modern fertilizing process" (l. 9), i.e. the mass production both of different types of human beings (from "Alphas" to "Epsilons", cf. ll. 24–25) and different numbers of embryos (up to "ninety-six human beings", ll. 31–32). Scientists have achieved the feat of genetic engineering through different processes of artificial insemination.

2. The Director addresses the students in a slightly condescending manner (cf. his opening words). He speaks as an expert who is in full command of his special field of knowledge, but willing to adapt to the students' level of understanding. However, his free use of the technical terms for talking about the process of fertilization (e.g. "incubators", "ova", "male gametes", etc.) presupposes at least a certain level of theoretical knowledge on the part of his listeners. Apparently, what they have come to see is the practical side of the process (cf. his opening of "an insulated door" at the beginning [l. 3], or later, when he leads "his charges to the work tables" and "actually show[s] them how this liquor [is] drawn off from the test-tubes" [ll. 15–16]).

3. The students react as awe-stricken, uncritical disciples of the technological advances they are witnessing (cf. "the more zealous students recorded his intention in their note-books", ll. 1–2; and "the students underlined the words in their little note-books", ll. 27–28).

4. The over-awed, but basically stupid reaction of the students (cf. their noting down the Director's opening platitude, their illegible handwriting) may influence the reader to adopt a much more critical attitude to the Director and the scientific feat he describes and praises than the students show. Not wanting to identify with the students, the reader is likely to begin to ask questions about the possible aims and effects of so-called "progress" (l. 32) in manipulating the human fertilizing process ; especially, whether all this is really, as the Director claims, "for the good of Society" (ll. 10–11). Thus the narrator moves the reader towards a more questioning attitude about what scientists and research institutes do in the name of scientific progress.

5. [He shows rather than tells the reader what students may consider characteristic of this area of research: first, the enormous possibilities of future developments; second, the scientist's complete disregard for the ethical and legal considerations involved in what he does. What blinds scientists, as Huxley shows in the fictional character of the Director, is a naive pride in what human ingenuity can achieve.]

6. These expressions are introduced as the climax of the Director's lecture and demonstration. The fictional term refers both to an outstanding discovery and to the scientist who made it. To the Director's visitors, this example is apparently intended to suggest that scientific research of the highest order may not only reward the scientist with a further insight into the workings of nature, but also, by permanently linking his name with this discovery, make him famous. To Huxley's readers, it may be intended to suggest that rewards such as this are at the root of a scientist's ambitions.

7. *What special dangers could you see in this kind of hatchery? Consider, for instance, the differences between Alphas, Betas, Gammas, Deltas and Epsilons (cf. Annotations).*
– –

8. *What may the changes in the Director's manner of presentation be intended to suggest to his listeners? Consider ll. 8–15 in comparison with ll. 15–26.*
In the two passages, the Director changes from what he *tells* the students over to what he mainly *shows* them, accompanied by a few words of explanation. This change suggests that, despite the immense complexity of the processes involved, complete mastery of the production of different kinds of normed human beings has been achieved, both theoretically and practically.

9. ***What signals does the narrator use in ll. 8–26 to suggest to the reader that he is closely following the Director's words and actions, without quoting every word?***
In the first part, the narrator regularly uses signals to show that he is summarizing the speaker's words, e.g. "spoke first, of course, of" (ll. 9–10), "continued with" (l. 11), "passed on to" (l. 13), "referred to" (l. 14). Thus the narrator indicates that he is following a chronological order (as characteristically used in narrative texts). He announces the major subdivisions of the Director's lecture. These subdivisions in turn correspond to and mark major stages in "the modern fertilizing process" (l. 9). In other words, the narrator reports in summary form what the Director said in his lecture.
In the second part, on the other hand, the main signals in the text all point to his explaining and, simultaneously, demonstrating things: "and ... showed them how this liquor" (l. 15), "how it was let out" (l. 16), "how the eggs" (l. 17), "how ... this receptacle" (ll. 18–19) "and how ... the container" (l. 21), "how ... it was" (ll. 22–23), "how the fertilized ova" (l. 23). Here the narrator follows the analytical order of expository texts, supporting it with a simple listing order introduced by anaphorical repetition of "how".

10. ***How does the narrator announce and mark the conclusion of the Director's lecture?***
He uses three devices both to announce the conclusion of the lecture and to mark it as a climax: a terminating signal for the conclusion to his summary of the Director's lecture and demonstration ("the D.H.C. concluded", l. 33); a summary expression to announce the conclusion to the Director's talk ("Essentially, ...", l. 33); and representation of the Director's words in direct speech, allowing him, as a climax to his talk and demonstration, to sum up for himself what "bokanovskification" is basically about.

2 Spencer Reiss et al.: High-Tech Babies

Didaktische Hinweise

Es bietet sich an, Text 2 mit seinem expliziten Bezug auf Huxleys Vision genormter Menschenproduktion (vgl. Z. 33 f., 95 f.) im Zusammenhang mit Text 1 zu diskutieren. Die Autoren zeigen, wie nahe heute bereits die Verwirklichung der von Huxley weit in die Zukunft projizierten Möglichkeiten steuernder Eingriffe in die menschliche Keimzelle gerückt ist. Dieser Sachtext, 1985 in *Newsweek* erschienen, kann zugleich dazu dienen, nach ersten Antworten auf die Frage nach einer nationalen wie internationalen Kontrolle gentechnischer Forschung zu suchen (vgl. auch A. Toffler: *Future Shock*. London, Pan Books 1971, S. 285 f.).

Background information

"with the techniques available today" (ll. 35–36): In April 1988, the US Patent and Trademark Office for the first time allowed the patenting of animals produced by bio-technical procedures: "Although humans were to be excluded as candidates for patent review, the Patent Office would consider all other animals – both new forms created in the laboratory and existing species that had been given new genetic traits" (*Encyclopaedia Britannica: 1988 Book of the Year*. Encyclopaedia Britannica, Chicago, p. 238).

Semantic and collocational field "Ethics and procreation"

the basic question of what constitutes life/of when life begins, the making of life, the (longstanding) debate over abortion/contraception, (to) be confronted by (pressing) medical/legal/ethical questions ◊ traditional law, conventional morality, the stricture against sex without procreation/procreation without sex, (to) oppose sth. across the board, (to) be viewed as ethically dubious, (to) regulate the new techniques ✧ artificial/alternative birth, a right to reproduce, (to) have obligations/rights to the eventual offspring ✧ a frozen embryo, (to) implant a living embryo in a womb, (to) donate/supply sperm and eggs ✧ a test-tube baby, in vitro conception, (to) mix sperm in a petri dish, (to) create a baby artificially, (to) be conceived in a petri dish, (to) owe one's existence to artificial insemination ✧ genetic manipulation, (to) be born deformed/retarded, (to) eliminate inherited diseases

Talking about the text – Suggested answers

1. The writers use Huxley's novel (here assumed to be known to the general British and American reader) as a backdrop, and a model of comparison, in order to assess the range of "powers over procreation" (ll. 24–25) that "doctors and clinical researchers" are acquiring today with alarming "speed" (cf. ll. 21–23). Using some of the concepts from Huxley's novel, the writers perceive "the dawning of an ominously engineered human future" (ll. 31–33). They view the present state of research as science's "brave new world", in the sense that this area of research is dangerously devoid of new legal and ethical guidelines (cf. ll. 50–51). They speak of "the use of high-tech baby-making" (l. 81) and "test-tube babies" (ll. 40–41), and they measure this development against "the infant assembly-line vision of *Brave New World*" (ll. 95–96).

2. Revolutionary aspects about "the techniques available today" (ll. 35–36) are the worldwide "routine" use (l. 47) of "artificial insemination" (l. 43), or, as they later put it, "procreation without sex" (l. 84); "the first hints of genetic manipulation" (ll. 37–38).

3. According to the writers, "the revolution that is now under way in the making of human life" (ll. 20–21) raises "pressing medical, legal and ethical questions" (ll. 50–51). In other words, the decision-making institutions in society – i.e. governments, law courts, the Church – are called upon to act.

4. – –

5. Throughout the article the writers have been concerned with "contemporary reproductive science" (l. 94). They write of progress coming along "with a speed that amazes some observers and alarms others" (ll. 21–23). The in vitro conception of "Louise Brown", an event that stunned the world a mere seven years before this article was written (cf. l. 27), already "looks positively quaint" (ll. 39–40). Considering this rapid progress readers may assume that scientists could very quickly reach the point described in Huxley's novel. The writers support this uneasiness by adding that "the foundations for something perhaps uncomfortably like [the infant assembly-line vision of Huxley's novel] are already clearly in place" (ll. 96–98).

6. – –

7. *Judging from what you read or hear in the media, can you see any signs that the "fundamental decisions" (l. 99) as to how to control this particular area of research are being made? Explain your view.*
   – –

8. *What difference does it make to current thinking and discussion that we are familiar with the concepts of "Brave New World"?*
   Present-day perception of what is happening in the field of reproductive science might indeed lack some important concepts if Huxley's novel had not been written. One can easily imagine that scientists, ethicists and even journalists might well see genetic research in a far more positive light if it were not for the warning contained in this fictional text of 1932. It was, in its way, even more revolutionary than the actual scientific developments of our time. Huxley pushed his readers' door of perception open even wider than science is doing now, and so he was able to influence future thinking and offer standards by which to evaluate developments in genetic science.

3 Varindra Tarzie Vittachi: The Sorcerer's Apprentice

Didaktische Hinweise

Text 3 spezifiziert die Frage nach der Verantwortung des Wissenschaftlers im Bereich der Nukleartechnologie. Der Eintritt in das atomare Zeitalter, so lautet Vittachis These, mache deutlich, daß naturwissenschaftliche Methoden der Menschheit keineswegs den Schlüssel zur vollständigen Beherrschung oder folgenlosen Manipulation der Natur liefern. In ihrer Auseinandersetzung mit dem Text sollen die Schüler/innen erkennen, daß jeder neue Triumph der Technik auch Komplikationen nach sich zieht, die sich in der Gegenwart zunehmend als lebens- und menschheitsbedrohend erweisen. Diese Erkenntnis sollte zu der Einsicht führen, daß das Postulat des wertfreien Forschens, das aus der Befreiung von kirchlicher Bevormundung und Zensur herrührt, nach dem Abwurf der Atombombe auf Hiroshima neu überdacht werden muß.

Eine fiktionale Auseinandersetzung mit diesem Thema findet sich in dem Drama von Howard Brenton: *The Genius* (1983), das als Klassenlektüre besonders geeignet ist (Frankfurt, Cornelsen Verlag Hirschgraben 1988. TAGS. SB Best.-Nr. 667305, LH 667365).

Background information

"But the value questions cannot be so peremptorily dismissed" (ll. 67–68): For a critical exposition of how mankind has lived with nuclear weapons in its midst since 1945, cf. J. Schell: *The Fate of the Earth.* Pan Books, London, 1982.

Semantic and collocational field "Science and responsibility"

a triumph of technology, a victory for science, (to) restrain progress ◇ (to) understand the value/purpose of sth., (to) answer for one's deeds, (to) disdain responsibility for how sth. (e.g. a technological artifact) is used ◇ (to) take moral considerations into account, (to) seek a new morality ◇ a universal sense of awe, a potential for deadly mischief, (to) be (deeply) disturbed by sth., (to) feel qualms about sth., (to) have the edge on destructiveness, (to) threaten to destroy life itself, (to) let the genie out of the bottle

Talking about the text – Suggested answers

1. The writer's illustrations are a) "the story of the Sorcerer's Apprentice" (ll. 1–7), b) H.G. Wells's "mordant comment" (l. 8) on "those rudimentary but marvelous airplanes" used in World War I (ll. 7–16), and c) the reactions to the dropping of "the first atom bomb" on Hiroshima (ll. 19–38).
    Each example shows the same serious deficiency in the human makeup, i.e. the naivety of human beings in extolling their technical constructions as "triumphs" or "victories" of technology (cf. ll. 23 and 24), and their failure to control their technical achievements so that they will not turn against humanity. In the writer's words: "When man's wisdom is overtaken by the cleverness of the tools he makes, he is in trouble" (ll. 17–19). The Sorcerer's Apprentice released an unstoppable flood of water, having used his master's magic formula "without understanding its value or purpose" (ll. 4–5). Wells's comment reveals that a "marvelous" invention, such as an "airplane" (l. 13), always tends to come under the control of people's animal instincts. They tend to use it for "deadly mischief" (l. 45), in the case of the airplane, "to drop poison gas on cities" (l. 14). And even the mixed reactions to the catastrophic effect of the first atom bomb show that the potential of

nuclear technology for "deadly mischief was given more attention" (ll. 45–46) than the
" 'peaceful' use of the atom" (ll. 42–43).

2. The differences between the three examples are above all those of an immense increase
in complexity and dangerousness as modern times are reached. While the fictional
Sorcerer's Apprentice here represents an early stage of technological inventiveness, the
airplane of World War I and the atom bomb of World War II show stages of the
increased pace of technological development in the twentieth century. Since Hiroshima
and the enhanced sophistication of later nuclear technology, the destructive potential of
nuclear weaponry has now become global.

On the other hand, people's powers of controlling their "technological artifacts" (l. 62)
have remained as deficient as at the beginning (cf. the writer's reference to Edward
Teller's lack of qualms about making "better and smaller bombs" despite his experience
of Hiroshima, ll. 32–38).

3. After the three illustrations, the writer continues by drawing his major conclusion. After
Hiroshima "science can no longer be value-free" (ll. 58–59); "its devotees and prac-
titioners can no longer disdain responsibility for how their technological artifacts are used"
(ll. 60–62). In their striving after ever more technological perfection in "unbottling" the
forces of nature, scientists are compelled to take one further dimension into account,
"moral considerations" (ll. 55–56), i.e. "the traditional questions 'Is it good or bad?' and 'Is
it right or wrong?' " (ll. 64–66).

4. The writer rejects the modern counter-argument that "progress could and should not be
restrained" (ll. 40–41) by pointing to the "catastrophic possibilities" (l. 53) that scientists
should have been able to recognize after Hiroshima. They can no longer be justified in
pursuing the goal of truth for truth's sake while placing responsibility for the use of their
"artifacts" on politicians. Their feeling sorry after producing their technological constructs,
as did Einstein, Oppenheimer and others, will no longer be acceptable. They will have to
control their own efforts in their laboratories – for the common good of humanity.

5. Obstacles to fundamental changes of attitude are the insatiable human drive towards
technological perfection (" 'Will it work?' ", l. 63), coupled with ever renewed greed (" 'Is it
profitable?' ", ll. 63–64). The first drive shows the human being as the distinctive tool-
making animal that cannot desist from tinkering with materials and the forces of nature.
The second drive shows that self-interest still tends to dominate people's feelings for "life-
enhancing values such as tolerance and cooperation" (ll. 81–82). In terms of an individual
scientist (such as Edward Teller), the personal ambition to succeed, to hold a well-paid job
and live a lavish life is apparently stronger than his or her impulse to say no to a dubious
scientific project, such as offered by the defence departments of governments.

6. In the writer's view, the chance for a return to "the value questions" (l. 67) lies with the
"millions of young people [who] are seeking a new morality" (ll. 77–78). Movements in
almost every country of the world, such as those linked with environmentalists and anti-
nuclear groups, may be mentioned to illustrate the writer's view. What they and others
may discover as sharing are "life-enhancing values such as tolerance and cooperation"
(ll. 81–82), combined perhaps with the desire to develop "the planet's resources to
alleviate unnecessary suffering and fulfill unmet human needs" (ll. 47–49).

7. *In contrast to the "hard-nosed questions" (ll. 62-63) of today's scientists, the
writer quotes "the traditional questions 'Is it good or bad?' and 'Is it right or
wrong?' " (ll. 64–66). How would you explain and view the writer's favourable
attitude to these questions?*

– –

8. *In ll. 18–19, the writer speaks of "the cleverness of the tools" that human beings
make, and in ll. 30–31 of "the genie [that] had been let out of the bottle". How*

does such language use tend to influence people's thinking about science and technology?

Use of language such as that quoted here personifies processes (e.g. the explosion of the atom bomb) and objects (e.g. an airplane). It suggests that these assume a life, will and ungovernable purpose of their own. Language use like this tends to delude people about what happens and why it happens since it does not name the master-mind behind the processes and technological "artifacts". The Enola Gay had a pilot who released the atom bomb it carried; the bomb had a limited number of individual scientists behind it, who had worked for years in the seclusion of the New Mexican desert to develop and test its destructive powers (among them Robert Oppenheimer and Edward Teller); and this team of scientists had a theoretical formula to work with and plenty of political supporters (most prominently, Albert Einstein and political figures such as Franklin Delano Roosevelt and Winston Churchill).

4 John Scott of Amwell: The Drum

Didaktische Hinweise

Ging es in Text 3 um die Verantwortung des Wissenschaftlers, insbesondere im Bereich der Kernforschung, so rückt mit den Texten 4 bis 7 das Teilthema „Krieg" in den Mittelpunkt, hier unter allgemeinem (und historischem) Aspekt, in den Folgetexten mit der spezifischen Fragestellung nach dem Selbstverständnis einer Wissenschaft, die sich vor allem in Kriegszeiten in der Gefahr befindet, im Dienste nationalstaatlicher Interessen eine verantwortungslose „Auftragsforschung" zu betreiben. Im Interpretationsgespräch über diese Textgruppe können Problembereiche wie die folgenden angesprochen werden: die verführerische Faszination, die von militärischer Macht und den jeweils neuesten Waffensystemen ausgeht (vgl. Text 4, 5 und 6); die verheerenden Folgen, die moderne Waffen für zunehmend größere Teile der Erdbevölkerung zeitigen (Text 5, 6 und 7); die Käuflichkeit wissenschaftlicher Erkenntnisse (Text 5 und 6) sowie die Gefahren, die sich daraus ergeben, daß Politiker auch im Zeitalter der Kernspaltung noch in den Kategorien nationalstaatlicher Grenzen denken (Text 7).

Text 4 eröffnet diese Textgruppe mit der Fragestellung, wie es in der Geschichte immer wieder zu der verhängnisvollen Verknüpfung von Ehrgeiz, Ruhm- und Gewinnsucht, Täuschung durch Ideologien und ein noch unausgebildetes Verantwortungsbewußtsein kommen konnte. Auch in den folgenden Texten werden einzelne dieser Aspekte immer wieder angesprochen, in Text 8 dann unter besonderer Akzentuierung dieser Gefahren auch bei friedlicher Nutzung der Kernenergie.

Background information

John Scott of Amwell (1730–1783) was born in Bermondsey, South London, the youngest son of a Quaker linendraper. In 1740 his family moved to Amwell, Hertfordshire. He had his first poems published in the "Gentleman's Magazine" between 1753 and 1758. His *Poetical Works* were first published in London in 1782, while his *Critical Essays* were published after his death.

"And when Ambition's voice commands, | To march, and fight, and fall, in foreign lands" (ll. 7–8): This sentence alludes to a common 18th century practice among

European monarchs to sell armies of mercenaries abroad (cf., e.g., Friedrich Schiller: *Kabale und Liebe* II,ii). Significantly, it is to the sounding of drums that the young men are marched away, and it is the sounding of drums that drowns out the cries of those they are torn away from.

Talking about the text – Suggested answers

1. The main connection that the speaker establishes between the two six-line groups in stanzas I and II is one of contrast. While the first stanza shows how "thoughtless youth" (l. 3) reacts to and becomes enticed by "the drum's discordant sound" (l. 1), the second shows the dreadful pictures of destruction and human misery the speaker has come to associate with it ("To *me* it talks of …", l. 11; "groans", l. 13; "moans", l. 14; "Misery's hand", l. 15; "human woes", l. 16). He speaks as an old and experienced person who has seen it all, again and again, in the course of his life. The drum's call has always called young men first to service, then to battle, death and destruction.

    A second, less obvious connection between the two stanzas is one of causes and effects. It is the young men's gullibility (cf. "*thoughtless* youth", l. 3) that becomes the cause of the destruction, of death and suffering which the old person has witnessed and recalls in stanza II on hearing "that drum's discordant sound". In other words, young people do not think of what the older person has come to know and see clearly.

2. In the speaker's view, young people characteristically fall for the promise of "pleasure" (l. 3) in various guises. Young people do not think ahead, and they forget to think of the duties that they are taking on. They are offered various "charms" and "tawdry lace" (ll. 5–6), such as a well-tailored uniform, glittering symbols of rank or special decorations; are given "glittering arms", always the latest and the most efficient products that the arms manufacturers have on offer (cf. l. 6). And young people, the speaker suggests, do not recognize that, in following "that drum's […] sound", they actually sell "their liberty" (l. 5), their freedom to decide about the use of their lives, and subject themselves to the commands of "Ambition's voice" (l. 7), i.e. of those few persons who pursue their own selfish goals of power and personal aggrandisement at the young people's expense. They think neither of their own seemingly distant tomorrow, i.e. their risking an untimely and ignominious death in some "foreign land" (l. 8) nor of the destruction and suffering they cause in civilized society around them, to individuals, couples and families (cf. ll. 11–16).

3. The speaker's reflections are apparently stirred when he perceives "that drum's discordant sound / Parading round, and round, and round". The speaker views the drum in two of its former uses as a means of communication: first, of rallying young people to the flag everywhere in the country (it "lures from cities and from fields", l. 4); second, of leading soldiers into battle on the battlefield and passing orders to them by different kinds of beat, "To march, and fight, and fall" (l. 8).

4. The "drum's … sound"/"parading round, and round, and round", "lur[ing]" and "charm[ing]", points to roles commonly associated with magic and seduction, beguiling and deceiving such as the legendary Pied Piper or an impersonation of Death. Such an evil-meaning person can lure and charm ever larger throngs of followers behind him as he passes through cities and countries, only finally and inevitably making them all fall in with the rigid pace of a dance of death.

5. By repeating the two opening lines in stanza II, the speaker appears to indicate that the drum's sound continues to be heard all the while he is speaking. Its sound is all-pervasive. The old speaker heard it when he was young, and he has heard it ever since, always sounding its unchanging beat to the march into action and inevitable death. Viewed against the background of a person's life span, the speaker's choice of the expression "parading" also assumes the meaning of the drummer strutting proudly round and round on the stage of the world, dominating people's lives from beginning to end. He starts a new show and cycle with each generation of "thoughtless youth" responding to his lure.

6. *How is the meaning of "round, and round, and round" reflected in the six-line units that follow this line in each stanza?*

   In the first stanza, the meaning of "round, and round, and round" is embodied in the life cycle leading from pleasure-seeking youth to ignominious death in "foreign lands" (l. 8). The drum's sound smoothly leads (cf. the spaced repetition of "and" as a sign of easy transition in ll. 4 and 7) from the pleasurable stage to the dreaded one. The cycle is inevitably terminated (cf. the quickening repetition of "and" in l. 8) by the individual's fall. In the second stanza, the drum's cyclical movement is reflected in how the old person scans ever narrower circles of the world around him. He starts with the widest circle of human vision ("plains", l. 11), then narrows it to "towns" (l. 12), and finally, to individual members of the family, to the young men ("swains", l. 12) and the mothers ("widows") and their children ("orphans", l. 14).

   In each circle, the speaker perceives the same effects of the drum's rallying sound to war and destruction (cf. "ravag'd", "burning", "ruin'd", "mangled", "dying", "tears" and "moans", ll. 11–14). His long series of "and"-expansions (added seven times) emphasizes how the destructive effects build up, one by one, to a mountain of "woes" (l. 16) at the end.

7. *How is similar formal symbolism used to reflect the meaning of "discordant" in the poem as a whole?*

   The meaning of the word "discordant" is reflected in the formal shape the speaker gives his text. The basic discord is that established between the two stanzas, i.e. between "thoughtless youth" in search of "pleasure" (l. 3) and an old person's knowledge that this will become the principal source of "human woes" (l. 16). The discord is further emphasized within each eight-line stanza by the discrepancy between the drum's unchanging "parading" round (in the opening two-line units) and the multiplicity ("catalogue", l. 16) of destructive changes it produces in the world.

8. *In sum, what aspect of human life and war does the poem elucidate?*

   All in all, the poem embodies an older person's lament over young people, generation after generation, falling prey to the lures of passing benefits, honours and "glittering arms" (l. 6). By remaining shortsighted, the speaker is saying, young people of every generation and country give the decisive support to the few power-hungry leaders in the world who, at any given moment, may command them "To march, and fight, and fall, in foreign lands" (l. 8).

9. *Would you say that the speaker's view of young people still applies? Explain your view.*

   – –

5 Ambrose Bierce: The Ingenious Patriot

Didaktische Hinweise

Am Beispiel dieser Parabel lassen sich Zusammenhänge aufzeigen zwischen technischem Erfindungsgeist, selbstsüchtigem Profitdenken einzelner Forscher, Erpressbarkeit der Mächtigen und den finanziellen Folgen eines skrupellosen Wettrüstens für die Gemeinschaft (vgl. Aufg. 3). Auch die im Zusammenhang mit Text 3 aufgeworfenen Fragen (vgl. LB, S. 252) können hier wieder aufgenommen werden. Sind die Schüler/innen an einer weiteren Diskussion der angesprochenen Probleme und ihrer Lösungsmöglichkeiten interessiert, kann anschließend auch Text 12 besprochen werden.

Background information

Ambrose Bierce (1842–1914?) was born in a log cabin by Horse Cave Creek, Meigs County, Ohio. He received no general education. After serving with distinction in the Civil War, he moved to San Francisco, where he worked as a journalist. He lived for several years in England, contributed articles to various periodicals and published three collections of mordantly humorous sketches that established his reputation as "Bitter Bierce". In 1876, he returned to San Francisco and became a major literary columnist. In 1896, he was sent to Washington as a correspondent for William Randolph Hearst's newspaper *Examiner*. Between 1909 and 1912 he published the twelve volumes of his *Collected Works*, but they proved to be a financial failure. The collection *The Cynic's Word Book* (1906) retitled *The Devil's Dictionary* (1911) is a volume of highly amusing, ironic definitions. In 1913, he settled his affairs and disappeared into warring Mexico.

For information on the actual defence budgets of the superpowers, cf. the yearly figures for the American and the Soviet defence budgets in *Encyclopaedia Britannica: Book of the Year*. Encyclopaedia Britannica, Chicago.

Semantic and collocational field "Armaments"

a gun, a missile, a warship ✧ a formula for constructing sth., the working plans of sth. ✧ (to) pierce armour plating, (to) avert a missile, (to) be invincible/invulnerable ✧ (to) attest the value of an invention, (to) adopt/construct sth.

Talking about the text – Suggested answers

1. The author's references to the most effective and up-to-date armaments remind us of the continuing arms race in our own times. As each new weapon is bought to replace the earlier one in the story, it is made clear that the real-life superpowers' search for the ultimate defence weapon, i.e. one that will give one nation a permanent strategic advantage over its rival or rivals, is futile.

2. The millions of "tumtums" paid by the King for the Patriot's offers point to the exorbitant sums that governments have to pay for the development, purchase and maintenance of the most recent and up-to-the-minute strategic arms systems. Sums like this constitute a nation's so-called defence budget. In some countries, defence takes the largest chunk out of the nation's total budget. This is earned and amassed by each individual taxpayer. Funds thus appropriated to defence, the story suggests, are lost to other sectors, such as social welfare, education, the arts and leisure, or simply projects aimed at improving conditions of life for people (e.g. health). Moreover, and this is what the title of the finance minister in the story indicates (cf. l. 8), these funds have to be "extorted" from the people by an endless series of tax increases. Every wage earner in the country is held to ransom for his or her country's costly arms systems.

3. – –

4. [In the story, the King acts as a politician, i.e. as someone who tries to match the scientist's ingenuity. He quickly realizes that outstanding "ingenuity" in some patriots has to be treated just like any other human foible. That is to say, some human faculty will sometimes run amok and commit criminal acts against others. These are commonly treated as "capital offences". On the other hand, governments do need citizens who are devoted to their community's welfare, i.e. "patriots", but they can well do without the misdirected "ingenuity" with which some citizens try to outwit the power élite. This is why the King's decree aims only at constraining "ingenuity" in his subjects.]

5. – –

6. **What solution may the author possibly be suggesting for dealing with similar "ingenious patriots" in our own times?**

   [Among other things, the following solutions may be considered: Governments ought to control misdirected "ingenuity" all over the world by no longer rewarding scientists and researchers for their destructive efforts, i.e. in terms of salaries, promotion, titles and opportunities. Defence budgets should be converted to constructive uses in societies. Governments, heads of state and/or politicians should pursue a common policy in research. They should seek to establish global control of destructive "ingenuity" and its products.]

7. **Despite its serious theme, the story comes across as a fairly humorous tale. How does the author achieve this effect?**

   Several aspects help to create the humorous effect, e.g. his choice of funny names for things or people, which sound as if they were chosen for children as readers (e.g. "tumtums", "the Emperor of Bang", "the Great Head Factotum", ll. 6, 11, 21); his concealed irony in these and other choices so as to ridicule persons or things (e.g. "the Lord High Treasurer of the Extortion Department", l. 8, for the Chief Minister); his choice of a fairy-tale setting, in an unspecified world where Kings and Emperors hold sway as absolute rulers.

6 Robert Waithman: Force of Nature Harnessed

Didaktische Hinweise

Text 6 illustriert am konkreten Beispiel, was in den Texten 4 und 5 in fiktionalen Wirklichkeitsentwürfen als Menschheitsproblem bereits thematisiert wurde: nationalstaatlich orientiertes Freund-Feinddenken, das ein wissenschaftsgestütztes Wettrüsten rechtfertigen soll; die verbreitete Euphorie über einen weiteren Fortschritt in der scheinbaren Beherrschung von Naturkräften, die Forscher und Politiker die Unkontrollierbarkeit der Folgen insbesondere dort übersehen läßt, wo Wisssenschaftler die denkbar tiefsten Eingriffe in Elementarstrukturen der Natur vornehmen (etwa in der Genforschung und der Atomtechnologie). Den Schülern/Schülerinnen wird es aus der zeitlichen Distanz zu 1945 leicht fallen, die in der Schlagzeile verkündete Behauptung "Force of Nature Harnessed" in Frage zu stellen, unter anderem mit dem Hinweis darauf, daß die Gefährlichkeit radioaktiver Strahlung (vgl. Text 7 und 8) erst Jahre später voll erkannt wurde. Inzwischen ist die Kontrollierbarkeit von Radioaktivität, etwa von radioaktivem Müll, zum brennenden Gegenwartsproblem geworden.

Background information

For a balanced assessment of what happened in August 1945, students may be acquainted with the historical circumstances that led to the development of the first atomic bomb: "Atomic weapons were born from the fear that Hitler's Germany would dominate the world with a monopoly of atomic bombs. The initiative for their development came from Dr Leo Szilard, a Hungarian-born refugee from fascism, who obtained the support of Albert Einstein. Einstein, a German-born Jew and a life-long opponent of German militarism, was then living in self-imposed exile in the United States of America. On 2 August 1939 he wrote to the President, Franklin D. Roosevelt, warning of the danger that Germany might develop the bomb. ... The USA was not at that time at war and so Einstein's warning did not meet with an energetic response. ... In fact the decision to go ahead and build an A-bomb was taken on 6 December 1941 – the day before the Japanese attack on Pearl Harbor which brought America into the war.

In the next four years the scientists worked feverishly to develop atomic weapons in advance of Germany. ... But by November 1944 it was clear that Germany was not in fact making such a bomb. ... In the spring of 1945 Szilard and Einstein again wrote to Roosevelt, this time with a quite different purpose: to warn him of the dangers which would face the post-war world from the development of atomic energy" (J. Cox: *Overkill: The Story of Modern Weapons.* Penguin Books, Harmondsworth, 1981, pp. 15–16).

For a documentary of what happened at Hiroshima, cf. J. Hersey: *Hiroshima* (Penguin Books, Harmondsworth, 1966). The book was first published in the US weekly magazine *The New Yorker* in August 1946.

Semantic and collocational field "The atomic bomb"

a war-time scientific discovery, the scientific processes/mechanics of the operation of the atomic bomb, (to) carry out work on the atomic bomb ✧ the military deployment of an atomic bomb, (to) obliterate an entire island, (to) release atomic energy/a bomb, an atomic bomb falls/explodes on a city ✧ an improved bomb, (to) increase the effectiveness of the present atomic bomb, (to) pose a tremendous aid in shortening the war ✧ an army base, a target area, (to) be covered with an impenetrable cloud of smoke and dust

Talking about the text – Suggested answers

1. President Truman had authorized the dropping of the most destructive bomb ever built on a city of "385,000 inhabitants". In view of this fact the following aspects of his announcement may be considered unusual: his praise of the scientific victory over "the basic power of the universe", thus placing the successful detonation of the first atomic bomb in the context of God's original command to humanity, namely to subjugate the earth to the will of humankind; his emphasis on the need to protect the Allies (cf. "us") and "the rest of the world from the danger of sudden destruction".
    As reported by the "News Chronicle" correspondent, the president played down references to the destruction that the Allies themselves had intended and had successfully demonstrated on a Japanese city. His words sound as if he and his advisers had felt a need to conceal from the public the evil use to which politicians had put scientific research and ingenuity.

2. The journalist's language does not differ very much from the tone set by the politicians. The journalist, too, is awe-stricken before the power that scientists had been able to derive from the forces of nature (cf. "This is something so much bigger than any of the stories of war-time scientific discoveries"; "the greatest scientific gamble in history"; and also the last subheadline, "Allies beat Germans in battle of science").
    Like the politicians, the journalist plays down references to ethically dubious political decisions: the bomb simply "had fallen on a Japanese city"; Hiroshima is referred to as "a Japanese army base", which would have made it a military target that calls for attack and destruction in times of war; and he brushes aside what may be the first stirrings of bad conscience about the civilians killed and maimed by the bomb: "its implications, for both good and bad, are still hidden" (cf. also the British War Secretary's reassuring reference to having found the means "of releasing atomic energy 'not explosively but in regulated amounts' "; and the journalist's reference to "what happened to the army base at Hiroshima", adding the qualifying comment, "and perhaps to the nearby city and its 385,000 inhabitants").

However, there is some indication that the journalist had at least a hunch that not all was aboveboard with the decision to build and deploy the first atomic bomb. He significantly comments on the politicians' statements "that much more has still to be learned about the use of information that has been produced by the greatest scientific gamble in history".

3. Science is given quite a positive image in this article. The atomic bomb, the latest in a series of "war-time scientific discoveries", has decisively helped the Allies to win World War II. In fact, scientific discovery pursued in service of a just war against the German and Japanese aggressors has become synonymous for the journalist with engaging in a "battle" (cf. the subhead-line). In "harnessing" the nuclear forces of nature, "British and American scientists, working together", gave politicians the means to contain the outbreak of evil forces in some quarters of human society.

4. The statement was apparently intended to give the decisive justification for the Allies' use of the atomic bomb against a Japanese city. Many servicemen's lives in the Pacific war arena would be saved by the Allies forcing Japan to surrender before they might have done otherwise. Japan did in fact surrender after a second atomic bomb was dropped on Nagasaki, another large Japanese city, on August 9, 1945. The need for the Allies to use the atomic bomb against civilian targets at that late stage of World War II has often been doubted.

5. In World War II, most workers in plants and factories engaged in the production of the first nuclear device apparently did not know what they were actually producing. The project was top secret and the production of parts had been "scattered" over several places. And even if the workers had known what they were producing, they could not possibly have imagined the destructive potential of such a weapon. This is not the case today. One might say that human beings have lost their innocence since Hiroshima.

6. [With regard to Britain, for instance, the Official Secrets Act still prohibits all reporting on the details (e.g. names, places, kind) of research connected with the armed forces. Reporting from the Falklands War in 1982, for instance, was strictly limited to verbal reporting without photographs (cf. Ch. X, Text 8). All reports were sifted by censorship. As occasional revelations by investigative reporters show, all governments still try to keep their military research secret. They do so in the hopes of frustrating foreign spies, but also of preventing their own citizens from asking awkward questions.]

7. *The journalist of the "News Chronicle" reports that the "innocuous title" of "Manhattan Engineer District" (also referred to as the Manhattan Project) was chosen for work on the first atomic bomb. Can similar examples of verbal camouflage still be found in the scientific, technological or military areas of the peacetime world today? Give reasons for your answer.*
[Among other things, the students may reflect on camouflaging terms such as "the European theatre" or the various abbreviations (e.g. "ABC weapons") that often make it difficult to get at the actual meanings behind them.]

8. *The journalist of 1945 hints that the bomb on Hiroshima may have changed "the course of world history". Later, he also speaks of "the greatest scientific gamble in history". Speaking from the vantage point of today, would you support his view? Write a personal comment.*

– –

7 Nevil Shute: Deadly Winds

Didaktische Hinweise

Auf dem Hintergrund eines fortdauernden Wettrüstens auch im Atomzeitalter entwirft Nevil Shute in seinem Roman *On the Beach* (1957) eine Welt, in der das mögliche Ende dieses Zeitalters vorstellbar ist. Nach der Arbeit an dem vorausgehenden Sachtext kann hier an einem fiktionalen Text deutlich werden, wie die letztlich nicht voll beherrschbare Wirkung eines Eingriffs in den atomaren Baustein der Materie die Welt in den Untergang führt, wobei selbst jene Gebiete betroffen sind, die wie hier nicht für die kriegerische Auseinandersetzung in einem anderen Erdteil verantwortlich sind.

Nevil Shutes Roman ist in einer Paperback-Ausgabe erhältlich (Pan Books, London) und zur Verwendung als Ganzschrift durchaus geeignet.

Background information

Nevil Shute (Norway) (1889–1960) was born in Ealing, London, and published his novels under his Christian names. From an early age he demonstrated a keen interest in aircraft and flying, but failed, due to his stammer, to join the Royal Flying Corps. In 1919, he went up to Oxford to read engineering science. While working as an aeronautical engineer, he wrote novels and short stories. During World War II he was in the Royal Naval Volunteer Reserve, working on the development of secret weapons. In 1944 and 1945 he was a correspondent, taking part in the Normandy landings and then observing the war in Burma. After demobilization in 1945 he emigrated to Australia. Many of his novels, among them *A Town Like Alice* (1949), *On the Beach* (1957) and *Requiem for a Wren* (1960), became bestsellers and were made into films.

Semantic and collocational field "Radiation"

radiation sickness, the background level of radiation, a heavy/light particle, radioactive dust from the fall-out, (to) drop a hydrogen/cobalt bomb ✧ (to) be carried by diffusion, (to) be blown about/carried on the wind, the wind carries/picks up the radioactive dust

Talking about the text – Suggested answers

1. First of all, it is spreading "southwards" (l. 4) along the east coast of Australia. It has probably reached Townsville by now, which lies south of Cairns and will eventually get to the speakers' town still further south. Secondly, there is nothing anybody can do about it (cf. ll. 7 ff., 36–37).
2. Since the nuclear war was fought "nine or ten thousand miles away from us" (ll. 40–41), she would still like to believe what "people were saying once that no wind blows across the equator, so we'd be all right" (ll. 11–12). Moreover, she considers it "bloody unfair" (l. 41), since the southern hemisphere had no part in the war ("We had nothing to do with it", ll. 39–40).
3. The submarine commander speaks "quietly" (l. 13), without any show of emotion. He fully understands what is happening (cf. especially ll. 25–35). Miss Davidson, on the other hand, repeatedly rebels against acknowledging their fate as inevitable. She speaks "bitterly" (l. 21), "vehemently" (l. 38), and "angrily" (l. 43), as if the situation were a question of having the more persuasive arguments. She is still clutching at straws of hope for their survival.

4. An all-out nuclear war in one hemisphere has global consequences. If one nation or one part of humanity misbehaves, all life on the planet will eventually be threatened with extinction.

5. The commander uses a simple, but basically objective, explanation to help Moira Davidson understand why the northern winds with radioactive dust a) take so long (cf. ll. 25 ff.) to reach the southern hemisphere, b) will inevitably pick up the radioactive dust "and carry it down here" (l. 34). His choice of words is factual but easy to understand, since the technical terms he uses ("a circulatory system of winds", "the Pressure Equator", ll. 27, 29) are explained by the simple explanatory context that he establishes for them. In thus making Moira Davidson understand the inevitability of their fate, the commander simultaneously makes the reader see what is bound to happen in the nuclear age if a nation begins to act irresponsibly. In other words, the reader, too, is placed in the position that Moira Davidson here assumes. He or she would like things to be different, but begins to understand that a nuclear war will release an irreversible process towards global destruction.

6. The characters are part of a fictional world that Shute has created. They experience events that the reader still fears may happen any time in the present world. Though the reader lives in fear of what might happen in a world full of nuclear weapons, he or she still has hope. In contrast to the fictional characters, the reader may still be able to prevent the extinction of the human species.

7. *In your opinion, has Shute's vision of the possible destruction of mankind become more or less likely than when the novel was first published in 1957?*
   – –

8 John Greenwald et al.: Something Was Wrong – Terribly Wrong

Didaktische Hinweise

Nach der fiktionalen Gestaltung einer nuklearen Katastrophe (Text 7) beschließt dieser Bericht aus *Time* (12.5.1986), die exemplarische Verdeutlichung des mit der Nutzung der Kernenergie auch in Friedenszeiten verbundenen Sicherheitsrisikos, die Textsequenz zum Thema „Wissenschaft und Technik in Krieg und Frieden". Eine Verknüpfung insbesondere mit Text 7 liegt nahe (vgl. auch unten, Aufg. 6 und 7). Daß nationalstaatliche Interessen nicht nur in der Sowjetunion während der kritischen Anfangsphase des Reaktorunfalls höchste Priorität erhielten, haben G. Neuberger und E. Sieker in ihrem Beitrag „Tschernobyl und die Folgen" (in: A.-A. Guha und S. Papcke [Hrsg.]: *Entfesselte Forschung*. Frankfurt, Fischer 1987, S. 134–151) dargelegt.

Background information

"A catastrophe had occurred" (ll. 66–67): "The accident at the Chernobyl nuclear power plant resulted from the combination of a reactor design with inherent control problems and the reckless and deliberate disregard of established safety procedures by the plant operators. The series of events leading to the explosion began with the initiation of a test to see how long the steam turbines would run (and thus provide power for emergency safety systems) while coasting to a stop when the reactor was suddenly shut off. ... In the Soviet Union the consequences of the explosion were severe. Their full extent was revealed at an international conference in August [1986] at which the Soviets gave the details of the accident. ... Evacuation of the 780 sq km (300 sq mi) area around the plant involved 135,000 people. ... The total cost of the

disaster was several billion dollars. … One beneficial result of Chernobyl was the establishment of new mechanisms for the international sharing of information on all future incidents and for cooperating in dealing with them" *(Encyclopaedia Britannica: 1987 Book of the Year.* Encyclopaedia Britannica, Chicago, p. 204 f.).

Semantic and collocational field "Nuclear power plant accident"

a nuclear power plant, a power station, atomic power ✧ a reactor meltdown/explosion, a reactor is damaged, an accident takes place, a catastrophe occurs ✧ a(n) disturbing/disquieting/alarming signal, (to) suspect difficulties in one's own reactors, (to) search for a leak, (to) take Geiger counter readings ✧ an abnormally high level of radiation, (to) spew radiation into the atmosphere, (to) give off radiation far above contamination levels, (to) show four times the normal amount of radioactive emissions ✧ the consequences of the accident, the prospect of long-term health and environmental damage, (to) cause (untold) death and suffering

Talking about the text – Suggested answers

1. The writers start their story by presenting individual effects and reactions in the West, so that the naming of the causes is considerably delayed. They thus create suspense and induce the reader to become more interested and involved in what happened, in particular in the growing sense of danger. The reversal of the cause-and-effect order is further enhanced by the writers starting far away from the source of the danger and only gradually bringing the reader nearer to it.

2. Both the effect-and-cause order and the widened focus here appear to underline the enormity of what has happened. Not only have the effects of "abnormally high levels of radiation" (ll. 6–7) travelled enormous distances, but the concomitant radioactive contamination has also affected a vast stretch of land, moving across the borders of several countries. Readers are given the information piecemeal so that they may form a mental image of the contaminated region in the northern hemisphere.

3. Disasters or explosions involving nuclear power make national borders meaningless. With nuclear power, scientists have only partly been able to control and contain nature's forces. Even in peacetime, the seemingly safe and harnessed power may become "unleashed" (l. 73) by accident, spread randomly and kill people who are completely uninvolved and unsuspecting.

4. When, for six hours, "the Soviets steadfastly maintained that nothing untoward had happened" (ll. 46–47), they showed both a lack of understanding for the dangers and dimensions involved in the accident and a disdain for the concerns of their neighbours. One sentence from the television announcement indicates that the Soviets did not fully understand the nature of the energy they had tried to harness in their nuclear reactor. "Measures are being taken to eliminate the consequences of the accident" (ll. 56–58) suggests (wrongly) that scientists and a "government commission" (ll. 59–60) can actually cope with the "long-term health and environmental damage" (ll. 71–72) caused by the spread of radioactive particles [cf. also Ch. XII, Text 7, l. 36.]

5. The important expression in the quoted reference is "long-term". Radioactivity is produced by isotopes with different half-lives. Among the isotopes that were discharged into the atmosphere from the Chernobyl reactor (according to the "International Herald Tribune" of April 22, 1987, p. 6, "no fewer than 100 million curies of radioactive isotopes"), iodine 131 had a half-life of only about eight days, but others have considerably longer half-lives: strontium 27.7 years; caesium 137.33 years. The "health and environmental damage" will thus have been done for many years to come, with an increase above all in cancer deaths and hereditary diseases.

6. *If you have read the text by Nevil Shute (cf. Ch. XII, Text 7), what similarities and differences between fact and fiction strike you as important?*
   [Similarities: the slow, but steady, spread of radioactive particles by winds; the helplessness of people who are threatened with disease and death; the irresponsibility that draws uninvolved people towards the same fate.
   Differences: in the fictional text, the deadly spread of radiation was unleashed by a war, in the real event of 1986, it was "unleashed by peaceful nuclear use" (ll. 73–74); in the fictional text, death is certain on a global scale, in the real event, it is not as certain and will affect a much smaller area of the earth.]

7. *Against the background of the picture that Nevil Shute paints (cf. Ch. XII, Text 7), what may the accident at Chernobyl tell us about nuclear energy?*
   Chernobyl has made clear that only a few more accidents of "peaceful nuclear use" (ll. 73–74), even if spread over years or decades, may suffice to make whole regions of the world uninhabitable. The peaceful use of nuclear power, too, poses a constant global risk to humanity.

9 The Preamble to the Charter of the United Nations

Didaktische Hinweise

Die letzte Textgruppe dieses Kapitels (Text 9 bis 12) stellt verschiedene Möglichkeiten und Denkansätze für eine globale Friedenssicherung vor. Zu den politisch bedeutsamsten Formen für die Vermeidung eines weltumspannenden Krieges gehören heute unbestritten die Menschenrechtsdeklaration der Vereinten Nationen sowie der fortdauernde Einfluß, den die Gremien der Vereinten Nationen nach 1945 gehabt haben (Text 10). Die beiden abschließenden Texte 11 und 12 lenken den Blick noch einmal auf die problematische Doppelnatur des Menschen: Seine auf Aggression und Zerstörung gerichteten Antriebe stellen die gegenwärtig erreichte Stufe seiner Kultur fundamental in Frage.

   Die Absichtserklärungen der Präambel zur Charta der Vereinten Nationen (Text 9) veranschaulichen, wie mit der Zunahme globaler Zerstörungspotentiale auch der Wunsch der Nationen gewachsen ist, solcher Zerstörung durch international getroffene Vereinbarungen entgegenzuwirken. Die Menschenrechtsdeklaration der Vereinten Nationen (1948) wurde Grundlage und Bezugspunkt für spätere völkerrechtliche Abmachungen, in denen sich Staaten verpflichteten, allen ihrer Hoheitsgewalt unterstehenden Personen menschliche Grundrechte zu gewährleisten: so insbesondere in der Europäischen Menschenrechtskonvention (1953), aber auch in den Erklärungen von Helsinki (1975) und Wien (1989).

   Ausgehend von Text 9 lassen sich vielfältige Verbindungslinien zu bereits angesprochenen Problembereichen ziehen, etwa zu den Themen „Recht auf Bildung", „Gleichberechtigung", „Schutz vor Diskriminierung", „Recht auf freie Meinungsäußerung", um nur einige zu nennen. Über Kombinationsmöglichkeiten gibt das „Didaktische Inhaltsverzeichnis" (LB, S. xxxiii) Auskunft.

Background information

Two of the six principal organs of the UN have been of primary importance in maintaining international peace and security: the General Assembly, which is the only body in which all of the UN member states (159 in 1988) are represented, and the Security Council, at present a 15-member body that consists of five permanent members: China, France, the United Kingdom, the U.S.S.R. and the United States, and ten non-permanent members. The non-permanent members are chosen so as to represent African and Asian states (five members), eastern European states (one), Latin-American states (two) and western European and other states (two). In the General Assembly, decisions on important issues are taken by a two-thirds vote, otherwise by a simple majority vote. In the Security Council, nine affirmative votes are required on a substantive question, including all the permanent members.

Over the years, the importance of the General Assembly has steadily increased as an organ of deliberation and political influence, while that of the Security Council has often suffered from an inability of the permanent members to cooperate.

Semantic and collocational field "International goals"

international law, (to) live together in peace as good neighbours, (to) maintain international peace and security, (to) save sb./sth. from the scourge of war ✧ the promotion of the economic and social advancement of all peoples, (to) promote social progress, (to) maintain justice/peace/security, (to) unite one's strength ✧ the dignity and worth of the human person, the equal rights of men and women, fundamental human rights

Talking about the text – Suggested answers

1. The representatives of the original member states of the UN had directly experienced death, destruction and suffering on a scale never before recorded in human history. They formally pledged themselves to combine their efforts to prevent such events in future.
2. A distinction is made between aims emphasizing the basic human rights of the individual (cf. ll. 4–7) and social aims (cf. ll. 8–16). [The group of individual rights was a dominant concern of Western democratic nations, while the group of social aims was a primary concern of Soviet bloc countries.]
3. Probably the following two aspects: first, that all considerations are to be based on the belief in fundamental human rights (especially, "the dignity and worth of the human person", ll. 4–5); secondly, that this is not a pledge agreed upon between only a few dominant nations in the world, but intended to be upheld internationally (cf. l. 12).
4. [They have been met in so far as an international war on the scale of World War II or greater has indeed been avoided, though for various other reasons not directly connected with the existence of the UN. However, local "surrogate wars", e.g. in Korea, Vietnam, Latin America and Afghanistan, have not been prevented.]
5. The writers have kept the basic structure of the sentence fairly clear by using parts of the main clause (the subject "We, the peoples of the United Nations", l. 1, and the predicate "have resolved to …", l. 17) to frame a dependent participle clause ("determined …", l. 1) with a list of eight to-infinitives in parallel sentence structures ("to save …", "to reaffirm …", "to establish …", etc.). This structure is supported by the layout of the sentence.
   From the point of view of its content, the list falls roughly into two helpful subdivisions, with the second and third to-infinitives emphasizing "fundamental human rights" (l. 4) of the individual, and the fourth to eighth concentrating on the promotion of social progress within a general international framework of "peace and security" (l. 12).
6. By condensing the contents within the framework of a single sentence (in the highly formal register of a legal text), the writers may have wished to underline the complex interdependence of all the aims listed, and to emphasize that all of these aims would have to be taken into account if war was to be prevented. The common resolution, like the subject and predicate of the main clause, had to embrace each of the listed aims.

7. *The writers of the UN Charter "neither foresaw the impact of nuclear weapons nor the consequences of decolonisation" ("The Observer", Oct. 27, 1985, p. 11). What lessons for our own world could be drawn from these observations?*
– –

10 Anthony Sampson: A Club for the Third World

Didaktische Hinweise

Anthony Sampson (vgl. LB, S. 71) zieht in seinem 1985 in *Newsweek* erschienenen Artikel das Resümee vierzigjährigen Einwirkens der UNO auf kriegerische Auseinandersetzungen in der Welt. Seine Überlegungen veranschaulichen die bisherige Leistung der Vereinten Nationen, verdeutlichen zugleich aber auch, in welche Richtung eine zukünftige Stärkung der Weltbehörde gehen sollte.

Über die laufende Arbeit der Vereinten Nationen berichten die Veröffentlichungen *Yearbook of the United Nations* (annually); *United Nations Chronicle* (monthly) and *Annual Report of the Secretary General on the Work of the Organization* (UN Sales Section, Publ. Div., New York, N.Y.).

Semantic and collocational field "United Nations"

a world forum, a global centre, an international political forum, a forum for judgment and debate, a forum between East and West, a meeting place for communication between continents, a club for Third World countries, a mediator between superpowers, a member state/government, the U.N. includes the major powers ✧ the effectiveness of the U.N., a body that can provide emergency action, a peace keeping force, (to) keep lines open, (to) look to the U.N. ✧ a crisis point, a crisis of non-communication and possible war, a time of deteriorating relations ✧ an overblown bureaucracy, absurd jargon, bombastic rhetoric ✧ an instrument of American policy, (to) become heavily influenced by sb./sth., (to) be infused with anti-colonial rhetoric, (to) be firmly controlled by sb./sth., (to) give sb./sth. more influence on sb./sth. else

Talking about the text – Suggested answers

1. Sampson's intention was to defend the UN against critics who consider it to be ineffective (cf. his reference to "every kind of hypocrisy and muddled thinking", ll. 4–5) and to inform them about its true nature and purpose.
2. (1) Sampson reminds the reader of the purpose of the United Nations "to be a meeting place for communication between continents" (ll. 15–17).
    (2) He explains that its change from a forum between East and West to "the chief club for Third World countries" (ll. 31–32) does not restrict its possibilities, but actually extends its functions by providing "a way to keep lines open at a time of deteriorating North-South relations" (ll. 39–40).
    (3) The "original geographical mistake of putting its headquarters, and those of the IMF and the World Bank, in the United States" (ll. 60–62) should not distract the reader from the fact that these institutions have by no means become instruments of American policy (cf. ll. 74–75).
    (4) In contrast to Americans, Europeans still look to the United Nations as "a body that can provide emergency action, including peacekeeping forces" (ll. 98–100).
    (5) At crisis points, all governments have to agree that the United Nations "remains the best, and indeed the only, genuinely international forum" (ll. 104–105) that they have.

3. The implication is that wars are not effectively prevented by the threat of force (think of the so-called nuclear deterrence), but by keeping lines of communication open between hostile nations at an institutionalized level, outside the sphere where national pride and emotions become involved. Put differently, the principle is to talk rather than to wall oneself in and prepare for the worst.

4. [Briefly, the student can be expected to point out that when Britain and France resorted to imperial gunpowder politics to keep the Suez Canal open after it had been seized by Egypt, it was the UN that brought about a cease-fire, disentangled Britain and France from the adventure, and installed the first peacekeeping force between the hostile armies.]

5. These sentences, among others, show that the writer is dealing with his subject [i.e. the role of the United Nations after 40 years] in an argumentative manner, i.e. by presenting his own view in opposition to different, highly critical views. In the first of the quoted sentences, Sampson expressly refers to the opposing view by "That attitude ...". In the second sentence, he makes use of a possibility [in the form of a conditional clause] that refutes any different view as irresponsible.

6. *Considering the writer's references to positions which are different from his own, why may the argumentative text type be considered more suited to this topic than other text types?*

   After 40 years, misconceptions and ignorance about the role and effectiveness of the UN are apparently so widespread that the writer has to express his ideas in a form that allows him to deal with the criticism he anticipates from his readers. Straightforward exposition, i.e. a systematic explanation of the organization, aims and activities of the UN, would not achieve this effect. Argumentation, however, is more likely to be successful, since it establishes a connection between opposing views on the same subject matter.

11 Robert Frost: Mending Wall

Didaktische Hinweise

Mit Text 11 wird die Reflexion über Möglichkeiten eines friedlichen Zusammenlebens der Völker aus dem Bereich politischen Handelns wieder zurückgelenkt auf den Einzelnen. Frosts Gedicht – eine vom Dichter gesprochene Aufnahme bietet die Textcassette *Selected Texts on Cassette* (Best.-Nr. 54861) – deutet an, daß der Mensch heute mehr als früher, will er überleben, zum kooperativen Miteinander ohne trennende Grenzen befähigt werden muß. In der Diskussion kann die "wall"-Metapher auf die gegenwärtige weltpolitische Situation übertragen werden unter der Fragestellung, ob die Entwicklung insgesamt mehr auf ein Errichten oder ein Einreißen von Mauern hinausläuft (vgl. unten, Aufg. 7). Auch eine Kombination mit Robin Knights Belfast-Bericht (Kap. IV, Text 9), dessen Titel sich auf das in Frosts Gedicht eine zentrale Rolle spielende Sprichwort bezieht, liegt nahe.

Background information

Robert (Lee) Frost (1874–1963) was born in San Francisco, Calif., but grew up in New England. He worked in various jobs, including farming and teaching, before going to Harvard in 1897 to study Classics. However, after two years, he became ill and started farming in New Hampshire. From 1912 to 1915 he lived in England, where he prepared the first collection of his poetry, *A Boy's Will* (1913) for publication. It was followed by many others, e.g. *North of Boston* (1914, where "Mending Wall" first appeared), *Collected Poems* (1930 and 1939) and *In the Clearing* (1962). Frost gained immediate fame and, on his return to New Hampshire, he divided his time between farming and teaching at several New England colleges and universities. He won four Pulitzer Prizes for poetry.

It is interesting to note that "Mending Wall", though quite apparently supporting the speaker's enlightened stance against having a wall, has also been read as favouring the neighbour's position for "good fences". In an essay on how American journalists use poetic allusion to give depth to their comments, William Safire, a Pulitzer Prize-winning columnist, sternly corrects such a reading: "In an Op-Ed article last year about Mexican fears of our immigration law, the political scientist Jorge G. Castaneda writes: 'Strong fences make good neighbors, but realism and humility make friendlier ones.' The common mistake here (beyond substituting *strong* for *good)* is assuming the poet meant 'good fences make good neighbors' to be his message; in fact, Frost put that statement in the mouth of a narrow-minded neighbor, and questioned the good-fences philosophy with 'Before I built a wall I'd ask to know/What I was walling in or walling out' " ("Journalists give Robert Frost an allusive workout". In: *Arizona Daily Star,* July 25, 1988; originally published by *The New York Times)* (cf. also the heading of the American journalist's report on Belfast, Ch. IV, Text 9).

Semantic and collocational field "Boundaries"

a neighbour, a fence, a stone, a boulder, (to) build a wall, (to) wall sth. in/out, (to) set/keep a wall between two people, (to) walk the line ✧ (to) make repairs, (to) mend a wall ✧ (to) make a gap, (to) leave not one stone on a stone, (to) want sth. (e.g. a wall) down

Talking about the text – Suggested answers

1. At first the speaker is alone with his reflections on a stone wall, later he is together with his neighbour; first the reader is made to listen to the speaker's reflections on the "gaps" (l. 4) in the wall, later the reader is made to see him engaged in the activity of closing the gaps together with his neighbour.
2. The speaker considers "set[ting] the wall between [them]" (l. 14) to be "just another kind of outdoor game" (l. 21) since "There where it is we do not need the wall" (l. 23). His neighbour, on the other hand, insists on having the wall as a dividing "fence" (l. 27), to make sure that they will get on as "good neighbors" (ll. 27 and 45).
3. The reader's impression of the speaker's neighbour is created above all by his reactions to the speaker's proposal to change things: they have different tree crops, with the perhaps more tempting "apple orchard" on the speaker's side; "there are no cows" (l. 31) that might cross the line to feed on the neighbour's grass; and the speaker freely reveals himself as what the other person might consider a "good neighbor" who wishes to be on good terms with his neighbour: "Before I built a wall I'd ask to know / What I was walling in or walling out" (ll. 32–33).
   Not yielding an inch to the speaker's persuasive arguments against the wall between them (cf. his stubborn repetition of the saying that "Good fences make good neighbors", ll. 27 and 45), the neighbour reveals himself to be somewhat narrow-minded, relying on conventional wisdom rather than on common sense as dictated by the situation. The reader is likely to share the speaker's impression that this man has not yet become a civilized human being, but still acts according to prehistoric behaviour patterns, "like an old-stone savage armed" (l. 40), moving in spiritual and moral "darkness" (l. 41). To such a person, the reader is made to realize, no bridge of trust and friendship is possible.

4. Drawing upon connotations of the word "spring", he suggests that this is a time of renewal and new beginnings in the world; a time when, after having been imprisoned in their houses for shelter against the winter cold and snow, people can move outdoors again and experience the freedom of movement as a liberation from constraining bonds and limitations. Springtime is thus experienced by the speaker as the most likely time for extending one's goodwill to others.

    In this the speaker may feel supported by the way even the forces of nature appear to conspire in the downfall of the wall, from deep below ("Something ... That sends the frozen-ground-swell under it", ll. 1–2) and from high above, in the form of the warming beams of "the sun" (l. 3). By contrast, his neighbour "moves in darkness" (l. 41), that is, adheres to the rules dictated by the dark season of winter as well as the supposedly dark ages of the beginnings of mankind.

5. [Taking into account the two immediately preceding lines, the student may interpret the repetition as lending the saying less weight. That the neighbour at this point in the conversation "will not go behind his father's saying" (l. 43) indicates that he now appears to be shutting out forcefully any responses he may be making in his own mind to the speaker's arguments. Simultaneously, the fact that the neighbour "likes having thought of it so well" (l. 44), shows how his pride in having hit upon one good answer is being challenged by some discomforting new notion that the speaker has tried to put "in his head" (l. 29).]

6. Perhaps "Before I built a wall I'd ask to know / What I was walling in or walling out, / And to whom I was like to give offense" (ll. 32–34). The neighbour might realize at this point that he is walling out the speaker's (i.e. his own neighbour's) different, but nonetheless interesting view of the world. The view he is "walling out" (l. 33) might conceivably supersede the dated wisdoms of darker and more violent ages.

7. *What walls in the real world, in history as well as in today's world, may come to the reader's mind as being rather like the wall between the speaker and his neighbour?*

    [E.g. the walls of Jericho, the Chinese wall, Hadrian's wall, the Berlin Wall, or the walls in Belfast, Cyprus or Korea (cf. also Ch. IV, Text 9).]

8. *How would you explain Frost's reference to the "Something" that there is in this world "that doesn't love a wall" (l. 1)?*

    [According to the poem, the desire for good neighbourliness, companionship, cooperation and freedom, but also wilful destructiveness (cf. ll. 5–9). More generally, progression of human history towards more civilized organizations of human togetherness – at least in intention, if not yet in actual political fact – on a worldwide basis.]

9. *Try to characterize the speaker in this poem.*

    [The speaker is the one who initiates the meeting to mend the wall ("I let my neighbor know", l. 12). He has the playfulness, or "mischief" (l. 28), of spring in him, and, as they are working, he begins to see the mending as "just another kind of outdoor game" (l. 21). He contemplates toying with his (less intelligent?) neighbour (cf. ll. 28–36), whom he obviously considers primitive, "like an old-stone savage" (l. 40). This display of contempt shows the speaker to be a bit arrogant and complacent.]

10. *In ll. 28–29 the speaker wonders whether it wouldn't be possible to "put a notion" in his neighbour's head, yet he doesn't try to do so. Later he says, "I'd rather / He said it for himself" (ll. 37–38). Do you agree with the idea of letting others move "in darkness" (l. 41), or do you believe it is better for people with "notions in their heads" to try to convince others of their point of view? Discuss.*

    – –

12 Richard Leakey: All of the Same Species

Didaktische Hinweise

Ähnlich wie Robert Frost entwickelt Richard Leakey hier seine Vorstellungen über die Möglichkeiten der menschlichen Spezies, zu einem insgesamt kooperierenden statt konkurrierenden Miteinander zu kommen. Seine Überlegungen zielen auf eine Symbiose zwischen den enorm gewachsenen technischen Möglichkeiten der Gegenwart und der Fähigkeit des Menschen, sie zu einem konstruktiven Umlernen nutzen zu können. Aus der Perspektive der Huxleyschen Glücksutopie (vgl. Text 1) mögen sich Leakeys Gedanken allerdings in der praktischen Realisierung als ebensowenig frei von neuen Gefahren für das freie Individuum erweisen wie beispielsweise die Huxleys, Bradburys (vgl. Kap. VIII, Text 4) oder auch Orwells, die vor der Gefahr eines alle Lebensäußerungen kontrollierenden Polizeistaates warnen.

Semantic and collocational field "Survival of the human species"

an instinctive response, crying, smiling, the suckling reflex, one's potential to learn, a pattern of behaviour like sharing/cooperation, (to) draw upon an attribute/an asset, (to) succeed where other animals failed, (to) avoid extinction, (to) bring sb. through to the present time, our success relates to our adaptability/flexibility as a species, (to) learn a lesson as a species ✧ (to) have few options if one is to survive, (to) become extinct, (to) fail one's own kind ✧ (to) ease suffering, (to) provide relief aid

Talking about the text – Suggested answers

1. The basic question can be given different forms, such as: Why do we seem to be unable to learn the lessons of "our prehistoric record" (ll. 59–60) and use them towards "the resolution of today's complex problems" (ll. 30–31)? Or: Is the human species doomed to become extinct? Or: How can the human species survive?

2. The following topics may be set down: 1) the human potential to learn (ll. 1–14); 2) the potential of human intelligence and technology (ll. 14–25); 3) conditions for the success and survival of the species (ll. 26–44); 4) ways of avoiding extinction in our age (ll. 45–64).

3. 1) Since the behaviour patterns of sharing and cooperation once secured the survival and expansion of the human species, these behaviour patterns should be taught to the young, with all the intelligence and technology at our disposal.
   2) Since we are the species with an immense potential to learn, we should exploit our inventiveness and adaptability and, in a global educational effort, replace our present acceptance of aggression and military expenditure.
   3) In order to succeed, we should also use our intelligence, resources and modern technology to help others who still face starvation and untimely death.
   4) In order to survive, we should use the vast supply of experiences men have made during the long periods of their development. It is men who have to decide the survival of the human species.

4. Although he does not refer to Darwin directly, the writer uses key expressions from the vocabulary that has become associated with Darwin: "species" (e.g. heading, ll. 11, 40), "survive" (l. 27), "become extinct" (ll. 48, 52, 54) and "extinction" (ll. 49, 57). However, rather than explaining the success of the human species in terms of its success in an aggressive fight for survival, Leakey bases his argument on the opposite, namely "patterns of behaviour, like sharing and cooperation, that lie deep in our past" (ll. 9–10).

5. *Compare Leakey's view of "today's world" (l. 26) with the message of Robert Frost's poem "Mending Wall" (cf. Ch. XII, Text 11).*
   – –